A PRACTICAL APPROACH TO
SENTENCING

A PRACTICAL APPROACH TO

SENTENCING

Martin Wasik

CBE

Barrister, Recorder on the Midland Circuit

Professor of Criminal Justice, Keele University

FIFTH EDITION

OXFORD

UNIVERSITY PRESS

OXFORD
UNIVERSITY PRESS

Great Clarendon Street, Oxford, OX2 6DP,
United Kingdom

Oxford University Press is a department of the University of Oxford.
It furthers the University's objective of excellence in research, scholarship,
and education by publishing worldwide. Oxford is a registered trade mark of
Oxford University Press in the UK and in certain other countries

© Martin Wasik 2014

The moral rights of the author have been asserted

First Edition published in 1985
Second Edition published in 1993
Third Edition published in 1998
Fourth Edition published in 2001
Fifth Edition published in 2014

Impression: 1

Published in the United States of America by Oxford University Press
198 Madison Avenue, New York, NY 10016, United States of America

British Library Cataloguing in Publication Data
Data available

Library of Congress Control Number: 2014934366

ISBN 978–0–19–969581–2

Printed and bound by
Lightning Source UK Ltd

PREFACE

There is never an ideal time to produce a new edition of a book on sentencing. This area of law is notorious for its technical complexity, and for the rapidity of change. Much of this change is driven by legislation. Ten years after the major changes wrought by the Criminal Justice Act 2003, the greater part of that legislative scheme has now been dismantled. Innovative ideas for custodial sentences of less than twelve months (so called 'custody plus') were never brought into force, nor were magistrates' powers to imprison for up to twelve months, and intermittent custody flickered briefly as a topic and then went out. Suspended sentences and community sentences have been heavily amended. Section 240 of the Act, which required judges to adjust their sentences to take into account days spent by the defendant on remand, turned out to be much more trouble than it was worth, and was repealed by the Legal Aid, Sentencing and Punishment of Offenders Act in 2012. The 2003 Act scheme for dangerous offenders misfired so badly and caused such injustice that it required radical surgery in 2008 and was abolished in 2012. There has been a steady increase in the range and complexity of ancillary orders which the courts may impose on sentence. The relevant chapter in the book has, in consequence, almost doubled in length since the last edition. New and unnecessary complexities have been introduced into the sentencing process as traps for the unwary. These include more prescribed minimum sentences, a requirement that at least one community order requirement is punitive in nature, and the need to add at the end of every sentencing delivery an instruction to the offender to pay up the required statutory surcharge. Some old traps remain in place. Despite many apparent indications to the contrary in later legislation, the sentence of imprisonment still starts at age twenty-one (and not age eighteen) because section 61 of the Criminal Justice and Court Services Act 2000 remains on the books but not in force.

One consistent and very positive achievement has been the continued development of sentencing guidelines. Most of the major areas of sentencing are now addressed by guidelines. They have been produced since 2009 by the Sentencing Council for England and Wales, in a new format and style but essentially building on what went before. Much of the judicial scepticism with respect to the sentencing guidelines project has now dissipated, and many judges (especially those who sit on a part-time basis, and the more recently appointed) appreciate the help that guidelines give, while recognizing their inherent flexibility. Guidelines are now central to practice in the criminal courts, and to Judicial College training. The prevalence of sentencing guidelines creates a technical difficulty for a book of this sort. The published guidelines now run to hundreds of pages of text, and it is not practical to include that material within its covers. Fortunately, the sentencing guidelines are very readily accessible online, at <http://sentencingcouncil.judiciary.gov.uk/> and in supplements to the major practitioner works. While, of course, much summary and analysis of the guidelines can be found in the pages of this book, practitioners should *always* refer to the full text of any particular guideline before relying on the guideline in court.

The volume of appellate case law continues unabated. Among the most important recent sentencing decisions discussed in this edition are *Caley* [2013] 2 Cr App R (S) 47 on discount for a guilty plea, *Blackshaw* [2012] 1 WLR 1126 on sentencing offences committed during widespread public disorder, *AG's Ref (No 60 of 2009)(Appleby)* [2010] 2 Cr App R (S) 286 on sentencing manslaughter, *Perkins* [2013] EWCA Crim 323 on victim personal statements, *Smith* [2012] 1 All ER 451 on sexual offences prevention orders, *Boakye* [2013]

1 Cr App R (S) 6, *Healey* [2013] 1 Cr App R(S) 176, and *AG's Refs (Nos 15, 16, and 17 of 2012)(Lewis)* [2013] 1 Cr App R (S) 289 on the proper approach to sentencing guidelines, and *Saunders* [2013] EWCA Crim 1027 and *Burinskas* [2014] EWCA Crim 334 on life sentences after LASPOA.

This fifth edition (the title of which now clearly reflects its *Practical Approach*) is the natural successor to *Emmins on Sentencing*. It will be clear from what has been said in this Preface that developments since the last edition have required, for most chapters, a completely fresh start. I have tried to describe and explain the law on sentencing as fully, clearly, and helpfully as possible. I have retained the gender-specific 'he' when referring to defendants and offenders, since the great majority of them are male. As always, I am grateful to the publishers for their efficiency, encouragement, and patience.

CONTENTS SUMMARY

DETAILED CONTENTS

TABLE OF CASES

TABLE OF STATUTES

TABLE OF STATUTORY INSTRUMENTS, CRIMINAL PRACTICE DIRECTIONS AND CRIMINAL PROCEDURE RULES

LIST OF ABBREVIATIONS

ASBO	Anti-Social Behaviour Order
CAA	Criminal Attempts Act
CAJA	Coroners and Justice Act
CCRC	Criminal Cases Review Commission
CDA	Crime and Disorder Act
CDDA	Company Directors Disqualification Act
CJA	Criminal Justice Act
CJPA	Criminal Justice and Police Act
CPR	Criminal Procedure Rules
CPS	Crown Prosecution Service
DPP	Department of Public Prosecution
DVCVA	Domestic Violence Crimes and Victims Act
ECHR	European Convention on Human Rights
ECtHR	European Court of Human Rights
FSA	Football Spectators Act
IA	Immigration Act
ISO	individual support order
LASPOA	Legal Aid, Sentencing and Punishment of Offenders Act
MCA	Magistrates' Court Act
MHA	Mental Health Act
MHRT	Mental Health Review Tribunal
NHS	National Health Service
OAPA	Offences Against the Person Act
PCC(S)A	Powers of Criminal Court (Sentencing) Act
PCMH	plea and case management hearing
PHA	Protection from Harassment Act
PSR	pre-sentence report
RTA	Road Traffic Act
RTOA	Road Traffic Offenders Act
RTRA	Road Traffic Regulation Act
SAP	Sentencing Advisory Panel
SC	Sentencing Council
SGC	Sentencing Guidelines Council
SOA	Sexual Offences Act
SOCPA	Serious Organised Crime and Police Act
SOPO	sexual offences prevention order
SVGA	Safeguarding of Vulnerable Groups Act
TA	Theft Act
TIC	taken into consideration

1

THE SENTENCING PROCESS

A AN OUTLINE OF PROCEDURE RELEVANT TO SENTENCING

Sentencing is closely connected with matters of criminal procedure. A general discus- **1.01** sion of criminal procedure lies outside the scope of this book, although an outline of procedure as it directly affects sentencing is given in the following paragraphs. Readers seeking detailed coverage are referred to *A Practical Approach to Criminal Procedure* by John Sprack.

Categories of offences

1.02 Sentencing is about the way courts deal with a person *after* he has pleaded guilty or has been found guilty. Criminal trials in England and Wales take one of two forms: they are either summary trials or trials on indictment. At the start it is important to distinguish between sentencing for:

(a) offences triable only on indictment,
(b) offences triable either way, and
(c) offences triable summarily.

1.03 Offences triable only on indictment must be dealt with in the Crown Court. Such offences include murder, manslaughter, rape, and robbery. Offences triable either way can, as their name implies, be dealt with either in the Crown Court or in a magistrates' court. An offence is triable either way if it is listed as such in the Magistrates' Courts Act 1980, schedule 1 or if the enactment which creates the offence specifies one penalty on summary conviction and one penalty on conviction on indictment. Offences triable either way include burglary, theft, and assault occasioning actual bodily harm. The decision over where an offence triable either way will be dealt with is known as the mode of trial decision. Basically an offence triable either way will be dealt with on indictment if either the accused relies on his right to Crown Court trial and 'elects' to be dealt with in the higher court, or the magistrates come to the view that the case is too serious for them; in particular, that the accused is charged with an offence which if convicted will result in a sentence in excess of their sentencing powers (normally six months' imprisonment). If they think that their powers would be inadequate to deal with the matter, they should send the case to the Crown Court for trial. As a matter of terminology, which often causes confusion, the term 'indictable offence' means an offence which is triable only on indictment or an offence triable either way (Interpretation Act 1978, schedule 1). Thus both murder and burglary are indictable offences. Similarly, a conviction in the Crown Court is referred to as a 'conviction on indictment' whether or not the offence involved was triable only on indictment or was an offence triable either way.

Two methods of trial

1.04 Summary offences are (with certain narrow exceptions) dealt with exclusively in the magistrates' courts. These are the least serious offences and include many road traffic offences, regulatory matters, and other assorted offences. Summary offences also include common assault, assault of a police officer in the execution of his duty, driving with excess alcohol, and taking a vehicle without consent. Summary offences are sometimes referred to as 'purely summary' or 'summary only' offences. These words add nothing, but are sometimes included to reinforce the distinction between a summary offence and one triable either way. 'Summary conviction' means conviction in a magistrates' court, whether for a summary offence or for an offence triable either way. There are two exceptions to the general rule that summary offences must be tried in the lower court. First, if magistrates are sending an either way offence to the Crown Court they may also send a summary offence at the same time so as to avoid splitting the sentencing function between the magistrates' court and the Crown Court. This can only be done if the summary offence is punishable with imprisonment and arose out of circumstances connected with the either way offence (CJA 1988, schedule 3, paragraph 6). Secondly, certain summary offences may be included by the prosecution in the indictment along with the indictable offence to be dealt with in the Crown Court. The summary offence must be founded on the same facts or evidence as the indictable offence or be part of a series of offences of the same character as, or a similar character to, the indictable offence (CJA 1988, section 40). An example would be three allegations of assault committed in a domestic context, two of assault occasioning actual bodily harm and one of common assault, against the same victim.

Summary trial takes place on a magistrates' court. Most judges in this court are lay (ie **1.05** unpaid) magistrates. Magistrates are also known as justices of the peace. They are not lawyers, but are people drawn from the local community. Upon appointment they are deployed to sit at the courts in the area in which they live or work. A much smaller number of judges in the magistrates' courts are professional lawyers, paid a salary to work full-time in that court. These are referred to as district judges or, more precisely, district judges (magistrates' courts), to distinguish them from district judges sitting in the county courts. A lay bench normally comprises three magistrates, although two are sufficient. District judges sit alone, although in the youth court they often sit with a lay colleague. Magistrates and district judges are assisted in their work in courts by a court clerk. Clerks are qualified either as barristers or solicitors. The clerk advises the magistrates or district judge on the law when it is appropriate to do so, but does not otherwise become involved in their decisions. Magistrates' courts are organized on the basis of local justice areas (Courts Act 2003, section 8). Magistrates may not try a case summarily unless the court is composed of a district judge or at least two lay justices (Magistrates Courts Act 1980, section 121(1)). Normally, three justices sit together, one of whom acts as the chairman of the bench. The decision of the magistrates may be arrived at by a majority, but in the event of a split in an even-numbered bench, the court must adjourn for rehearing before a differently constituted bench. Some powers of a magistrates' court may be exercised by a single lay justice, but these do not extend to sentencing matters and so are not covered here.

A summary trial commences with the charge or information being put to the accused by the **1.06** clerk. Where it is alleged that two or more persons acted together in committing the offence they may be jointly charged in one information, and will normally be tried together. If the accused pleads guilty there is no need for evidence about the offence to be called, and the magistrates or district judge can commence the procedures leading up to sentence being passed. Trial on indictment takes place in the Crown Court. In theory the Crown Court is a single court which sits in many different geographical locations. In the past trial on indictment has been preceded by committal proceedings taking place in the magistrates' court. Committal proceedings were abolished in respect of offences triable only on indictment fifteen years ago. By the Crime and Disorder Act 1998, section 51 if the accused is charged with an offence which is triable only on indictment the magistrates should send him 'forthwith' to the Crown Court for trial. More recently committal proceedings have also been abolished for offences triable either way, initially only in parts of the country but nationally by 2013. Now, in the case of an offence triable either way the magistrates will send the matter 'forthwith' to the Crown Court under section 51 when, after hearing from the accused whether he intends to plead guilty or not guilty, they decide that the matter is too serious to be dealt with in the lower court or the accused has elected to be tried on indictment. The procedure which must be adopted in determining whether bail is granted or not is set out in the Sentencing Guidelines Council (SGC) guideline on *Allocation*, together with the *Criminal Practice Directions*, paragraph 9A.1. The details are outside the scope of this book and are not considered further here. The accused will be sent to the Crown Court remanded in custody or on bail. The outcome of that decision is, however, important when it comes to sentence. Any days which have been spent by the defendant in custody on remand are deducted automatically from any custodial sentence which is imposed for the offence, and credit must be given by the sentencing judge for days which have been spent by the defendant on bail under a particular form of qualifying curfew. These matters are considered at 3.15 and 3.20 in this book.

1.07 Once the accused has been sent for trial in the Crown Court the indictment is drawn up. This is done by a Crown Prosecution Service (CPS) lawyer. An indictment contains one or more counts, each count charging the accused with a single indictable offence. The indictment should contain sufficient counts to represent fairly the criminal conduct alleged against the accused. It is not good practice to include counts for all offences which might conceivably be made out on the alleged facts. It is ultimately for the prosecutor drafting the indictment to decide whether an additional count would genuinely add something to the prosecution case or would merely overload the indictment. An overloaded indictment tends to lead to longer and more complex trials and runs the risk of confusing the jury.

1.08 A trial on indictment begins with the clerk to the court putting the counts on the indictment to the accused. If the plea is guilty to all counts the court embarks on the procedures leading up to pronouncement of sentence. As we shall see, if the accused decides to admit his guilt at an early stage of the proceedings, well before the matter comes to trial, he can expect to receive a substantial discount on the sentence that he would have received had he pursued the case to trial and been convicted. Sometimes the accused is prepared to admit to his involvement in what happened, but through his lawyer suggests that this amounts in law to a lesser offence that appears on the indictment. This lesser offence must be an indictable offence which is expressly or implicitly included in an offence on the indictment. An example is a plea of guilty to theft on a charge of robbery. Another is a plea of guilty to manslaughter on a charge of murder. The prosecution may then consider whether a plea of guilty to that lesser offence might be acceptable in fairly reflecting the seriousness of the matter. Conviction for a lesser offence is likely to restrict the sentencing options available to the court, and so that will always be an important consideration when deciding whether to accept a plea to a lesser offence. A slightly different situation is where the accused admits that he committed the offence charged on the indictment, but disagrees with the way in which the prosecution says the incident took place. In other words, the accused disputes the 'factual basis' of the offence. If there is a marked divergence between what the prosecution and the defence say took place then, if the judge thinks that the sentence would be different in accordance to which version is correct, a short hearing (without a jury) is required to resolve that narrow issue. This procedure is known as a 'trial of issue' or a '*Newton* hearing', and is considered further at 1.46 in this Chapter.

Age categories of offenders

1.09 A matter which may well have a crucial impact on where the offence is to be tried and sentenced, and the powers available to the sentencing court, is the offender's age. Several age groups need to be distinguished. The terminology used is as follows:

Adult offenders	
Aged 21 and over	Adults
Aged 18, 19, or 20	young adults
Young offenders	
Aged 14, 15, 16, or 17	young persons
Aged 11, 12, or 13	Children

For the purposes of determining the method of trial and the appropriate sentencing court, the crucial dividing line is between adult offenders and young offenders. Adult offenders are dealt with in the Crown Court or in a magistrates' court, depending on the seriousness of the offence charged. Young offenders are usually dealt with the youth court, but occasionally in the Crown Court.

The determining factor in sentencing is usually, but not always, the age of the offender on the date when they are convicted (or plead guilty). Thus if an offender is aged seventeen when charged with an offence, but aged eighteen when he is convicted or pleads guilty, the court's powers to deal with eighteen-year-old young adults, and not seventeen-year-old youths, are available. So, a birthday between conviction and sentence will make a difference. As far as a custodial sentence is concerned, the court would pass a sentence of detention in a young offender institution (available for young adults) rather than a detention and training order. In this situation, however, it would be right for the sentencing court to bear in mind that this important age milestone has just been passed and think carefully about imposing a much greater punishment than would have been available if the offender had been only seventeen years old when convicted. On the other hand a birthday between conviction and sentence will not make a difference. If an offender is aged seventeen when convicted but turns eighteen before being sentenced the court's powers are those applicable to a seventeen-year-old. This would mean that the appropriate custodial sentence would be a detention and training order and not detention in a young offender institution. See further 3.09 and 3.10, Chapter 3 in this book. **1.10**

One exception to this general rule stated is murder. A person who is under eighteen at the time of committing the offence of murder must be sentenced to detention during Her Majesty's pleasure rather than to a life sentence. Here the crucial date is the date of the offence and not the date of conviction. So, a person who commits murder when aged under eighteen years old must be sentenced to detention during Her Majesty's pleasure whatever their age when convicted. Two men convicted of the racially motivated murder of Stephen Lawrence received the sentence of detention even though they were in their late thirties before they were convicted at trial (*Dobson and Norris*, WL 14586, 4 January 2012). **1.11**

There is usually no doubt how old the offender actually is, but occasionally there can be uncertainty. If so, the court must determine the offender's age before passing sentence having considered any evidence which is available to it: Powers of Criminal Courts (Sentencing) Act 2000, section164(1). If there is a disagreement about the offender's age, it would be sensible to adjourn for inquiries to be made (*Steed* (1990) 12 Cr App R (S) 230). If the court passes a sentence on an assumption which later turns out to be incorrect it seems that the sentence is not rendered void by that mistake (*Brown* (1989) 11 Cr App R (S) 263), but it would have to be corrected on appeal. **1.12**

Courts sentencing adults

Adult offenders are sentenced either by the Crown Court or by a magistrates' court. When magistrates convict an adult offender summarily of an offence triable either way they may pass a sentence of up to six months' imprisonment and/or a fine up to £5000. There are provisions in statute for increasing the six-months limit to twelve months (CJA 2003, section 282(1)), but these have not been brought into force and the government said in summer 2013 that there were no plans to do so. As the law currently stands, however, when sentencing an adult for two offences either way magistrates do have power to pass an aggregate sentence of up to twelve months. Most methods of dealing with adult offenders are available in broadly the same circumstances as they are available to the Crown Court, except that magistrates cannot add a restriction order to a hospital order in the case of a mentally disordered offender. **1.13**

1.14 The decision over mode of trial has already been mentioned. The level of gravity at which magistrates should refuse jurisdiction in respect of an offence triable either way is not susceptible to precise calculation, but it is possible to gauge the kind of conduct which can properly be punished with a sentence of six months imprisonment or less. By section 17A of the Magistrates' Courts Act 1980 the court having read the charge to the accused will then ask him whether he intends to plead guilty or not guilty. Section 19 of the Magistrates' Courts Act 1980 requires magistrates to consider information from the prosecutor as the accused's previous convictions, to allow both prosecutor and accused opportunity to make representations, and then to make its decision on the basis of the sentencing powers available to the court and to the SGC guideline on *Allocation*. By section 20, if the court decides that summary trial is more suitable it must explain this to the accused and proceed to summary trial if the accused agrees. If he wishes, he may be tried on indictment instead. At this point the accused may request an indication of whether a custodial or non-custodial sentence would be the more likely outcome if he were to be dealt with summarily and to plead guilty. Advance indications of sentence are considered at paragraph 1.33 following. If the accused agrees to be tried summarily the court proceeds to summary trial of the information. If he does not agree then the court sends the case to the Crown Court in accordance with section 51 of the Crown and Disorder Act 1998.

1.15 So, where a person aged eighteen or over is dealt with summarily, pleads guilty, or is found guilty after a summary trial, the magistrates will normally pass sentence. Sometimes, however, where the offence is triable either way the magistrates may commit to Crown Court for sentence. The magistrates' decision on mode of trial is, of course, based on the view that their sentencing powers would be adequate in light of the information available to them at the time of the mode of trial decision. It may turn out, after hearing more facts, or after presiding over the trial, that the offence is more serious than it first appeared to be, and it needs to be committed to the higher court for sentence. This will normally be done under section 3, 3A, or 4 of the Powers of Criminal Courts (Sentencing) Act 2000. Section 3 covers the more common situation where the magistrates are now of the view that the offence (or the combination of the offence and associated offences) is (or are) so serious that the Crown Court should sentence the offender. Magistrates should always think carefully before accepting a case which on the face of it will require a sentence close to their limit, also bearing in mind that their maximum sentence is closer to four months rather than six if a timely guilty plea has been entered. Magistrates are, however, entitled to change their minds about the nature of the case and commit for sentence. One possible reason for doing so is the offender asking for a number of other offences to be taken into consideration on sentence. Section 3A covers the unusual case of an offender who has committed a 'specified offence' and qualifies as a 'dangerous offender' who may require the imposition of an extended sentence to protect the public. Information about the potential risk posed by the offender might only emerge when further details about the offender's background and past offending are revealed to the court. Section 4 applies where several either way offences have been charged, to some of which the accused pleads guilty and some of which he intends to contest. If the magistrates send the disputed matters to the Crown Court for trial they can also commit for sentence those matters to which he pleads guilty, even if those offences standing alone would not have been serious enough to justify committal under section 3.

1.16 Whenever an offender is committed for sentence under section 3, 3A, or 4 it is important to understand that the Crown Court is *not* limited to magistrates' court powers. They can impose any sentence which the Crown Court has available to it, whether the magistrates could have passed that sentence or not (PCC(S)A 2000, section 5). In addition to these main powers of committal the magistrates may also commit for sentence under section 6. Typically, alongside committal under section 3 the lower court may additionally commit another less serious indictable offence, or a summary offence, of which the magistrates have proceeded to convict the offender. The important difference here is that the Crown Court when sentencing for an offence committed under section 6 is limited to magistrates' court powers; they can only impose a sentence which the magistrates had available to them (PCC(S)A 2000, section 7).

Sometimes mistakes occur in the operation of these provisions. In *Ayhan* [2012] 1 WLR **1.17** 1775 the magistrates purported to commit the offender to Crown Court for sentence under section 3 in respect of three offences, one of which was triable either way and the other two were summary. That was defective in that summary offences cannot be committed under section 3. The Court of Appeal said that it was essential to look beyond the form to the substance of the matter. If the magistrates were vested with power to commit all three matters to the Crown Court then a mistake in recording the statutory basis for committing the summary offences did not invalidate the committal. The Court confirmed that in respect of the matters committed in law under section 6 the higher court was bound by the sentencing powers of the magistrates. It seems that if there has been a procedural error in the magistrates' court and the defendant has been committed for sentence under the wrong provision, the Crown Court judge can exercise the power which exists under section 66 of the Courts Act 1971, by sitting as a district judge and committing the defendant under the correct section and then reconstituting himself as a Crown Court judge to deal with the same matter once properly committed. Section 66 states that all judges who sit in the Crown Court possess all the powers of a District Judge (Magistrates' Court) in relation to criminal causes and matters. In *Ashton* [2007] 1 WLR 181 it was held that a Crown Court judge exercising his powers under section 66 could properly determine mode of trial, commit the defendant for sentence, and may then (sitting again as a Crown Court judge) sentence the defendant. This is a very useful power which avoids the Crown Court having to send the matter back to the magistrates' court for the mistake to be rectified. It does not, however, affect the rule that where an offence is properly committed under section 6 the Crown Court is limited to magistrates' court powers.

Magistrates' courts have the important function of enforcing the payment of fines, whether **1.18** these have been imposed in a magistrates' court or in the Crown Court. They are also responsible for enforcing other financial orders, such as compensation orders and surcharges. Magistrates' courts act as supervising courts for community orders and if an offender is brought before the court for an alleged breach of the order then the magistrates deal with the breach and sentence for it if it is proved, but if the original order was made in the Crown Court the magistrates will generally be required to commit the matter to Crown Court for it to be dealt with there.

Courts sentencing young offenders

Members of the public are excluded from the youth court courtroom. This position is in **1.19** contrast to cases where a juvenile appears in an adult magistrates' court or in the Crown Court, where the public has a right to be present. Further, no report of the proceedings in a youth court can be broadcast or published which reveals the name, address, or other identifying detail of any juvenile concerned in the proceedings (CYPA 1933, section 49). The ban on publicity operates only for so long as the young person concerned is under eighteen. Their eighteenth birthday automatically brings the protection under section 49 to an end, even if proceedings are continuing (*T v DPP, North East Press Ltd* (2004) 168 JP 194).

The court may choose to lift the ban on publicity, but only if it is necessary to avoid injustice to the juvenile concerned or, if the juvenile is convicted, the court is satisfied after hearing representations from prosecution and defence that it is in the public interest to do so. The discretion to dispense with anonymity in the latter situation should, according to the Divisional Court in *McKerry v Teesdale and Wear Valley Justices* (2000) 164 JP 355 only be exercised after very careful thought.

1.20 Young offenders are normally sentenced in a youth court. Sometimes, however, they may be sentenced in an adult magistrates' court or in the Crown Court. The maximum custodial sentence which can be passed in a youth court is a detention and training order for two years. When a juvenile (person aged under eighteen) charged with an offence is the only accused involved in the proceedings (or when any other accused are juveniles as well) he (or they) must be tried in a youth court unless:

(a) the offence charged is a form of homicide (murder, manslaughter, causing death by dangerous driving, etc) or certain firearms offences which carry mandatory minimum sentences, or

(b) the young offender is charged alongside an adult, or

(c) the young offender is charged with a 'specified offence' triggering the dangerous offender provisions, or

(d) the magistrates in the youth court consider that the prosecution allegations are such that, if convicted on indictment, the Crown Court could order the young offender to be detained under the PCC(S)A 2000, section 91.

Section 91 empowers the higher court to order that young offenders convicted of certain 'grave crimes' be detained for a period of time not exceeding the maximum prison term which could be imposed on an adult for that offence. Orders under section 91 are clearly appropriate only in very serious cases, where the magistrates think that the juvenile, if convicted, will receive a sentence in excess of two years. If so, the youth court should not try the matter and must send the case to the Crown Court to be dealt with there.

1.21 When dealing with a young offender, magistrates technically do not 'convict' him, but record a 'finding of guilt'; and rather than 'sentencing' him they 'make an order upon a finding of guilt' (Children and Young Persons Act 1933, section 59). Nothing of practical importance turns upon this difference in terminology.

1.22 A juvenile who has a finding of guilt recorded against him in a youth court is also sentenced there. The sentencing powers of the youth courts are substantial. The power to impose a custodial sentence of up to two years stands in contrast to the power of the adult magistrates' court to sentence up to six months in respect of those aged eighteen and over. While at first sight this may look odd, the higher maximum for the youth court is designed to ensure that as many young offenders as possible are sentenced in the court which is designed to deal with them.

1.23 When a juvenile pleads guilty or is convicted on indictment, all the sentencing powers available by law in respect of those under eighteen years of age are at the Crown Court's disposal, save for the referral order, which is not available in the higher court. Section 8 of the PCC(S)A 2000 provides that, except in cases of homicide, if a juvenile is convicted in a court other than a youth court he shall be remitted to that court for sentence unless the convicting court is 'satisfied that it would be undesirable to do so'. The undoubted rationale of section 8 is that youth court magistrates have greater experience in dealing with young offenders than an adult magistrates' court or the Crown Court. Accordingly Crown Court judges may feel that this is appropriate unless the young offender is to be sentenced in a manner beyond the youth court's powers. In practice, however, the young offender often falls to be sentenced in the Crown Court alongside older offenders involved in the same offence, and it will often be better to sentence all the offenders in the Crown Court on the same occasion. In the important decision in *Lewis* (1984) 6 Cr App R (S) 44 Lord Lane LJ said that the Crown Court would be justified in *not* remitting young offenders to the youth court in at least the following cases:

(a) where the judge, having presided over the young offender's trial, feels that he is better informed as to the facts and circumstances of the case than a youth court could be;
(b) where an adult has been convicted as well as the juvenile, and remitting the juvenile might lead to disparity of sentence through different co-defendants being sentenced by different courts;
(c) where remitting the juvenile would lead to delay, duplication of proceedings, and fruitless expense.

These reasons, taken together, might apply in almost any case, so the effect of the decision has been that, notwithstanding section 8, Crown Court judges as a general rule themselves sentence young offenders convicted on indictment and do not remit them for sentence. Since section 8 does not apply to cases of homicide, juveniles convicted of offences involving death will always be sentenced in the Crown Court.

Where a young offender is convicted in an adult magistrates' court, the court's sentencing **1.24** powers are quite limited. The magistrates may impose a referral order, a fine, a discharge, bind over the juvenile's parents, and make some ancillary orders such as orders for compensation or costs (section 8(7) and (8)). If these options are not appropriate, it will be necessary to remit the young offender to the youth court. An adult magistrates' court cannot remit to the Crown Court.

Sentencers in the Crown Court

Sentence in the Crown Court is pronounced by a Crown Court judge. Normally the judge **1.25** alone will conduct the trial and deal with sentencing. There are three varieties of Crown Court judge: High Court judges, Circuit judges, and Recorders. High Court judges are based in London but a number of them spend time 'on circuit' and deal with the most serious criminal cases. Circuit judges and recorders handle the great bulk of Crown Court business. The difference is that Circuit judges, like High Court judges, are full-time judges, while recorders sit part-time, usually spending the remainder of their professional lives in practice. Some Circuit judges and recorders also sit in county courts, but the way the judge's time is split varies quite widely. An experienced recorder may be appointed to sit as a deputy High Court judge, which is also a part-time appointment.

The training of all judges is overseen by the Judicial College (formerly known as the **1.26** Judicial Studies Board). After induction training following initial appointment all judges are required to attend regular refresher courses. If major statutory change is pending then compulsory training of all members of the judiciary may be required. This was the case with the Criminal Justice Act 2003, which changed the law of evidence and procedure very substantially along with the law on sentencing. The Judicial College gives particular prominence to training on sentencing matters. In addition, a one-day conference which focuses on sentencing is provided by the College for full-time and part-time members of the judiciary on each circuit every year.

When hearing appeals from a magistrates' court, whether against conviction, sentence, or **1.27** both, the Crown Court is composed of a Crown Court judge and two lay justices.

Sentencers in the magistrates' courts

1.28 Most magistrates are lay men or women, often referred to as 'lay justices' or, in their more formal title, 'justice of the peace'. Justices are appointed by the Lord Chancellor on advice from local advisory committees. Although unpaid, magistrates are entitled to an allowance for travelling and subsistence, and to compensation for loss of earnings (Courts Act 2003, section 15). Some lay justices are in full-time employment away from the court and so their availability to sit is strictly limited. Normally magistrates are required to sit once a fortnight, but this varies across the county in accordance with the level of work required. In recent years the amount of work has been declining, largely due to the increased use of out-of-court sanctions such as cautions and fixed penalty notices. Many minor matters that used to come before the lower courts are now dealt with otherwise.

1.29 A small minority of magistrates are appointed to sit full-time in the lower courts. They were formerly known as stipendiary magistrates, properly entitled District Judges (Magistrates' Courts). Unlike lay justices, District Judges are qualified lawyers who are paid a salary. Provisions relating to their appointment, removal, and remuneration can be found in the Courts Act 2003, sections 22 to 26. There are a number of deputy District Judges, who perform the same duties but on a part-time basis.

1.30 At each sitting of a magistrates' court the magistrates are assisted by a clerk. Justices' clerks are appointed by the Lord Chancellor (Courts Act 2003, section 27(1)). The duties of the clerk include putting the charge to the accused, noting the evidence, explaining the procedure of the court to a party who is not legally represented, and, most importantly, advising the magistrates in matters of law. The justices' clerk is also required to carry out a range of administrative and managerial duties. In most court centres assistant justices' clerks may also be appointed. The clerk will often be asked by magistrates whether a particular form of sentence is open to them or whether they have power to commit a matter to the Crown Court. This advice should be given in open court. As far as sentencing is concerned, the clerk may properly advise the magistrates when asked, but should not seek to influence them on the actual sentence to be passed. The sentencing guidelines applicable to magistrates' courts are of great practical importance in this context.

1.31 When magistrates are appointed they undergo a course of basic training which is organized locally though overseen by the Judicial College. There will be follow-up training on a regular basis and additional training is required when a magistrate assumes additional responsibilities, such as chairing the magistrates in court or starting to sit as a youth court magistrate. A justice may be removed from office by the Lord Chancellor for incapacity or misbehaviour, or for failing to carry out his or her duties as a magistrate but otherwise retains the status of justice of the peace for life. On attaining the age of seventy a justice's name is placed on the 'supplemental list' which effectively means retirement.

Sentencers in youth courts

1.32 Trial in a youth court is simply a special form of summary trial, so that the sentencers in youth courts are magistrates. Not all magistrates are entitled to sit in a youth court. Those that have been authorized by the Lord Chief Justice and have received additional training to do so are termed the youth court panel, and only members of that panel are eligible to sit in the youth court. A youth court must consist of two or three magistrates, with both genders represented. It must be chaired by a youth court justice who is an approved youth court chairman. A district judge will be a member of the youth court panel and may sit alone in the youth court.

B ADVANCE INDICATION OF SENTENCE (*GOODYEAR*)

In what circumstances may a magistrate or Crown Court judge give an indication of the **1.33** sentence the defendant may expect to receive? Everyone understands that if the defendant admits his guilt he can expect to receive a lower sentence than he would receive if he contested the case and was convicted. The level of 'discount' for guilty plea depends upon the stage at which it is made and the circumstances existing at that time. The earlier the plea, the greater the discount, up to a recommended maximum of one-third, if the plea is entered at 'the first reasonable opportunity'. This issue is of much practical importance, and is considered in detail in 2.54 in the following Chapter. About two-thirds of all defendants in the Crown Court plead guilty, and nine out of every ten accused in the magistrates' courts do so. It is one of the tasks of the defence lawyer to explain the sentencing discount fully and fairly to the accused. The Code of Conduct of the Bar confirms that defence counsel should explain to his or her client the advantages and disadvantages of pleading guilty. Strong advice to enter a guilty plea is permissible, but should not be so strong as to effectively deprive the accused of his free choice as to how he pleads. The danger, of course, is that an innocent defendant may feel under great pressure to plead guilty believing that the plea will make the difference between a custodial and a community sentence. Such pressure is all the greater if the accused comes to believe, rightly or wrongly, that the judge is involved as well.

Choosing to plead guilty

In *Nightingale* [2013] EWCA Crim 405 the Court of Appeal said that in our criminal **1.34** justice system, a defendant charged with an offence is personally responsible for entering his plea, and that in exercising his personal responsibility he must be free to choose whether to plead guilty or not guilty. The principle applies whether or not the judge or counsel thinks that the case against the defendant is weak, or even unanswerable. The principle does not mean, however, that the defendant must be free from the pressure of the circumstances in which he is forced to make his choice. The defendant will be advised by his lawyers about his prospects of successfully contesting the charge and the implications for the sentencing decision if the contest is unsuccessful. Even if the defendant has indicated to or instructed his lawyers that he intends to plead not guilty, in his own interests he is entitled to be given, and should receive, realistic, forthright advice on these and similar questions. These necessary pressures do not deprive the defendant of his freedom to choose whether to plead guilty or not guilty; rather, the provision of realistic advice about his prospects helps to inform his choice. In marked distinction, the judge, subject only to express exceptions, must maintain his distance from and remain outside this process. The defendant's plea of guilty in *Nightingale* was found to be a nullity because of the Judge Advocate's uninvited indication that there would be a very substantial difference in the level of sentence which the defendant would receive, depending upon whether he pleaded guilty or was convicted after a trial.

There is a narrow and specific exception to this general rule. In the old case of *Turner* [1970] **1.35** 2 QB 321 the Court of Appeal said that the only circumstance in which the judge may give an advance indication of sentence is to say that the sentence will (or will not) take a particular form irrespective of the plea. So, if the judge felt able to say that the accused would not receive a custodial sentence, irrespective of plea, that might give an accused who was very scared of going to prison the necessary courage to plead guilty. In this narrow respect *Turner* remains the law, but otherwise it has been superseded by the important decision in *Goodyear* [2005] 1 WLR 2532.

Goodyear indications

1.36 From this case a number of key points emerge:

(a) A court should never give an indication of sentence unless one has been asked for by the accused. In *Nightingale* it was said that it is open to a judge to remind the defence advocate that he is entitled, if the defendant wishes, to seek a *Goodyear* indication, but this is as far as any judge should go. The judge 'should not give an advance indication of sentence unless one has been sought by the defendant'. A request for an indication may be made at the plea and case management hearing (PCMH) but sometimes happens on the morning of the trial. The hearing should take place in open court. *Turner* considers situations in which counsel might meet with the judge in chambers to discuss the issue, but this carries obvious dangers and hearing the matter in open court is a much better way to proceed. In the unlikely event of a meeting in judge's chambers both counsel must be there as well as a note-taker to make sure that an accurate record in made. If the case is going to be a complex one, and there are several matters in dispute, there should normally be an advance application from the defence served on the prosecution and the court.

(b) If an advance indication of sentence is requested, there is never an obligation on the court to provide one. There is some difference in judicial practice in this area. Some judges are quite prepared to give an indication where appropriate, while others seem to have a policy of never doing so. There are a number of particular types of case where the giving of a *Goodyear* indication is ill-advised. In particular, one should not be given in any case where the defendant is charged with a specified offence and the 'dangerous offender' provisions may come into play. In some cases the likely application of these provisions would be clear from the serious nature of the violent or sexual offence charged, and from the defendant's previous convictions, in which case an indication should never be given. The Court of Appeal in *Kulah* [2008] 1 WLR 2517 observed that, even if the dangerousness issue was not clear from the start of the case, there were obvious risks in giving a sentence indication where a pre-sentence report might later disclose material sufficient to show that the offender represented a real risk to the public and the sentence indication was therefore too low.

(c) Before a *Goodyear* indication can be given there must be a basis of plea agreed by the defence and the prosecution, reduced to legible written form. Clearly, if the defendant is prepared to admit guilt but only on a much less serious version of the facts than the prosecution continue to allege, no indication can be given. The basis of plea should, according to the *Criminal Practice Directions*, Sentencing, paragraph B.8, be signed by the defendant and by both defence and prosecution counsel. This is so that there can be no later argument about the facts upon which the indication was sought. If there is a sharp divergence between the prosecution and defence versions of the facts of the offence then a *Newton* hearing will be needed to resolve the issue (see paragraph 1.51 following). As we will see, the outcome of a *Newton* hearing may affect the level of reduction which the defendant receives for his plea of guilty, and so it seems clear that a *Goodyear* indication should not be given in such a case. It may be, however, that the disagreement over the facts of the offence is not sufficiently wide enough to make a real difference to the sentence outcome, and the judge might proceed to give an indication. Initiation of the process of seeking an indication lies with the defence, and the prosecution respond to it. The prosecution may wish to draw the judge's attention to relevant matters likely to affect sentence, such as items of evidence which the prosecution intended to rely upon at trial, a victim's personal statement, and the defendant's previous convictions. As usual, it is expected that any definitive sentencing guidelines or appellate sentencing authority will be brought to the judge's attention by both counsel prior to any indication being given. There is no need for an opening statement by the prosecution, and a plea in mitigation would be out of place at this stage. If appropriate the prosecution may wish to remind the judge that the power of the Attorney General to refer a sentencing decision as unduly lenient is unaffected by a sentencing indication having been given, and the prosecutor should not say anything which might give the impression that the sentence indication has the support or approval of the Crown.

(d) If an indication is given, it should be an indication of the sentence which the judge would impose on the basis of the agreed facts if the defendant was to plead guilty straight away. Matters of personal mitigation should not be considered at this stage, and may in due course cause the judge to come down from the original indication in order to take them into account. The judge should also make it clear that the sentence indication relates to the main punishment for the offence, and does not make reference to any ancillary orders which may be appropriate, such as disqualification of one kind or another, or a restraining order.

(e) Once an indication has been given it is binding on the court. To follow up on the point in the last paragraph, it is clear from *McDonald* [2008] 1 Cr App R (S) 91 that if a judge has given a clear indication that the highest sentence he would pass would be five years it was not then open to him to pass an indeterminate sentence for public protection in light of the reports. It may be that the indication could cease to be binding if the Sentencing Council issued a new definitive guideline on the offence in question or the Court of Appeal issued guidance to alter the previously appropriate sentencing level. The indication is binding on the judge who has given the indication and it binds any other judge who later assumes responsibility for sentencing the case, irrespective of whether he would have given the same or a similar indication, or would have given an indication at all. In practice it is much better for the judge who has given the *Goodyear* indication also to be the judge who passes sentence. This may sometimes be inconvenient, particularly where the judge is a recorder who may have to come back to sentence on another occasion.

(f) If the defendant after due consideration decides not to plead guilty, the indication ceases to have any effect and the trial proceeds on a not guilty plea. This eventuality makes it important for the judge to ensure that the proceedings which form part of the *Goodyear* indication are subject to reporting restrictions.

The right of a defendant to appeal against his sentence, or the right of the Attorney General **1.37** to refer a sentence to the Court of Appeal as being unduly lenient, are unaffected by the process of advance indication of sentence.

The Court of Appeal in *Goodyear* said that it would be impractical for the same arrange- **1.38** ments for advance indication of sentence to apply in the magistrates' courts. In the lower courts, where the offence is triable either way, the magistrates invite an indication from the defendant as to whether he intends to plead guilty or not guilty before deciding whether the case is suitable for summary trial or whether it should be sent to the Crown Court under the CDA 1998, section 51. The first part of this process is known as 'plea before venue'.

C ADJOURNMENT BEFORE SENTENCE

The court does not necessarily sentence the offender on the day on which he pleads guilty **1.39** or is found guilty. It has power to adjourn prior to passing sentence. This is frequently done, particularly for a period to allow preparation of a pre-sentence report and sometimes other reports. The Crown Court's power to adjourn is one which it possesses by virtue of common law. It is distinct from its statutory power to defer sentence (see *Annesley* (1975) 62 Cr App R 113 and paragraph 8.01, this book). A magistrates' court's power to do so is governed by the MCA 1980, section 10(3), which permits a magistrates' court to adjourn 'for the purpose of enabling inquiries to be made or of determining the most suitable method of dealing with the case'. Adjournment for some other reason, such as putting off a difficult decision, or to allow the passage of time so that the young offender will mature in the meantime (as in *Arthur v Stringer* (1986) 8 Cr App R (S) 329), is unlawful. During the period of an adjournment the offender will be remanded in custody or on bail. Where an offender remanded for reports to be prepared is granted bail the court has power to include a condition that the offender makes himself available 'for the purpose of enabling inquiries or a report to be made to assist the court in dealing with him for an offence' (Bail Act 1976, section3(6)(d)).

Adjournment for reports

1.40 Independent reports on offenders are often a vital factor in the sentencing decision. The most frequently encountered are pre-sentence reports (PSR) and medical reports. Where the accused indicates an intention to plead guilty and it seems likely that the court will need reports before passing sentence, the reports are prepared before the hearing if possible. If, however, the accused is pleading not guilty it is unlikely that reports can be prepared. This is because an important element in the PSR is the consideration of the accused's attitude to the offence. If the accused is pleading not guilty then obviously this aspect cannot be investigated. Even if the accused is pleading guilty the preparation of reports is not automatic. The circumstances in which a court is required by law to obtain a PSR or a medical report are laid down by statute, and are considered in paragraphs 1.74 and 1.82 following.

1.41 The current norm is an adjournment for three weeks for preparation of a PSR. In the magistrates' courts 'stand-down' reports are common, being reports prepared in short order on the day on which the offender has pleaded guilty or been convicted. Preparation of a medical report, especially a psychiatric report, can take several weeks.

Adjournment where there are several offenders

1.42 There is a strong argument to be made that offenders who have jointly committed an offence, or offenders who have committed separate offences which arose out of the same circumstances or which were otherwise factually linked, should be sentenced together by one judge on one occasion. To do so should ensure consistent treatment for them all, with any differences in the sentences imposed being designed to reflect the different roles played in the offence(s) and other material differences between the offenders. If the defendants plead guilty together, or all elect trial together there is likely to be no problem. If, however, A pleads guilty and B pleads not guilty, then clearly B cannot be sentenced unless and until he is convicted. This may not happen for some weeks or months. The desirability of sentencing A and B together means that generally it is better to adjourn sentence on A until the outcome of B's trial is known. It may be that A is to give evidence at B's trial, in which case there is the general advantage that the judge will have the benefit of hearing evidence as to which of them played the leading role in the offence. This general preference for adjournment was established in the old case of *Payne* [1950] 1 All ER 102 and it still represents the law. There are some situations, however, in which the judge should consider sentencing A straight away, before the trial of B takes place. According to the Divisional Court in *Sheffield Crown Court ex pate Brownlow* [1980] QB 520 the following matters (amongst others) might be relevant to whether or not to adjourn sentence upon A:

(a) A would have a very long time to wait before sentence could be passed upon him, such as where B has absconded; or
(b) A's offence was trivial in comparison with the charge against B; or
(c) there are more than usually strong reasons to think that A might perjure himself by colouring his evidence in the trial of B.

The situation discussed in this paragraph can also create difficulties where the sentencer comes to determine the factual basis for passing sentence on the two offenders. Comments adverse to A's role in the offence may be made at B's trial which A may have little opportunity to refute. This issue is considered at paragraph 1.58, this Chapter.

Adjournments where there are outstanding charges

It is desirable that an accused with several charges outstanding against him should be **1.43** sentenced on one occasion for all matters in respect of which he is ultimately convicted. Watkin J in *Bennett* (1980) 2 Cr App R (S) 96 said that there was an obligation 'on solicitors, counsel, and judges alike to do all within their power to ensure that as far as possible all outstanding charges against a defendant are dealt with in the same court, by the same judge upon a single occasion'. If the offender is sentenced piecemeal by different judges (or by the magistrates for one matter and the Crown Court for another) there is a danger that the aggregate sentence will be out of proportion to the overall gravity of the offending. There is also a danger that the first sentencer, dealing perhaps with the less serious matters, will pass a community order and thus create a dilemma for the second sentencer. The latter may feel that a custodial sentence is required for the offence with which he is dealing, but to pass such a sentence would prevent the earlier community sentence running its natural course. To avoid these problems it is generally better that one sentencer should deal with everything on one occasion, even if these means adjournments and extra administrative work behind the scenes. Adjournment in these circumstances is entirely at the discretion of the court, and the accused may be remanded in custody or on bail.

Sentence indications on adjournment for reports

Where the Crown Court or a magistrates' court adjourns for reports in circumstances which **1.44** justifiably lead the offender to think that, if the report turns out to be favourable, a community order will be passed, then the court is bound by the implied promise which it has given. To resile from the promise would leave the offender with a legitimate sense of grievance. This principle was first stated in *Gillam* (1990) 2 Cr App R (S) 267 and has been followed in many later cases. An example is *Gibson* [2004] 2 Cr App R (S) 84, a case where the offender had committed his third domestic burglary and so attracted a prescribed minimum sentence of three years (under the PCC(S)A 2000, section111) unless there were particular circumstances relating either to the offences or to the offender which in the view of the court would render such a sentence unjust. The court adjourned for an assessment of the offender's suitability for drug treatment under a community order. The Court of Appeal held that this approach had given rise to a legitimate expectation on the part of the offender that a community sentence would be passed if the report was a favourable one. It was favourable, and so the eventual imposition of a custodial sentence under section 111 was 'unjust'.

The problem in *Gillam* only arises if something in the nature of a promise has been made. If **1.45** the judge ordering the adjournment makes it clear that no such promise is being made, even if the report turns out to be favourable, then no sense of grievance can arise even if the outcome is a custodial sentence. This is the reason why judges and magistrates ordering a report commonly indicates that 'all options are open', indicating that a favourable report will not necessarily mean a community sentence. Such a statement is not very helpful to the probation officer who is to write the PSR, who no doubt would prefer some provisional indication of the court's thinking at the time of adjournment. The SGC guideline on *New Sentences* suggests that if the court has reached the provisional view that a community sentence is appropriate then the sentencer should assist the probation officer by explaining what purpose the community order is intended to fulfil, and whether the offence falls towards the top, middle, or bottom of the community offence range. It is also suggested that such remarks should be committed to writing. In many cases, however, especially in the Crown Court, the case lies near the custody threshold and the judge in ordering the PSR is seeking further information about the background of the offender and the circumstances before deciding whether custody can be avoided. In such a case it is safer to adopt the course approved by the Court of Appeal in *Chamberlain* (1994) 16 Cr App R (S) 473, where the defendant was told that he should not assume that he is likely to receive any particular form of treatment, or that a custodial sentence is ruled out, whatever the further report or inquiry might reveal.

D SETTLING THE FACTUAL BASIS FOR SENTENCE (*NEWTON*)

1.46 Before selecting the appropriate sentence the judge or magistrates will require further information about the offence and about the offender. From the moment when the offender pleads guilty or is found guilty to the moment when the judge or bench passes sentence, there is a period of time in which this information will be adduced. In simple, straightforward cases, particularly in the lower courts the decision on sentence can be reached almost immediately. In more complex cases the procedure between conviction and sentence may take several hours, involving the calling of witnesses and close investigation of disputed facts. If there has been a trial it is very much to be preferred that the judge who presided over the trial should also pass sentence. This may be inconvenient for a part-time judge, such as a recorder, who may have to make a special trip to that court to sentence an offender over whose trial he presided three weeks earlier. The matter is important, however, since the judge will have had the advantage of hearing the detail of the evidence and forming a view as to the witnesses in the case, especially the offender if he chose to give evidence.

1.47 It may seem odd, at first sight, that an accused can be found guilty of an offence when important factual issues remain unresolved. It should be remembered, however, that when the accused has pleaded guilty there will have been no trial and hence no examination of the offence in court. Even where there has been a trial, it will have been confined to issues in dispute between the parties and relevant to guilt. Other matters, not relevant to that issue, may still require examination before the proper sentence can be fixed. Consider offences of strict liability. Whether the accused committed the offence knowingly or not is irrelevant to his liability for the offence but it is of central importance when fixing the punishment. An example is *Sandhu* [1997] Crim LR 288 where the offender pleaded guilty to strict liability offences under the Trade Descriptions Act 1968 and was sentenced on the assumption that he had *mens rea*. The Court of Appeal said that the assumption should not have been made without the offender having been given a chance to give evidence on the matter, and reduced the sentence from six months imprisonment to a fine of £280. A more recent one is *Jackson* [2007] 1 Cr App R 28 where at a Court Martial the offender had pleaded guilty to flying his aircraft too low (under 100 feet, which is forbidden by service regulations) with the result that he had hit a tower and caused considerable damage to the aircraft. He was fined £2500 and severely reprimanded. The Court of Appeal found that the offence was one of strict liability and said that when sentencing it is important to determine the level of culpability to the criminal standard. A pilot who knowingly or recklessly flies his plane at an altitude of less than 100 feet may expect a higher sentence than one who does so negligently, which was the case with this offender.

Prosecution duties

If the accused pleads guilty the first stage in the procedure between conviction and sentence **1.48** is the summary by the prosecutor of the facts of the offence. This summary is designed to assist the court and to inform the offender, the public, and the press of the basis of the prosecution case. If the accused has pleaded not guilty this summary may be dispensed with, but where the court is convening for sentence after a period of adjournment to obtain reports, it will still be appropriate for the prosecution to outline the agreed facts. The impact of the offence upon the victim is clearly an important consideration when the court is assessing the seriousness of the offence. In some cases the court may have the benefit of a victim personal statement (see paragraph 1.84, this Chapter) but whether or not there is such a statement the prosecutor should be in a position to explain to the court the impact of the offence upon the injured party. The prosecution is required to take a measured and fair attitude during the stage between conviction and sentence. It is not their task to persuade or encourage the sentencer to pass a severe sentence. The *Code of Conduct of the Bar*, paragraph 11.8(a) says that 'prosecuting counsel should not attempt by advocacy to influence the court with regard to sentence'. The prosecution has a duty to point out aggravating features of the case, but it should also be frank in drawing attention to any matters within its knowledge which reflect to the offender's credit, such as a plea of guilty at the first reasonable opportunity. It is no longer the case, if it ever was, that the prosecutor should be entirely neutral at sentence. It is the responsibility of the prosecutor to refer the judge to any one or more of the following matters which may arise:

(a) It is clear that the prosecution as well as the defence is responsible for making the court aware of any limitations on sentencing powers which arise in the particular case. It is particularly the role of the prosecutor to be aware of the maximum penalty available to the court for the offence being dealt with. An experienced prosecutor will be aware of areas where a mistake is perhaps more likely to be made—such as where the Crown Court is limited to magistrates' court's powers in sentencing, or where a prescribed minimum sentence applies. There is no doubt that sentencing has become technically more complex over the last twenty years or so, with numerous pitfalls and potential for errors to be made. In cases where sentencing mistakes have been made, the Court of Appeal has frequently observed that the judge did not receive the assistance from counsel that he or she was entitled to expect. A clear statement to this effect can be found in *Cain* [2007] 2 Cr App R (S) 135 where Lord Phillips CJ said: '[S]entencing has become a complex matter...it is unacceptable for advocates not to ascertain and be prepared to assist the judge with the legal restrictions on sentence that he can impose...This duty is not restricted to defence advocates'.

(b) The prosecutor should be ready, without prompting from the judge, to refer the court to any relevant definitive sentencing guidelines and appellate case law. The prosecutor should indicate to the judge the prosecutor's view as to how the guidelines apply to the case in hand. It is perfectly appropriate, for example, for the prosecutor to assert that the case falls within category 1 at step 1 of the Sentencing Council's definitive guideline on *Assault*, and to identify the presence of particular statutory and other aggravating factors which are relevant at step 2. The judge is entitled to expect assistance from the prosecution as well as from the defence on these matters. The Court in *Cain* said that 'the advocate for the prosecution should always be ready to assist the court...and in a position to draw the judge's attention to any relevant sentencing guidelines or guideline decisions of this court'.

(c) In any case where the court has power to make an order ancillary to sentence, such as a compensation order, a restitution order, or a restraining order, prosecution counsel must be ready to provide all relevant information. None of these orders can be made without an adequate factual basis being made for them. In the case of a compensation order, for example, the court is under a duty to make an order whenever it reasonably can do so, but since the victim is not a party to the proceedings and may well not be present in court at the sentencing hearing, it is incumbent on the prosecutor to adduce the amount, such as receipts showing the cost of property damaged. In a case where the Crown seeks an order for forfeiture of an item of property from the offender as part of the sentence for the offence, then according to the Court of Appeal in *Pemberton* (1982) 4 Cr App R (S) 328, 'it is incumbent upon the prosecution to justify the application, and it is incumbent upon the trial judge to put the prosecution to proof if they simply state baldly, without any supporting evidence, that they seek an order for forfeiture'. It is not, however, the duty of the prosecution to investigate the offender's means (*Phillips* (1988) 10 Cr App R (S) 419). The defence should be in a position to provide that information and, if necessary the court may require the offender to complete a means assessment.

1.49 The Court of Appeal has made it clear in a number of decisions, especially *Underwood* [2005] 1 Cr App R 178, now confirmed and re-stated in *Cairns* [2013] EWCA Crim 467, that a basis of plea must never be agreed by the prosecution on a misleading or untrue set of facts and must take proper account of the victim's interests; in cases involving multiple defendants, the bases of plea for each defendant must be factually consistent with each other. The following points in particular are set out in that decision:

(a) The written basis of plea must be scrutinized by the prosecution with great care.

(b) The prosecution must ensure that the defence is aware of the basis on which the plea is accepted and the way in which the case will be opened. Where a basis of plea is agreed, having been reduced into writing and signed by advocates for both sides, it should be submitted to the judge prior to the opening. It should not contain matters which are disputed.

(c) Both sides must ensure that the judge is aware of any discrepancy between the basis of plea and the prosecution case that could potentially have a significant effect on sentence so that consideration can be given to holding a *Newton* hearing (see paragraph 1.51, following). Even where the basis of plea is agreed between the prosecution and the defence, the judge is not bound by such agreement. If the judge is minded not to accept the basis of plea in a case where that may affect sentence, he should say so and the judge is entitled to insist that any evidence relating to the matters in dispute should be called. The defendant can thereby be given an opportunity to present evidence that what he has asserted in the basis of plea is in fact true. The judge is, however, not entitled simply to reject the basis of plea without a *Newton* hearing unless the judge makes a finding that the basis is manifestly false.

Establishing the facts after a guilty plea

1.50 By pleading guilty the offender does not necessarily admit that the prosecution case against him is correct in its entirety. He admits, of course, that he committed the offences described in each of the counts to which he enters a guilty plea. Many modern offences are broadly drafted, and the particulars in the offence are likely to reveal little about whether the offence is a serious or trivial one of its type. It sometimes happens that an offender pleads guilty but denies that the crime was as serious as the prosecution asserts, or might be assumed. A wide variety of situations may arise. Examples include where the offender admits an assault but then denies the prosecution assertion that he used a weapon, or admits the assault but claims that it was committed only after significant provocation from the injured party. Although in these cases the offender is clearly guilty as charged, the sentence might well be quite different depending upon whether the judge accepted the prosecution statement of facts or the defence version of what happened.

The leading case in this area is *Newton* (1982) 4 Cr App R (S) 388. The offender pleaded **1.51** guilty to a sexual offence committed on his wife. As the law stood at that time the offence was committed whether or not the wife consented to the sexual activity. Defence counsel made clear in mitigation the offender's assertion that his wife had consented, but the judge passed a sentence of eight years' imprisonment which was clearly based upon an acceptance of the prosecution version of the facts, that the activity had been without consent. On appeal against the sentence the Court of Appeal reduced the sentence to one year, resulting in Newton's immediate release from prison (he had by that time served ten months in prison). Lord Lane CJ in the Court of Appeal said that in such a case, where a vital issue of fact was unresolved by the plea, the judge must come to a clear view on the facts. In some circumstances it might be possible to obtain the answer from the jury. That was not possible here, since the offender had admitted the offence. The second option was for the judge to hear evidence from one side, then the other, and come to his own conclusion, acting as his own jury. The third option was to hear no evidence but to listen to submissions from counsel and come to his conclusion that way. But if there remains a substantial conflict between the two sides the version of the defendant must be accepted so far as possible. The basic propositions advocated in *Newton* have been elaborated in later appellate decisions including *Cairns* [2013] EWCA Crim 467 and in the *Criminal Practice Directions*, paragraphs Sentencing B.1 to B.14. The practice advocated by Lord Lane has become known as a '*Newton* hearing' or sometimes as a 'trial of issue'. The following main points have emerged over the years:

(a) In *Newton* cases the burden of proof rests on the prosecution to establish its version of the facts to the normal criminal standard of 'beyond reasonable doubt'. In criminal trials this phrase has now generally been replaced by the requirement that the jury must be 'sure' of guilt. The equivalent in a *Newton* hearing is that the judge must be sure that the prosecution version of the disputed fact is the correct one. According to the Court of Appeal in *Ahmed* (1984) 6 Cr App R (S) 391 the court should direct itself 'that the accused's account must be accepted unless that court is sure that it is untrue'. It is important that the judge directs himself or herself openly and for the record as to the relevant burden and standard of proof.

(b) A *Newton* hearing is necessary only where there is a 'substantial conflict between the two sides', according to Lord Lane. It follows that where the factual different is insignificant and would make no discernible difference to the sentence to be passed a *Newton* hearing would be a waste of time. If the judge takes that view it is still good practice to make it clear that the defendant is being given the benefit of any doubt on the matter (*Hall* (1984) 6 Cr App R (S) 321). Neither is a *Newton* hearing necessary if the defence version of what happened is so implausible that the judge can safely reject it out of hand rather than being obliged to conduct a hearing on the matter. The old case of *Hawkins* (1985) 7 Cr App R (S) 351 is a good example. The offender's account of his involvement as the get-away driver in a joint offence of burglary, committed by himself and two others, was that he was unaware until the very end of the incident why the others had asked him to drive them to specified premises and then collect them an hour later. The judge declined to hear evidence on the matter and sentenced Hawkins on the prosecution version of the facts, which was that he had been a knowing participant throughout. The Court of Appeal upheld the judge's decision, agreeing that the defendant had made an 'incredible assertion'. Even so, a decision to strike out the defendant's version of the facts in this way must not be taken lightly. In a case where a *Newton* hearing really is necessary the judge is under a duty to hold one.

(c)   The initiative to raise the matter of a *Newton* hearing usually rests with the defence, who will draw the issue to the attention of the prosecution and the court. It is, however, in the end a matter for the judge. As we have seen, there may be circumstances in which prosecution and defence declare themselves sufficiently agreed on the material facts, but the judge is not prepared to accept without further inquiry the factual basis agreed by the two sides. In *George* [2006] 1 Cr App R (S) 683 the Court of Appeal said that if a judge, on reading the papers, came to the view that the basis of plea was unrealistic, he was bound to say so. The same line was taken in *Cairns* [2013] EWCA Crim 467. In *George* the judge had used robust language to reject the basis of plea, but an appeal on the basis that the judge was thereafter biased against the offender was rejected. It was clear that the resulting *Newton* hearing had been carried out with scrupulous fairness. If the judge decides that a hearing is necessary the parties are given the opportunity to call witnesses if they wish to do so, and to cross-examine the witnesses of the other side. There may be circumstances where the judge, in order to get to the truth of the matter, may direct the attendance of witnesses if the parties have not done so (*Sheard* [2013] EWCA Crim 1161). The defendant is a competent witness for the defence but cannot be called by the prosecution (or by the judge). The whole *Newton* process has more in common with a contested trial than the usual arrangements between conviction and sentence. The hearing should follow adversarial lines. The judge should preside over the hearing as if he were presiding over a trial. He or she should not adopt an inquisitorial role and, if asking questions, should wait until both counsel have finished their questions (*Myers* [1996] 1 Cr App R (S) 187). The Court in *Cairns* made the point that a *Newton* hearing need not be a lengthy affair. In that case the judge was concerned that the defendant was, in truth, the equivalent of a street dealer (given the quantity of drugs and money in his possession). It would have taken only a few minutes for the defendant to be given the opportunity to provide evidence to support his contention that his supply of drugs to others was to friends only. The judge would then have been in a position to decide the issue to the usual criminal standard.

(d)   One result of contesting the facts by way of a *Newton* hearing is that the offender will, if the judge in the end accepts the prosecution version of the facts, lose some of the discount which he would otherwise have received for pleading guilty. The SGC guideline on *Reduction in Sentence for a Guilty Plea* simply states that the matter should be 'taken into account' in determining the appropriate level of reduction. In *Caley* [2012] EWCA Crim 2821, Hughes LJ said that the loss of discount following an unproductive dispute on the facts was 'only common sense', and that it was important that unrealistic bases of plea should receive no incentive. The Court said that what (if any) reduction for plea should survive an adverse *Newton* finding would depend on all the circumstances, including the extent of the issue determined, whether lay witnesses had to give evidence and on the extra time and effort involved for the court. In so far as the rationale for the reduction in sentence for a guilty plea is the saving of cost, the same principle applies here. The defendant ought to be made aware from the outset of the risk that he may lose some, or all, of the discount if a *Newton* hearing is required, but the judge should be careful not to give the impression that he or she has already decided against the defendant's version of the facts (*Satchell* [1997] 2 Cr App R (S) 258).

(e) Finally, according to *Cairns*, the Court of Appeal will not interfere with a finding of fact made in a *Newton* hearing, provided that the judge has properly directed himself (in accordance with the burden and standard of proof) unless, exceptionally, the Court is satisfied that no reasonable finder of fact could have reached that decision.

Sentencing only for offence admitted

It is one of the most fundamental principles of sentencing that an offender who has pleaded **1.52** guilty to an offence must only be sentenced for that offence. Where the prosecution accepts a plea of guilty to a lesser offence, or accepts a plea of guilty to one of several counts which were originally preferred against the accused, the judge must be careful to sentence only for the matters admitted or specifically proved against the offender. A simple example is *Lawrence* (1983) 5 Cr App R (S) 220, where the offender pleaded guilty to possession of cannabis, in light of which a count of possession with intent to supply did not proceed. The Court of Appeal varied a short prison sentence to a fine because it was felt that the sentencer had failed to 'banish from his mind' the possibility that the defendant was growing the cannabis in order to sell it. Another clear example is where the offender has pleaded guilty to the 'basic' form of an offence which also has a racially or religiously aggravated form which carries a higher maximum penalty. It is wrong for the judge to sentence on the basis that the 'basic' offence was racially or religiously aggravated since that would be to sentence him for an offence with which he had not been charged and convicted. The point was made clear in *McGillivray* [2005] 2 Cr App R (S) 366, which is discussed at paragraph 2.41, this book.

Sample counts

A difficult problem can be posed by the bringing of sample counts against an accused. The **1.53** prosecution opts to proceed on sample counts in a case where the defendant is alleged to have committed an offence on a very large number of occasions, and it makes practical sense to prosecute a representative sample of those instances rather than all of them. An example is an allegation of repeated instances of benefit fraud, a fresh offence technically having been committed every time the offender claimed benefit knowing that he was not entitled to it. To prosecute all the offences would be pointless because if convicted the sentence is unlikely to be much greater than it would be for a modest number of such offences. It would therefore also be very wasteful of court time and resources. It was established in *Canavan* [1998] 1 Cr App R 79 that, consistent with the principle referred to in the last paragraph, the sentencer is bound to impose sentence purely on the basis of the sample counts proved against the offender or admitted by him, unless the defence concedes that the counts are indeed part of a wider pattern, or asks for the other counts to be treated as offences to be taken into consideration. Another way of putting this is to say that any offence which is not included on the indictment and has not been taken into consideration is not an 'associated offence' within the terms of the PCC(S)A 2000, section 161, and so the offender cannot be sentenced for it. In most cases the rule in *Canavan*, which has been endorsed in subsequent cases including *Povey* [2005] 2 Cr App R (S) 100, should cause few practical problems. The prosecution will just need to ensure that there is a sufficient number of sample counts on the indictment so that upon conviction they will attract an appropriate level of sentence. As Lord Woolf CJ put it in *Povey*, at paragraph [33]:

> ...the problem will be most satisfactorily alleviated by the appropriate framing of the indictment...In preparing the indictment the prosecution should always have in mind...the need to provide the sentencing judge

…with sufficient examples (and no more) of the offending behaviour to enable the judge to impose a sentence which properly reflects the offender's criminal behaviour…[T]he presence of more counts than necessary will only result in concurrent sentences.

The importance of the principle in *Canavan* should not lead to overly technical drafting of charges against the accused. The Court in *Povey* said that a single count might properly reflect the alleged theft of several different articles from the same place, or the illegal felling of ninety trees over a number of days.

1.54　A narrow statutory exception to the rule in *Canavan* is provided by the Domestic Violence, Crime and Victims Act 2004, section 17. This allows the prosecution in certain cases to apply for trial by jury on sample counts, with the judge alone trying the remaining counts. The prosecution must make advance application under this rarely used provision, and the judge may grant leave to proceed in this way if it is in the interests of justice to do so.

Establishing the facts after a guilty verdict

1.55　Post-conviction disputes about the circumstances of the offence are not limited to cases where the offender pleads guilty, for a jury's guilty verdict after a trial is not necessarily a total vindication of the prosecution's case. Consider for example the position of an accused who denies a charge of assault occasioning actual bodily harm. The victim gives evidence for the prosecution that he was attacked with a knife, and the accused admits striking the victim but says that he was acting in self-defence and did not use a weapon. A verdict of guilty will merely show that, in the jury's view, the admitted assault was not a justified act of self-defence. It will not resolve the issue, highly relevant to sentence, of whether a weapon was used. In such cases it is usually for the judge to form his or her own view of the evidence adduced during the trial, and decide what the facts of the offence were. If necessary the judge can embark upon a *Newton* hearing, but this would only really be appropriate if the issue which now arose as relevant to sentence was not properly considered during the trial because it was not relevant to guilt. A good example is *Finch* (1993) 14 Cr App R (S) 226, where the accused claimed that he had been entrapped by the police into committing the offence. Entrapment is not a defence in English law, and so was not relevant to guilt. Circumstances of entrapment, however, might constitute substantial mitigation, and the Court of Appeal said that a *Newton* hearing should have been held to resolve the issue.

1.56　In general the judge should not ask the jury the reasons for its verdict or ask what facts it finds proved. In earlier times it was common practice for the judge to ask a jury to elaborate on the factual basis for its decision, to deliver a 'special' rather than a 'general' verdict. A case cited as authority for the proposition that this should no longer be done is *Larkin* [1943] KB 174, although there are examples of trial judges doing it in later cases, and the possibility of a judge receiving assistance from the jury was left open in *Newton* as a permitted way of establishing the factual basis for sentence. Most of the later cases in which judges have sought assistance from the jury are manslaughter cases, a crime which may be legally established in a number of different ways. It may be that manslaughter represents an exception to what the Court of Appeal in *Stosiek* (1982) 4 Cr App R (S) 205 (at page 208) called 'the usual and proper practice' of 'refrain[ing] from inviting juries to explain their verdicts'. The reason for doubting this practice in England is the rather strange ground that investigation by the judge into the precise basis for the jury's decision may reveal that different members of the jury have based their conviction on materially different versions of the facts. If it emerges that this has happened the accused's conviction must be quashed (see *Brown* (1984) 79 Cr App R 115). There remains the possibility that a jury may, unsolicited, volunteer its reasoning to the judge, or make its opinion clear in some other way, such as by adding a rider to its verdict. The judge may take such an indication into account, but is not bound by it (*Mills* [2004] 1 Cr App R (S) 332). One way of avoiding the practice of the judge questioning the jury to determine the facts is for the prosecution to anticipate the problem, by inserting an additional count in the indictment which is designed to resolve the ambiguity on the main count. While this is possible in theory it may be difficult to achieve in practice. Thus, it has been suggested that if in *Newton* the prosecution had included an additional count of assault occasioning actual bodily harm the jury's verdict on that count might have resolved the issue of whether the sexual offence was consensual or not. Even so, on the prosecution version of the facts, the wife had received other injuries consistent with an attempt to escape from her husband, so it seems that a verdict of guilty on the assault charge would not necessarily have settled the 'vital issue of consent'.

The most important matter is that the view of the facts which the judge adopts must be **1.57** consistent with the jury's verdict. If the jury refuses to find the accused guilty as charged but convicts him of a lesser offence, the sentence must of course be appropriate to that lesser offence, notwithstanding that the judge is convinced that there should have been a conviction for the more serious offence. A clear example is where the prosecution has charged a racially aggravated form of the offence but the jury returns a conviction for the basic (ie non-racially aggravated) form of the offence. In those circumstances it would be quite wrong for the sentencer to sentence on the basis that a racial element was present (*McGillivray* [2005] 2 Cr App R (S) 366). Where more than one interpretation of the jury's verdict is possible the judge is not necessarily bound to accept that version of events which is the most favourable to the offender. In *Triumph* (1984) 6 Cr App R (S) 120 the jury found the offender not guilty of attempted murder but guilty of causing grievous bodily harm with intent. The accused maintained in his evidence that the gun had gone off accidentally. The judge sentenced on the basis that the offender had shot the victim on purpose, even though he had not intended to kill. The decision was upheld by the Court of Appeal, but should be read in the context of other cases, particularly *Stosiek* (1982) 4 Cr App R (S) 205, which makes it clear that the judge should always be careful to give the benefit of any real doubt to the offender.

Establishing the facts after a conviction, where a co-accused pleaded guilty

The procedures outlined earlier in this Chapter have caused difficulty in the case where **1.58** A has pleaded guilty but is not sentenced, and B, who has pleaded not guilty, is convicted after a trial. The problem is that when sentencing B the judge is, of course, under a duty to determine the proper factual basis for sentencing both offenders. In *Smith* (1988) 10 Cr App R (S) 271, the leading case on the matter, the offender pleaded guilty to involvement in the supply of stolen credit cards to the three co-accused. One of the co-accused pleaded guilty, while the other two were found guilty by a jury after their defence that they had acted under duress from Smith, was rejected. At sentence, the judge stated that he had taken the view that Smith was the ringleader in the scheme, based in part on the evidence which the co-accused had given in their own defence. The judge offered Smith the chance to testify in his own defence at the sentencing stage, but this was not taken up. A sentence of twenty-one months' imprisonment was passed on Smith, while the three co-accused were all given community sentences. The Court of Appeal upheld the sentences, saying that the sentencer was entitled to take account of all the evidence he had heard at the trial of B in fixing the sentence on A. It was important that A be given a chance to give evidence about the extent of his involvement, and this had been done. Lord Lane CJ said that the judge must bear in mind that self-serving statements made by the offenders might be untrue. In this case the judge had 'handled this difficult situation impeccably'.

1.59 In *Winter* [1997] 1 Cr App R (S) 331 six offenders were charged with conspiracy to cause grievous bodily harm with intent. One offender pleaded guilty while the others were convicted after a trial and received eight-year or six-year prison sentences. The offender who had pleaded guilty appealed against his six-year sentence on the basis that he had been given no proper credit for his plea, which had been tendered and accepted on the basis that he had used no violence against the victim. The Court of Appeal reduced the sentence to one of five years saying that the offender should at least have been given the opportunity to give evidence if he had wished to do so. This had not been done.

E OFFENCES TAKEN INTO CONSIDERATION

1.60 As we have seen, the offender must be sentenced only for those offences for which he has been found guilty or to which he has pleaded guilty. There is a limited exception to this principle, which applies where other offences are taken into consideration. Offences taken into consideration when sentence is passed (or TICs as they are generally known) are offences of which the offender is never convicted, but which are admitted by him in court and, at his request, are borne in mind by the sentencer when sentence is passed for the offences in respect of which there is a conviction (hereinafter called the 'conviction offences'). The sequence of events leading up to offences being taken into consideration is a matter of convention rather than statutory regulation, although the Sentencing Council issued a guideline dealing with *Offences Taken into Consideration* in 2012. The practice is of long standing. Typically it will involve a suspect, who has been arrested on suspicion of one or more crimes, admitting at the police station that he committed the crimes alleged and making it obvious that he intends to plead guilty. The police may then ask him about other similar offences which they believe he might have committed, but which, in the absence of an admission by him, they would find difficult to prove. Since he is resigned to pleading guilty to the offences for which he was arrested the suspect often decides to make a clean breast of everything on the understanding that some or all of the offences he is now being asked about will not be the subject of separate charges but will merely be taken into consideration. A list is then drawn up of the offences to be taken into consideration and the suspect signs the list. The offences for which he was arrested and with which he was charged are then prosecuted in the normal way. Copies of the list of TICs are given to the prosecutor and to the defence. The list should set out the nature and date of each offence and brief relevant details (monetary value of items stolen, addresses of properties burgled, and so on).

1.61 At court the accused duly pleads guilty. Then at some stage during the prosecutor's statement of the facts the prosecutor will mention to the sentencer that the offender wants to have other matters considered. The sentencer will then be handed the list of offences signed by the offender and the sentencer, or court clerk, will ask the offender in open court whether he admits them and whether he wants them taken into consideration (*Anderson v DPP* [1978] AC 964). If the offender answers 'yes' to both questions the sentencer may, and usually will, comply with the request. Agreement must come from the offender personally, and not from his lawyer. Care must be taken with offenders who are unrepresented or where there may be doubt as to their understanding of the process. The offender should admit the offences in open court, but it is not necessary to put all the offences (there are sometimes very many) to the offender one by one. Usually the offender is asked whether he has signed the list, whether he agrees that he committed the offences, and whether he wants them taken into consideration. Any offences which he then denies should be deleted. All this assumes that the offender pleads guilty, and that is the situation for which offences TIC is principally designed. There is, however, nothing to stop the prosecution requesting an adjournment after the accused had been convicted following a trial, to ask him whether, given that outcome, he now wishes to have other offences considered. The prosecution should be in a position to provide the sentencer with brief details of any of the offences TIC. The sentence which is eventually passed will be somewhat more severe than it would have been in the absence of the TICs. The addition to the sentence will, however, be considerably less than the penalty would have been if they had been prosecuted separately. If in a magistrates' court the new information about TICs now makes the case one which should attract a punishment greater than the magistrates have power to impose, and provided the offence is triable either way, and the offender is aged eighteen or over the case may be committed to the Crown Court for sentence (PCC(S)A 2000, section 3).

The system of taking offences into consideration has advantages for offenders. It allows **1.62** them to 'clear the slate' and to receive a lesser sentence than might otherwise have been the case. It also has advantages for the police, because they 'clear up' offences which otherwise might have remained unsolved. The victim of an offence which is 'merely' taken into consideration rather than being the subject of a distinct charge and conviction might feel somewhat aggrieved by the process. As explained in the following, the court may make a compensation order in favour of the victim of an offence TIC but the reality is that this is rarely done. The following additional points about taking offences into consideration should be noted:

(a) When the sentencer is deciding whether an offence is, or offences are, so serious that neither a fine alone nor a community sentence can be justified, the court may consider the conviction offences, or a combination of the conviction offences and the offences taken into consideration (CJA 2003, section 161). If the sentencer decides than a custodial sentence is inevitable on that basis then all the conviction offences and all the TICs should be weighed when determining the shortest custodial term which is commensurate with the seriousness of the offences (CJA 2003, section 153(2)). If the sentencer decides that the offence is, or the offences are, not so serious as to require custody, a community sentence may be imposed, but only where serious enough to justify that course. When deciding whether the offence is, or the offences are, serious enough for a community sentence to be justified, the court may similarly have regard to the TICs as well as the conviction offences (CJA 2003, section 148(1)). The Sentencing Council guidelines are structured in such a way that the sentencing starting point for the conviction offence(s) should be determined first, initially without reference to the TICs. The presence of the TICs will then 'generally be treated as an aggravating factor'.

(b) The sentence the court may pass is restricted to the maximum permissible for the offence(s) of which the offender has been convicted (*Hobson* (1944) 29 Cr App R 30) and, for custodial sentences, CJA 2003, section 153(2). In practice it is almost always possible to add something to the sentence for the conviction offences to reflect the existence of the TICs without approaching the maximum sentence. The Sentencing Council's guideline states that 'When sentencing an offender who requests offences to be taken into consideration, courts should pass a total sentence which reflects all the offending behaviour. The sentence must be just and proportionate and must not exceed the statutory maximum for the conviction offence.' While the presence of the TICs must normally increase the overall sentence, the guideline expects the court to 'consider the fact that the offender has assisted the police (particularly if the offences would not otherwise have been detected) and avoided the need for further proceedings demonstrat[ing] a genuine determination by the offender to "wipe the slate clean".'

(c) Since the taking of an offence into consideration does not, as a matter of law, amount to a conviction for that offence, the offender would not be able to resist a subsequent prosecution for the offence by reliance upon a plea of *autrefois convict* (that he has already been convicted of that offence, and so cannot be charged again) (*Nicholson* [1947] 2 All ER 535). In practice, however, prosecution should never be brought for offences which have already been taken into consideration. In a case where, by error, one was brought, the Court of Appeal recommended that there should be 'no additional penalty' for it (*North* (1971) CSP L.31B01).

(d) The court is not obliged to comply with a request to take offences into consideration. A number of sensible and fairly obvious limitations apply. Magistrates should not take offences into consideration which are triable only on indictment (*Simons* [1953] 1 WLR 1014). More generally, it is bad practice to take offences into consideration which are more serious than the conviction offences. The court should never take offences into consideration which carry endorsements or disqualification unless the conviction offences are also so punishable (*Collins* [1947] KB 560) because the sentencing powers of the court are limited to those it possesses in respect of the conviction offences. Nor should a court take into consideration an offence which is a breach of an earlier sentence (*Webb* (1953) 37 Cr App 82). The Sentencing Council guideline also suggests that an offence should not be taken into consideration if it is not founded on the same facts or evidence, or is not part of a series of offences of the same or similar character as the conviction offence(s) unless the court is satisfied that it is in the interests of justice to do so.

(e) A compensation order may be passed by a court in respect of an offence taken into consideration (PCC(S)A 2000, section 130(1)). Until recently, in a magistrates' court, the total sum which might be ordered by way of compensation where the offender had TICs could not exceed the maximum which could be ordered for the offences apart from the TICs, which was £5000 (PCC(S)A 2000, section 131(2)). That maximum figure has now been removed by the Courts and Justice Act 2013, as far as it applies to offenders aged eighteen years and over. This means that the limit on the total compensation for all offences including those taken into consideration has also been removed, but again limited to offenders aged eighteen years or over. There has never been an upper limit on compensation orders made in the Crown Court. A restitution order may be used in respect of an offence taken into consideration (PCC(S)A 2000, section 148(1)). A deprivation order may be imposed, *inter alia*, where the offender asks to have an offence taken into consideration which involves unlawful possession of property which has since been lawfully seized from him or was in his possession or under his control when he was apprehended (PCC(S)A 2000, section 143(2)).

F ANTECEDENTS AND CRIMINAL RECORD

1.63 The antecedents material is set out on a set of standard forms prepared in advance by the police, subject to guidance provided and set out in the *Criminal Practice Directions* 10A.1 to 10A.8. In the magistrates' courts the antecedents will be prepared by the police and submitted to the CPS with the case file. Five copies will be prepared, one for the CPS, one for the defence, one for the probation service, and two for the court. In the Crown Court the antecedents are prepared by the police immediately following hearing in the magistrates' court. Seven copies are prepared. Two are sent to the CPS directly. Of the remaining five, one goes to the defence, one to the probation service, and the others to the court. The antecedents must be provided within twenty-one days of the case being sent to the Crown Court. Seven days before the hearing the police will check the record of convictions. Details of any additional convictions will then be provided and attached. Details of any matters outstanding against the accused must also be provided at this stage. The antecedents must contain personal details relating to the defendant. This will include name (and aliases where appropriate), address, and date of birth. The antecedents must also contain information about the defendant's previous convictions, if any, drawn from the Police National Computer. Spent convictions may be marked as such on the record, but are not erased. Details of any police caution, warning, reprimand, or youth caution will appear on a separate sheet. The antecedents should also contain information on the date of last discharge from any custodial sentence and any court orders to which the defendant is currently subject. If conviction for the offence now charged would also constitute breach of a sentence currently being served, details of the offence which gave rise to that earlier offence should also appear. In the Crown Court the police should provide brief details of the circumstances of the last three similar convictions and/or of convictions likely to be of interest to the court, this being judged on a case-by-case basis (*Criminal Practice Directions*, paragraph 10A.6). This information should be provided separately and attached to the antecedents. Any points of dispute about the accuracy of the antecedents should be raised with the police by the defence at least seven days before the hearing, so that the matter can be cleared up if possible.

Previous convictions

Evidence of the offender's previous convictions, if there are any, is always made available **1.64** to the court when it turns to consider sentence. The relevance of previous convictions (or lack of them) to the sentence decision is considered in the CJA 2003, section 143(2) and in Chapter 2, paragraph 2.33. The discussion in this section focuses on the provision of the relevant material and any dispute relating to it. The CJA 2003, section143(4) makes it clear that 'previous convictions' means a previous conviction by a court in the United Kingdom, or a previous conviction of a service offence within the meaning of the Armed Forces Act 2006, or a previous conviction in another European Union Member State of a 'relevant offence'. 'Relevant offence' means one which would constitute an offence under the law in any part of the United Kingdom if it were committed in that part of the United Kingdom at the time when the defendant was convicted of the offence in question. By section 143(5), this does not prevent the court from treating a previous conviction by a court outside the United Kingdom and European Union, or a conviction in a Member State which is not a relevant offence, as an aggravating factor in any case where the court considers it appropriate to do so.

Attached to the antecedents will be the list of the offender's previous convictions. The list **1.65** also contains previous 'findings of guilt'. A finding of guilt is the equivalent of a conviction, but made against a young offender (CYPA 1933, section 59). For each conviction the previous convictions form sets out the court at which the offender was convicted, the date of the conviction, the offences of which the offender was convicted, and the sentence passed for each offence (generally including the amount of any fine, the duration of any custodial sentence, the form of any community sentence with the specific requirements, and any alteration made as the result of an appeal). The date of release from the last custodial sentence, if any, is also given. Offences taken into consideration are not convictions, and those incurred by the defendant on previous occasions should simply be referred to by number against the conviction offence. It will be clear from the list of previous convictions whether the offender has committed the latest offence within the operational period of another sentence, such as a conditional discharge or a community order, or within the licence period following his release from a custodial sentence. The offender must be asked whether he admits the breach of the earlier order or licence condition, and if so the court can then deal with him for that matter as well, in accordance with the statutory provisions dealing with breach of the particular conditional order, or by taking the breach of licence into account as an aggravating factor.

1.66   Previous convictions are taken to be those in existence before the commission of the offence for which the offender is now to be sentenced. Any convictions between the commission of the offence and the hearing relating to that offence should, technically, not appear in the list of previous convictions, but should still appear in the antecedents. There should be no mention on the form of any arrest, charge, or prosecution which did not proceed to court and end in a conviction (*Burton* (1941) 28 Cr App R 89). The Rehabilitation of Offenders Act 1974, section 7(5) says that: '[n]o order made by a court with respect to any person otherwise than on a conviction shall be included in any list or statement of that person's previous convictions given or made to any court which is considering how to deal with him in respect of any offence'. It follows from this that an acquittal on the ground of insanity would not appear in the list of convictions but since the fact and circumstances of that acquittal might well be of importance in deciding on the sentence for the latest offence, such an acquittal would appear elsewhere in the antecedents. There are some disposals, such as a restraining order, or a bind over to keep the peace, which can be imposed upon an acquitted defendant, and again it would seem important for these to be included in the antecedents even though not in the convictions list. Cautions, warnings, and reprimands are not convictions, but any which have been incurred by the offender during the last three years will appear in a separate list. The payment of a fixed penalty without prosecution is not a conviction and so should not appear in the convictions list. Mention should also be made of absolute and conditional discharge. The effect of the PCC(S)A 2000, section 14 is that, for a range of purposes an offender who is so sentenced is deemed not to have been convicted of the offence. However, the ROA 1974, section 1(4) defines 'conviction' so as to include conviction followed by a discharge, so these sentences are routinely listed in the previous convictions of offenders.

1.67   In most cases the information about previous convictions is clear and not disputed by the prosecution or the defence. Sometimes, however, there can be difficulty. The prosecution may wish to show that the offender has convictions which do not appear on the list, such as very recent ones typically acquired in a magistrates' court while the offender was on bail awaiting trial or sentence at the Crown Court. Records can sometimes be inaccurate or incomplete in other ways, and for other reasons. An alleged conviction which is disputed by the offender must be drawn to the attention of the prosecution straight away (*Criminal Practice Directions*, paragraph 10A.3) and the prosecution will be required to prove it. This will normally be done by:

(a)   producing a certificate of conviction signed by the clerk of the court in which the disputed conviction is said to have occurred, or the equivalent court officer if that court is a Member State outside the United Kingdom (Police and Criminal Evidence Act 1984, section 73) and, where the conviction was for an offence relating to a prescribed minimum sentence for drug trafficking or domestic burglary, by the PCC(S)A 2000, section 113, and

(b)   adducing evidence to show that the person named in the certificate is the person whose conviction it is sought to establish.

It will thus be for the prosecution to prove (to the criminal standard) that the offender before the court is the person named in the certificate of conviction that has been produced. According to *Pattison v DPP* [2006] 2 All ER 317 this proof may come from an admission by the accused, by fingerprint evidence, or by the evidence of someone who was in court at the time. In practice a clear match between the personal details of the accused and the personal details recorded on the certificate will suffice. Endorsements on a driving licence may be produced as prima facie evidence of the matters endorsed (Road Traffic Offenders Act 1988, section 31(1) and section 44(1)). An order of disqualification from driving may be proved by the production of an extract from the court register certified by the clerk of the court.

If there is other material in the antecedents which is disputed by the defence then it must be **1.68** proved by admissible evidence or ignored by the sentencer (*Van Pelz* [1943] KB 157). If the offender admits a previous conviction but wishes to be allowed to explain it more fully, he should be allowed to do so (*Metcalfe* (1913) 9 Cr App R 7). This is perhaps more conveniently done in the plea of mitigation rather than by challenging the antecedents.

A person who in the past has been convicted of, or cautioned for, an offence under the **1.69** Sexual Offences Act 1956, section 12 (buggery) or section 13 (gross indecency between men) may apply to the Secretary of State to have that conviction or caution 'disregarded', under the Protection of Freedoms Act 2012, section 92. A conviction or caution will become disregarded if the Secretary of State decides that the other person involved in the conduct consented to it and was aged sixteen or over and that such conduct would not now amount to an offence under the SOA 2003 (sexual activity in a public lavatory).

Previous cautions, warnings, and reprimands

As an alternative to initiating a prosecution the police, working together with the CPS, **1.70** may decide to issue a formal caution. A caution can be a simple caution, or may be a conditional caution, such condition being designed to achieve an element of reparation or rehabilitation. The criteria for issuing a caution rather than prosecuting, and the procedures that must be followed, are set out in various Ministry of Justice Circulars. In particular, the person cautioned must admit responsibility for the offence. The Crime and Disorder Act 1998 set up a stepped system of reprimands and warnings to replace formal cautions for those under eighteen. The provisions of the 1998 Act have recently been replaced by a new 'youth caution', introduced by the Legal Aid Sentencing and Punishment of Offenders Act 2012 inserting sections 66ZA and 66ZB into the CDA 1998. The details of these arrangements lie outside the scope of this book. It is sufficient here to note that none of these alternatives to prosecution are convictions, and so none should appear in the list of previous convictions. All such schemes do require, however, that the caution etc be formally recorded by the police. These records are kept, and if the defendant is prosecuted for a later offence any caution etc issued for an offence committed by that person (whether as a juvenile or an adult) may be cited in court. Any caution etc will appear in a separate list in the antecedents. One particular sentencing implication is that where a person who has been given a final warning under the CDA, or has received two more youth cautions, is convicted of an offence committed within two years the court cannot impose a conditional discharge unless it is of the opinion that there are exceptional circumstances relating to the offence or the offender which justify such a course of action (section 66(4) and section 66ZB(5) and (6)).

Spent convictions

The Rehabilitation of Offenders Act 1974 was passed with the aim of helping ex-offenders **1.71** to 'live down' the stigmatizing effect of previous convictions. The main effect is that, once a specified period of time (the rehabilitation period) has elapsed from the date of the offender's conviction, the conviction becomes 'spent' and the offender, in respect of that conviction is 'a rehabilitated person' (ROA 1974, section 1(1)). As a rehabilitated person he is for many purposes treated as if he had never committed or been convicted of the offence (section 4(1)). 'Conviction' is, for the purposes of the ROA 1974, widely defined to include 'any finding in criminal proceedings other than one linked with a finding of insanity' (section 1(4)). This includes findings of guilt made against young offenders. Whether a previous conviction is capable of becoming spent and, if so, the length of the rehabilitation period, are governed by the sentence imposed for the offence. A full list of the rehabilitation periods is given at paragraph 15.60 in this book, together with some other provisions of the Act. Cautions etc as well as convictions come within the scope of the 1974 Act. A further complexity of the ROA 1974 lies in the wide range of exceptions to its out-of-court application to the employment of ex-offenders.

1.72 On its face the ROA 1974 does not apply to a wide range of judicial proceedings, including criminal proceedings (section 7(2)). This is misleading. In the case of criminal proceedings, the *Criminal Practice Directions,* paragraphs 35A.1 to 35A.3, state that both the court and advocates should give effect to the general intention of Parliament by never referring to a spent conviction when such reference can reasonably be avoided. The list of the defendant's previous convictions should contain all convictions, but those which are spent should, so far as practicable, be marked as such. When passing sentence the judge should make no reference to a spent conviction unless it is necessary to do so for the purpose of explaining the sentence to be passed. This approach, as set out in the *Practice Directions*, is applicable to all criminal courts.

G REPORTS

1.73 Once evidence has been given as to the offender's antecedents and previous convictions the sentencer will turn to consider any reports which have been prepared on the offender. In general terms the purpose of reports is to provide additional factual information for the sentencer about the circumstances of the offence and the character of the offender. Sometimes sentence may properly be passed without the benefit of reports, but there are several occasions upon which the court is placed under an obligation to obtain and consider them and many other cases in which it is undoubtedly good sentencing practice to do so.

The relevant reports may have been obtained prior to conviction or hearing, in which case, in the Crown Court, they will have been read by the judge in advance. If they have not been obtained it may be appropriate for the sentencer to adjourn for them to be prepared. This matter was considered in paragraph 1.40, this Chapter. A pre-sentence report on an accused who intends to plead not guilty will not generally have been prepared in advance. This is because to do so would be a wasted effort if the accused is acquitted, and because important information which should appear in the report, such as the extent of the accused's culpability and the accused's attitude to the offence, cannot be investigated. In these cases, adjournment after conviction is the general rule. In what follows the main emphasis is placed upon the pre-sentence report because this is the document which is most commonly encountered in practice and in many cases will be the only report which the court will have. Depending on the issue raised by the case, however, the pre-sentence report may be supplemented by other reports.

Pre-sentence reports

1.74 Section 158(1) of the CJA 2003 provides that a PSR is a report:

    (a) with a view to assisting the court in determining the most suitable method of dealing with an offender, is made or submitted by an appropriate officer, and

(b) contains information as to such matters, presented in such manner, as may be prescribed by rules made by the Secretary of State.

Formerly, a PSR had to be in written form, and that is still generally the case, but the rules now allow for an oral 'stand-down' report, prepared very quickly following a discussion with the offender, and delivered orally in open court (section 158(1A)). Stand-down reports are quite common in the magistrates' courts, and they provide useful additional information for the bench in what is in other respects a straightforward sentencing exercise. In more serious or complex cases, where a custodial sentence or perhaps a community sentence is being considered, the court may wish to have a written report. In any event the magistrates must have a written report before them before imposing a custodial sentence on an offender under 18 (section 158(1B)).

Where the offender is aged eighteen or over the report is prepared by a probation officer, **1.75** and if the offender is under eighteen a PSR can be prepared by a probation officer, a social worker of a local authority, or a member of a youth offending team (section 158(2)). Whenever a court requests a report it is the duty of the relevant service to provide one. A copy of the PSR must be given to the offender or to his lawyer so that any controversial matters in it can be challenged, and a further copy should be given to the prosecutor. In the case of a young offender a further copy should normally be provided for any parent or guardian of his who is present in court (section 159). The contents of the PSR are often referred to by defence counsel, and sometimes by prosecution counsel. It is not appropriate to read out lengthy extracts from a PSR, but a key finding or recommendation by the report writer may be read out. Occasionally matters in the report are in dispute, or some aspect of the report is unclear. The report writer is unlikely to be present in court, and if the court probation liaison officer is unable to clarify the issue it may be necessary in the last resort to call the probation officer to answer questions. This will necessitate adjournment and some consequential delay. In practice defence lawyers often base their pleas in mitigation on material in the PSR. This is natural, but sometimes occasions criticism from the bench.

Important provisions in section 156 of the CJA 2003 require a court to obtain and consider **1.76** a PSR before making a decision to impose a custodial or a community sentence (section 156(3)). However, in either case the court has discretion to dispense with that requirement whenever it appears to the court to be 'unnecessary' to obtain one (section 156(4)). This appears to confer a general discretion on the court, and there is very little authority on the question of when a court may properly choose to press ahead without a report. In any event the discretion is subsequently narrowed (in section 156(5)) in respect of young offenders, so that the court cannot sentence a young offender without ordering a report unless there is a previous report to hand, and the court has had regard to that one. Section 156(6) states that no custodial sentence or community sentence shall be invalidated by the failure of a court to obtain a report when it should have done so under section 156(3), but if the court has so sentenced without a report and the offender appeals against sentence, the appeal court should obtain and consider one (section 156(6)) unless again the appeal court thinks it unnecessary to obtain one (section 156(7)).

The content of all pre-sentence reports is governed by national standards. These require **1.77** that reports should be prepared as quickly as possible and should, in any event, normally be completed within fifteen working days. They must be objective, impartial, free from discriminatory language, and factually accurate. Every PSR must set out the basic factual information about the offender and the offence(s) and list the sources used to prepare the report. There should be an offence analysis, including the offender's attitude to the offence(s) and awareness of the consequences for the victim. There should be an offender assessment, including the relevant personal background, such as accommodation or employment problems, or substance misuse. Then there should be an assessment of risk and likelihood of re-offending. The PSR should conclude by making a clear and realistic proposal for sentence. This is particularly valuable where a community sentence or a suspended sentence with community requirements is in the offing. The report writer can explain fully the requirements which seem most appropriate to the offender's case, and whether the offender is suitable. Nowadays it is common for the report writer to specify, should the judge choose to go down that path, when the offender's first appointment with the probation officer or relevant provider will be.

1.78   When might it be appropriate to proceed without a PSR? The basic answer is, whenever the court is of the view that no PSR could possibly make a difference to the sentencing outcome. An obvious point is that the valuable time and resources of the probation service should not be wasted in preparing a report that can make no difference. In the Crown Court a judge might dispense with a report in a case where a low-tariff disposal such a conditional discharge or a small fine is the inevitable outcome. The SGC guideline, *New Sentences: CJA 2003* suggests that imposing a community sentence without ordering a report is likely to be 'infrequent', but that a report might be dispensed with if the case fell just over the community sentence threshold and only a single requirement was necessary which did not require the involvement of the probation service. Or, the offender might be facing a custodial sentence but has already served a substantial period in custody on remand, so that when the sentence is passed it will result in the offender's immediate release. Sometimes, if the offender is clearly facing a long custodial sentence, a PSR might not be especially helpful. In *Armsaramah* [2001] 1 Cr App R (S) 467 the Court of Appeal approved the decision of the trial judge to sentence the offender to a custodial term of five years without a report. The Court noted that defence counsel had not asked for a report and the offender had been convicted after a trial so the judge was fully familiar with the circumstances of the case. Occasionally defence counsel will say to the judge that their client realises that custody is inevitable and wishes to be sentenced straight away without the benefit of a report. Of course the judge is not bound by that suggestion. It should be remembered that information in the report may well be relevant to determining the length of a custodial sentence. It will be crucial if the offender has been convicted of a specified offence thereby triggering the dangerous offender provisions. The sentencer will then always wish to consider what the PSR writer has to say about the risk to the public which the offender represents. The pre-sentence report is perhaps at its most valuable when the case sits near the custody threshold. In this kind of case the court will need to know in some detail the background, circumstances, and motivation for change on the part of the offender before deciding whether, instead of immediate custody, a suspended sentence or a community order with the appropriate balance of requirements is the preferable course to take.

Medical reports

1.79   The CJA 2003, section 157(1) states that in any case where an offender is or appears to be mentally disordered, the court must obtain and consider a medical report before passing any custodial sentence apart from the mandatory life sentence for murder. This is subject to the exception, similar to that which operates in pre-sentence reports, which is that the court may dispense with the medical report if in the circumstances of the case it considers that it is not necessary to obtain one. 'Medical report' is defined as a report as to an offender's mental condition made or submitted orally or in writing by a registered medical practitioner who is approved for the purposes of the Mental Health Act 1983, section. 12, as having special experience in the diagnosis or treatment of mental disorder (section 157(6)). The section also makes it clear that a medical report is not the same thing as a pre-sentence report, and the ordering of a medical report does not displace the need to order a PSR under section 156. In some cases a medical report will have been ordered and prepared well in advance of sentencing, such as where there may be a question over the defendant's fitness to stand trial, or where the nature or circumstances of the offence charged cause concern. It would be quite usual for the defence to order a report in the case of a defendant charged with homicide, a serious violent or sexual offence, or arson. Apart from those cases the defence may initiate a report, as may the court. It is well known that a high percentage of defendants appearing before the criminal courts are suffering from some degree of mental disorder. Occasionally defence counsel will sometimes say to the judge that his client appears to be disturbed or seriously distressed and is unable to communicate his instructions properly. A request for an adjournment to investigate, and to order a report may well follow. A court must obtain and consider medical reports before it can make a hospital order or a guardianship order under the Mental Health Act (MHA) 1983, section 37, and it will usually be appropriate though not essential before a court inserts a requirement of medical treatment into a community order or a youth rehabilitation order.

1.80 The court may adjourn for the purposes of preparation of a medical report. This is likely to involve a delay of several weeks. Adjournment for reports is considered at paragraph 1.40, this Chapter. When the report has been prepared, a copy should be given to the court and a copy to the defence. The offender will not see the report, but if he is not legally represented he should be told the gist of what is in it (MHA 1983, section 54(3)). Although the report should not be read out in court there may of course be discussion of its contents. The defence may require the report writer to be present in court and to give evidence, and evidence can be called to rebut what appears in the report. In the Crown Court the vast majority of requests for medical reports come from the defence, in the context of providing material for mitigation. Reports are given considerable weight by judges, but there are some circumstances where a custodial sentence (especially an indeterminate one) may properly be preferred to a medical disposal because of the seriousness of the offence and the degree of responsibility which attaches to the offender despite the presence of mental disorder. An example would be sentencing for manslaughter on the ground of diminished responsibility. If the court is minded to impose a hospital order it may order a medical report if one has not already been provided, and the court has power to require information to be provided by the hospital as to the arrangements which will be made for the defendant. If a hospital order is made the court will provide the hospital with a copy of the court's order containing such information that the court has relating to the circumstances of the offence and the defendant's mental condition and other circumstances (CPR 2013, 42.8 and 42.9).

1.81 Apart from the case of an offender who is, or appears to be, mentally disordered, the issue of the health or well-being of the offender may arise in other ways at the sentencing hearing. If the offender is seriously ill it may affect the choice of appropriate requirements in a community order or a suspended sentence—the offender may be unfit to carry out physical work under an unpaid work requirement, for example. It may also be argued by the defence that the nature and severity of offender's physical affliction means that it would be very difficult for him to receive proper medical care in prison, or that his medical condition would be adversely affected such that the prison sentence would have a disproportionate impact upon him. Such issues may properly form part of the plea in mitigation, and they are considered fully in Chapter 2 at paragraph 2.52 at point (iv).

Other reports

1.82 Information may sometimes be derived from other sources. Before certain requirements can be inserted into a community order or a suspended sentence, the court must be satisfied that the relevant arrangements are in place. Usually there will be a pre-sentence report before a community order is made, and the PSR can cover all required matters, but if for some reason there is no PSR the other information still has to be provided. Section 160 of the CJA 2003 deals with the disclosure of reports (other than pre-sentence reports) by probation officers, social workers, or members of youth offending teams made to the Crown Court or to an adult magistrates' court with a view to assisting the court to determine the most suitable disposal. The court must give a copy of that report to the offender or his legal representative. Unlike pre-sentence reports, there is no provision in section 160 for the disclosure of these reports to the prosecutor, no doubt because these matters are outside the sphere of influence of the prosecutor.

1.83   Quite often on hearing an appeal against sentence the Court of Appeal has information before it from the custodial establishment where the offender is serving his sentence, which relates to his behaviour so far, whether positive or negative. Sometimes information about an offender's reaction to his first few weeks of custody is a factor which weighs with the appeal court in deciding whether to reduce sentence.

H VICTIM PERSONAL STATEMENTS

1.84   A victim personal statement is a formal written statement by the victim of the offence which the court is about to sentence. There is also a family impact statement, which is written by surviving members of the family of a deceased victim, and a business impact statement where the victim is a corporate entity. These statements allow victims a structured opportunity to explain how they have been affected by the crime. They provide a practical way of ensuring that the sentencing court will consider the evidence of the victim about the specific and personal impact of the offence or offences, or in the cases of homicide, on the family of the deceased. It was said in *Nunn* [1996] 2 Cr App R (S) 136 to be 'an elementary principle of sentencing' that if the impact of the offence upon the victim has been especially severe, then that should be made known to the judge or magistrates and taken into account by them. In what is now the leading case on the matter, *Perkins* [2013] EWCA Crim 323, Lord Judge CJ said that properly formulated statements provide 'real assistance' for the court. The statement provides victims with an opportunity to make an input in the process, but no pressure should be placed on them by the police or anyone else to do so. It is important to note that the statement does not provide an opportunity for the victim to suggest the type of sentence, or level of sentence, which they would like the court to impose. The Court of Appeal in *Perks* [2001] 1 Cr App R (S) 66 said that the opinion of the victim or members of the victim's family about the appropriate level of punishment for the offender could not provide a sound basis for sentencing. Otherwise, cases with identical features would be dealt with in widely different ways. Some other jurisdictions do allow victims to have their say on sentencing, but there are obvious dangers with that approach. The victim is hardly likely to bring the necessary degree of detachment or understanding of sentencing rules and conventions, and a criminal offence is a wrong against society at large as well as against the individual victim. That is the whole point of the Crown taking on prosecution of offenders, rather than leaving matters to the aggrieved individual. To these points may be added the further important reason mentioned in the SGC guideline on *Domestic Violence*, that 'it is undesirable that a victim should feel a responsibility for the sentence imposed' (paragraph 4.1, SGC guideline on *Domestic Violence*).

1.85   Detailed provisions relating to the way in which victim personal statements should be approached by the sentencer are set out in the *Criminal Practice Directions*, paragraphs F.1 to F.3 (on victim personal statements), and paragraphs G.1 to G.3 (on families bereaved by homicide). The principles were revisited and re-stated by the Court of Appeal in *Perkins* [2013] EWCA Crim 323. The following points emerge from this guidance:

(a) Except where inferences can properly be drawn from the nature of, or circumstances surrounding, the offence a sentencer must not make assumptions unsupported by evidence about the effects of a particular offence on the victim. This point emerges clearly from *Hobstaff* (1993) 14 Cr App R (S) 605 and was approved in *Perkins*.

(b) When a police officer takes a statement from the victim the victim will be told about the scheme and given the chance to make a victim personal statement. The decision whether or not to make a statement is entirely up to them and must be made by them personally. They must be provided with information which makes it clear that they are entitled to make a statement but need not do so. The perception should not be allowed to emerge that if they do not the court may misunderstand or minimize the harm caused by the crime. It should clearly be explained to the victim that their opinion about the sentence which ought to be passed must not be included. The statement can be made or updated at any time prior to the disposal of the case. The victim personal statement will be placed in the judge's file of papers for sentencing, alongside the PSR and other information. The court should pass what it judges to be the appropriate sentence having regard to all matters and taking account, so far as the court considers it appropriate, of the impact on the victim. Where it becomes clear from the information in the statement that the impact on the particular victim has been greater than might have been expected or assumed, such as where the effects of a house burglary on an elderly person has been to destroy their self-confidence and independence, then the offence becomes all the more serious and so may properly be reflected in the sentence to be passed.

(c) The Court in *Perkins* stressed that the effects of an offence on the victim contained in the victim personal statement constitutes evidence which is clearly relevant to sentence, and so must be presented in proper form and treated as evidence. Responsibility for presenting the evidence lies with the prosecution. The statement should be served upon the defendant's solicitor, or the defendant if he is not represented, prior to sentence and in good time for any objection to the use of the statement, or any part of it, if necessary, to be prepared. The Court expressed concern that in some cases statements are handed over too late, in a haphazard manner. Evidence emanating from the victim alone should always be treated with care, especially if it relates to matters which the defence have no realistic way of challenging. The Court said that the contents of a victim personal statement may be contested in cross-examination, may give rise to disclosure obligations, and may be used after conviction to deploy an argument that the credibility of the victim is open to question. It seems likely that these statements in *Perkins* will be further explored in later cases. While of course an assertion made in a victim personal statement may amount to an exaggeration, or even be completely untrue, there are obvious dangers in defence counsel seeking to challenge what the victim has said, and thereby blackening their reputation.

(d) When the statement is put before the court some part or parts of it may be read out by the prosecutor. The judge may also choose to quote a relevant passage. Clearly, in the selection of any passages for quotation the advocate and judge must be very sensitive to the position of the victim, and the need to respect their privacy. If the victim wishes to read out a statement in court, or wants to nominate someone else to do so, the court should always do its best to accede to that wish, unless it would require adjournment and delay (*Criminal Practice Directions,* paragraph F.3(c)).

(e) While the guidance is clear that the victim should never be permitted in his statement to argue for a tough sentence (and that if, by oversight, such comment has slipped through, the judge should make it clear that he or she has ignored it), there is somewhat less clarity over the approach where a victim makes clear the preference for a lenient sentence. Such preference should not appear in the victim personal statement either, but occasionally a victim will contact the prosecution or defence to express a view which is then made known to the court through the plea in mitigation. The Court of Appeal in *Nunn* said that a sentencer should be 'very cautious' about paying attention to such an expressed wish for leniency, however that came before the court, but if there was evidence that the passing of a severe sentence on the offender would aggravate the victim's distress, then sentence *might* be moderated to some degree. Such a case might arise in a case of causing death by dangerous driving, where the young and inexperienced defendant driver is responsible for causing the death of his close friend, who was a passenger in the car. The parents of the deceased now express the view that sending the offender to prison would make their own loss even harder to bear. The court's prime concern, however, is to pass a sentence appropriate to the seriousness of the offence and the culpability of the offender. Again, there is good reason for caution in such cases because, as the SGC guideline on *Domestic Violence* makes clear, 'there is a risk that a plea for mercy made by a victim will be induced by threats made by, or a fear of, the offender' (paragraph 4.1, SGC guideline on *Domestic Violence*).

I PLEA IN MITIGATION

1.86 The defence will always have the opportunity to provide a plea in mitigation. The purpose of the plea in mitigation is to make known to the sentencer any aspects of the case which tend to reduce its gravity, whether these relate to the facts of the offence (bearing in mind that any significant differences between the prosecution and defence versions of the facts should already have been resolved), the offender's attitude to the offence, his individual personal background and circumstances, any indications of remorse, willingness to make reparation to the victim, and so on. This is also the opportunity to draw to the judge's attention any 'references' or letters of support about the offender written by members of the public. These might include material emphasizing the good qualities of the offender, or it might contain an offer of new or continued employment. Sometimes there can also be a personal letter expressing regret from the offender, addressed to the judge. There is no set pattern for mitigation, but these days it is always expected that defence counsel will engage with the relevant sentencing guidelines to draw from them any points which reflect to its client's favour and, where appropriate, taking issue with the prosecution's interpretation of the guidelines. It is common, for example, for the prosecution to say that the case falls within a higher offence category than the defence accepts, or that prosecution and defence take somewhat different views as to the balance between applicable aggravating and mitigating factors. While the aim of the plea in mitigation is to persuade the judge to impose a lower sentence, or a different kind of sentence, from that which the judge might originally have had in mind, it is also important that defence counsel be 'realistic' and frank about the aggravating features of the case as well. Defence counsel is likely to draw the attention of the sentencer to material in the pre-sentence report, or in a medical report if there is one, particularly where the case is a 'borderline custody' one and the report writer makes a reasoned proposal for a non-custodial disposal. This should not be overdone, however. It can properly be assumed that the judge or magistrates will have read the relevant report, and will not find it helpful simply to be told what it says. A skilful plea in mitigation will be independent of the report, but will draw upon one or two telling passages in support of the submissions being made.

There is considerable variation in the content, style, and approach of pleas in mitigation. **1.87**
There is no set pattern. According to Comyn J in *Gross v O'Toole* (1982) 4 Cr App R
(S) 283, mitigation is 'purported to be the province of the most junior of counsel' but is in
fact 'amongst the most difficult tasks'. What ought to be said will obviously vary considerably from case to case, and the lawyer's common sense and experience will be the guide as
to what is better left unsaid. Even where there is little to be said in favour of the offender, it
is the lawyer's duty to present whatever mitigation can be found, and it is the judge's duty
to listen to those representations patiently and without excessive interruption (*Jones* [1980]
Crim LR 58). Sometimes the judge may intervene to comment that, for example, he is not
now thinking of a custodial sentence, so that counsel can concentrate on the requirements
to be written into a community order rather than spending further time pushing against
an open door. Obviously, what is relevant in a plea in mitigation is highly case specific.
There are, however, a number of issues which crop up on a regular basis, which are generally accepted to be relevant to personal mitigation. These are dealt with in paragraph
2.51, this book. It is important always to remember that it is up to the judge or the bench of
magistrates to decide how important the mitigation is in the context of the case as a whole.
Clearly, the more serious the offence the less room there is for personal mitigation to make
a real difference to the sentencing outcome. Judges and magistrates always have to take
mitigating (and aggravating) factors into account when these impinge directly upon the
seriousness of the offence itself, but the extent to which factors personal to the offender will
affect the ultimate outcome is less certain. This is an area of sentencing where the quality of
the advocacy can make quite a difference. The plea in mitigation usually takes the form of a
single address, but it is open to the defence to call witnesses to speak to the offender's good
character, such as an employer prepared to continue employing the offender. Sometimes it
may be appropriate at this time to assist the judge by calling as a witness a probation officer,
social worker or mental health worker who is offering to be involved in the future care of
the offender should the judge select a community disposal rather than a custodial one. Such
evidence may be called at any point in the plea in mitigation, whenever convenient (according to Comyn J in *Gross v O'Toole*). The offender will not normally be called as a witness
at this time, unless perhaps this is a case subject to mandatory disqualification from driving
and the offender wishes to show special reasons for not being disqualified.

Sometimes difficulties arise where an assertion is made in the plea in mitigation which is **1.88**
hard for the sentencer to accept, either because it conflicts with other information which
has been given, or simply because it appears far-fetched. The case of *Gross v O'Toole* itself
provides a good example. The offender was convicted of offering his services as a driver
at Heathrow Airport contrary to a by-law. In mitigation it was contended that he had
offered his services innocently, and free of charge. Before passing sentence the magistrates
commented that they disbelieved the mitigation, no doubt because the offender had many
previous convictions for the same sort of offence. One of the points argued on appeal was
that the bench should have given counsel warning that they were minded to reject the mitigation. The Divisional Court said that the prime responsibility was on defence counsel to
'make good the submission' whether by a speech or by calling evidence. The bench was not
obliged to warn counsel of its provisional view but, according to *Tolera* [1999] 1 Cr App R
(S) 25, it is good practice to do so. A problem which frequently arises is the submission of
an item of personal mitigation unrelated to the offence itself, which the prosecution finds
itself unable to contest. It has been held that in such a case the burden of proof is on the
defence to prove their version of events, on the balance of probabilities. It will be seen that
this situation is different from the *Newton* type of case, where prosecution and defence put
forward sharply different versions of what happened. Here the prosecution is unable to
help, and it is up to the defence to prove what they assert. The case of *Underwood* [2005] 1

Cr App R 178 provides assistance here. The Court of Appeal said that if the matter raised by the defence is outside the knowledge of the prosecution it should say so, rather than simply accepting it as true. Although a full *Newton* hearing is inappropriate in such a case, the judge is entitled to invite defence counsel to call his client to give evidence and to provide details. The judge is equally entitled to dismiss the defendant's assertion if the argument is absurd or untenable, but the judge should explain why that view has been reached. It should be noted that in recent decisions the Court of Appeal has deprecated the practice of Crown counsel simply saying that they cannot 'gainsay' the defence mitigation. In *AG's Reference (No 23 of 2011)(Sanchez Williams)* [2012] 1 Cr App R (S) 266 the offender had pleaded guilty at a late stage to murder, but denied that he had the intention to kill (a relevant issue in sentencing for murder by virtue of schedule 21 to the CJA 2003). When the judge asked prosecution counsel what the Crown's view on that matter was, he replied that he could 'not gainsay' the offender's denial of the intent to kill. Lord Judge CJ said that as an answer to a direct question those words were meaningless, and that they should be 'eliminated from the prosecuting advocate's lexicon'. Similar comments were made by Hallett LJ in *Flynn* [2013] EWCA Crim 653.

1.89 If the defendant contested the case at trial but was convicted it is wrong for counsel to renew assertions of innocence in the plea in mitigation (*Wu Chun-Piu v The Queen* [1996] 1 WLR 1113). Of course if the offender continues to assert his innocence there can be no evidence of remorse. During the speech in mitigation counsel must not make any statements which are 'merely scandalous or intended or calculated to vilify, insult or annoy' any person (*Code of Conduct of the Bar*). Section 58 of the Criminal Procedure and Investigations Act 1996 states that the judge may make an order to prevent the reporting by the press of any false or irrelevant assertions made during a speech in mitigation. Of particular concern here are assertions made in the speech that the victim was a person of less than upright character, or was at least partly responsible for what happened. The section is designed to eliminate gratuitous remarks. It does not prevent defence counsel referring to established facts in the case, such as that the victim was the initial aggressor in the assault by the offender, or that he offered considerable provocation before the offender over-reacted. It is also clear from *Perkins* (considered at paragraph 1.85, this Chapter) that the defence is perfectly entitled to challenge assertions made in a victim personal statement, on the basis that they are untrue or exaggerated.

1.90 Occasionally a matter to be put forward in mitigation is one which the offender does not wish to have made public. If the offender seeks mitigation on the basis that he has assisted the prosecution or the police behind the scenes by providing them with information about other offences which have taken place or are planned, then there is a set procedure for that information to be received. The rules are considered at paragraph 2.68, this book. A different kind of example would be the fact that the offender, or a close member of his family, has been diagnosed with a terminal illness. Such information might already have been mentioned in the pre-sentence report. If so, counsel can make sure that the judge has seen that information, without having to refer to it directly or in detail in open court. If the material does not appear in the pre-sentence report, the best course is for the matter to be written down and given to the judge, with a copy to the prosecution. If the facts are in dispute and if accepted would affect the sentence to be passed, inquiries may have to be made and an adjournment may be necessary for that to be done. In an extreme case the court can be cleared and matters in mitigation heard in camera, but this is a 'wholly exceptional' course to take (*Ealing Justices, ex parte Weafer* (1981) 3 Cr App R (S) 296).

1.91 In a case where the judge may have in mind a sentence which counsel might not have considered, the judge should give the defence lawyer notice of that fact before mitigation is begun.

It will normally be obvious to an experienced defence lawyer from the context of the case, the outline given by the prosecution, and the reports before the court, that the judge will be considering (for example) the application of the dangerous offender provisions, the making of a hospital order, or the making on a specific ancillary order, such as a company director disqualification or a sexual offences prevention order. It is nonetheless good practice for the judge to point out, before the plea in mitigation begins, any approach which counsel genuinely might not have considered. A possible example is deferment of sentence, the initiative for which usually comes from defence counsel, but sometimes from the judge. If a financial order is likely to be made, such as a fine or an order for compensation, it is usual for the judge to ask defence counsel to provide some information concerning his client's ability to pay.

J PASSING SENTENCE AND GIVING REASONS

Pronouncing sentence

In a straightforward case a Crown Court judge sitting alone may pronounce sentence immediately after the defence mitigation is concluded. This used to be the norm, but the increasing complexity of sentence decision-making means that in many more cases judges will now rise from the courtroom and retire for a few minutes, or sometimes longer, to reflect on their sentence and set out their sentencing remarks in written form. This is increasingly common in cases such as: **1.92**

(a) where there are more than usually complex issues of sentencing law or practice, or
(b) where there are multiple defendants (especially where one or more defendant is a young offender and one or more is an adult and so different sentencing rules and conventions apply), or
(c) the case is one which has aroused strong feelings, or
(d) the case requires very careful handling and the sympathetic use of words in explanation (such as a case of causing death by dangerous driving).

In such cases judges will prepare detailed written sentencing remarks, and sometimes make these available to the parties and to the press to ensure so far as possible that everyone can understand the way in which the sentence has been reached. A very good example is the detailed sentencing remarks of Treacy J when sentencing defendants Dobson and Norris at the Central Criminal Court in January 2012 for their part in the racially motivated murder of teenager Stephen Lawrence almost twenty years earlier. This was a case involving unprecedented public and media interest, as well as some unusual and complex sentencing issues (see *Dobson and Norris*, WL 14586, January 4, 2012).

It is customary to require the defendant in the dock to stand to receive sentence. Again, as a result of the lengthy sentencing remarks which are now necessary and common to many cases, many judges do not require the defendant to stand until these explanations have been offered. Some judges take the view that it is better for the sentence to be announced at the start of the sentencing remarks, with the defendant standing, and then to invite him to be seated while the fuller explanation is given. If a Crown Court judge is sitting with lay magistrates on an appeal against sentence unless the decision is very clear and straightforward they will retire to consider the sentence. Similarly, a lay bench of magistrates may wish to retire to consider the sentence. The magistrates may ask the clerk to advise them on their powers but the sentencing decision must be theirs. In a magistrates' court (or in the Crown Court when hearing an appeal) the decision on sentence may be taken by a majority but is pronounced by the chairman of the bench without any mention of the fact that it is not **1.93** unanimous. The same convention applies in the Court of Appeal, where sentence is upheld or varied in a speech given by one member of the Court without any mention of whether this was unanimous or by a majority.

Giving reasons

1.94 Sentencers have always been encouraged wherever possible to give full reasons for deciding upon a particular sentence. There are now a large number of statutory provisions requiring the court to explain why a particular sentence has been passed (or not passed) or why a particular approach to sentence has been taken, or how a sentencing guideline has been applied. These are in addition to the overarching obligation to give reasons implicit in the provisions of Article 6 of the European Convention of Human Rights (ECHR). There are also several sentencing provisions requiring the court to explain matters to the offender in ordinary, non-technical language. Occasionally the agreement of the defendant is required before a particular form of sentence can be passed. These matters are considered in this book, paragraphs 6.10 et seq. In earlier times it was common for judges to deliver 'sentencing homilies' upon an offender, during which a judge might express a view about the offender's general moral character, and suggest ways in which he should adjust his behaviour. Some of these statements travelled well beyond the facts of the offence. Such gratuitous remarks run the risk of being picked up and misquoted, or used out of context by the media, and sentencing homilies are now much rarer than they once were.

1.95 Section 174 of the CJA 2003 sets out the following duties on the court passing sentence on an offender:

(a) The court must state in open court, in ordinary language, and in general terms, the court's reasons for deciding on the sentence (section 174(2)).

(b) The court must explain to the offender in ordinary language the effect of the sentence, the effects of non-compliance, any power of the court to vary or review any part of the sentence, and the effects of failure to pay a fine, if the sentence consists of or includes a fine (section 174(3)).

In complying with its duty under (b) the court must, in particular, comply with the following.

- By section 174 (6), the court must identify any definitive sentencing guidelines relevant to the offender's case and explain how the court discharged the duty imposed on it by section 125 of the Coroners and Justice Act 2009 (duty to follow guidelines unless satisfied it would be contrary to the interests of justice to do so). If the court was satisfied it would be contrary to the interests of justice to follow the guidelines, it must state why.
- By section 174(7), where as a result of taking into account any matter referred to in section 144(1) (guilty pleas), the court imposes a punishment on the offender which is less severe than the punishment it would otherwise have imposed, the court must state that fact.
- By section 174(8), where the court imposes a sentence that may only be imposed in the offender's case if the court is of the opinion mentioned in section 1(4)(a) to (c) of the Criminal Justice and Immigration Act 2008 (offender aged under eighteen years old and a custodial sentence would otherwise be appropriate), or section 148(1) of the CJA 2003 (offender aged eighteen years or over) and the offence is serious enough to warrant a community sentence, or section 152(2) of the CJA 2003 (the offence is so serious that neither a fine alone nor a community sentence can be justified), the court must state why it is of that opinion.

The specific requirements to give reasons as set out in section 174 are certainly not exhaustive. Other statutory examples include:

(a) the duty imposed by the PCC(S)A 2000, section 130(3) to give reasons in any case in which a court does not make a compensation order in favour of the injured party;
(b) the duty imposed by the Football Spectators Act where the offender is convicted of a relevant offence to give reasons if it is not making a football banning order;
(c) the duty imposed under the Crime and Disorder Act 1998, section 9 to impose a parenting order on the parent or guardian of a young offender aged under sixteen unless the court is satisfied that such an order would not be desirable in the interests of preventing the young offender from offending.

Failure to give reasons

What is the effect of a failure by the court to comply with any of the requirements to give **1.96** reasons, whether set out in section 174 or otherwise? There is no mention of this issue in the section. It is clear from the case law that a failure to follow the requirements would not render the sentence unlawful but, on the other hand, a failure to give adequate reasons for the sentence passed might well cause the Court of Appeal to think that the judge had failed to address a relevant issue such as application of a relevant offence guideline or the appropriate reduction for a guilty plea. Lord Taylor CJ in *Baverstock* (1993) 14 Cr App R (S) 471 said (at p. 475) that the statutory provisions were 'not to be treated as a verbal tightrope for judges to walk', and that even if judges made a mistake and failed to explain something they should have explained, the Court of Appeal would not interfere with the resultant sentence 'unless it is wrong in principle or excessive'. So, in *Giga* [2008] 2 Cr App R (S) 638, the judge made a mistake when explaining to the offender how long he could expect to serve in custody. He said that the offender would serve half the sentence before being released on licence but in fact, because of the date on which the offences were committed, a previous version of the early release provisions applied and the offender would in fact serve two-thirds of the sentence before being released. The matter was referred to the Court of Appeal by the Criminal Cases Review Commission as amounting to a miscarriage of justice, but the Court said that the judge's error did not make the sentence unfair, nor could it found the basis for an appeal. The fact is that the sentence was the correct one and the operation of early release rules was not, in principle, a matter for the judge. He was required to explain their effect to the sentenced offender, and an error in that explanation could not render the sentence unlawful or unfair. The decision in *Bright* [2008] 2 Cr App R (S) 578 is to the same effect. Of course matters would be different if, in giving the explanation in open court for proceeding to sentence in the way in which he had done, the judge thereby revealed an error in his application of the relevant law.

K COMMENCEMENT OF SENTENCE

A sentence imposed by the Crown Court takes effect from the beginning of the day on **1.97** which it is imposed, unless the court directs otherwise (PCC(S)A 2000, section 154). The court can never order a sentence to take effect *earlier* than the day on which it was passed. In *Whitfield* [2002] 2 Cr App R (S) 186 the judge dealt with an offender who was serving a custodial sentence of seventeen months following breach of a community order, and who now fell to be sentenced for a number of offences committed before the breach proceedings. The judge passed a sentence of twenty-seven months, concurrent with the existing sentence and designed to extend the overall term by ten months. The Court of Appeal said that the new sentence could not be backdated in that way, and would be treated as running from the date on which it was imposed. The actual effect was therefore more severe than the judge had meant and the Court of Appeal reduced sentence to achieve the effect which the judge intended. Had the error come to light within fifty-six days it would have been open to the judge to correct the sentence without the need for an appeal (see paragraph 1.99, this Chapter). In *AJ* [2013] EWCA Crim 908 the judge imposed a custodial sentence and directed that it should run concurrently with a sentence which the offender was already serving, but such that the release date from the earlier sentence would be unaffected. Because of a miscalculation the new sentence did require the offender to spend additional time in prison. The Court of Appeal said that the new sentence could not be backdated because of section 154, so it was reduced accordingly to give effect to the judge's intention. Again, had the matter come to light within fifty-six days it could have been corrected without troubling the appeal court.

1.98 There is by section 154 a limited discretion to order the sentence to start at a later specified date, such as the date on which an existing sentence is going to expire. In *Anomo* [1998] 2 Cr App R (S) 269 the Court of Appeal upheld a direction that a custodial sentence should start on the date when the offender had completed a custodial term imposed by a civil court for contempt of court. The power to commence sentence at a later date is, however, subject to the important rule in the CJA 2003, section 265, that a court imposing a custodial sentence cannot direct that it shall take effect from the expiry of any other custodial sentence *from which he has already been released*. This provision has caused practical difficulty for Crown Court judges. The offender, who has committed an offence while on licence and has now had his licence revoked and been recalled to prison may, in practice, serve no additional time in prison as a result of the sentence for the new offence. The offender may well be released at the end of the original licence period. The offender in *Whittles* [2009] 2 Cr App R (S) 673 had been released halfway through a five-year sentence for domestic burglary. Licence was revoked four months later, and two months after that he was sentenced to fifty-six months for domestic burglary (with five similar offences TIC). The Court said that the new sentence had clearly been inflated in an attempt to ensure that Whittles would serve time in custody beyond the expiry of the original sentence. The Court of Appeal sympathized with the approach of the judge, and with the view that section 265 should be repealed, but said that for as long as the section remained the law it was unlawful to pass a disproportionately long sentence to ensure that the offender served additional time in custody. *Whittles* was approved in *Costello* [2010] 2 Cr App R (S) 608, the Court observing that the problem might be solved by repeal of section 265 or, better still, the reinstatement of the power under section 116 of the PCC(S)A 2000, which the Crown Court formerly enjoyed, to order that part of the period of licence from the first sentence should now be served in custody in addition to the term imposed for the new offence.

L VARIATION OF SENTENCE

1.99 The Crown Court may vary or rescind a sentence imposed or other order made within 56 days of its being passed (PCC(S)A 2000, section 155). This is a very useful practical power, often avoiding the need for an appeal against sentence to be brought where a mistake in sentencing comes to light and can be corrected quickly. The section, known colloquially as 'the slip rule', is subject to some important procedural limitations. The variation must be made by the judge who originally passed the sentence (section 155(4)). This applies no matter how inconvenient it might be, such as where a recorder passed the sentence and is now engaged in a long trial in a different part of the country, or where the judge who passed the sentence has since retired. If the judge was sitting with lay magistrates when sentence was passed (following an appeal from the magistrates' court), it is not necessary for the lay justices to be present. The offender should be present in court (or by way of a link to the prison if a custodial sentence was passed) when sentence is varied (*Cleere* (1983) 5 Cr App R (S) 465). This does not apply if there is some good reason for his absence, such as that he has absconded, as was the case in *McLean* (1988) 10 Cr App 18. In one case, *Shacklady* (1987) 9 Cr App R (S) 258, the Court of Appeal upheld a variation of sentence where the offender had not been present in court but had been represented by counsel, the Court taking the view that the variation had not taken place behind the offender's back, and there had been no breach of natural justice. Any variation of sentence under section 155 should be made in open court so that nobody can be in any doubt as to what sentence has been passed—this process cannot be done 'behind the scenes', or by sending a message (*Dowling* (1988) 88 Cr App R 88). The power under section 155 cannot be exercised if an appeal, or an application for leave to appeal, the sentence has been determined (section 155(1A)).

The power to vary sentence may be used to correct a straightforward error in the original **1.100** sentence. Thus where the sentencer by a slip of the tongue has mistakenly passed a sentence of imprisonment on an offender aged twenty years of age, where the proper sentence was detention in a young offender institution, this can be corrected under section 155. Similarly, the section may be used where the sentencer has been misled by information concerning the number of days which the offender has spent on bail under a qualifying curfew, but where that information has been corrected within the statutory period. Adjustment of the length of a custodial sentence now occurs automatically to take account of days spent on remand, and so this problem remains only in relation to days spent on qualifying curfew. The best way for a sentencer to avoid the need to fall back on section 155, and avoid the need for an expensive appeal to correct the arithmetic, is to use the formula in *Nnaji* when dealing with this issue. The matter is discussed fully at paragraph 3.22, this book. If the Crown Court judge forgets to make an order which he should have made, such as a surcharge, this error is unlikely to be remediable on appeal and so the omission should be dealt with under section 155, provided it comes to light in time.

The section may also be used to replace one form of sentence with a different (even in- **1.101** cluding a more severe) one, but there are limits to the circumstances in which this can be done. If the sentencer simply has second thoughts, and decides that the sentence passed was, on reflection, too low, there is authority in *Nodjoumi* (1985) 7 Cr App R (S) 183 and in *Evans* (1992) 13 Cr App R (S) 377 that the power under section 155 is unavailable. These case may be contrasted with the view taken in *Hadley* (1995) 16 Cr App R (S) 358 where the judge substituted a higher sentence after realizing that he had made a mistake about his sentencing powers. Here the Court agreed with the approach of the judge who had increased the sentence but tempered the increase to allow for the fact that the offender had been sentenced twice and clearly felt hard done by. Glidewell J in the Court of Appeal said that if such a case was to recur the sentencer might ask himself whether his original sentence was 'unduly lenient', applying the test applicable on an Attorney General's Reference to the Court of Appeal. If the answer to that question is 'yes', and the statutory period has not expired, the sentence may properly be increased under section 155. The Court has upheld other variations of sentence to the detriment of the offender under section 155 where new information has come to light within the fifty-six-day period. Thus in *Sodhi* (1978) 66 Cr App R 260 a prison sentence of six months was replaced by a hospital order with a restriction order in light of late evidence arriving as to the mental condition of the offender. In *Hart* (1983) 5 Cr App R (S) 25 the offender was given a suspended sentence, partly on the basis of evidence that he was about to leave the country and start a new life abroad. Shortly afterwards a newspaper reported Hart as saying that this had been a lie to trick the judge into passing a lenient sentence. The judge brought the offender back and imposed an immediate custodial sentence. The sentence had to be quashed because it had not been done within the statutory time period, but the Court of Appeal said that otherwise it was a 'plain case' for variation of sentence.

1.102 In *Reynolds* [2007] 2 Cr App R (S) 553 the Court dealt with a number of appeals where mistakes had been made by sentencers over the complex provisions relating to dangerous offenders. The Court said that if the mistake, such as a failure to realize that the offence was a 'specified' offence was spotted quickly enough, correction could be made under the slip rule. If the fifty-six days had expired, however, the only remedy was an appeal to the Court of Appeal. It should be appreciated, however, that it may not always be open to the Court of Appeal to remedy a mistake or omission in the Crown Court, because of the rule that the Court of Appeal cannot increase the overall severity of a sentence on appeal (see paragraph 15.28, this book, for discussion of this rule). So, in *Stone* [2013] EWCA Crim 723, the Court of Appeal pointed out that if the Crown Court has forgotten to make the appropriate order for surcharge, it is not open to the appellate court to add the surcharge where that would increase the overall severity of the sentence. Once the statutory period for variation has expired, a court may not vary its sentence even if, through inadvertence, it has failed to include something (such as an ancillary order) which it really should have dealt with. Any variation made after the statutory period is void, according to the House of Lords in *Menocal* [1980] AC 598. In the view of the Court of Appeal in *Reynolds* [2007] 2 Cr App R (S) 553, however, if the error has been recognized and the original sentence is rescinded within the fifty-six days it is open to the court to adjourn to pass sentence on a day more than fifty-six days from the day when the original sentence had been imposed.

1.103 Magistrates' courts may also vary sentence. This power, under the MCA 1980, section 142, is broader than the Crown Court equivalent in that it allows for a conviction or a sentence to be re-opened. There is no formal time limit within which this can be done, provided that it appears to the court to be in the 'interests of justice' to take that course. Delay is not in itself a factor for refusing an application to re-open (*R (Dunlop) v DPP* [2004] EWHC 225), but the bench is entitled to take all relevant matters into account in deciding whether to do so, such as inconvenience that would be occasioned to any witnesses who would be required to attend. The power in section 142 'extends to replacing a sentence or order which for any reason appears to be invalid by another which the court has power to impose or make' (section142(1)), but the 'interests of justice' test will allow re-opening in a wide range of cases. Section 142 may be used to review an incorrect sentence and either reduce it or increase it. If a person has been convicted in the magistrates' court and it later appears to the court that it would be in the interests of justice for the matter to be reheard by a different bench, the court may direct that that should be done (section 142(2)). According to Bean J in *Zykin v CPS* [2009] EWHC 1469 the power under section 142 is 'to be used in a relatively limited situation, namely one which is akin to mistake or the slip rule'. In any event, power to re-open under section 142 can no longer be exercised once the matter has been the subject of an appeal to the Crown Court or has been considered by the High Court on a case stated.

M REWARDS

1.104 The Crown Court has power to order the payment of a sum of money to any person who has been 'active in or towards the apprehension of any person charged with an arrestable offence' (Criminal Law Act 1826, section 28). The amount of any such reward should be sufficient to compensate that person for any 'expenses, exertions, and loss of time' involved in that apprehension. Such an award might well be made at the time of sentencing the offender. Technically, the judge directs the High Sheriff of the county in which the offence has been committed to pay the person who is to receive the reward, and then the High Sheriff is reimbursed from public funds by the Lord Chancellor (CLA 1826, section 29). For an example of a reward being ordered see *Alexander* [1997] 2 Cr App R (S) 74.

KEY DOCUMENTS[1]

John Sprack, *A Practical Approach to Criminal Procedure*, 14th edition (OUP, 2012).

Sentencing Guidelines Council, Definitive Guideline, *New Sentences: CJA 2003* (December 2004).

Sentencing Guidelines Council, Definitive Guideline, *Domestic Violence* (effective 18 December 2006).

Sentencing Guidelines Council, Definitive Guideline, *Magistrates Sentencing Guidelines* (effective 4 August 2008).

Sentencing Guidelines Council, Definitive Guideline, *Allocation* (effective 11 June 2012).

Sentencing Council, Definitive Guideline, *Assault (Crown Court)* (effective 13 June 2011).

Sentencing Council, Definitive Guideline, *Offences Taken into Consideration* (effective 11 June 2012).

Criminal Practice Directions [2013] EWCA Crim 1631 (effective 7 October 2013), amended by [2013] EWCA Crim 2328 (effective 10 December 2013).

Criminal Procedure Rules 2013 (SI 2013, No 1554) (effective 7 October 2013).

European Convention on Human Rights, Article 6.

---

[1] All sentencing guidelines can be found on the Sentencing Council website: <http://sentencing council.judiciary.gov.uk/>.

2

GENERAL PROVISIONS IN SENTENCING

A PURPOSES OF SENTENCING

2.01 The Criminal Justice Act (CJA) 2003, section 142(1) sets out a list of the 'purposes of sentencing'. It provides that:

> any court dealing with an offender in respect of his offence must have regard to the following purposes of sentencing:
>
> (a) the punishment of offenders,
> (b) the reduction of crime (including its reduction by deterrence),
> (c) the reform and rehabilitation of offenders,
> (d) the protection of the public, and
> (e) the making of reparation by offenders to persons affected by their offences.

This rather compendious list is restricted in a number of ways. It does not apply where the penalty for the offence is fixed by law (murder) or in any of those cases where statute sets a required custodial sentence. Nor does section 142(1) apply where the court is sentencing a mentally disordered offender.

2.02 The list in section 142(1) has been criticized for providing little practical help for sentencers, particularly in cases where the purposes conflict, or point towards different sentencing outcomes. When sentencing a case of domestic burglary, for example, punishment of the offender, deterrence of him and others, and protection of future victims, are likely to be uppermost in the sentencer's mind. However, there are some less serious cases of burglary where the court might hear that the offender has committed the offence in order to obtain money to buy drugs, and avoid an immediate custodial sentence in favour of a suspended one, or a community order, containing a drug treatment and testing requirement. Here reform and rehabilitation of the offender (and perhaps the longer-term protection of the public) may take priority over punishment. Section 142(1) does not really assist the sentencer with that decision—as the Sentencing Guidelines Council (SGC) points out in the sentencing guideline *Overarching Principles: Seriousness*, the section: '…does not indicate that any one purpose should be more important than any other and in practice they may all be relevant to a greater or lesser degree in any individual cases—the sentence has the task of determining the manner in which they apply' (paragraph 1.2).

The Court of Appeal has occasionally referred to section 142. In *Seed* [2007] 2 Cr App R **2.03** (S) 436 Lord Phillips CJ said that '[u]nless imprisonment is necessary for the protection of the public the court should always give consideration to the question of whether the aims of rehabilitation and thus the reduction of crime cannot better be achieved by a fine or a community sentence rather than by imprisonment, and whether punishment cannot adequately be achieved by such a sentence'. In *Wilkinson* [2010] 1 Cr App R (S) 628 the Court agreed with the SGC's observation, but added that in some cases, such as gun crime, protection of the public must be the paramount consideration. In *Blackshaw* [2012] 1 Cr App R (S) 677 the Court used section 142 to support its view that deterrent sentencing was necessary in the context of widespread offending in the context of public disorder, and noted that none of the offenders involved were children or young offenders (for whom different sentencing considerations apply). In *Sellafield Ltd* [2014] EWCA Crim 49 the Court noted that the purposes of sentencing in this section applied just as much to corporate offenders as to individuals.

Purposes of sentencing: young offenders

Section 142(2) states that the list of purposes in section 142(1) does not apply to offenders aged under eighteen at the time of conviction. There is a section 142A (inserted by the **2.04** Criminal Justice and Immigration Act 2008, section 9) which specifies a similar but not identical list of purposes when sentencing young offenders, but section 142A has not been brought into force. The relevant provisions for young offenders, then, are the Crime and Disorder Act 1998, section 37, which states that the principal purpose of the whole of the youth justice system including the sentencing of young offenders, 'is to prevent offending by children and young persons', and there is also a long-standing statutory duty under the Children and Young Persons Act 1933, section 44, to 'have regard to the welfare of the child or young person'. Most offenders under the age of eighteen are sentenced in the youth court. The proper approach to sentencing young offenders is set out fully in the SGC guideline, *Sentencing Youths*. That guideline notes that, in addition to the statutory provisions just referred to, a court sentencing a young offender must be aware of obligations under a range of international conventions which emphasize the importance of avoiding criminalization of young people whilst ensuring that they are held responsible for their actions and, where possible, take part in reparation to the victim of their offence. Young offenders require a different, individualistic, approach from adults, and the guideline stresses that even within the category of 'youth' the response to an offence is likely to be very different depending on whether the offender is at the lower end of the ten to seventeen years-of-age bracket, in the middle, or towards the top. In many instances the maturity of the offender will be just as important as the chronological age.

B SENTENCING GUIDELINES

2.05 Reference has already been made to some sentencing guidelines, and it is appropriate now to explain what these are, the various authorities under which they have been produced, and their particular importance to the practice of sentencing.

A brief history

2.06 Sentencing guidelines were originally developed in the 1980s, with the Magistrates' Association producing written voluntary guidance for the lower courts on the sentencing of motoring offences, and the Court of Appeal occasionally issuing what are called 'guideline judgments' which went beyond the facts of appeal before them and laid down general considerations relating to sentencing for the kind of offence in question. For the purposes of a guideline judgment the Court tended to pull together a number of appeal cases falling into the offence category in question and, having explained the appropriate sentence range(s) and starting point(s) applicable, proceeded to dispose of that group of cases in line with the stated principles. The guideline judgments were conventionally issued by the Lord Chief Justice or a senior Lord Justice and soon became key reference points for practitioners. In the Crime and Disorder Act 1998 Parliament created a new body called the Sentencing Advisory Panel (SAP), which conducted research and consultation before advising the Court on the content of new sentencing guidelines and the revision of old ones. The Court of Appeal guideline judgment in *Webbe* [2002] 1 Cr App R (S) 82, on handing stolen goods, is an example. Arrangements changed in Criminal Justice Act 2003 with the creation of the Sentencing Guidelines Council (SGC), a statutory body chaired by the Lord Chief Justice, which took over from the Court of Appeal the task of issuing sentencing guidelines. The SGC was advised by the SAP. Most of the guidelines referred to in this book came about this way, and these include the guidelines on *Robbery* and *Reduction in Sentence for a Guilty Plea*, as well as *Overarching Principles: Seriousness*, and *Sentencing Youths*, mentioned earlier in this Chapter. As the name implies, *Robbery* is an offence guideline, whereas the other three deal with broader sentencing issues which can crop up across a wide range of offence categories. Once the SGC took over the task of issuing guidelines it was no longer necessary to wait for a relevant case to come before the Court of Appeal to which a guideline judgment could be attached. Guidelines could now be issued as and when they were complete, and the SGC could issue more generic guidelines as well as offence-based ones. The sentencing courts were required, by the CJA 2003, section 172, to 'have regard to' sentencing guidelines. Parliament changed things again in the Coroners and Justice Act 2009, which abolished both the SGC and the SAP, and replaced them with the Sentencing Council for England and Wales.

The Sentencing Council guidelines

2.07 The Sentencing Council has been operational since 2010 and has issued a number of offence guidelines, principally on *Assault, Burglary, Drugs Offences* and *Sexual Offences* (which all replaced earlier SGC guidelines), and a generic guideline on *Offences Taken into Consideration, and Totality*. The Coroners and Justice Act 2009, sections 118 to 136 creates the Sentencing Council and sets out its remit and responsibilities. Section 120 requires the Council to prepare sentencing guidelines, which may be general in nature or limited to a particular offence, particular category of offence, or particular category of offender. By section 121, the offence sentencing guidelines should specify the 'offence range' appropriate for a court to impose on an offender convicted of that offence and, if the guidelines describe different categories of case, specify for each category a 'category range' within the offence range. The guidelines should also specify the 'starting point' within the offence range or within each category range. This general approach is consistent with earlier offence guidelines, but the terms 'offence range' and 'category range' now have a clear and distinctive meaning. The offence range embraces all the category ranges (typically there are three or four for each offence guideline). To take the example of burglary in a dwelling, the three offences categories are (1) two to six years' imprisonment, (2) high-level community order—two years' imprisonment, and (3) low-level community order—twenty-six weeks' imprisonment. The offence range therefore runs from 'six years down to low-level community order'. Section 125 sets out the duty of the court in relation to the guidelines, and states that: '[e]very court (a) must, in sentencing an offender, follow any sentencing guidelines which are relevant to the offender's case, and (b) must, in exercising any other function in relation to the sentencing of offenders, follow any sentencing guidelines which are relevant to the exercise of that function, unless the court is satisfied that it would be contrary to the interests of justice to do so'. It is important to note that this requirement applies not just to the Sentencing Council guidelines but to all the earlier guidelines, whether issued by the SGC or by the Court as guideline judgments (Coroners and Justice Act 2009, Commencement No 4, Transitional and Savings Provisions Order 2010, paragraph 7).

The duty on courts in section 125 to 'follow' the Sentencing Council guidelines looks, on **2.08** the face of it, to be a tighter requirement for the court than the former requirement to 'have regard to' the SGC guidelines. However, closer reading of the CJA 2009, section 125 shows that the duty is to impose a sentence within the overall 'offence range' (*not* the particular 'category range'). The duty then extends to deciding which of the categories most resembles the offender's case (unless none of the categories sufficiently resembles the offender's case) but does *not* extend to sentencing within the 'category range'. The duty on the court to impose a sentence which is within the offence range is expressly stated to be subject to the CJA 2003, section 144 (reduction in sentence for guilty pleas), and the Serious Organised Crime and Police Act (SOCPA) 2005, sections 73 and 74 (assistance by defendants: reduction of sentence). It is implicit from these references that a court may pass a sentence below the lower end of the offence range for one or other of these reasons. The duty imposed by section 125 is also subject to various other statutory provisions including those setting out a mandatory sentence (murder), or a required minimum sentence. Also, nothing in section 125 is to be taken as restricting any power to deal with a mentally disordered offender. The duty to 'follow' any sentencing guideline is of course limited to the final, or 'definitive', version of the guideline. It does not apply to drafts, or to consultation documents (see *Valentas* [2010] 2 Cr App R (S) 477).

The *Crown Court Sentencing Survey*, available on the Sentencing Council website, covered **2.09** the whole of 2011 and suggests that departures from the guidelines (by passing a sentence outside the offence range) are relatively rare. For the offence of assault occasioning actual bodily harm, which has an offence range of three years to a fine, 97 per cent of sentences fell within the offence range, 2 per cent above the range and 1 per cent below it. For causing grievous bodily harm with intent (Offences Against the Person Act 1861, section 18), which has an offence range of sixteen years to three years, 92 per cent of sentences fell within the offence range, 7 per cent below and 1 per cent above. The Court of Appeal in *Blackshaw* [2012] 1 Cr App R (S) 677, an important decision dealing with sentences imposed in the context of widespread public disorder, upheld a number of severe sentences for a range of offences including burglary of commercial premises and handling stolen goods, on the ground of general deterrence. The relevant offences had all been committed during a time of widespread rioting and looting in a number of English towns and cities during the summer of 2011. Lord Judge CJ noted that a sentencing court could depart from the guidelines 'in the interests of justice' and concluded that in the present context 'sentences beyond the range in the guidelines for conventional offending...was not only appropriate, but...inevitable' (at paragraph [16]). His Lordship said that the requirement to 'follow' the guidelines did not require 'slavish adherence' to them, and stressed (not for the first time) that 'guidelines are guidelines and not tramlines'. The decision in *Blackshaw* is controversial, and has been the subject of academic critique. In any event Sentencing Council guidelines which have been issued after the decision in *Blackshaw* include 'context of general public disorder' among the step 1 factors indicating greater harm. It follows that a future court would probably have no need to depart from the guidelines to take that matter into account.

2.10 As part of the statutory duty on the court to give reasons for sentence, the CJA 2003, section 174(2) requires that a court, when passing sentence on an offender, must state in open court, in ordinary language, and in general terms, its reasons. In particular, by section 174(6), it must identify any definitive sentencing guidelines relevant to the offender's case and explain how the court discharged any duty imposed on it by the Coroners and Justice Act 2009 (CAJA), section 125 and, where the court did not follow any such guidelines because it was of the opinion that it would be contrary to the interests of justice to do so, state why it was of that opinion. It follows from what has been said already that a sentencer cannot refuse to follow a relevant guideline because for some reason he disagrees with it (see *Heathcote-Smith* [2011] EWCA Crim 2846 for an example). Hughes LJ in *Healey* [2013] 1 Cr App R (S) 176 noted, in the context of the Sentencing Council guidelines on *Drug Offences*, that it was not open to a sentencing judge to disregard the guideline because the judge preferred earlier Court of Appeal authority. On the other hand, sentencing guidelines can, and do, become out of date. This may be as a result of legislative change, or for other reasons. An obvious example is that Sentencing Council guidelines prior to *Sexual Offences* all remind the court to make adjustment to sentence for any time served by the offender on remand in custody. That requirement has now been repealed by statute and such time is deducted automatically. In *Thornley* [2011] 2 Cr App R (S) 361, a case which engaged the SGC guideline on *Manslaughter by Reason of Provocation*, but after reform had taken place of that partial defence by the CAJA 2009, Lord Judge CJ said that the 'interests of justice' test required the sentencing court to consider a guideline taking into account any later statutory changes and appellate case law, adding this time: '[g]uidelines are not tramlines— nor are they ring-fenced'.

2.11 Guidelines always make clear on their face the date upon which they come into effect, and generally require that they apply to all offenders sentenced on or after that date, irrespective of the date upon which the offence was convicted or the date upon which the offender was sentenced. If a sentencing guideline has the effect of increasing the sentencing tariff for a particular offence, either generally or in a particular respect, it is clear that a judge should apply the guideline to all offenders, and that there is no infringement of Article 7 of the European Convention on Human Rights (ECHR) if the offender was convicted before the guidelines came into effect but sentenced afterwards. This is because Article 7 is concerned with retrospective changes to the law, and the guidelines change sentencing conventions and practice but do not change the law (see *Bao* [2008] 2 Cr App R (S) 61). If a sentencing guideline has the effect of reducing the sentencing tariff in whole or in part (as the Sentencing Council's guideline on *Drug Offences* does in respect of a limited category of drug courier) it is not open to offenders sentenced under the former sentencing conventions to appeal on the basis they might be more leniently dealt with if sentenced today. This issue arose in *Boakye* [2013] 1 Cr App R (S) 6, where the Court of Appeal said that if changes in sentencing practice were treated as retrospective courts would be deluged with applications relating to cases long since closed.

In *AG's Ref (Nos 73, 74, and 3 of 2010)* [2011] 2 Cr App R (S) 555, Lord Judge CJ said **2.12** that nothing in the legislative provisions establishing the Sentencing Council prevented the Court of Appeal from issuing a definitive sentencing guideline of its own. This is controversial. Although there is no statutory bar to the Court issuing a sentencing guideline, there is a strong argument that it should not do so now that the Sentencing Council is charged by statute with that task. The senior judiciary might well say that there can be circumstances in which sentencers require advice and assistance more quickly than the Sentencing Council process can provide. The Council offered no guidance to courts on sentencing in the period immediately after the summer riots in 2011, preferring to leave it to the Court of Appeal. While the Court in *Blackshaw* approved sentences outside the guidelines, the practice of judges developing their own local sentencing guidelines to deal with the immediate aftermath of the offending was deprecated. In fairness, judges clearly felt it necessary to fall back on their own resources when faced with a highly unusual and serious spate of offending, with no guidance from either the Council or the Court until months after the events.

In line with section 174 of the CJA 2003, which sets out a series of duties the court should **2.13** comply with when explaining the sentence to be passed to the offender and others, the Court of Appeal has emphasized on many occasions the importance of sentencers making it clear in their sentencing remarks that they have properly considered the applicable guideline, explained their reasoning and, where appropriate, made it clear into which offence category the instant offence falls. The Court of Appeal has also often stressed that it is the duty of counsel to bring the relevant sentencing guidelines to the attention of the judge, and this is crucial now that guidelines cover the majority of criminal offences. It should be the norm that prosecution counsel at the sentencing hearing will not only draw the court's attention to the guidelines, but will make submissions as to the relevant offence category and any important aggravating features of the case. It can also be expected that as part of any plea in mitigation the defence will engage with the guideline and identify any relevant mitigation, as well as reminding the judge of the appropriate recommended discount for a plea of guilty.

The structure of the guidelines

The structure of Sentencing Council guidelines is different from earlier guidelines in some **2.14** important respects. As time goes on the Sentencing Council will issue further guidelines and replace earlier ones, so that the Sentencing Council guidelines will become the dominant model. It is necessary, therefore, to say a little more about their structure here. In particular, the Sentencing Council guidelines involve an explicit stepped process.
Step 1 requires the court to match the case to one of three categories of seriousness. The highest is category 1, which involves a finding by the judge that the offence displayed both 'greater harm' and 'higher culpability'. Category 2 is appropriate if the offence involved *either* greater harm and lower culpability *or* lesser harm and higher culpability. Category 3 involves lesser harm *and* lower culpability. Step 1 of the guideline sets out an *exhaustive* list of factors which should be used to determine which of the three categories is most appropriate for the particular offence. These are the principal factual elements of the offence. Step 1 factors include important aggravating circumstances, such as targeting a vulnerable victim or planning of the offence. Lower culpability factors include factors such as offence committed on impulse. Having determined the applicable category range the court then uses the relevant starting point for that range to move towards a sentence which is shaped by the remaining steps in the guideline.

Step 2 involves a fine-tuning of harm and culpability by reference to a *non-exhaustive* list of aggravating and mitigating factors related to crime seriousness, culpability, or personal mitigation. The Sentencing Council guidelines state clearly that, in a particular case, there may be aggravating features of sufficient weight to justify moving up not just from the starting point in the category range identified at step 1 but from that category range to the next higher category range. Similar logic applies if there are weighty matters in mitigation, so as to move the sentence down not just from the starting point but to the next lower category range. As we have seen, a move from one category range to another in this way does not amount to a 'departure' from the guideline. Only a move outside the whole offence range is a departure, requiring a statement that to sentence within the guidelines would be contrary to the interests of justice.

2.15 It is important to note that the Sentencing Council guidelines, unlike all previous guidelines, make no assumption as to the offender's criminal record. Previous guidelines all assume that the court is dealing with a 'first-time offender', so that it may be appropriate to increase the sentence from the starting point to take account of relevant and recent previous convictions. Under a Sentencing Council guideline, however, movement up *or down* from the starting point may be appropriate to take account of relevant and recent previous convictions, *or their absence*. This change risks creating some degree of confusion, but in principle it is an improvement on earlier guidelines. Most offenders appearing before the courts have criminal records, so it was a little unrealistic for all guidelines to be premised on the assumption that the courts would be dealing with a previously unconvicted offender.

2.16 Step 3 in the process requires the court to take into account statutory provisions which permit a court to reduce sentence in cases where the offender has provided or offered to provide assistance to the prosecution or police. This issue will only be relevant in a small number of cases, and is discussed further at paragraph 2.68 in this Chapter. Step 4 requires the court to take into account any reduction of sentence which is appropriate to reflect the offender's plea of guilty. This is of course relevant in many cases, and requires the sentence to consult a separate guideline, the SGC guideline on *Reduction of Sentence for a Guilty Plea*, to determine the appropriate reduction to give. A reduction of one-third from the sentence arrived at in step 2 is, for example, recommended if the offender has pleaded guilty 'at the first reasonable opportunity'. This important issue is considered in detail at paragraph 2.54 in this Chapter. In respect of step 4 the Sentencing Council guidelines are consistent with all earlier guidelines in that the category ranges and starting points all assume that the offender has been convicted after a trial, so that these figures must be adjusted downwards to take the guilty plea into account.

2.17 There are five further steps in the Sentencing Council guideline process, some or all of which will be relevant to every case:

Step 5 involves consideration of whether a discretionary life sentence or an extended sentence is appropriate in the case of a 'dangerous offender';

Step 6 is relevant when sentencing an offender for more than one offence, and requires the sentencer to have regard to the principles of concurrent and consecutive sentencing and 'totality';

Step 7 involves consideration of whether a compensation order, or other ancillary order, should be made;

Step 8 requires the giving of reasons for the sentence passed, in accordance with the CJA 2003, section 74, and

Step 9 requires the court to taking into account time spent by the offender on remand under qualifying bail conditions.

These matters will all be considered in their appropriate places later in the book.

C OFFENCE SERIOUSNESS

Section 143 of the CJA 2003 states that:

2.18

> In considering the seriousness of any offence, the court must consider the offender's culpability in committing the offence and any harm which the offence caused, was intended to cause or might foreseeably have caused.

The SGC guideline, *Overarching Principles: Seriousness*, explains that '[t]he sentencer must start by considering the seriousness of the offence, the assessment of which will determine which of the sentencing thresholds has been crossed, indicate whether a custodial, community or other sentence is the most appropriate, be a key factor in determining the length of a custodial sentence, the onerousness of the requirements to be incorporated in a community sentence and the amount of any fine imposed' (paragraph 1.3). Section 143 makes it clear that, despite the range of purposes of sentencing set out in section 142(1) (paragraph 2.01, this Chapter), the sentencing court should always in practice start by considering the seriousness of the offence.

Seriousness: harm and culpability

It is very difficult to define 'seriousness' in the abstract, but sentencers must gauge the seriousness of one kind of offence against another, and to distinguish within each offence; for example, one case of burglary as against another case of burglary. Distinctions also need to be drawn between the respective roles played by co-defendants in the same case. Of course, sentencers do not start with a blank sheet, because they can derive great assistance from the available range of sentencing guidelines and related case law. The Sentencing Council guidelines, as we have seen, require the judge at step 1 explicitly to allocate the particular offence to one of three categories of seriousness: a category 1 case is one which displays both greater harm and higher culpability; category 2 is appropriate if the offence involves *either* greater harm and lower culpability *or* lesser harm and higher culpability; category 3 involves lesser harm *and* lower culpability. The exhaustive list of step 1 factors determine into which offence category the case should go.

2.19

The SGC guideline on *Seriousness* goes on to consider various levels of culpability, and varieties of harm. In levels of culpability they identify cases where the offender (i) has the intention to cause harm, with the highest culpability where an offence is planned; (ii) is subjectively reckless as to whether harm is caused even though the extent of the risk would be obvious to most people, (iii) has knowledge of the specific risk, and (iv) is negligent. Of course there are many offences of strict liability, where none of these states of mind need to be established by the prosecution in order to obtain a conviction, but culpability will still be highly relevant as to the sentence passed (see *Sandhu* [1997] Crim LR 288). In relation to harm, the SGC notes that the types of harm recognized by criminal law are diverse, and individual victims may suffer physical injury, sexual violation, financial loss, damage to health, or psychological distress. Some offences may cause harm to the community at large (instead of or as well as harm to an individual), such as economic loss, harm to public health, or interference with the administration of justice. Damage to the environment might also have been included here. Other forms of harm are more difficult to categorize, such as the

2.20

supply of prohibited drugs, and cruelty to animals. The SGC goes on to say that assessing seriousness is always difficult, particularly where there is an *imbalance* between culpability and harm, where either the harm that results is much greater than the harm intended, or where the culpability is at a higher level than the harm resulting. An example of the former would be a momentary driving error which results in multiple deaths, and an example of the latter is an attempt to kill which miscarries so that the intended victim is physically unscathed. These are examples which cause problems in the substantive criminal law, and those problems re-emerge at the sentencing stage. The SGC cannot provide an answer to these acute sentencing dilemmas, but in the end concludes that '[t]he culpability of the offender in the particular circumstances of an individual case should be the initial factor in determining the seriousness of an offence'.

2.21 Assessing the seriousness of the offence is the first step in determining the appropriate sentence. Matching the offence to a type and level of sentence is a separate exercise assisted by the application of the 'threshold' tests for the imposition of custodial and community sentences.

The custody threshold

2.22 Section 152(2) of the CJA 2003 provides that:

> The court must not pass a custodial sentence unless it is of the opinion that the offence, or the combination of the offence and one or more offences associated with it, was so serious that neither a fine alone nor a community sentence can be justified for the offence.

This is a very important provision but, as usual in sentencing, there are exceptions. It does not apply where the penalty for the offence is fixed by law (murder) or in any of those cases where statute sets a required minimum sentence. Another possible exception (in theory, although hardly ever applicable in practice) is that a custodial sentence may be passed in a case where the court would have passed a community sentence containing a requirement to which the offender must express a willingness to comply, and he has failed to do so. This matter is referred to in section 152(3). In forming its opinion under section 152(2) the court must take into account all such information as is available to it about the circumstances of the offence (or offences) including any aggravating or mitigating factors affecting the seriousness of the offence (section 156(1)), any appropriate reduction to reflect a plea of guilty or giving of assistance to the authorities, and may take into account any matters which are relevant in personal mitigation (section 166(1)). The clear purpose of this subsection is to reserve prison as a punishment only for the most serious offences or, to put it another way, only when all other sentencing options have been considered and rejected. Custody is 'a last resort'. As Lord Woolf CJ observed in *Kefford* [2002] 2 Cr App R (S) 495, 'the message is imprisonment only when necessary...'. The point was reinforced in *Seed* [2007] 2 Cr App R (S) 436, when Lord Phillips CJ said that this provision required the court, when looking at the particulars of the offence, to decide whether the 'custodial threshold' had been crossed—'[i]f it has not, then no custodial sentence can be imposed'. His Lordship also noted that at times of prison overcrowding the custodial regime would be harsher in its effects, and the opportunities for rehabilitative intervention in prison more restricted than usual. It has to be said, however, that over the years these exhortations appear to have had little effect, since the prison population has continued to rise steadily to its current record levels.

2.23 When, exactly is the custody threshold crossed? At one time it was suggested by the Court of Appeal that the test was whether this was the kind of case which '...would make all right-thinking members of the public, knowing all the facts, feel that justice had not been done by the passing of any sentence other than a custodial one' (Lawton LJ in *Bradbourn* (1985) 7 Cr App R (S) 180). Although these words were endorsed by Taylor LCJ in *Cox* [1993] 1 WLR 188, Lord Bingham CJ accepted in *Howells* [1999] 1 WLR 307 that the test was unhelpful, that there was 'no clear bright line' between cases that deserved custody and those that did not, and that in reality a court was bound in each case to give effect to its own assessment of what justice required. The SGC in the guideline *Overarching Principles: Seriousness* agreed (at paragraph 1.32) that it is impossible to determine definitively which features of a particular offence make it serious enough to cross the custody threshold. The Sentencing Council guideline on *Domestic Burglary* contains three category ranges, two of which straddle the custody threshold. The guideline states that: 'when sentencing category 2 or 3 offences, the court should also consider the custody threshold as follows: has the custody threshold been passed? If so, is it unavoidable that a custodial sentence be imposed? If so, can that sentence be suspended?'

The last cited question demonstrates an important point that, even though an offence is judged sufficiently serious to have crossed the custody threshold, an immediate custodial sentence is still not inevitable. There may be other reasons, such as the appropriate reduction for a plea of guilty, or the presence of powerful personal mitigation, which means that custody can still be avoided. The court may then step back from immediate custody to a community order or (where available) a suspended sentence. This principle can be found in the CJA 2003, section 166(2), but has been clear at least since the decision in *Cox* [1993] 1 WLR 188. There, the eighteen-year-old offender pleaded guilty to theft and reckless driving. He had been riding a motorcycle without lights and carrying a pillion passenger. In attempting to avoid a pursuing police car, he mounted the pavement, which he drove along for 50 metres, ignored a 'Give way' sign, and then fell off. He had with him when arrested at the scene various items of stolen property, which he had taken from a garage earlier that evening. The Court of Appeal agreed with the judge that the offences crossed the custody threshold, but that the judge had given insufficient attention to matters of mitigation, including the guilty plea, the offender's age, the fact that there was only one offence on his record and that a community order had been recommended in the pre-sentence report. The custodial sentence was quashed and a community order for twelve months was substituted. At the time of *Cox* the suspended sentence was not available in a case of this sort, but if the facts recurred today a sentencer would have that method of avoiding an immediate custodial sentence available as well as the community order. The circumstances which justify a sentencer in deciding against custody in a 'borderline custody' case are classically a matter for the judge to weigh up, where the statutory framework, sentencing guidelines, and the 'custody threshold' provide the context within which that decision has to be made.

Seriousness and multiple offences

The preceding discussion of the CJA 2003, section 152(2) has been based on the assumption that the offender has been convicted of, or pleaded guilty to, just one offence. The subsection also refers to the judgment of seriousness being made on the basis of 'the combination of the offence and one or more offences associated with it'. When considering the gravity of a combination of offences, the PCC(S)A 2000, section 161(1) provides that one offence is to be regarded as 'associated with another' offence 'if the offender is convicted of it in the proceedings in which he is convicted of the other offence, or (although convicted of it in earlier proceedings) is sentenced for it at the same time he is sentenced for that offence', or when convicted and sentenced he asks to have one or more offences taken into consideration. Obviously, a custodial sentence may be justified when the court is looking at more than one offence when it would not be so justified in respect of any one of the offences standing alone.

2.26   The meaning of 'associated with' is important. It will be seen that there is no need for any link between the offences save that they are being sentenced on the same occasion. It is normal good practice for all outstanding matters against an offender to be dealt with together (see paragraph 1.43, this book). In *Baverstock* [1993] 1 WLR 202 the offender was dealt with for two offences, the second having been committed while the offender was on bail in respect of the first. The offender was sentenced for the two offences on the same occasion; hence, they were 'associated' for the purposes of section 161(1). The case of *Godfrey* (1993) 14 Cr App R (S) 804 makes it clear that where a sentencer is sentencing for a new offence, and at the same time revokes a community sentence passed on the offender on an earlier occasion, and he re-sentences that earlier offence, they are 'associated offences'. The same applies if the sentencer deals with a new offence and passes a sentence for breach of a conditional discharge. In *Godfrey* itself, however, the judge decided to impose 'no separate penalty' for the breach of the conditional discharge. This meant that the earlier offence was not being sentenced on the same occasion as the new offence, and thus the two offences could not be regarded as associated. In *Cawley* (1994) 15 Cr App R (S) the judge was dealing with an offender for two offences which placed him in breach of a suspended sentence. The judge imposed a prison sentence for the new offences and activated the suspended sentence to run consecutively. In the Court of Appeal it was pointed out that the new offences were not 'associated' with the original offence, because activation of a suspended sentence did not amount to the passing of a sentence. Finally, if an offender has been convicted in respect of a number of charges which were represented by the prosecution as 'sample counts', other offences which have not been included on the indictment, or formally taken into consideration, are not associated offences (*Tovey* [2005] 2 Cr App R (S) 606). Once the court has decided that the offence (or offences) was (or were) so serious that neither a fine alone nor a community sentence can be justified, the next question is how long that custodial sentence may properly be. That issue is considered at paragraph 2.30 later in this Chapter. First we need to look at the community sentence threshold.

The community sentence threshold

2.27   The CJA 2003, section 147 states that a 'community sentence' is a sentence that consists of, or includes a 'community order' or a 'youth rehabilitation order'. The community order applies to offenders aged eighteen years and over, and the youth rehabilitation order applies to offenders under eighteen years old. For a detailed explanation of these sentences see Chapter 6. Here we are simply concerned with the justification for imposing such a sentence. This can be found in section 148(1) of the CJA, which states that:

> [a] court must not pass a community sentence on an offender unless it is of the opinion that the offence, or the combination of the offence and one or more offences associated with it, was serious enough to warrant such a sentence.

The similarity between this provision and section 152(2) which deals with the custody threshold (at paragraph 2.22, earlier in this Chapter) is clear. The main difference is that section 148(1) says that the offence(s) must be 'serious enough', whereas section 152(2) says that the offence(s) must be 'so serious' that nothing less will do. As for the custody threshold the court must consider the offender's culpability in committing the offence and any harm which the offence caused, was intended to cause or might foreseeably have caused (CJA 2003, section 143). In forming its opinion under section 148(1) the court must take into account all such information as is available to it about the circumstances of the offence (or offences) including any aggravating or mitigating factors affecting the seriousness of the offence (section 156(1)), any appropriate reduction to reflect a plea of guilty, and may take into account any matters which are relevant in personal mitigation (section 166(1)). The CJA 2003, section 150A limits the power to pass a community sentence to cases where the offence is punishable with imprisonment.

The SGC guideline, *Overarching Principles: Seriousness* says that sentencers should con- **2.28** sider the disposals available within or below the community sentence threshold before reaching the provisional conclusion to pass a community sentence so that 'even where the threshold for a community sentence has been passed, a financial penalty or discharge may still be an appropriate penalty' (paragraph 1.36). This seems comparable to the section 166(2) proviso in relation to the custody threshold. In the context of the community sentence threshold, however, the phrase 'serious enough' implies that offence seriousness is a necessary but not a sufficient condition for passing a community sentence. In practice this wording seems to create no difficulty, and there is no case law to speak of in relation to the community sentence threshold. The subsection also refers to the judgment of seriousness being made on the basis of 'the combination of the offence and one or more offences associated with it'. This phrase was considered in relation to the custody threshold at paragraph 2.25, this Chapter. Again, there appears to be no case law on this criterion in the context of the community sentence threshold so one can only assume that it has created no practical difficulty.

For the sake of completeness we should mention the CJA 2003, section 150 states that **2.29** power to pass a community sentence is not available where the penalty for the offence is fixed by law (murder) or in any of those cases where statute sets a required minimum sentence or where the dangerous offenders provisions apply. Section 151 of the CJA 2003 relates to imposing a community order for persistent offenders who have previously been fined. This section is not in force and is not considered here.

Seriousness and custodial sentence length

Of course in any case the sentencing court must ensure that it sentences within the max- **2.30** imum custodial term permitted by statute and, if sentence is being passed in a magistrates' court, it must accord with the restrictions on the powers of that court. Different statutory maxima may apply to young offenders, and these must also be borne in mind. Apart from these general limitations, the CJA 2003, section 153(2) states that:

> ...the custodial sentence must be for the shortest term (not exceeding the permitted maximum) that in the opinion of the court is commensurate with the seriousness of the offence, or the combination of the offence and one or more offences associated with it.

As usual, this provision is subject to cases where the penalty for the offence is fixed by law (murder) or in any of those cases where statute sets a required minimum sentence or where the dangerous offenders provisions apply.

The wording in section 153(2) is a clear reflection of the well-established principle that, **2.31** when it is necessary to impose a custodial sentence, that sentence should be as short as possible to achieve the aims of that sentence. In forming its opinion under section 153(2) the court must take into account all such information as is available to it about the circum- stances of the offence (or offences) including any aggravating or mitigating factors affecting the seriousness of the offence (section 156(1)), any appropriate reduction to reflect a plea of guilty, and may take into account any matters which are relevant in personal mitigation (section 166(1)). The Court of Appeal in *Ollerenshaw* [1999] 1 Cr App R (S) 65 said that when a court is considering imposing a custodial sentence of about twelve months or less, it should ask itself (especially where this will be the offender's first prison sentence) whether a shorter period might be equally effective. According to Rose LJ in that case, 'six months may be just as effective as nine, or two months may be just as effective as four'. In fact there is a great deal of doubt amongst criminologists of the rehabilitative value of custodial sentences of less than twelve months, so perhaps the reference to 'effectiveness' is misplaced here. The point really is that a custodial sentence must be as short as it can be. In *Kefford* [2002] 2 Cr App R (S) 495, Lord Woolf CJ said that the overcrowding of the prison system was a matter of grave concern, and that all courts should heed the message, which was 'imprisonment only when necessary, and for no longer than necessary'. Similar remarks were made in *Mills* [2002] 2 Cr App R (S) 229, with respect to the female prison population, and more generally again in *Seed* [2007] 2 Cr App R (S) 436. In the last case Lord Phillips CJ said that section 153(2) was an important provision and that '[i]n times of prison overcrowding it is particularly important that judges and magistrates pay close regard...the court should properly bear in mind that the prison regime is likely to be more punitive as a result of prison overcrowding'.

2.32 Section 153(2) states that the court may have regard to 'the combination of the offence and one or more offences associated with it' when determining the length of a custodial sentence. The PCC(S)A 2000, section 161(1) (see paragraph 2.25, this Chapter), defines when one offence may be regarded for these purposes as 'associated with' another. If the offender is being sentenced for several offences, it is well established that the court should not simply add together the custodial sentences imposed for the offences to reach a grand total. Such an approach could lead to a total sentence which is disproportionate to the overall seriousness of the offending behaviour. The CJA 2003, section 166(3)(b), in an attempt to avoid this, declares that nothing shall prevent a court 'in a case of an offender who is convicted of one or more other offences, from mitigating his sentence by applying any rule of law as to the totality of sentences'. This provision gives statutory recognition to the 'totality principle' developed over many years by the Court of Appeal. Where appropriate, in order to keep within totality, a sentencer should pass concurrent custodial sentences (which run at the same time as one other) rather than consecutive custodial sentences. The Sentencing Council has issued a guideline on this issue: *Offences Taken into Consideration and Totality*. For full discussion of concurrent and consecutive sentencing, and totality, see paragraph 3.33 in the following Chapter.

Previous convictions

2.33 There are some situations where the presence of a particular conviction in the offender's antecedents will trigger a prescribed custodial sentence, leaving the judge with little room for manoeuvre on sentence. For example, an offender convicted for the third time for an offence of domestic burglary must receive a custodial sentence of at least three years unless there are particular circumstances which would render such a sentence unjust. The effect of such a statutory rule is to enhance significantly the usual role of criminal record in sentencing. The so-called 'three strikes' rule in cases of domestic burglary is considered in Chapter 5, along with other prescribed custodial sentence provisions. A second point is that when a sentencer is considering whether to impose an indeterminate sentence on a dangerous offender, the court must always have regard to the offender's criminal record, among other matters in assessing whether he poses a significant risk to members of the public of serious harm. Here the record provides material on which the sentencer must come to a judgment of risk. This issue is dealt with in Chapter 3.

Leaving aside these special cases, the great bulk of sentencing decisions are driven by the **2.34** normal requirements of offence seriousness. Section 143(2) of the CJA 2003 provides that:

> [i]n considering the seriousness of an offence ('the current offence') committed by an offender who has one or more previous convictions, the court must treat each previous conviction as an aggravating factor if (in the case of that conviction) the court considers that it can reasonably be so treated having regard, in particular, to—
>
> (a) the nature of the offence to which the conviction relates and its relevance to the current offence, and
> (b) the time that has elapsed since the conviction.

The CJA 2003, section 143(3) explains that 'previous conviction' in this context means a previous conviction returned by a court in the United Kingdom, a previous conviction of a service offence within the meaning of the Armed Forces Act 2006, or a previous conviction in another EU Member State of a 'relevant offence'. By section 143(5) this does not prevent the court from treating a previous conviction by a court outside the UK as an aggravating factor in any case where the court considers it appropriate to do so. An old conviction may be 'spent' under the Rehabilitation of Offenders Act 1974 and while such a conviction will still be made known to the sentencing court it may well be appropriate to accord it little or no relevance. Out of court disposals, such as cautions, reprimands, and warnings, are not previous convictions but are kept on record and may appear in a separate part of the antecedents of the offender. For further details of these matters see paragraph 1.64 earlier in this book.

Section 143(2) is the most recent attempt by Parliament to capture the idea that previous **2.35** convictions aggravate the seriousness of the latest offence. Earlier versions have been repealed. In the views of some it is illogical to regard previous wrongdoing as relevant to the seriousness of the offence since the fact that the offender has broken the law before cannot increase the harm caused by the instant offence, nor (it is argued) can it increase the culpability of the offender. In any event, past offences have been dealt with by the court, and the offender should not be subjected to further penalty for that reason. On the other hand in practice courts have always tended to increase punishment for persistent offenders. That seems to make sense if the sentencing purpose which is being pursued is the reduction of crime by deterrence or the protection of the public. The Crown Court Sentencing Survey found, unsurprisingly, that heavier sentences are imposed on offenders with 'recent and relevant' previous convictions (which is a conventional, shorthand way of referring to the requirements expressed in section 143(2)). The likelihood of being sentenced to immediate custody increases with the number of previous convictions being taken into account. The survey found, however, that there is an inverse relationship whereby offenders convicted of less serious offences, such as petty theft, are more likely to have committed a number of previous similar offences. Those convicted of more serious offences, such as serious assault, are much less likely to have committed a number of similar offences. The Sentencing Council guidelines at step 2 specify as a 'statutory aggravating factor', previous convictions, having regard to (a) and (b) as specified in section 143(2). Additionally, as for example in the *Burglary* guideline, sentencers are specifically reminded that 'relevant recent convictions are likely to result in an upward adjustment' either within the category range selected at step 1 or, perhaps, as justifying a movement to a higher category range.

There is no sentencing guideline on the subject of the relevance of previous convictions, or **2.36** the weight to be attached to them, and the Court of Appeal has never issued general guidance. Whether a previous conviction is 'relevant' is essentially a matter for the sentencer to decide, but obviously similar offences are more likely to be relevant than offences of an entirely different type. It is also clear from the section that, other things being equal, an old conviction is less likely to be relevant than a recent one. There is case authority which indicates that it is wrong to impose a sentence which is disproportionate to the seriousness of the offence purely on the basis of a bad record. In *Neasham* [2012] EWCA Crim 542 the thirty-six-year-old offender was convicted of burglary. He had numerous previous convictions, including twenty-nine for theft and similar offences, and fourteen for burglaries of dwelling houses. The present offence was the offender's third conviction under the minimum sentence provision and so attracted a minimum sentence of three years. The facts were that residents were disturbed at 1 o'clock in the morning by a man in their backyard, and they called the police. When the police arrived they found the defendant in the conservatory of a house normally occupied by students, but empty at the time. He told officers he was looking for somewhere to sleep. He had with him a multi-tool penknife, a torch, and a pair of gloves. In the event no property was taken. He was sentenced to six years' imprisonment. On appeal against sentence, the Court of Appeal said that the sentence was manifestly excessive in the circumstances. According to Singh J, '[e]ven though the appellant has a poor record for similar offences, he was being sentenced for the particular offence of which he had been convicted on this occasion. Relevant previous convictions are a statutory aggravating factor, but there is still a need for the punishment to be proportionate...this was not the most serious offence of burglary'. The sentence of six years was quashed and replaced with a term of four years. Another example is *Byrne* [2012] EWCA Crim 418, where brothers Ryan and Anthony pleaded guilty to burglary of commercial premises. Entry had been forced and computers worth £6000 were moved to the doorway for later collection, but when the offenders came to collect them the police were waiting and arrested them. Both offenders had records of dishonesty. Ryan had twenty-five previous convictions for burglary, and at the time of the offence was in breach of a pre-release licence from a sentence of nine years' imprisonment. He had failed to return from licence at the time he committed the burglary. He recruited his brother to commit the offence with him. Anthony was younger and had six previous convictions for burglary. The applicable sentencing guidelines at the time were the SGC, *Theft and Burglary in a Building Other than a Dwelling*, which indicated a sentencing range for an offence of this description after a trial of a high community order to twelve months, with a starting point of eighteen weeks. In passing sentence the judge said he was passing sentence outside the guidelines (by which he clearly meant the category range rather than the offence range) because of the defendant's previous convictions. The Court of Appeal said that the sentences were out of proportion to the offence that was committed. According to Saunders J, '[w]hile a judge can sentence outside the guidelines any determinate sentence should bear some relationship to the seriousness of the offence for which it is passed'. Sentences were reduced to three-and-a-half years and eight months respectively. These reduced sentences are still well above the normally applicable category range, especially bearing in mind that the starting point was twelve rather than eighteen months because of the pleas of guilty. On the other hand there were significant aggravating factors in Ryan's case as well as the previous convictions. The sentencing guidelines used in this case have now been replaced by the Sentencing Council's guideline on *Burglary Offences* with effect from January 2012.

2.37 Section 143(2) deals with the circumstances in which an offender's poor record may be taken to aggravate the seriousness of the offence. If the offender has a clean record, or has no 'relevant or recent' convictions, then this may be regarded as a significant mitigating factor and may be taken into account under the CJA 2003, section 166(1) as a matter of personal mitigation. This issue is considered at paragraph 2.52 at point (ii).

Offending on bail

Section 143(3) of the CJA 2003 states: '[i]n considering the seriousness of any offence com-   **2.38**
mitted while the offender was on bail, the court must treat the fact that it was committed
in those circumstances as an aggravating factor'. It is clear that where the defendant has
offended in this way the matter is made worse by his breach of the trust reposed in him by
the court. Logic would suggest that matters would be made worse in a case where the second
offence was committed only shortly after bail was granted, and/or was an offence of the
same type as that for which bail was granted. An example is *Jeffrey* [2004] 1 Cr App R (S)
179, where the offender admitted an offence of inflicting grievous bodily harm which was
committed while he was on bail awaiting sentence for other offences of assault committed
only a month earlier. Mance LJ said that the offending on bail was 'a serious aggravating
element' but, taking everything in the round, the original sentence of three-and-a-half years
was reduced to two-and-a-half years. In *Jeffrey* the offender was on bail awaiting sentence
but the same principle clearly applies where the offender is on bail awaiting trial.

Section 143(3) is expressed in mandatory terms and, as a statutory aggravating factor, is for-   **2.39**
mally referred to in all sentencing guidelines. It should, however, be set against another sentencing principle, that consecutive sentences are appropriate where one offence is committed
while the offender is on bail in respect of another. Clearly, operation of these rules together
would involve 'double-counting' and would result in a disproportionately severe sentence. As
a practical matter it seems that offending on bail is much more routinely taken into account
as aggravating the new offence rather than to justify the passing of consecutive sentences.

Racial or religious motivation as aggravating factors

Parliament has created a number of 'racially or religiously aggravated' versions of crim-   **2.40**
inal offences in the Crime and Disorder Act 1998, sections 29 to 32. These cover certain
aggravated forms of assault, aggravated criminal damage, certain aggravated public order
offences, or aggravated harassment. The racially or religiously aggravated versions of these
offences all carry higher maximum penalties than the 'basic' offence. By section 28(1) of
the 1998 Act, an offence is racially or religiously aggravated if:

(a) at the time of committing the offence, or immediately before or after doing so, the offender demonstrates towards the victim of the offence hostility based on the victim's
membership (or presumed membership) of racial or religious group, or
(b) the offence is motivated (wholly or partly) by hostility towards members of a racial or
religious group based on their membership of that group.

The cases of *Saunders* [2000] 1 Cr App R (S) 548 and *Kelly* [2001] 2 Cr App R (S) 341,
both involving racially aggravated actual bodily harm, provide sentencing guidance for
cases involving racial aggravation. *Kelly* is a guideline case, issued by the Court of Appeal
on advice from the SAP. In line with this case law the Sentencing Council guideline on
Assault states, for each of the racially aggravated assaults, that 'the court should first determine the appropriate sentence for the offence without taking account of the element
of aggravation, and then make an addition to the sentence, considering the level of aggravation involved. It may be appropriate to move outside the category range, taking
into account the increased statutory maximum'. In addition to this *Kelly* suggests that
the court should state what the basic sentence was and the extent of the uplift, and that
even if the basic offence did not cross the custody threshold, the aggravated offence may
do so. Also in *Kelly* it was said that the extent of the uplift might be enhanced where the
racist element was a planned part of the offence, the offence was part of a pattern of racist

offending, the offender was part of a racist group, or where the victim had been deliberately set up so that the accused could humiliate or offend him. The impact on the victim was also important, such as where he was vulnerable, or providing a service to the public, or where particular distress had been caused to the victim, his family, or the community.

2.41 It is important to note that if the offender has been convicted of a basic offence where a racially or religiously aggravated version exists, it is wrong for the court to sentence on the basis that there was a racial or religious element to it. This is one aspect of the fundamental principle that the offender must only be sentenced for offences proved against him or formally admitted, which is considered at paragraph 1.52 in the previous Chapter. In *McGillivray* [2005] 2 Cr App R (S) 366 the offender pleaded guilty to assault occasioning actual bodily harm. The racially aggravated version of that offence had originally been charged as well, but no evidence was adduced on that count and a verdict of not guilty was entered. The judge passed a sentence of three years' imprisonment on the basis that the assault had been racially aggravated. The Court of Appeal said that it had not been open to the judge to sentence on that basis, since the offender had not been convicted of the racially aggravated form of the offence. The sentence was reduced to two years, a sentence appropriate for the basic offence.

2.42 The CJA 2003, section 145 applies where a court is considering the seriousness of an offence other than one of the offences under sections 29 to 32. The sentence must decide on the evidence whether the offence was racially or religiously motivated and, if it was, must treat that fact as an aggravating factor on sentence and must state in open court that the offence was so aggravated. For the definition of 'racial or religious aggravation', see above. Much of the guidance given in *Kelly* seems equally applicable in this context. In *Morrison* [2001] 1 Cr App R (S) 12, the Court of Appeal said that the appropriate additional punishment to reflect racial aggravation would depend on all the circumstances, but in that case approved the enhancement by two years of a nominal sentence of four-and-a-half years for burglary committed in circumstances of racial aggravation.

Other statutory aggravating factors

2.43 Building upon the original categories of racial and religious aggravation in section 145, section 146 of the CJA 2003, section146 extends the categories of a case where, when considering the seriousness of the case, the court must treat as an aggravating factor:

(a) a demonstration of hostility towards the victim, or where the offence was motivated by hostility towards the victim, based upon the sexual orientation (or presumed sexual orientation) of the victim, or

(b) a demonstration of hostility towards the victim, or where the offence was motivated by hostility towards the victim, based upon the disability (or presumed disability) of the victim, or

(c) a demonstration of hostility towards the victim, or where the offence was motivated by hostility towards the victim, based upon the victim being transgender (or presumed to be transgender).

In addition, by the Counter-Terrorism Act 2008, section 30, where an offence listed in schedule 2 to the Act appears to the sentencing court to have a 'terrorist connection', that fact must be treated as an aggravating factor.

It should be noted in relation to (a) above, that in *B* [2014] EWCA Crim 91 the Court of Appeal held that an assault committed because the offender believed the victim to be a paedophile was not an offence aggravated within the meaning of section 146.

General aggravating factors

The SGC guideline, *Seriousness* sets out a list of aggravating factors generally relevant to **2.44** sentencing, applicable across many, but not necessarily all, offences. Some of these reflect higher culpability on the part of the offender; others reflect a more than usually serious degree of harm. It is clear from the wording of the CJA 2003, section 156(1) that aggravating factors affecting the seriousness of the offence should always be taken into account when deciding, amongst other things, whether an offence is 'serious enough' to warrant a community sentence (CJA 2003, section 148(1)) or 'so serious that neither a fine alone nor a community sentence can be justified' (CJA 2003, section 152(2)), or in determining the length of a custodial sentence (section 153(2)). These matters were all considered earlier in this Chapter. The list of factors in the guideline is set out here. The guideline states that these are not intended to be comprehensive and are not listed in any particular order of priority.

Factors indicating higher culpability

- Offence committed whilst on bail for other offences
- Failure to respond to previous sentences
- Offence was racially or religiously aggravated
- Offence motivated by, or demonstrating, hostility to the victim based on his or her sexual orientation (or presumed sexual orientation)
- Offence motivated by, or demonstrating, hostility based on the victim's disability (or presumed disability)
- Previous conviction(s), particularly where a pattern of repeat offending is disclosed
- Planning of an offence
- An intention to commit more serious harm than actually resulted from the offence
- Offenders operating in groups or gangs
- 'Professional' offending
- Commission of the offence for financial gain (where this is not inherent in the offence itself)
- High level of profit from the offence
- An attempt to conceal or dispose of evidence
- Failure to respond to warnings or concerns expressed by others about the offender's behaviour
- Offence committed whilst on licence
- Offence motivated by hostility towards a minority group, or a member or members of such a group
- Deliberate targeting of vulnerable victim(s)
- Commission of an offence while under the influence of alcohol or drugs
- Use of a weapon to frighten or injure victim
- Deliberate and gratuitous violence or damage to property, over and above what is needed to carry out the offence
- Abuse of power
- Abuse of a position of trust

Some of these aggravating factors are listed in statute, and have already been mentioned.

Factors indicating a more than usually serious degree of harm

- Multiple victims
- An especially serious physical or psychological effect on the victim, even if unintended
- A sustained assault or repeated assaults on the same victim

- Victim is particularly vulnerable
- Location of the offence (for example, in an isolated place)
- Offence is committed against those working in the public sector or providing a service to the public
- Presence of others (eg relatives, especially children or partner of the victim)
- Additional degradation of the victim (eg taking photographs of a victim as part of a sexual offence)
- In property offences, high value (including sentimental value) of property to the victim, or substantial consequential loss (eg where the theft of equipment causes serious disruption to a victim's life or business)

2.45   Occasionally the Court of Appeal has indicated that other matters, not specifically referred to here, should be regarded as general aggravating or mitigating factors. In *A-G's Reference (Nos 73, 75, and 03 of 2010)* [2011] EWCA Crim 633, for example, Lord Judge CJ emphasized that, at least in the context of sexual offences, invasion of the victim's home to commit the offence was an aggravating factor. In the same case his Lordship said that the taking of photographs of the victim of a sexual offence was a seriously aggravating factor, but did not refer to that factor's inclusion in the SGC's list.

Prevalence of the offence

2.46   When can an offence be regarded as more serious by virtue of its prevalence—being committed by many offenders? The SGC sentencing guideline, *Seriousness* tries to deal with issue, but does not offer particularly clear advice. On the one hand the guideline states (at paragraph 1.38) that the seriousness of an individual case should be judged on its own dimensions of harm and culpability, rather than being seen as part of a collective social harm. On the other hand, it also says (in paragraph 1.39) that it is legitimate for the overall approach to sentencing levels for particular offences to be guided by their cumulative effect. What this seems to mean is that an individual case of, say, theft from a shop, needs to be sentenced on its merits rather than by reference to the overall scale of financial loss occasioned to retail outlets generally. Sometimes, though, an escalation in a particular form of serious offending (such as knife crime) may prompt an overall reassessment of the way in which such crimes have been sentenced in the past. An increase in sentencing levels here may be taken either as a recalibration of seriousness or an effort at general deterrence. What this seems to boil down to is that Parliament (through raising maximum penalties) or the Court of Appeal (by announcing a change in sentencing approach) may alter general sentencing levels for a particular form of law-breaking. An example of the former is the substantial and successive increases in maximum penalties for driving offences causing death. An example of the latter is, indeed, knife crime, where the Court in *Povey* [2009] 1 Cr App R (S) 228 said that such offences should be sentenced more severely than before across the board, because knife crime was now a very serious social problem. It is more difficult for individual judges and magistrates to do that because they will see only a small part of the whole picture. The decision in *Blackshaw* [2012] 1 C r App R (S) 677 makes it clear, if there was ever a doubt, that it is wrong for judges in one court or one area of the country to set their own sentencing guidelines on a particular issue.

2.47   The SGC guideline does recognize, however, that there may be exceptional circumstances that lead a court to decide that local prevalence should influence sentencing levels. The issue in such cases is the harm being caused to the local community. Where such a situation arises the SGC guideline states that before proceeding to impose a higher sentence the judge must have supporting evidence from an external source. The *Criminal Practice Directions* paragraphs H.1 to H.6 refer to the possibility of a 'community impact statement' being drawn up by the police 'to make the court aware of particular crime trends in the local area and the impact of these on the local community'. In *Oosthuizen* [2006] 1 Cr App R (S) 385 the judge had passed a deterrent sentence on offenders for committing robberies by grabbing handbags from women in the street, saying that such crime was a particular problem in that area. The Court of Appeal said that every court must 'have regard to' the guideline (as the requirement was phrased at that time) and that it was 'hazardous' for a judge to assume without supporting evidence that an offence was more prevalent in his area than nationally, especially where there was a sentencing guideline in place for that offence. In *Lanham* [2009] 1 Cr App R (S) 592 sentences of thirty months for theft of lead from a roof were 'reluctantly' reduced to sixteen months by the Court of Appeal since the judge had cited no evidence to support the claim of local prevalence. The judge had not been referred to the guideline. Finally, in *Moss* [2011] 1 Cr App R (S) 199, a thirty-month sentence for theft of copper cabling from a telephone installation was reduced to two years on appeal. In that case the judge had been told that there had been about twenty similar offences in that part of the country within a relatively short period of time, but Pitchford J in the Court of Appeal said that this had been insufficient material upon which to include a deterrent element in the sentence.

General mitigating factors

The SGC guideline, *Seriousness* also provides a list of mitigating factors generally relevant **2.48** to sentencing, applicable across many, but not necessarily all, offences. The SGC states that some factors reflect unusually low culpability on the part of the offender; others show that the harm caused by an offence is less than usually serious. The list, however, contains only four factors in the former category and none at all in the latter.

Factors indicating significantly lower culpability

- A greater degree of provocation than normally expected
- Mental illness or disability
- Youth or age, where it affects the responsibility of the individual defendant
- The fact that the offender played only a minor role in the offence

Factors indicating that harm caused is less than usually serious

None

This list provides a striking contrast to the long list of general aggravating factors. This is **2.49** probably because the majority of mitigating factors in sentencing related to harm or culpability are offence-specific, rather than the generic factors referred to in this list. Offence-specific aggravating and mitigating factors relevant to seriousness of offence are set out in the individual offence guidelines. Provocation has long been recognized as a mitigating factor, although of course it operates as a partial defence to murder, now in the form of 'loss of control'. There is an SGC guideline on *Manslaughter by reason of provocation*, which sets out various degrees of provocation. The guideline needs updating to take account of the change in the substantive law, but aspects of the guideline are still helpful in distinguishing provocation cases generally. In *AG's Reference (No 23 of 2011)* [2011] EWCA Crim 1496 the Court of Appeal noted that the partial defence of loss of control addressed the question whether sexual infidelity might form the basis for a defence to murder, but even if not amounting to a defence circumstances of provocation might still provide mitigation in a case of murder and, by implication, in offences other than murder. Clearly the weight to be attached to the provocation varies from case to case, with a sudden and impulsive reaction being generally regarded as less blameworthy than a planned retaliation. The phrase 'greater degree of provocation than normally expected' is rather oddly expressed, but it perhaps serves to indicate that provocation only above a certain level of seriousness should sound in mitigation at all. Generally speaking, people should keep their tempers. In *Collis* [2012] EWCA Crim 1335 a man called Scott pushed past the offender into his flat and attacked the offender's wife. Collis and Scott started to fight, in the course of which Collis grabbed a kitchen knife and stabbed Scott in the neck, causing serious, life-threatening injury. A sentence of eight years was reduced to six on the basis of the 'considerable provocation'.

2.50   Alongside provocation the SGC guideline on *Seriousness* might have recognized circumstances of severe intimidation and pressure, but falling short of a defence of duress. Thus in *Robinson* [2004] 2 Cr App R (S) 392, a case involving importation of drugs where the defence of duress had failed at trial, the Court of Appeal observed that it may still be necessary for the judge to hold a Newton hearing (as to which see paragraph 1.51, previous Chapter in this book) to determine whether there had been coercion short of duress which ought to be recognized on sentence. Another example is *Jones* [2012] 1 Cr App R (S) 150, where the Court of Appeal reduced a prescribed sentence of five years for harbouring firearms to six months, partly because although her defence of duress failed at trial it was accepted that she was in fear and her will was overborne by threats. There was also powerful personal mitigation in that case. Logically, although a mistake of the criminal law cannot found a defence, a genuine mistake by the offender on such a matter ought to sound in mitigation. In *Universal Salvage v Boothby* (1983) 5 Cr App R (S) 428, a fine imposed on a company for breach of regulations was reduced when the appeal court heard that the company had reasonably relied on official advice that the regulations did not apply to them. In certain narrow circumstances mental disorder will amount to a defence. Otherwise, evidence that the defendant was mentally disordered falls to be taken into account by the sentencer.

D PERSONAL MITIGATION

2.51   Section 166(1) Criminal Justice Act 2003 makes provision for a sentencer to take account of any matters that 'in the opinion of the court, are relevant in mitigation of sentence'. This is a very broad provision allowing a sentencer to take into account in principle any matter which seems relevant in reduction of the sentence. It will be seen that this section provides a power to take personal mitigation into account, and is quite different from the statutory and other aggravating factors set out earlier. Personal mitigation is not an entitlement. It is always open to a judge to decide not to take an item of personal mitigation into account, or to decide that the mitigation is eclipsed by the seriousness of the offence. As Scarman LJ said when sentencing a first-time offender in the old case of *Inwood* (1974) 60 Cr App R 70, '. . . in the balance that the court has to make between the mitigating factors and society's interest in marking the disapproval for this type of conduct, we come to the irresistible though unpalatable conclusion that we must not yield to the mitigating factors'. Sometimes a judge may doubt the truthfulness of the offender's mitigation and, if so, the case of *Guppy* (1995) 16 Cr App R (S) 25 says that the burden of proof is on the defence to satisfy the judge on the balance of probability. There might be no point in ordering a *Newton* hearing in such a case, but it is always open to the judge to invite the offender to give evidence to support what he claims.

2.52   Although the category of personal mitigation is wide open, it may nonetheless be helpful to set out a range of commonly encountered examples. Information on these matters is likely to emerge from the pre-sentence report or the plea in mitigation. In some cases the judge may be provided with references or testimonials about the offender.

(i) *remorse*

Numerous cases indicate that where the court is persuaded that the offender has experienced genuine remorse in the period following the commission of the offence, that can provide significant personal mitigation. The Crown Court Survey found that this was the most frequently cited form of personal mitigation. What is at issue here is 'genuine' remorse, which is a difficult matter for the judge to assess. Offenders often express remorse through a plea in mitigation and not uncommonly the judge may receive a letter from the offender saying much the same. Sometimes it is clear from the circumstances of the offence and the offender that expressions of remorse are entirely genuine and heartfelt. An example is *Larke* [2010] 1 Cr App R (S) 5, where the elderly female offender had made a momentary but catastrophic misjudgment while driving and had caused the deaths of two people. The offender had a clean driving record which stretched back many years, and her expressions of regret and remorse were undoubtedly heartfelt. In the case of *Claydon* (1994) 15 Cr App R (S) 526, the offender had voluntarily come to the police station and admitted the offence even before it had been reported. This was taken to be clear evidence of genuine remorse. In other cases matters are not so clear. At one time remorse as a mitigating factor was associated with the rationale for reduction of sentence for a guilty plea, but following the SGC guideline on reduction for plea the two issues must now be treated as separate. Clearly a guilty plea may sometimes reflect remorse, but offenders who plead guilty are often doing so for pragmatic reasons and may not be remorseful at all. It may be that by the time of sentence the offender has made some voluntary restitution to the victim, such as by paying back some of benefits sum which has been obtained by fraud. The strength of the mitigation here varies according to the relative difficulty for the offender in paying the money, rather than the amount paid. It can give rise to a danger that such mitigation is available only to offenders who have the money to pay (or have relatives able to help them out). The Court of Appeal was aware of this in *Crosby* (1974) 60 Cr App R 234, and pointed out that to impose a prison sentence on one defendant but suspend sentence on his co-defendant because he had repaid £3600 to the victim 'does not seem to us to be a firm foundation for the administration of justice'.

(ii) *clean record*

One of the most powerful matters which can generally be advanced in mitigation is the offender's good character and clean criminal record. An absence of previous convictions is a key factor, but in addition it may be possible to assert that the offender is a person of 'positive good character' in that (apart from having a clean record) they are morally upstanding, do good work in the community, and so on. The Sentencing Council guideline on *Sexual Offences* makes this point clearly when stating that 'previous good character/exemplary conduct is different from having no previous convictions'.

Section 143(2) on previous convictions as an aggravating factor was considered at paragraph 2.33, this Chapter. In a sense this is now the reverse of that section. Even if the offender does have previous convictions, they will carry less weight if they are old or very different in nature from the latest offence. There are also occasions on which a conviction-free gap in the offender's record may be evidence of effort to rehabilitate himself in which the latest offence might be seen as a lapse rather than a reversion to bad old ways. Something can be made of a slowdown in offending of a persistent offender.

Although in principle good character is potentially relevant across the full range of offences, there are some exceptions. Clearly, the more serious the offence the less relevant this matter can be. Previous good character provides no personal mitigation in homicide or in rape. In other cases, however, it is likely to make a significant difference, and may mean that an otherwise deserved custodial sentence can be avoided, according to the Court of Appeal in *Seed* [2007] 2 Cr App R (S) 436. There is a particular issue is relation to cases of domestic violence. The SGC guideline on *Domestic Violence* points out (at paragraph 3.20) that as a general principle of sentencing, a court will take account of an offender's positive good character. In that particular context, however, '...one of the factors that can allow domestic violence to continue unnoticed for lengthy periods is the ability of the perpetrator to have two personae. In respect of violence is a domestic context, an offender's good character in relation to conduct outside the home should generally be of no relevance where there is a proven pattern of behaviour'. The Sentencing Council guideline on *Sexual Offences* takes the point further, and says that where an offender has used his previous good character etc to provide the opportunity to commit a sexual offence then it can provide no mitigation and may constitute an aggravating factor. There has also been a long-standing policy that personal mitigation should be given much less weight than usual when sentencing drug couriers. This is because a policy of deterrence has been uppermost, and it is recognized that people of good character often in considerable financial and personal difficulties are recruited to transport drugs. There has been a change of policy in relation to so-called 'drug mules' in the SC guideline *Drug Offences*, which is considered further in Chapter 14.

(iii) *youth*

Youth has often been referred to as mitigating factor in sentencing, but this is a little misleading as a general statement. On some occasions youthfulness and immaturity may show reduced culpability, in which case it comes within the SGC list set out above. In other cases youth is probably better seen as personal mitigation and as signalling a different, more individualized sentencing approach. In *N, D & L* [2011] 1 Cr App R (S) 155 Lord Judge CJ said that it is an old and well-established principle of sentencing that the youth of an offender should normally lead to a lower sentence. The youth of an offender is widely recognized as requiring a different approach from that which would be adopted in relation to an adult. This is clear from the different sentencing aims set out in statute (see paragraph 2.04, this Chapter), and the fact that lower maximum custodial sentences are generally set for offenders aged under eighteen years of age. Even in murder a shorter minimum term is appropriate for a juvenile. The SGC guideline on *Sentencing Youths* provides a detailed treatment of this issue. The guideline says that individual sanctions are likely to have a greater impact on a young person, especially custodial sentences because of the exposure to influences likely to entrench criminal conduct and the greater risk of self-harm that exists in young people. Factors regularly present in the background of juveniles who commit offences include low family income, poor housing, poor employments records, low educational attainment, experience of offending by other family members, or of violence and abuse. Young people should be given greater opportunity to learn from their mistakes. In particular, by paragraph 11.16, the guideline says:

> Where the offender is aged 15, 16 or 17 the court will need to consider the maturity of the offender as well as chronological age. Where there is no specific offence guideline it may be appropriate, depending on maturity to consider a starting point from half to three quarters of that which would have been identified for an adult offender. Where the offender is aged 14 or less the sentence should normally be imposed in a youth court and the length of the custodial sentence should normally be shorter than for an offender aged 15–17 convicted of the same offence.

Obviously, youth gathers extra strength as a mitigating factor if associated with other matters, such as good character and remorse. All of the above reflects the normal discounted approach when sentencing young offenders. However, as Lord Judge CJ pointed out in *N, D & L*, the maturity of some young offenders is well in advance of that to be expected of youths of that age. Maturity, as well as chronological age is relevant because in some cases mitigation arising from youth can be reduced or diminished, sometimes to virtual extinction.

(iv) *old age/illness*

On occasions (such as where there is evidence of senility or disordered thinking) it is arguable that the offender's age might tend to reduce culpability, together with the matters mentioned at paragraph 2.48 in this Chapter. Ordinarily, though, age does not affect culpability, so it is better regarded as personal mitigation. An elderly person with a short life expectancy can sometimes make an argument for a reduction in sentence but, again, this always has to be balanced against the seriousness of the offence. In *Heron* [2009] 2 Cr App R (S) 362 the seventy-seven-year-old offender who was registered as disabled and suffered from asthma, hypertension, diabetes, and osteoarthritis was convicted of importing 16 kilograms of a Class A drug, cocaine, with a street value of £1 million. The Court of Appeal said that numerous authorities establish that regard must be had to the fact that, owing to age and ill-health, the offender may become ill or die in prison. According to David Clarke J, '[i]t is a not a risk that can be avoided, but it is one to be taken into account in sentence. Any such discount is case-specific. There is still some room in the sentencing process for the exercise of a modicum of mercy'. The sentence of thirteen years was reduced to ten years. The case can be compared with the extraordinary case of *Hall* [2013] 2 Cr App R (S) 68, where a desperately sick man who was confined to a wheelchair went on holiday with his carer to South America and returned with a large quantity of cocaine hidden in the wheelchair. The Court reduced a merciful sentence of three years still further to eighteen months.

In *Qazi* [2010] EWCA Crim 2579 the Court of Appeal considered in some detail the state of health care provision in English prisons, and concluded that only in highly exceptional circumstances could the imposition of a prison sentence on a seriously ill offender breach that person's rights under Article 3 of the ECHR. On that basis the court should not concern itself with the allocation of the offender to a specific prison or other administrative matters. Once the sentencing court had concluded that a prison sentence was necessary, it should have regard to the principles laid down in the leading case of *Bernard* [1997] 1 Cr App R (S) 135. In that case the offender suffered from narrowing of the oesophagus, diabetes, and hypertension, conditions aggravated by imprisonment such that he was at greater risk of a heart attack or stroke. The Court of Appeal said that in such a case it would not interfere with a proper sentence although it might be a matter for the Home Secretary to consider in relation to his powers to order early release on compassionate grounds. A serious medical condition would not automatically entitle an offender to a shorter sentence, but might enable the court, as an act of mercy, to impose a shorter sentence. That approach was taken by the judge in *Hall*, and further extended by the appeal court.

(v) *severe collateral impact of the sentence*

According to Swinton Thomas LJ in *Whitehead* [1996] 1 Cr App R (S) 111 'the courts are always very reluctant to send the mother of young children to prison'. In that case both parents were given short prison sentences for doing acts tending to pervert the course of justice (the wife told the police that she was driving the car at the time of an accident when a motorcyclist was injured, but in fact the husband had been driving). Sentence was varied in the wife's case from two months imprisonment to a community order. More recently, in *Boakye* [2013] 1 Cr App R (S) 6 the Court of Appeal said that in each case the question whether a deserved custodial sentence could be avoided because of the collateral impact on the children was a matter for the judge to decide, having heard all the facts. In the leading case of *Petherick* [2012] EWCA Crim 2214 the Court of Appeal dealt with a case in which the twenty-two-year-old defendant had pleaded guilty to causing death by dangerous driving and driving with excess alcohol, and had advanced by way of personal mitigation the deleterious effect which her imprisonment would have upon her sixteen-month old child, and upon her relationship with that child. The defendant had separated from the child's father before the date of the offences, and the defendant was effectively a single parent. The Court considered the decision of the Supreme Court in *HH v Deputy Prosecutor of the Italian Republic of Genoa* [2012] UKSC 25, which dealt with extradition of one or more parent and the impact of that process upon the Article 8 rights of dependent children. Lord Justice Hughes in *Petherick* accepted that the sentencing of a defendant inevitably engages that person's rights under Article 8, as well as their family, including dependent children. A sentencing court should always be informed of these matters and take account of them where the seriousness of the offence and other relevant matters permit that to be done. The graver the offence, the more inevitable it is that a custodial sentence must be imposed, and the less scope there can be for the impact upon the family to have a mitigating effect. The mitigating factor was 'infinitely variable and nature and must be trusted to the judgment of experienced judges'. Having considered this matter and other personal mitigation in the case, the overall sentence was reduced from one of four years and nine months to one of three years and ten months.

There can be other forms of severe adverse impact on the offender and on others. The courts have, for example, sometimes taken account of the fact that the offender will be discharged from the army as a result of the offence, but in *Ranu* [1996] 2 Cr App R (S) 334 Stuart-Smith J cautioned against accepting such mitigation on face value since the Army has some discretion in the matter. In *Richards* (1980) 2 Cr App R (S) 119 a general medical practitioner was sentenced to thirty-months' imprisonment for making false claims for professional duties. The Court of Appeal said that the judge had not given sufficient weight to the fact that the offender would probably be struck off the medical register and his pension rights would be affected. In addition, he had been a man of positive good character (there had been a petition signed by 700 supporters), there had been a four-year delay in bringing the matter to the courts, and that his wife had committed suicide. Sentence was reduced to twelve months. This form of personal mitigation operates unpredictably in practice. In some cases it seems to make a substantial difference to the outcome, but in other cases the court takes the view that the offender should have considered the consequences before breaking the law. It may be noted that the SGC guideline on *Causing Death by Driving* includes as a mitigating factor the fact that the 'offender was seriously injured in the collision'. It is difficult to see how this factor impinges on harm or culpability, so to the extent that it is relevant it really ought to be a matter of personal mitigation.

(vi) *lapse of time since commission of the offence*

In some cases the passage of time since the offence may be relevant to the eventual punishment, especially where there has been fault on the part of the prosecuting authorities and the matter has been hanging over the offender's head for an inordinate amount of time. Generally such mitigation will not be available in cases where the offender himself has occasioned the delay, whether by covering his tracks, delaying the investigation, or absconding from the jurisdiction. An exceptional case is *Bird* (1987) 9 Cr App R (S) 77 where the offender committed a robbery but absconded when granted bail and was not arrested until ten years later. The Court said that 'the offence had not changed by the passage of time, but the man had', and sentence was reduced from five years to three years. More generally, where many years have elapsed and the offender is now elderly, that aspect may affect sentence. Such problems are commonly encountered in 'historic' cases, particularly of sexual abuse. The leading case is *H* [2012]2 Cr App R (S) 88, where Lord Judge CJ said that in such cases due allowance for the passage of time may be made. The offender might have been young and immature at the time when the offence was committed, and he may have led an unblemished life over the years since. Such mitigation always has to be balanced against the seriousness of the offence(s) and the impact on the victim. In *Matthews* [1999] 1 Cr App R (S) 309 the offender admitted offences of attempted rape and indecent assault committed thirty years earlier on a ten-year-old girl when he was aged eighteen. Taking account the offender's remorse, the exceptional delay and other personal mitigation, the Court of Appeal varied a sentence of thirty months to one of twelve months.

(vi) *meritorious conduct*

This category overlaps with 'positive good character', above. In the case of *Jones* [2012] 1 Cr App R (S) 149, where sentence was slashed on appeal from five years to six months, the personal mitigation included the fact that the twenty-two-year-old offender had worked in a youth parliament, had represented young people in her area, had been instrumental in opening youth clubs in the area, and was described as an outstanding conscientious student who was about to graduate from university. She had also dedicated herself to the care of her older sister with Down's syndrome. The Court of Appeal said that 'if ever there was a case of exceptional circumstances, this is it'. Occasionally a court will have regard to a particular feature of the offender's conduct which is unrelated to the offence but which shows him in a good light and deserving of some credit on that basis. Sentences have been reduced in cases where the offender has shown great courage in apprehending armed men carrying out a robbery (*Alexander* [1997] 2 Cr App R (S) 74), or failed in a valiant attempt to rescue three children from a burning house (*Reid* (1982) 4 Cr App R (S) 280).

2.53 Finally on the topic of personal mitigation it may be noted that there is no category of 'personal aggravation'. Positive features of the offender's character and behaviour may, in the discretion of the court, be given appropriate weight, but not negative features. So it is wrong to increase sentence because (as was wrongly done in *Spinks* (1980) 2 Cr App R (S) 335) the offender chose to contest the case or (as in *Evans* (1986) 8 Cr App R (S) 197) because of the manner in which the defence was conducted. It was said in *Loosemore* (1980) 2 Cr App R (S) 172 that a judge should deal with an offender on the basis of his offence, and not on the basis of his 'feckless character and general behaviour'.

E REDUCTION IN SENTENCE FOR A GUILTY PLEA

The general principle

2.54 Reduction in sentence for a guilty plea is one of the most important principles in sentencing, and since it arises in the majority of cases falling to be sentenced in the courts, it is of the greatest practical importance. All judges and advocates in criminal cases need to fully aware of the relevant law and sentencing guideline in this area. Section 144(1) of the CJA

2003 provides that in determining what sentence to pass on an offender who has pleaded guilty to an offence in proceedings before that or another court, a court must take into account—

(a) the stage in the proceedings for the offence at which the offender indicated his intention to plead guilty, and
(b) the circumstances in which this indication was given.

The *Criminal Practice Directions*, paragraph D.1 states that whenever a defendant pleads guilty to an offence for which he is to be sentenced the prosecution must state the facts of the offence in open court before sentence is passed, to enable the press and public to know what were the circumstances of the offence(s).

2.55 The SGC sentencing guideline *Reduction in Sentence for a Guilty Plea* explains that a reduction in sentence is appropriate in such circumstances 'because a guilty plea avoids the need for a trial (thus enabling other cases to be disposed of more expeditiously), shortens the gap between charge and sentence, saves considerable cost, and, in the case of an early plea, saves victims and witnesses from the concern about having to give evidence' (paragraph 2.2). It is important to understand that the reduction for plea is a separate matter from remorse, and from other aspects of mitigation, and is separate from any reduction which may be appropriate to reflect assistance to the prosecuting authorities. Remorse as a matter of personal mitigation was dealt with at paragraph 2.52(i) earlier in this Chapter. Reduction to reflect assistance to the authorities is dealt with at 2.66 later in this Chapter. Although the distinctive nature of the guilty plea reduction is (at least since the SGC guideline) quite clear, it is still sometimes misleadingly referred to as 'mitigation'. As we have seen, the Sentencing Council offence guidelines are set out in a series of steps. Consideration of reduction for plea comes at step 4, after step 1 (determining the offence category), step 2 (starting point and category range), and step 3 (consider any factors which indicate a reduction, such as assistance to the prosecution). Aggravation and mitigation (including personal mitigation) should all be dealt with at step 2, before the question of reduction for a guilty plea arises.

2.56 Whenever a court takes a plea of guilty into account it is a statutory requirement for the judge to say that this has been done (CJA 2003, section 174(2)(d)), and the guideline requires that the judge should also indicate what scale of discount has been given. It is not sufficient for the judge to refer to the plea and simply say that it has been 'taken into account'. The judge should indicate what starting point has been adopted before reduction for plea, how much credit has been accorded and why, and what the resulting sentence therefore is. While this represents proper practice, a lapse on the part of the sentencer in making these matters clear does not necessarily mean that the sentence will be reduced on appeal. The Court will not interfere if it is clear from what has transpired that the proper discount has been given (*Bishop* [2000] 1 Cr App R (S) 432).

2.57 The guideline makes it clear that the principle of a reduction for plea applies in the Crown Court, a magistrates' court, and, whenever practicable, in a youth court (paragraph 1.1). The slightly reduced relevance in youth court sentencing reflects both the more individualized nature of sentencing young offenders and also the idiosyncratic structure of the detention and training order, which is the main custodial sentence for those aged under eighteen years of age. Detention and training orders are considered at paragraph 4.06, this book. The guideline goes on to say that the principle of reduction for plea should be applied to any of the punitive elements of a sentence, but not to the rehabilitative elements, nor to any ancillary order including a disqualification from driving (paragraph 2.5). It follows from this that the sentence reduction for plea applies to all custodial sentences, to fines, and to the 'punitive elements' in a community sentence, such as the number of hours of unpaid work required of the offender. While this is clear in principle, in practice the main impact of the reduction is in the area of custodial sentences, and it is unusual, to say the least, to hear sentencers adjusting hours of unpaid work in this way. The contrast is with a 'rehabilitative element' in sentence. A good example would be a domestic violence programme inserted into a community order. Such programmes are designed to last a certain number of weeks, and it clearly would not make sense for it to be curtailed to make allowance for plea. The guideline specifically mentions that there should be no reduction for plea in the case of a driving disqualification (paragraph 2.5), and again this makes good sense although it might be more accurate to say that the reason here is protection of the public rather than rehabilitation. Some might argue that a driving ban is a punishment (and it would certainly feel like one to the offender) but for these purposes it is regarded as a preventive rather than a punitive measure. It is clear from the guideline that the effect of the plea may, in an appropriate case, be to change a community sentence to a fine or discharge, or to change a custodial sentence to a community one. If that happens, the change in form of the sentence itself constitutes the reduction for plea, and of course it is not necessary to reduce further the scale of the lesser punishment. To do so would be to give a double reduction.

Determining the discount

How much reduction should be given? The guideline indicates that the level of reduction **2.58** should be a proportion of the total sentence imposed, with the proportion calculated by reference to the two criteria in section 144(1)—the circumstances in which the guilty plea was indicated and, in particular, the stage in the proceedings in which it was made. There is a sliding scale, with the greatest reduction (a recommended one-third off the sentence) given where the plea was indicated at the 'first reasonable opportunity'. This drops to a recommended one-quarter (where a trial date has been set) to a recommended one-tenth (for a guilty plea entered at the 'door of the court' or after the trial has actually started (paragraph 4.2)). This guidance is set out in both narrative and diagrammatic form in the guideline, and is central to it. What is meant by the 'first reasonable opportunity'? The guideline itself in Annex 1 says that this time will vary and the court must make a judgement in each case. The guideline says that the first reasonable opportunity 'may' be the first time that a defendant appears before the court and has the opportunity to plead guilty, and if a case which is triable either way is committed to the Crown Court and the defendant pleads guilty at the Crown Court the reduction will be less than if an indication of guilt had been given before the magistrates. Further assistance has been given by the Court of Appeal in the important case of *Caley* [2013] 2 Cr App R (S) 305. Hughes LJ in that case said that the first reasonable opportunity for most offenders appearing at Crown Court was at the magistrates' court or immediately upon arrival at the Crown Court. It would *not* normally be at the plea and case management hearing (PCMH). The effect of this ruling in *Caley* was to alter Crown Court practice, where many judges had previously been giving maximum credit for a plea tendered at that stage. Of course, an admission of guilt at the police station is not a 'guilty plea'—that can only be tendered before a court. The guideline, however, speaks of the stage at which the offender demonstrated 'a willingness to admit guilt', which would include admissions made to the police. If made very early, and on the offender's own initiative, the offender may be allowed some reduction for personal mitigation based on remorse as well as being entitled to the full reduction for plea. The Court in *Caley* said that, leaving aside the rare cases where the defendant simply did not know whether he was guilty or not before receiving legal advice or disclosure of evidence from the prosecution, there was nothing to stop the great majority of defendants from admitting guilt (or at least admitting what they had done) before receiving legal advice. The Court also recognized that there were some exceptional 'late plea' cases where a larger than normal discount might be appropriate. These would include cases such as *Girma* [2010] 1 Cr App R (S) 172, where the Court of Appeal said that in a multi-handed trial set to last for many months, at great public expense, a guilty plea entered shortly before trial when savings can still be made might attract a reduction in the order of 20 per cent rather than the recommended 10 per cent. There are also cases where a late plea might still attract a substantial discount because it saves the complainant from having to give evidence. It should be remembered that the timing of the guilty plea is not the only consideration—the 'circumstances' in which the plea was made are also relevant. However, Hughes LJ stressed, larger discounts must not become routine because they would undermine the whole scheme of graduated discounts.

2.59 In *Caley* the Court referred to the now widespread use of 'early guilty plea schemes' at court centres across the country. The *Criminal Practice Directions*, paragraphs 3A.6 to 3A.8 state that there may be an early guilty plea hearing, in accordance with directions given by the presiding judges, where a guilty plea is anticipated to allow the Crown Court to deal promptly with the case. Sentence will be passed at that hearing and the parties should be ready, so that all the usual matters such as agreeing a basis of plea, ordering and receiving reports for sentence have been completed in advance.

Offering to plead guilty

2.60 An offer to plead guilty is not quite the same thing as a plea of guilty before a court. It was held in *Birt* [2011] 2 Cr App R (S) 82 that no credit should normally be given for a pre-trial offer to plead guilty which did not ripen into a guilty plea, but that the sentencing judge does have discretion to allow credit according to the circumstances. In *Caley* the view was taken that the defendant might 'indicate a plea of guilty' by notifying the Crown that he would plead guilty perhaps to a lesser charge. Credit would be given if the position taken by the defendant was a realistic one. An example is *Knowles* [2008] EWCA Crim 2647 where the offender was charged with murder and offered to plead guilty to manslaughter. The prosecution rejected that offer, the murder trial went ahead, but the jury failed to agree. The matter was adjourned for a retrial, but subsequently the prosecution accepted the offender's offer to plead guilty to the lesser offence. The judge gave a discount of 15 per cent to reflect the defendant's original indication, and that was upheld on appeal.

2.61 In certain prescribed circumstances it is possible for a judge, if asked by the defendant or his legal representative, to give an advance indication of sentence to a defendant. This indication will be confined to the highest sentence which the defendant would receive if he were to plead guilty at that time. This procedure, which is subject to rules laid down in the Court of Appeal case of *Goodyear* [2005] 1 WLR 2532, is considered in detail at paragraph 1.33, this book.

Overwhelming prosecution case

2.62 A particular issue which has caused contention is whether an offender who is caught 'red-handed' at the scene of the crime, or who for some other reason has no realistic option other than to plead guilty, should still receive credit for their guilty plea. The pre-guideline cases suggested that a reduction was not merited in such a case. The guideline now says that in a case where 'the prosecution case is overwhelming' it may not be appropriate to give the full reduction. While there is a presumption in favour of doing so, if the case is indeed overwhelming then that may be a reason for giving a lesser reduction, of 20 per cent for a plea at the first reasonable opportunity. A relevant case is *Wilson* [2012] EWCA Crim 386, where the Court of Appeal said that even in an overwhelming case the guilty plea had a distinct public benefit. The Court understood why the judge had refused to give any credit for guilty pleas in a dreadful case involving two counts of rape of a child, but it would create inconsistency and confusion if judges ignored the guideline unless there was a specific reason to conclude that it was in the interests of justice to do so. The approach in *Wilson* was endorsed in *Caley*. While there were cases in which the offender had been caught red-handed and in reality had little option but to plead guilty, there was a 'wider lesson', which was that the public benefits which underlay the practice of reducing sentence for a guilty plea applied just as much to overwhelming cases as to weak ones. Hughes LJ said that it could not be assumed that defendants would make rational decisions or ones which were born of any inclination to cooperate with the system, but those who did cooperate merited recognition for that.

Maximum sentence and the guilty plea

It follows from what has been said so far that for a court to impose the maximum sentence **2.63** on an offender who has pleaded guilty would almost always be a wrong sentence. It perhaps goes without saying that a sentencer should not ignore the usual principles on reduction for a guilty plea and pass the maximum sentence because he thinks the maximum penalty is too low to reflect the seriousness of the offence. This issue arose in *Simpson* [2009] 2 Cr App R (S) 492 where the offender pleaded guilty to a very bad offence of aggravated vehicle taking, which carries a maximum penalty of two years. The judge said that the maximum sentence was inadequate, and he would have given five years if he could. In the event he passed a sentence of twenty-three months, allowing just one month's reduction for plea. The Court of Appeal said that in the circumstances a 20 per cent reduction was required, and sentence was reduced to twenty months. In some such cases it may be that the offender has been undercharged, or was fortunate with his jury in being convicted of a lesser offence, but the judge cannot remedy a perceived defect of that kind by refusal of the appropriate discount. There are a couple of situations where it has been accepted that a court may properly impose the maximum sentence on an offender who has pleaded guilty. The first arises in the magistrates' court where the maximum custodial sentence for an adult is normally six months. If the magistrates conclude that, had the offender been convicted after a trial it would have been necessary to send him to Crown Court for a sentence just above six months but that in light of his plea a sentence of six months is appropriate, they may pass such a sentence. Obviously such a course would not be open to magistrates if the offence was a summary one. The second arises in the Crown Court, where the court is dealing with an offender under the age of eighteen. The normal maximum custodial sentence is a detention and training order for two years, but for some very serious offences the Crown Court has power to impose a sentence of detention under section 91 of the Powers of Criminal Court (Sentencing) Act 2000. That section allows the court to pass a much longer sentence where appropriate, in principle up to the maximum available for an adult convicted of that offence. If the judge concludes that if there had been a trial the proper sentence would have been detention under section 91 for a period of a little over two years, then on a plea of guilty it may turn out that the offender can be dealt with by the maximum two-year detention and training order. These examples are provided in the SGC guideline on *Reduction in Sentence for a Guilty Plea*, paragraphs 5.7 to 5.9.

Prescribed sentences and the guilty plea

Section 144(1), which was set out earlier in this Chapter, is the main statutory provi- **2.64** sion in relation to reduction for a guilty plea. Section 144(2) deals with the narrower question of the operation of the guilty plea discount in those circumstances where there is a prescribed custodial sentence paid down by Parliament (such as the 'three-strikes' domestic burglary). In those special circumstances the reduction for guilty plea must not produce a final sentence which is less than 80 per cent of the prescribed sentence (three years in the domestic burglary example). This matter is considered further in Chapter 5, where the prescribed sentences are dealt with. It should also be noted that there is only one situation in which *no* discount for a guilty plea can be given (apart from the whole-life minimum term imposed in a murder case). This is where an offender is convicted and sentenced for one of certain firearms offences specified in the Firearms Act 1968, section 51A.

Reduction in discount following *Newton* hearing

2.65 If the defendant is prepared to plead guilty to the charge but his version of the facts of the offence is substantially at odds with the prosecution's alleged facts a *Newton* hearing (also known as a trial of issue) will be ordered by the judge in order to resolve the factual basis upon which the defendant should be sentenced. If the defendant's version of events is rejected by the judge at the *Newton* hearing then some portion of the discount for the guilty will be lost. See further paragraph 1.51(d), this book.

F REDUCTION IN SENTENCE FOR ASSISTING THE AUTHORITIES

2.66 It has long been accepted that some reduction in sentence is appropriate where an offender has disclosed information to the authorities which has led to the apprehension of others and the bringing against them of serious charges. The extent of the discount varies, depending upon the degree of assistance given, the seriousness of the offender's offence, and the seriousness of the other offences cleared up. An example is *Saggar* [1997] 1 Cr App R (S) 167, where sentence was reduced from seven years to four-and-a-half years because of the help given by the offender, including testifying for the prosecution in related matters. On the other hand, in *Debbag* (1991) 12 Cr App R (S) 733 no discount at all was appropriate. The offender only offered up information to the police after he had vigorously contested his own trial and been convicted and sentenced. The information, when eventually produced, was already known to the police in any event.

The statutory scheme

2.67 The scheme for reduction of sentence in circumstances such as these was placed on a statutory footing by the Serious and Organised Crime and Policing Act 2005. Section 73 says that if a defendant, following a plea of guilty, has entered into a written agreement with the prosecution assisting or offering to assist in relation to that offence or another offence, the court may take the nature and extent of that assistance into account when sentencing the offender (section 73(1) and (2)). If it does so the court should state in open court that it has passed a lesser sentence than it would otherwise have passed, and what the sentence would otherwise have been (section 73(3)). However, this requirement of statement in open court does not apply if 'it would not be in the public interest to disclose that the sentence has been discounted', but if so the court must provide written notice of the details to both the prosecution and the defence (section 73(4)). Section 73(4) is important, because there are some cases where the offender has placed himself or his family at real risk of reprisal for assisting the police. Such an offender will not want an explanation to be given in open court. Where that is the case it is clear that the statutory scheme does not replace the traditional common law arrangement, under which the offender will ask a senior police officer to produce a written 'text' which acknowledges the assistance which the police have received and sets out the details there. The judge will be invited by the prosecution to read this material in chambers, in advance of the sentencing hearing. Normally the defence advocate will also be fully aware of the content of the text, but very occasionally difficulty can arise where the offender does not wish his lawyer to know about the information he has provided to the police lest this might somehow be discovered by those against whom he has given information, which might include former co-defendants. This written material is retained and kept secure in its 'brown envelope' for the future. The judge may then choose to make no reference to the matter at all when passing sentence on the offender, or perhaps make some guarded remark in reference to the unexpectedly lenient sentence, such as 'taking into account all the information which I have received about your case', before imposing sentence. It should be noted that the operation of the statutory scheme overrides the prescribed minimum sentence provisions (section 73(5)). These provisions include the prescribed minimum sentence of three years for the third domestic burglary, and they are considered in Chapter 5. The operation of this rule might place the sentencing judge in a slightly different position, since if the judge decides that the minimum sentence would be unjust because of the substantial assistance rendered by the offender to the authorities, he would naturally be expected to explain how that view had been reached. It may be significant that the CJA 2003, section 174 (the general provision requiring the court to give reasons) makes no specific mention of the SOCPA, section 73.

Any reduction on this ground is separate from, and additional to, the appropriate discount **2.68** for a plea of guilty. This was made clear in *Wood* [1997] 1 Cr App R (S) 347 and in the SGC guideline in *Reduction for a Plea of Guilty* (paragraph 2.4, although the SGC warns that there is a risk here of 'double-counting' the same factor). It is also clearly set out within the series of steps laid down in the Sentencing Council's guidelines. According to those, any adjustment by way of a reduction for assistance to the authorities should be made at step 3, before at step 4 making any appropriate reduction for a plea of guilty.

Section 74 provides for a subsequent review of a sentence passed on (a) an offender who **2.69** received a discount on sentence under section 73 on the basis of a promise which he did not fulfil, or (b) on an offender who received a discount at the time but has gone on to provide further assistance, or (c) on an offender who did not receive a discounted sentence at the time but who has later provided, or offered to provide, assistance (section 74(2)). In case (a) the prosecutor may refer the case back to the Crown Court if the offender is still serving his sentence and the prosecutor thinks it is in the interests of justice to do so. The case must if possible be heard by the judge who passed the original sentence. If the court is satisfied that a person whose sentence has been discounted has knowingly failed to give the assistance promised then it may increase the original sentence but not to a level above the sentence it would have passed if the agreement had not been made. In case (b), again the case may be referred back to the Crown Court for review and a greater reduction if appropriate. In case (c), again the sentence may be referred back to the Crown Court for review and a reduction if appropriate. It should be noted that case (c) comprises the only circumstances under the statutory scheme where a reduction may be given despite the offender having been convicted after a trial. Even so, there is an exception where the offender has been convicted of murder, where no reference can be made. The issues of confidentiality which crop up in this context at the sentencing hearing can recur on the hearing of a reference. For that reason the Crown Court may exclude from the proceedings anyone other than an officer of the court, a party to the proceedings and their representatives, and may give such direction as it thinks fit prohibiting the publication of any matter relating to the proceedings including the fact that the reference has been made. Such an order should only be made to the extent that it is necessary to do so to protect the safety of any person, as is in the interests of justice (section 75). According to the Court of Appeal in *P* [2008] 2 Cr App R (S) 16, the power in section 75 to remove the media from the review should be used with great caution, and any other practicable alternatives should be used first.

2.70 The offender, or the prosecutor, has a right of appeal to the Court of Appeal in respect of the outcome of a referral under this section (section 74(8)).

Extent of the discount

2.71 Sections 73 and 74 of the SOCPA 2005 say nothing about the appropriate extent of any reduction to reflect actual or promised assistance by the offender. It is clear that the extent to which the assistance given or offered may affect sentence is a matter for the court. There are a number of long-standing Court of Appeal authorities which, according to the leading decision of the Court of Appeal in *P* [2008] 2 Cr App R (S) 16, are still relevant despite the introduction of the statutory scheme. In *P* the Court made the following points:

(a) While the statutory scheme did not abolish the old 'text' system, which may still be used when appropriate, a discount of sentence under the non-statutory arrangements is likely to be less than one consequent upon the operation of section 73. That is because the earlier process lacks some of the safeguards of the statutory scheme, and is more open to manipulation by the offender.

(b) The principles governing the appropriate level of discount for assisting the authorities were not altered by the introduction of the statutory scheme. There is no 'tariff', and every case depends upon its own facts. Having said that, the 'normal' level of reduction should be one which produces a sentence of between one-half and two-thirds of what the sentence would otherwise have been. This was later confirmed in *Hood* [2012] EWCA Crim 1260 to be the reduction appropriate in the paradigm case of a professional criminal who gives evidence against dangerous people, and who puts himself at considerable risk as a result. Reduction by one-half is certainly not to be taken as an entitlement (*Ford* [2011] 2 Cr App R (S) 64). Reduction by only 10 per cent may well not be enough, since it does not provide sufficient incentive for offenders to enter into section 73 agreements (*McGarry* [2012] 2 Cr App R (S) 60). Further, in *Dougall* [2011] 1 Cr App R (S) 37 the appropriate sentence for the offence would have been two years, but was reduced under section 73 to twelve months. The Court accepted that there was a strong argument that this scale of reduction was not enough in a case where the offender had cooperated fully with the authorities and had agreed to cooperate in future prosecutions. In such a case the practical reality was that suspension of the custodial sentence was required.

(c) If the offender has placed himself at considerable risk of reprisal for assisting the authorities that would usually attract a greater discount than where he has not. The seriousness of the offence admitted by the offender is relevant to the extent of the discount, as is the seriousness of the offences in respect of which the offender has agreed to assist the authorities. The offender's motive for entering into the agreement was not relevant to his eventual sentence, since in most cases it is bound to be wholly or substantially geared towards securing for himself a lower sentence. The strength of the prosecution case against the offender is not normally of much relevance, though where the offender had been caught red-handed that may impact upon the separate question of the reduction for guilty plea.

KEY DOCUMENTS[1]

Sentencing Guidelines Council, Definitive Guideline, *Overarching Principles: Seriousness* (effective December 2004).

Sentencing Guidelines Council, Definitive Guideline, *Manslaughter by Reason of Provocation* (effective 28 November 2005).

Sentencing Guidelines Council, Definitive Guideline, *Robbery* (effective 1 August 2006).

Sentencing Council, Definitive Guideline, *Domestic Violence* (effective 18 December 2006).

Sentencing Guidelines Council, Definitive Guideline, *Reduction in Sentence for a Guilty Plea* (effective from 23 July 2007).

Sentencing Guidelines Council, Definitive Guideline, *Causing Death by Driving* (effective 4 August 2008).

Sentencing Guidelines Council, Definitive Guideline, *Theft* (effective 5 January 2009).

Sentencing Guidelines Council, Definitive Guideline, *Sentencing Youths* (effective 30 November 2009).

Sentencing Council, Definitive Guideline, *Assault (Crown Court)* (effective 13 June 2011).

Sentencing Council, Definitive Guideline, *Drug Offences* (effective 27 February 2012).

Sentencing Council, Definitive Guideline, *Burglary Offences* (effective 16 January 2012).

Sentencing Council, Definitive Guideline, *Offences Taken into Consideration* (effective 11 June 2012).

Sentencing Council, Definitive Guideline, *Totality* (effective 11 June 2012).

Sentencing Council, Definitive Guideline, *Sexual Offences* (effective 1 April 2014).

Crown Court Sentencing Survey (published 2012) <http://www.sentencingcouncil.judiciary.gov.uk/facts/sentencing-survey.htm>.

European Convention on Human Rights, Articles 3, 7, and 8.

Criminal Practice Directions [2013] EWCA Crim 1631 (effective 7 October 2013), amended by [2013] EWCA Crim 2328 (effective 10 December 2013).

---

[1] All sentencing guidelines can be found on the Sentencing Council website: <http://sentencincouncil.judiciary.gov.uk/>.

3

CUSTODIAL SENTENCES: ADULT OFFENDERS

A AVAILABLE CUSTODIAL SENTENCES

3.01 The imposition of custodial sentences, whether by a magistrates' court or the Crown Court, is governed by the general statutory sentencing framework consolidated in the PCC(S)A 2000 and the CJA 2003, and a range of specific statutory provisions and case law dealing with particular forms of custodial sentences. The general restrictions which apply in relation to imposing any discretionary custodial sentence and in determining the length of such sentence (to be found in sections 152 and 153 of the CJA 2003) were considered at paragraphs 2.22 and 2.30 in the previous Chapter. These are important and should be borne in mind throughout this Chapter.

By the PCC(S)A 2000, section 76(1), the term 'custodial sentence' means: **3.02**

(a) a sentence of imprisonment,
(b) a sentence of detention under the PCC(S)A 2000, section 90 or 91,
(c) a sentence of custody for life under the PCC(S)A 2000, section 94,
(d) a sentence of detention in a young offender institution, or
(e) a detention and training order.

The term 'sentence of imprisonment' does not include a committal for contempt of court or any kindred offence (section 76(2)). A suspended sentence is a custodial sentence.

All these custodial sentences are discussed in detail in this Chapter, as far as they apply to offenders aged eighteen years and over, and for those under eighteen, in Chapter 4. They are all properly described as 'discretionary' custodial sentences, and can be contrasted with the 'mandatory' life sentence for murder and the 'prescribed' custodial sentences such as the 'three-strikes' provision in domestic burglary. It should be noted that offenders aged under twenty-one years at the date of conviction cannot be sentenced to imprisonment (PCC(S)A 2000, section 89(1)). Those who are under twenty-one cannot be committed to prison for any reason, such as non-payment of a fine, but if a person under twenty-one is remanded in custody for trial or sentence, or sent in custody for trial under the CDA 1998, section 51, he may be committed to prison for the period before his case is disposed of (PCC(S)A 2000, section 89(2)).

Of the sentences listed in section 76(1) (a) is applicable to offenders aged twenty-one years **3.03** or over, (b) and (e) are applicable to offenders under eighteen, and (c) and (d) are applicable to offenders aged eighteen, nineteen, or twenty years old. The sentences under (c) and (d) are prospectively repealed by the Criminal Justice and Court Services Act 2000, section 61, but given that this change has still not taken place, the sentences seem likely to survive and so are fully covered in this book. If detention in a young offender institution is abolished, then imprisonment would start at eighteen, rather than twenty-one years of age. By far the most frequently used of these sentences are imprisonment and detention in a young offender institution. Some sentences of imprisonment and detention in a young offender institution can be suspended.

B GENERAL REQUIREMENTS

Offence must be imprisonable

The most obvious limitation on the availability of any custodial sentence is that the offence **3.04** must be an imprisonable offence in the case of an adult. All common law offences are punishable with imprisonment. A statutory offence is so punishable if the statute creating it specifies imprisonment as one of the methods of dealing with offenders who commit the offence. Many offences are punishable with imprisonment and/or a fine. If the statute mentions only a fine as the penalty for the offence, then it is not imprisonable. Virtually all indictable offences are imprisonable, but there are some exceptions, such as the offences under the Forgery and Counterfeiting Act 1981, sections 18 and 19, which proscribe the putting into circulation of imitation currency and coins. Many summary offences are not imprisonable, but the more serious ones are, such as common assault, assaulting a police officer in the execution of his duty (each carrying six months maximum), and interfering with a motor vehicle (three months). Most summary road traffic offences (such as driving without due care and attention, speeding, using a vehicle without insurance, and failing to stop after an accident) are not imprisonable. A great mass of minor offences, such as dropping litter, are non-imprisonable. If an offence is not imprisonable in the case of an adult a custodial sentence cannot be imposed on an offender aged under eighteen (and see PCC(S)A 2000, section164(2)).

Legal representation

3.05　Section 83 of the PCC(S)A 2000 provides that a magistrates' court or the Crown Court shall not pass a sentence of imprisonment on an offender who:

(a)　is not legally represented, and
(b)　who has not been previously so sentenced by a court in any part of the UK unless, section by section 83(3) applies.

Section 83(3) applies to a person if either:

(a)　representation was made available to him for the purposes of the proceedings under Part 1 of the Legal Aid, Sentencing and Punishment of Offenders Act 2012 but was withdrawn because of his conduct or because it appeared that his financial resources were such that he was not eligible for such representation;
(b)　he applied for such representation and the application was refused because it appeared that his financial resources were such that he was not eligible for such representation; or
(c)　having been informed of his right to apply for such representation and having had the opportunity to do so, he refused or failed to apply.

3.06　For the purposes of this section a person is to be treated as legally represented in a court if, but only if, he has the assistance or counsel or a solicitor to represent him in the proceedings in that court at some time after he is found guilty and before he is sentenced (section 83(4)). A clear application of the rule is *Hollywood* (1990) 12 Cr App R (S) 325, where the defendant was represented by counsel and a solicitor when he pleaded guilty but when he was sentenced two days later neither was present. The sentence was therefore invalid. Lord Bridge explained the importance of this right for the unrepresented defendant in *McC (A Minor)* [1985] AC 528:

> No one should be liable to a first sentence of imprisonment...unless he has the opportunity of having his case in mitigation presented to the court in the best possible light. For an inarticulate defendant, such presentation may be crucial to his liberty.

This issue is most likely to arise in the magistrates' court, where unrepresented defendants are frequently encountered, or in the Crown Court on appeal from the magistrates (see for a recent example *R (Ebert) v Wood Green Crown Court* [2013] EWHC 917 (Admin)). The practical effect of the section is that where the court is considering imposing a first prison sentence it should inform the unrepresented defendant of his right to representation, and grant an adjournment for that to be obtained. A suspended sentence of imprisonment is a prison sentence for the purposes of section 83, and it seems clear that a suspended sentence should not be passed unless the defendant has had the opportunity to avail himself of legal representation. The statute states in section 83(5) that, for the purpose of deciding whether the defendant has previously been sentenced to imprisonment, a suspended sentence which has not been activated does not count, but the context suggests that this is a reference to an old-style suspended sentence passed under the 2000 Act and not the much more frequently encountered new-style suspended sentence under the CJA 2003.

3.07　Section 83(2) extends the effect of this provision to custodial sentences other than imprisonment—detention in a young offender institution (including a suspended sentence), detention under the PCC(S)A 2000, section 91, custody for life, and the detention and training order. There is an important difference here, however; the court must, if considering the imposition of any of these sentences, comply with section 83 even if the defendant has had a prior custodial sentence.

A custodial sentence which is passed in contravention of section 83 is unlawful, but in the **3.08** case of a sentence passed by the Crown Court it has been held that on appeal it may be corrected by the substitution of a lawful sentence by the Court of Appeal (*Howden* [2007] 1 Cr App R (S) 164). If the sentence was passed by a magistrates' court and the defendant appeals against sentence, it was held in *Birmingham Justices, ex parte Wyatt* [1976] 1 WLR 260 that the Crown Court must pass a sentence which the lower court could lawfully have passed, which must necessarily be a non-custodial one.

Age of the defendant

In deciding upon the sentence available, given the defendant's age, the relevant date is the **3.09** date of conviction. This issue may in principle arise in relation to other sentences, such as whether the offender is eligible for a youth rehabilitation order (for those under eighteen) or a community order (for those aged eighteen and over), but in practice is most likely to be encountered in relation to custodial sentences and so is dealt with here. As we shall see, the crucial age thresholds are twelve years and fifteen years (in relation to the detention and training order, dealt with in Chapter 4), eighteen years (the age of eligibility for detention in a young offender institution) and twenty-one years (the age of eligibility for imprisonment). In *Danga* [1992] QB 476, where the offender was aged twenty when convicted but aged twenty-one when sentenced, it was held that the relevant age of the offender, for the purposes of the PCC(S)A 2000, section 96(1), was the age at the date of conviction, so that the proper sentence was one of detention in a young offender institution rather than imprisonment. In *Robinson* [1993] 1 WLR 168 it was held, following *Danga*, that, in determining whether an offender was aged under eighteen and eligible for a sentence under the PCC(S)A 2000, section 91, the issue was the age of the defendant at the time of conviction rather than at the time of sentence.

The decision in *Ghafoor*

This point is clear, but is made more complicated in practice by the decision in *Ghafoor* **3.10** [2003] 1 Cr App R (S) 428. There, the offender, who was seventeen years old when the offence was committed but eighteen when convicted, pleaded guilty to riot. It was noted that the maximum penalty for the offence was ten years' detention in a young offender institution but, had the offender been convicted when still seventeen, the maximum penalty would have been a detention and training order of twenty-four months, less an appropriate discount for guilty plea. The Court of Appeal said that the offender clearly fell to be sentenced by way of a detention in a young offender institution, but that when fixing the appropriate length of that sentence a 'powerful', albeit not determining, factor would be the term which the offender would have been likely to receive if he had been sentenced at the date of the commission of the offence. The sentence of four-and-a-half-years' detention in a young offender institution was reduced to eighteen months on that basis. The decision has been followed and applied in many later cases, including *Britton* [2007] 1 Cr App R (S) 745. The SGC guideline *Sentencing Youths* provides further guidance on sentencing in cases where the young offender has crossed a significant age threshold between commission of an offence and date of sentence. The guideline, endorsing *Ghafoor*, says that whenever an offender crosses a relevant age threshold between the date on which the offence was committed and the date of conviction a court 'should take as its starting point the sentence likely to have been imposed on the date on which the offence was committed' (paragraph 5.2). The guideline also says that it will be rare for a court to pass a sentence more severe than the maximum it could have imposed if the offender had been a year younger, but a sentence at or close to that maximum may be appropriate for a serious offence. On this particular point, in *Bowker* [2008] 1 Cr App R (S) 412 it was held that there was no infringement of the ECHR, Article 7(1), in a case where the sentence imposed on an eighteen-year-old offender was greater than the maximum sentence which could have been imposed on him at the time of the offence, when he was aged seventeen. That is clearly right, since Article 7 is only engaged where there has been a change in the law, while in *Bowker* all that had changed was the penal regime to which he would be subject having reached the age of eighteen.

Age of the offender unclear

3.11 In the unusual situation that the age of the offender is unclear, the first course of action is likely to be to adjourn for further inquiries to be made and if necessary evidence to be called to resolve the issue. If no satisfactory answer is forthcoming, PCC(S)A 2000, section 164(1) applies. This states that:

> For the purposes of any provision of this Act which requires the determination of the age of a person by the court or the Secretary of State his age shall be deemed to be that which it appears to the court or the Secretary of State (as the case may be) to be after considering any available evidence.

If a court imposes a sentence on an assumption of the offender's age made under section 164(1), it has been held that the sentence is not rendered unlawful if it is later discovered that the assumption was incorrect. The subsection (in fact an earlier identically worded version) was relied upon in *Brown* (1989) 11 Cr App R (S) 263 where, because of an error in the paperwork before the court, the offender was sentenced as a twenty-one-year-old whereas in fact he was only twenty. Ognall J, in the Court of Appeal, said that there was nothing wrong with the length of the sentence but if the judge had been properly informed he obviously would have passed a sentence of detention in a young offender institution instead of imprisonment. If the offender had been seventeen but sentenced by mistake as an eighteen-year-old, given *Ghafoor* and the SGC guideline, it seems likely that sentence would have to be adjusted. Section 164(1) means that the sentence imposed in error is not a nullity, and can normally be adjusted on appeal when the mistake comes to light. In *Harris* (1990) 12 Cr App R (S) 318, however, the offender was sentenced as a twenty-one-year-old although the antecedents form indicated that he was only twenty, and the judge passed a suspended prison sentence, which at that time was available only to offenders aged twenty-one years and over. When the mistake came to light, section 164(1) could not rescue the sentence, and it had to be quashed.

Limit on powers of magistrates' courts

3.12 By the PCC(S)A 2000, section 78(1) a magistrates' court does not have power to impose imprisonment or detention in a young offender institution for more than six months for any one offence. This normal maximum of six months is of course subject to the operation of a shorter maximum sentence provided by statute. An example is criminal damage (if the damage was not more than £5000 in value), where the maximum prison sentence is three months. The six months' limit does not apply to non-payment of a fine. The powers of a youth court are different (up to two years for a single offence). The minimum term of imprisonment that a magistrates' court can pass is five days (MCA 1980, section 132). There are some situations in which the Crown Court is limited to magistrates' courts sentencing powers, and so cannot impose a prison sentence in excess of six months.

The normal six months' figure is clearly very important. If the offence being dealt with is **3.13** a summary offence then no sentence in excess of six months can be imposed. If there has been a plea of guilty or there is other significant mitigation in the case, then the maximum penalty should not normally be imposed in any event. If the offender has pleaded guilty at the first reasonable opportunity and the magistrates would otherwise have passed the maximum sentence, the greatest sentence they can pass must normally be no more than four months. If the magistrates are sentencing for more than one summary offence the aggregate term is still six months even if consecutive terms are imposed. In such a case the SGC guideline on *Reduction in Sentence for a Guilty Plea* says at paragraph 5.7 that some reduction from the total aggregate term of six months must still be given. The six-month maximum also applies to an offence which is triable either way, but the maximum sentence may be imposed despite a guilty plea in a case where the magistrates would otherwise have committed the defendant to Crown Court for sentence with a view to receiving a sentence of more than six months (SGC guideline, paragraph 5.8). Clearly in such a case the magistrates must explain their reasons for passing the maximum sentence. If magistrates are dealing with two or more offences which are triable either way the maximum aggregate term goes up to twelve months (MCA 1980, section 133). All these provisions apply to sentences of detention in a young offender institution as well as to prison sentences. Detention and training orders operate in a different way.

A magistrates' court having power to imprison a person may instead order him to be detained **3.14** within the precincts of the court-house or at any police station until such hour, not later than 8 o'clock in the evening on the day on which the order is made, as the court directs (MCA 1980, section 135). Such order must not operate to deprive the person (who must be aged eighteen years or over) of a reasonable opportunity of returning home on the same day (section 135(2)). The power to order detention in this way is not a sentence of imprisonment, but it is a sentence, and is widely used in practice either as a penalty in its own right or as a means of dealing with fine default. The magistrates' courts also have power under section 136 of the same Act to order the detention overnight of a person aged eighteen years or over to discharge responsibility for payment of a fine. The person must be released by 8 o'clock in the morning on the following morning. The Crown Court does not have these powers.

C TIME SPENT ON REMAND OR UNDER QUALIFYING CURFEW

Time spent on remand

Until 2012, a judge passing a sentence of imprisonment or detention in a young offender **3.15** institution was required under section 240 of the CJA 2003 to give a direction in open court adjusting that sentence, to take into account any period of time which the offender had already spent in custody on remand in respect of that offence. Section 240 was replaced in 2012. The Legal Aid, Sentencing, and Punishment of Offenders Act (LASPOA) in that year repealed the section and replaced it with a new section 240ZA, which provides that the time served by the offender on remand in custody is now to be *deducted automatically*. The requirement for judges to adjust sentence under section 240 caused considerable practical problems, often because there was incomplete or inaccurate information available about the days which the offender had served on remand by the time of sentence. It is much better for an appropriate deduction to be made administratively, which is what now happens under section 240ZA.

3.16 Section 240ZA applies to imprisonment and to detention in a young offender institution and to the extended sentence of imprisonment or detention in a young offender institution. It also applies to detention under the PCC(S)A 2000, section 91, but *not* to the detention and training order, where a different statutory provision operates. For the last two sentences, available only to offenders aged under eighteen years, see Chapter 4. The new section does not apply directly to the setting of a minimum term in an indeterminate sentence case. The court will still have to make an appropriate adjustment under the PCC(S)A 2000, section 82A when setting the minimum term. This is considered at 3.72 later in this Chapter.

3.17 Section 242 of the CJA 2003 defines 'remanded in custody'. It provides that 'remanded in custody' means remanded in or committed to custody by order of a court, remanded or committed to local authority accommodation and kept in secure accommodation, or remanded admitted or removed to hospital under the Mental Health Act 1983. While nothing which falls outside this definition counts as 'remanded in custody' it has always been open to a judge where appropriate to adjust a custodial sentence by taking into account periods of time spent by the offender under detention of various kinds falling outside section 242. This discretion surely remains after the repeal of section 240. An example is *Al Daour* [2011] EWCA Crim 2392 where the defendant had been subject to a period of police detention under the Terrorism Act 2000. The Court of Appeal said that such detention did not come within section 242, but could be taken into account by the judge, as could police detention under the Police and Criminal Evidence Act 1984. Further, in *Watson* [2000] 2 Cr App R (S) 301 the Court of Appeal said that, although not falling within section 242, it was right to take into account a period of eleven months spent by the offender on remand in a bail hostel under restrictive conditions.

3.18 Although the introduction of section 240ZA means that the judge no longer has to make any adjustment to take remand days into account, the judge will still need to know whether, and if so for how long, the defendant has been held on remand for the offence about to be sentenced. This is because the information may affect whether a custodial sentence is now appropriate at all. There is Court of Appeal authority in *Barrett* [2010] 2 Cr App R (S) 551 that a prison sentence of (say) six months should not be passed on an offender who has already spent three months (the equivalent of a six-month sentence) in custody on remand and (in effect) has already served his sentence on remand. Clearly the judge will need to have reliable information on the time served on remand in order to pass a proper sentence. The position in *Barrett* was that a suspended sentence of twelve weeks was imposed on an offender who had already spent the equivalent of the maximum available sentence in custody on remand. On appeal the Court of Appeal dealt with the case by quashing the custodial sentence and substituting a conditional discharge. By contrast, the advice of the SGC in the guideline *New Sentences: CJA 2003*, paragraph 1.1.39, is that the best way for the sentencer to deal with this problem is to pass the appropriate custodial sentence (so that the correct penalty is reflected on the defendant's record) but to order that, having regard to the time served on remand, he is to be released immediately. This approach was not open to the Court of Appeal in *Barrett*, since the Court is not permitted to increase the severity of the penalty passed by the sentencing judge.

3.19 How should the court deal with the issue of time served on remand when imposing a suspended sentence, or a community order? These issues are considered later in this Chapter at paragraph 3.42, and later in this book at paragraph 6.06, respectively.

Time spent under qualifying curfew

3.20 Section 240A of the CJA 2003 states that, where an offender has been remanded on bail and that bail was subject both to a 'qualifying curfew condition' (requiring that person to remain at one or more specified places for a total of not less than nine hours in any given day) and an 'electronic monitoring condition' (imposed under section 3(6ZAA) of the Bail Act 1976), the court must normally direct that the 'credit period' is to count as time served by the offender as part of the sentence. Section 240A, unlike section 240, was not repealed by the LASPOA 2012 but amended in some of its details, and so in every case the judge must still be alert to the issue of whether the defendant has been subject to a qualifying curfew to make sure that he or she gives the appropriate allowance. The term 'imprisonment' includes in this context sentences of detention in a young offender institution, extended sentences of imprisonment or detention in a young offender institution, and determinate sentences of detention under the PCC(S)A 2000, section 91. It does not apply to the detention and training order.

The period to be credited is basically determined by first adding up the number of days on **3.21** which the offender's bail was subject to these two conditions. Any days on which the offender was found to be in breach of one or both of the conditions do not count, and must be deducted from the total. The total (adjusted if necessary) is then divided by two and rounded up to the nearest whole number. The judge should then credit the total against the custodial sentence which is to be passed.

The Court of Appeal in *Monaghan* [2010] 2 Cr App R (S) 343 said that any period of time **3.22** spent by the offender on electronically monitored curfew of less than nine hours was not a qualifying curfew under section 240A but the judge might well make some reduction where the offender had spent a significant period of time subject to those conditions. Most recently the Court in *Hoggard* [2013] EWCA Crim 1024 considered in detail the provisions as amended in 2012. The Court stressed that it was the responsibility of counsel appearing before the court to ensure that the judge was provided with accurate information about the number of days spent under a qualifying curfew. The Crown Prosecution Service should ensure that the form which contained those details was complete and up to date and that it followed the defendant as necessary from court to court. It was the responsibility of the defence team to ask the defendant about days spent under qualifying curfew. The Court also said that in a case where the judge intends to give full credit for the days spent under a qualifying curfew but there is some uncertainty as to how many days have actually been spent, the judge might make a statement along the lines that '[t]he defendant will receive credit for...half the time spent under curfew if the curfew qualified under the provisions of section 240A. On the information before me the total period is N days, but if this period is mistaken this court will order an amendment of the record for the correct period to be recorded'. This is a version of the form of words originally approved by the Court of Appeal in *Nnaji* [2009] 2 Cr App R (S) 700. The Court said that if that form of words is used, any error can be corrected in the court office, even after the expiry of the fifty-six days allowed under the slip rule, thereby avoiding the need for an expensive trip to the Court of Appeal to adjust the number of days. The Court also observed that in a case where there was dispute over one or two day's credit, and it would be expensive of court time to adjourn and make further inquiries to resolve it, it was acceptable to give the offender the benefit of the doubt. That was done by the Court itself in *Hoggard*. Finally, the Court issued warning in *Hoggard* and again in *Leacock* [2013] EWCA Crim 1994, that the Court would not be sympathetic to appeals brought solely on the basis of errors having been made on this issue, and would be very reluctant to grant leave for extensions of time to appeal where the mistake came to light weeks or months later.

How should the court deal with the issue of time spent under a qualifying curfew when **3.23** imposing a suspended sentence, or a community order? These issues are considered in this book at paragraphs 3.42 and 6.06 respectively.

D IMPRISONMENT AND DETENTION IN A YOUNG OFFENDER INSTITUTION

Maximum penalties

3.24 A determinate sentence of imprisonment is the normal custodial sentence for offenders aged twenty-one years and over, and a determinate sentence of detention in a young offender institution is the normal custodial sentence for an offender aged eighteen, nineteen, or twenty years old. The maximum terms of imprisonment which may be imposed for a statutory offence is almost always laid down by the statute which creates that offence. For summary offences and for offences triable either way which are tried summarily general limits on the power of magistrates' courts to impose imprisonment are specified by the PCC(S)A 2000, section 78(1): see paragraph 3.03 of this Chapter. The maximum term of imprisonment which can be passed by a magistrates' court is less, indeed often much less, than the Crown Court can impose. The maximum term of detention in a young offender institution that a court may impose is the same as the maximum term of imprisonment (PCC(S)A 2000, section 97(1)).

3.25 The system of maximum penalties is not the product of a rational and consistent scheme, but rather the result of piecemeal legislation over the years. For some reason, there is a preponderance of maxima of two, five, ten, and fourteen years, but there are some other examples. Some of the available maxima are very high and for many offences nothing like the maximum sentence is approached in day-to-day Crown Court sentencing practice. The maximum penalty available in the Crown Court is therefore no real guide to the normal sentencing bracket for the offence. It should be noted that in the Sentencing Council guidelines there is often a substantial gap between the top of the offence range and the maximum penalty for the offence. In the guideline for domestic burglary, for example, the category 1 range is two to six years while the maximum penalty is fourteen years. For non-domestic burglary the category 1 range is one to five years while the maximum penalty is ten years. For assault occasioning actual bodily harm the category 1 range is one to three years while the maximum penalty is five years. It will be recalled that if the sentencer intends to pass a sentence above the category 1 range (and hence outside the offence range) this will involve a departure from the guideline and it will be necessary to state that not to do so would be contrary to the interests of justice (Coroners and Justice Act 2009, section 125(1)).

3.26 It is a long-standing principle of sentencing that the maximum sentence should be reserved for 'the worst example of that offence which is likely to be encountered in practice' (*Bright* [2008] 2 Cr App R (S) 578), but when considering whether a particular offence actually is one of the worst examples the judge should have regard to the range of cases encountered in practice rather than to very unlikely or purely hypothetical examples. Clearly if there is substantial mitigation in the case, or if the offender has pleaded guilty, it will be very rare for the imposition of the maximum to be a correct sentence. Such cases do arise, however. In *Badland* [2012] EWCA Crim 1516 the maximum sentence of seven years for conspiracy to steal was upheld on appeal. The offender was described as a professional criminal who had taken no notice of previous sentences. He had contested the case and there was no mitigation. The maximum sentence of twelve months' imprisonment for failure to surrender to bail was upheld in *Chowdhury* [2013] EWCA Crim 943 where the defendant had absconded before his original trial, been at large for thirteen years, and was convicted of the offence after a trial. Sometimes sentencers find themselves dealing with an offence where the maximum penalty seems too low for the seriousness of the particular offence to be sentenced. This was the case in

Carroll (1995) 16 Cr App R (S) 488, where the judge, after passing the maximum sentence of two years which was then available for an offence of aggravated vehicle taking, complained that the maximum was too low. The Court of Appeal reduced the sentence on appeal, commenting that the judge must abide loyally by the maximum sentence. Problems of this kind usually arise because an inadequate charge has been brought in the first place. The SGC guideline on *Reduction of Sentence for a Guilty Plea* reinforces the principle in *Carroll*. Occasionally the Court of Appeal will suggest to Parliament that a particular maximum sentence is too low and ought to be revised. An example is *Kayani* [2011] EWCA Crim 2871, where Lord Judge CJ said that the maximum of seven years for an offence under the Child Abduction Act 1984 was too low to cater for the worst cases now coming before the courts.

Particular rules on maximum penalties

There are a number of special rules relating to maximum penalties: **3.27**

(a) No maximum specified

There exist a number of common law offences where no maximum penalty is specified. These include kidnapping, perverting the course of justice, and misconduct in a public office. For any such offence the penalty is at the discretion of the court. That does not entail a sentencing free-for-all, and clearly the judge would follow any relevant sentencing guidelines, or otherwise have regard to applicable appellate decisions on sentencing for that offence. Although murder is a common law offence the penalty for it is prescribed as the mandatory sentence of life imprisonment by the Murder (Abolition of Death Penalty) Act 1965. In the unlikely event that the defendant is convicted of a statutory offence but the statute is silent as to the maximum penalty, the maximum is deemed to be two years (PCC(S)A 2000, section 77).

(b) Inchoate offences

(i) **Conspiracy**   Under the Criminal Law Act 1977, section 3, a person guilty of conspiracy to commit murder, conspiracy to commit any offence for which the maximum penalty is life imprisonment, or conspiracy to commit any indictable offence punishment with imprisonment where no maximum term is specified, is subject to a maximum penalty of life imprisonment. The maximum penalty for other statutory conspiracies is the same as the maximum period provided by the relevant offence. Conspiracy is triable only on indictment. These provisions do not apply to common law conspiracies (preserved by the CLA 1977, section 5) which are subject to a penalty at the discretion of the court. By the CJA 1987, section 12, however the maximum penalty for conspiracy to defraud is ten years.

(ii) **Attempt**   Section 4 of the Criminal Attempts Act 1981 provides that the maximum penalty for attempted murder is life imprisonment; other indictable offences are subject to the same maximum penalty as applies on conviction on indictment for the offence attempted. If the offence is triable either way the maximum penalty on summary conviction is the same as the maximum penalty available for that offence tried summarily. It seems clear that the sentence for a give attempt should almost always be less than the sentence which would have been imposed if that offence had been completed, but much will depend on the stage at which the attempt failed and the reason(s) for its non-completion. The proper approach to sentencing for the offence of attempted murder is set out in the SGC guideline, *Attempted Murder*.

(iii) **Encouraging or assisting an offence etc**   The common law offence of incitement was abolished by the Serious Crime Act 2007, which creates three offences of intentionally encouraging or assisting an offence (under section 44 of that Act), encouraging or assisting an offence believing it will be committed (section 45), and encouraging or assisting offences believing one or more will be committed (section 46). Section 58 of the 2007 Act provides that if a person is convicted of an offence under section 44 or 45 or is convicted of an offence under section 46 by reference to only one offence (the 'reference offence') if the anticipated or reference offence is murder, he is liable to imprisonment for life. In any other case he is liable to any penalty for which he would be liable on conviction of the anticipated or reference offence. If a person is convicted under section 46 by reference to more than one offence then the maximum penalty is the same as the longer or longest which attaches to those offences.

(iv) Assisting an offender   The offence of assisting an offender under section 4 of the Criminal Law Act 1967 is subject to a uniquely complex set of provisions relating to the maximum penalties. By section 4 of that Act, if the principal offence is murder the maximum penalty for assisting under section 4 is ten years. If the principal offence carries fourteen years the maximum under section 4 is seven years (or six months, summarily). If the principal offence carries ten years the maximum under section 4 is five years (or six months, summarily). In other cases the maximum under section 4 is three years (or six months, summarily). There are no sentencing guidelines for this offence, but Court of Appeal guidance can be found in *A-G's Reference (No 16 of 2009)(Yates)* [2010] 2 Cr App R (S) 64, where it was said that the first consideration when sentencing for assisting an offender is the nature and extent of criminality of the principal offender, then the nature and extent of the assistance provided, then the extent to which the actions of the offender had damaged the interests of justice. Other relevant decisions are *Khatab* [2008] 2 Cr App R (S) 530 and *Urwin* [1996] 2 Cr App R (S) 281.

Retrospective penalties

3.28   It is an important principle that an offender who falls to be sentenced after the maximum penalty for the offence has been increased but in respect of an offence committed before that increase, must be sentenced on the basis of the former maximum sentence. This is a long-standing principle of English law, but Article 7 of the ECHR provides that no heavier penalty shall be imposed than the one applicable at the time the offence was committed. The principle can cause considerable difficulty when sentencing so-called 'historic' cases—ones committed many years ago but which have only recently come to light. This is most commonly encountered in sexual offences, where offences committed against young victims may not be revealed until years later. A good example is *Street* [1997] 2 Cr App R (S) 309, where the seventy-three-year-old offender pleaded guilty to several counts of indecent assault committed on a girl many years before. The Court of Appeal reduced the custodial sentences imposed because the sentencer had overlooked the fact that the offences had been committed before the maximum penalty for indecent assault had been increased from two years to eight years by the CJA 1988. The Court of Appeal issued detailed guidance on the approach to these cases in *H* [2012] 2 Cr App R (S) 88. Lord Judge CJ said that, inevitably, sentence had to be passed after conviction, on the basis of the current legislative provisions. Although sentence must be limited to the maximum sentence at the date when the offence was committed, it was unrealistic to attempt an assessment of what the sentence for the offence would have been if it had come to light at the time. Sometimes, again most likely in sexual offence cases, the exact date of the offence, or the exact dates of an admitted series of offences, are unclear. If the maximum penalty was increased at around that time and it is unclear which maximum penalty should apply, the offender should be given the benefit of the doubt and the lower maximum should apply.

If the maximum penalty for the offence has been reduced by Parliament at some time be- **3.29**
tween the commission of the offence and the defendant's conviction for it Article 7 is not
engaged. In *H* Lord Judge CJ said that in historic cases the defendant fell to be sentenced
today and even if there was evidence that there had been a more severe attitude to the
particular offence in earlier years than there was now, the earlier attitude was not now
relevant.

Minimum periods

The minimum period of imprisonment which can be imposed by a magistrates' court is five **3.30**
days (MCA 1980, section 132). There is no lower limit in the Crown Court. For detention
in a young offender institution, a court must not pass a sentence of less than twenty-one
days, and this applies both to Crown Court and to magistrates' courts (PCC(S)A 2000,
section 97(2)). In *Kent Youth Court, ex parte Kingwall* [1999] 1 Cr App R (S) 263 the
Divisional Court held (construing similarly worded earlier legislation) that where consecutive sentences of detention in a young offender institution had been imposed, section
97(2) applied to each of those sentences, rather than to the aggregate term. In other words
consecutive terms of ten days and twelve days would contravene the provision and be unlawful sentences.

Custodial regime and early release

A sentencer should not make any recommendation that the offender should serve the cus- **3.31**
todial sentence at a specified prison, since it may not be possible for this to be arranged
(*Lancaster* (1995) 16 Cr App R (S) 184). The fact that the prisoner will, by virtue of his
offence, be required to serve his sentence in isolation for his own protection is not normally
a matter to be taken into account when passing sentence (Parker [1996] 2 Cr App R (S) 275).
It is an important principle of sentencing that in setting the length of a custodial sentence
the court should ignore considerations of early release, licence, and home detention curfew.
These are all matters for the executive authorities, and it would be contrary to principle to
increase a sentence in an attempt to bring the offender within more rigorous early release
provisions. In *Al-Buhairi* [2004] 1 Cr App R (S) 496 the Court of Appeal held that it was
not proper for a judge to adjust sentence to take account of the fact that the offender may
be released early on the home detention curfew. The basic principle was confirmed by the
Court of Appeal in *Round* [2010] 2 Cr App R (S) 292. In some cases, however, it has been
held that a sentencer is entitled to adjust sentence length to avoid an unusually adverse
effect upon an offender's release date. An example is *Harrison* [1998] 2 Cr App R (S) 174.
It has been held that these decisions should not involve the judge in passing an unduly lenient sentence to avoid that result (*Parker* [2000] 2 Cr App R (S) 295). These cases generally
arose because the offender's sentence placed him on the borderline between two statutory
schemes for early release which operated differently from each other. That problem has
now been removed by statute.

Recommendation on licence conditions

If the Crown Court imposes a sentence of imprisonment or detention in a young offender **3.32**
institution of twelve months or more the offender will normally be released from custody at
the half-way point of the sentence (or earlier if released subject to home detention curfew).
Release is subject to licence on certain standard conditions and sometimes additional
special conditions which are determined shortly before release. The sentencing court has

power under the CJA 2003, section 238, to make a non-binding recommendation as to the content of those licence conditions. The recommendation is not part of the sentence as such (section 238(3)) and so cannot be the subject of an appeal against sentence. The SGC guideline, *New Sentences: CJA 2003* states that a court 'may sensibly suggest interventions that could be useful when passing sentence, but should only make specific recommendations about the requirements to be imposed on licence when announcing short sentences and where it is reasonable to anticipate their relevance at the point of release' (paragraph 2.1.14). The relevant prison governor and the probation service must have due regard to any recommendations made. It is thought that this power is rarely exercised in practice.

Concurrent and consecutive sentences

3.33   Where an offender is convicted on more than one count the court must impose separate sentences on each count, although occasionally a particular count may be dealt with by marking it with 'no separate penalty'. Sentences of imprisonment or detention in a young offender institution may run concurrently (at the same time) or consecutively (one after the other), or there may be a mix of concurrent and consecutive sentences. Similarly, where a court passes a custodial sentence on a person who is already serving one or more custodial sentences, it must make clear whether the fresh sentence is to be served concurrently with, or consecutively to, the existing sentence or sentences. It is unlawful to pass a sentence which is overlapping (ie partly concurrent and partly consecutive) with another sentence: *Salmon* [2003] 1 Cr App R (S) 414. The court must always make it clear which sentence relates to which count, and whether the sentences are concurrent or consecutive. If it fails to do so, it is presumed that the sentences are concurrent.

3.34   Terms of imprisonment may be ordered to run consecutively even where that results in a total term greater than the maximum which could have been imposed for any of the offences standing alone (eg *Prime* (1983) 5 Cr App R (S) 127). However, according to *Ralphs* [2009] EWCA Crim 2555, it is not permissible to impose consecutive sentences for offences which were committed at the same time (and hence would normally attract concurrent sentences) in order to evade the maximum penalty.

3.35   While there has been long-standing authority that a determinate sentence should not run consecutively to an indeterminate sentence (such as life imprisonment), in *Hills* [2009] 1 Cr App R (S) 441 the Court of Appeal said that since the CJA 2003 had created a sentencing regime for indeterminate sentences in which it was possible to identify with precision the date upon which the minimum term would expire, it was possible to order that a determinate sentence imposed on a serving prisoner should take effect at the expiry of the minimum term. The question of concurrent and consecutive sentences in the context of indeterminate sentences is dealt with in more detail at paragraphs 3.54 and 3.71, this Chapter.

3.36   There is a particular rule which has caused considerable difficulty, that a court imposing a prison sentence or sentence of detention in a young offender institution cannot direct that the new sentence shall commence at the expiry of an existing sentence from which the offender has already been released on licence and that licence has been revoked (CJA 2003, section 265). At one time judges had power to require the offender to serve in custody the whole or part of the unexpired portion of the original sentence, but the provision which allowed that to be done (section 116 of the PCC(S)A 2000) was repealed by the CJA 2003. In *Whittles* [2009] 2 Cr App R (S) 673 the offender still had two years of his licence period to complete when he was recalled to prison and subsequently sentenced for domestic burglary. The Court of Appeal noted and understood the judge's regret that the sentence imposed for the burglary would in practice result in no additional time being served by the offender. The Court thought that section 265 ought to be repealed. While it was still in place, however, it would be wrong in principle and contrary to section 153(2) of the CJA 2003 to pass a disproportionate sentence for the new offence simply designed to ensure that the offender would serve a period of time in prison longer than the remainder of the licence period for the original offence. Some other appellate decisions have conflicted with *Whittles*, but Court of Appeal in *Costello* [2010] 2 Cr App R (S) 608 said that it was correct. That appears to settle the matter, and the problem can only be resolved by legislation.

Concurrent and consecutive sentences, and totality

The SC guideline on *Totality* sets out the following general principles. All courts, when senten- **3.37**
cing for more than a single offence, should pass a total sentence which reflects all the offending behaviour before it and is just and proportionate. This is so whether the sentences are structured as concurrent or consecutive. Therefore, concurrent sentences will ordinarily be longer than a single sentence for a single offence. It is usually impossible to arrive at a just and proportionate sentence for multiple offending simply by adding together notional single sentences. It is necessary to address the offending behaviour, together with the factors personal to the offender, as a whole. The general approach, according to the guideline, is to first consider the sentence for each individual offence, referring to the relevant sentencing guidelines, and then to determine whether the case calls for concurrent or consecutive sentences.

Concurrent sentences will ordinarily be appropriate where:

(a) offences arise out of the same incident or facts

The guideline gives the following examples:

  (i)   a single incident of dangerous driving resulting in injuries to multiple victims (*Lawrence* (1989) 11 Cr App R (S) 580);
  (ii) robbery with a weapon where the weapon offence is ancillary to the robbery and is not distinct and independent of it (*A-G's Reference (Nos 21 and 22 of 2003)* [2003] EWCA Crim 3089);
  (iii) fraud and associated forgery;
  (iv) separate counts of supplying different types of drugs of the same class as part of the same transaction

(b) there is a series of offences of the same or similar kind, especially when committed against the same person

The guideline gives the following examples:

  (i)   repetitive small thefts from the same person, such as by an employee;
  (ii) repetitive benefit frauds of the same kind, committed in each payment period

Where concurrent sentences are to be passed the sentence should reflect the overall criminality involved. The sentence should be appropriately aggravated by the presence of the associated offences.

Consecutive sentences will ordinarily be appropriate where:

(a) offences arise out of unrelated facts or incidents

The guideline gives the following examples:

  (i)   where the offender commits a theft on one occasion and a common assault against a different victim on a separate occasion;
  (ii) an attempt to pervert the course of justice in respect of another offence also charged (*A-G's Reference (No 1 of 1990)* (1990) 12 Cr App R (S) 245);
  (iii) a Bail Act offence (*Millen* (1980) 2 Cr App R (S) 357);

(iv) any offence committed within the prison context;

(v) offences that are unrelated because whilst they were committed simultaneously they are distinct and there is an aggravating element that requires separate recognition, such as an assault on a constable committed to try to evade arrest for an offence also charged (*Kastercum* (1972) 56 Cr App R 298)

(b) offences that are of the same or similar kind but where the overall criminality will not sufficiently be reflected by concurrent sentences

The guideline gives the following examples:

(i) where offences are committed against different people, such as repeated thefts involving attacks on several different shop assistants (*Jamieson* [2008] EWCA Crim 2761);

(ii) where offences of domestic violence or sexual offences are committed against the same individual

(c) one or more offences qualifies for a statutory minimum sentence and concurrent sentences would improperly undermine that minimum (*Raza* (2010) 1 Cr App R (S) 56).

Where consecutive sentences are to be passed add up the sentences for each offence and consider if the aggregate length is just and proportionate. If the aggregate length is not just and proportionate the court should consider how to reach a just and proportionate sentence. There are a number of ways in which this can be achieved.

The guideline gives the following examples:

(i) When sentencing for similar offence types or offences of a similar level of seriousness the court can consider:
whether all of the offences can be proportionately reduced (with particular reference to the category ranges within sentencing guidelines) and passed consecutively;
whether, despite their similarity, a most serious principal offence can be identified and the other sentences can all be proportionately reduced (with particular reference to the category ranges within sentencing guidelines) and passed consecutively in order that the sentence for the lead offence can be clearly identified

(ii) When sentencing for two or more offences of different levels of seriousness the court can consider:
whether some offences are of such low seriousness in the context of the most serious offence(s) that they can be recorded as 'no separate penalty' (for example technical breaches or minor driving offences not involving mandatory disqualification);
whether some of the offences are of lesser seriousness and are unrelated to the most serious offence(s) that they can be ordered to run concurrently so that the sentence for the most serious offence(s) can be clearly identified.

Finally, the guideline states that the overall sentence(s) should be tested against the requirement that they be just and proportionate and whether the sentence is structured in a way that will be best understood by all concerned with it.

E SUSPENDED SENTENCE OF IMPRISONMENT OR DETENTION IN A YOUNG OFFENDER INSTITUTION

Power to impose suspended sentence

3.38 The power to suspend a custodial sentence is available only in relation to determinate sentences of imprisonment or detention in a young offender institution. An indeterminate or extended sentence cannot be suspended, nor can a detention and training order. In the

Crown Court a sentence of up to two years but not less than fourteen days can be suspended, for an operational period of between six months and two years. In the magistrates' court a sentence of up to six months can be suspended, again for an operational period of between six months and two years. If the court orders the sentence of imprisonment or detention in a young offender institution to be suspended it does not take effect unless the offender commits a further offence (whether or not it is punishable with imprisonment). The further offence must be committed within the operational period of the suspended sentence. The court dealing with the further offence may also order the suspended sentence to be activated and take effect (CJA 2003, section 189(1)).

The court imposing the suspended sentence in the first place may (and usually will) also **3.39** require the offender to comply with one or more requirements to be completed within the duration of the order. The period during which the stated requirements must be completed is known as the supervision period. A supervision period cannot be for less than six months. In many cases the operational period and the supervision period are of the same duration. Occasionally the operational period is longer than the supervision period, but never the other way round (see *Lees-Wolfenden* [2007] 1 Cr App R (S) 119). If the offender fails during the supervision period to comply with a requirement imposed by the court then that is a breach of the suspended sentence and the court dealing with the breach may order the suspended sentence to be activated and take effect (section 189(1A) and (1B)). If a suspended sentence is imposed by the Crown Court the court should always consider whether to direct that a failure by the offender to comply with a requirement should be dealt with by a magistrates' court. If no such direction is given any alleged breach of the community requirement will be brought back before the Crown Court.

It is important to understand that a suspended sentence is a custodial sentence and *not* a **3.40** community order. A suspended sentence therefore cannot be ordered unless all the statutory provisions as to the imposition of a sentence of immediate imprisonment have been observed. Before a suspended sentence can be passed, the court must take account of the relevant provisions of the CJA 2003, sections 152 and 153, which must be complied with before any custodial sentence is passed. The power to impose a suspended sentence in a magistrates' court is limited in the same way in which magistrates' powers to impose prison sentences are limited. The SGC guideline, *New Sentences: CJA 2003* explains that while there are some similarities between the suspended sentence and the community order, the real difference is that the suspended sentence is only appropriate for an offence that has crossed the custody threshold and for which custody is the only option (paragraph 2.2.10). As far as the length of the sentence is concerned, before making the decision to suspend the sentence, the court must first have decided that a custodial sentence is justified and also have decided on its length, which should be the shortest term commensurate with the seriousness of the offence if it were to be imposed immediately. The decision to suspend the sentence should not lead to a longer term being imposed than if the sentence were to take effect immediately (paragraph 2.2.12). If the court imposes two or more custodial sentences to run consecutively the power to suspend the overall term is only available if the aggregate term does not exceed two years.

Since the main reason for imposing a suspended sentence is to avoid immediate custody for **3.41** the offender, a court should not impose a suspended sentence at the same time as an immediate custodial sentence (*Sapiano* (1968) 52 Cr App R 674). A suspended sentence and a community order cannot be passed at the same time (CJA 2003, section 189(5)). A fine may be added to a suspended sentence. There is no restriction to passing any of the ancillary orders at the same time as a suspended sentence.

Time spent on remand or under qualifying curfew

3.42 The procedure appropriate where the offender has spent time on remand or has spent time under a qualifying curfew before being sentenced were discussed earlier in this Chapter at paragraphs 3.15 and 3.20. As we saw, time spent on remand is by section 240ZA deducted automatically from any sentence of imprisonment or detention in a young offender institution, while the sentencer should adjust the sentence under section 240A to make allowance for time served under a qualifying curfew. Section 240ZA(7) provides that, for the purpose of the section, a suspended sentence:

(a) is to be treated as a sentence of imprisonment when it takes effect under paragraph 8(2) (a) of (b) of schedule 12, and

(b) is to be treated as being imposed by the order under which it takes effect.

This clearly means that an offender will automatically be given credit for days spent on remand if and when the suspended sentence is activated. When it is activated the judge dealing with the breach has no discretion in relation to the matter, and the days will be deducted. However, in some cases the Court of Appeal has said that if an offender has spent a considerable period in custody on remand, and has in fact served the equivalent of a short custodial sentence, it would be wrong to pass a custodial sentence at all, whether immediate or suspended. A good example is *Barrett* [2010] 2 Cr App R (S) 551 the Court of Appeal varied a sentence of twelve weeks' imprisonment suspended for twelve months to a conditional discharge, since the maximum available sentence was six months and the offender had spent almost four months in custody on remand. In *Maugham* [2011] 2 Cr App R (S) 493 the Court said that where the offender had spent 198 days on remand (the equivalent of a thirteen-month sentence) it was wrong to pass a sentence of six months' imprisonment suspended for two years. The sentence should have been constructed in a way which would have given the offender the benefit of the time served on remand. As far as section 240A is concerned, the judge will have to make adjustment to take account of days spent under qualifying curfew. It seems that the same principles should apply. Normally the judge should adjust custodial sentence length only in the event of breach and activation of the suspended sentence, but in a case where the offender merits a short sentence and has spent a long time under a qualifying curfew that may mean that a custodial sentence is not appropriate at all.

Requirements in suspended sentence

3.43 Section 190(1) of the CJA 2003 lists the requirements with which the court may order the offender to comply during the supervision period of the suspended sentence. Prior to December 2012 it was always necessary for the court to impose at least one such requirement into a suspended sentence. That legal obligation was removed in December 2012, so that a suspended sentence may now contain no requirement at all (save for the basic obligation to commit no offence during the operational period of the order). The available requirements are:

(a) an unpaid work requirement
(b) an activity requirement
(c) a programme requirement
(d) a prohibited activity requirement
(e) a curfew requirement
(f) an exclusion requirement
(g) a residence requirement
(ga) a foreign travel prohibition requirement

(h) a mental health treatment requirement
(i) a drug rehabilitation requirement
(j) an alcohol treatment requirement
(ja) an alcohol abstinence and monitoring requirement
(k) a supervision requirement
(l) in a case where the offender is aged under twenty-five, an attendance centre requirement, and
(m) an electronic monitoring requirement

In the list in section 190(1) the clumsy numbering of (ga) and (ja) reflects the creation of new forms of requirements, inserted by LASPO 2012. Requirement (m) is also new, at least as a free-standing requirement, and was inserted by the Crime and Courts Act 2013. It has always been possible to impose an electronic monitoring requirement as a means of ensuring the offender's compliance with one or more other requirements (such as a curfew). The requirements available for a suspended sentence are the same as those which are available in respect of a community order, and subject to the same conditions. These are dealt with in detail at paragraphs 6.11 to 6.32, later in this book. The view is expressed in the SGC guideline, *New Sentences: CJA 2003* that because a suspended sentence contains a very clear deterrent threat the requirements imposed within a suspended sentence should generally be less onerous than those which might be imposed within a community order, and that if a judge is intending to impose onerous requirements into a suspended sentence it may be worth considering again whether a community order might be a more suitable disposal.

Power to order periodic review

If the offender is subject to a suspended sentence which contains a drug rehabilitation **3.44** requirement, the court has power to order that the requirement shall be subject to court review hearings under the CJA 2003, section 210. The court may order the offender to attend those hearings, and it may order the responsible officer, before each review, to provide to the court a report on the offender's progress. A review hearing is conducted by the court responsible for the order. There is an obvious advantage if the review hearings are held before the same judge who imposed the suspended sentence, but that may not always be possible to arrange. For detailed consideration see paragraphs 6.22 to 6.25 in this book. Section 191(1) of the CJA 2003 confers discretion on the court to provide that a suspended sentence containing one or more other requirements may be made subject to periodic review, at review hearings, at specified intervals of time. It is thought, however, that review hearings are utilized almost exclusively for drug rehabilitation requirements.

Section 192 sets out the procedure at review hearings. Section 192(1) permits the court, **3.45** after consideration of the report from the supervising officer, to amend any requirement of the suspended sentence, although the court cannot amend the order by adding a requirement of a different kind unless the offender consents. The offender's consent is always required before the court amends a drug rehabilitation requirement, an alcohol treatment requirement, or a mental health treatment requirement (section 192(2)). The court may also extend the supervision period, but not so that it infringes the normal maximum of two years. If the court is of the opinion that the offender is making satisfactory progress, it can adjust the intervals of time between review hearings or may amend the order so that subsequent reviews can be held by considering the papers rather than by a full hearing. If performance under the order regresses, the review hearings can be reinstated.

Breach of suspended sentence

3.46 Breach of suspended sentence may occur either as a result of the offender's failure to comply with a requirement during the supervision period of the order or the offender's commission of a further offence within the operational period of the sentence. Care must always be taken to ensure that the relevant event occurred during the relevant period. There has still been a breach of the suspended sentence provided one of the above events has occurred, even though the overall term of the suspended sentence has come to an end by the time the matter is before the court dealing with breach. On the other hand if the offender is brought before the court to be sentenced for an offence which was committed before the suspended sentence was imposed the commission of that offence is not a breach of the suspended sentence.

3.47 Schedule 12, paragraph 8 to the CJA 2003 describes the powers of the court when it deals with (by 8(1)(a)) an offender who has failed without reasonable excuse to comply with any of the community requirements of the suspended sentence order, or (by 8(1)(b)) an offender convicted of an offence committed during the operational period of a suspended sentence order. The court *must* deal with him in one of the following ways, set out in paragraph 8(2):

(a) order that the suspended sentence takes effect with the original term unaltered, or

(b) order that the suspended sentence takes effect with the substitution for the original term of a lesser term, or

(c) the court may order the offender to pay a fine of an amount not exceeding £2500, or

(d) in the case of a suspended sentence order that imposes one or more community requirements the court may amend the order by doing any one or more of the following—

    (i) imposing more onerous community requirements which the court could include if it were then making the order,

    (ii) extending the supervision period, or

    (iii) extending the operational period, but not beyond two years from the date of making the order.

(e) in the case of a suspended sentence order that does not impose any community requirements, the court may, subject to section 189(3) amend the order by extending the operational period.

The court must make an order under (2)(a) or (b) unless it is of the opinion that it would be unjust to do so in view of all the circumstances, including the following matters:

(a) the extent to which the offender has complied with any community requirements of the suspended sentence order, and

(b) in a case falling within sub-paragraph (1)(b) the facts of the subsequent offence.
    If it decides not to proceed under (2)(a) or (b) the court must state its reasons.

It should be noted that where the offender is before the court in respect of breach of a suspended sentence order the court *must* deal with him in one of the ways listed in paragraph 8. It is not permissible simply to revoke the order, or to make no order with respect to it. There is no power under the CJA 2003, schedule 12, paragraph 8(2), for the court dealing with a breach to impose a custodial term longer than that originally suspended (see *Cassidy* [2011] 2 Cr App R (S) 240). In *Phipps* [2008] 2 Cr App R (S) 114 the Court of Appeal observed that the power of the court to impose custody when dealing with breach of a requirement attached to a suspended sentence was thereby more restricted than its power when dealing with breach of an equivalent requirement in a community order. Where the offender has breached the order by commission of a further offence, any activated term of the suspended sentence will normally be required to run consecutively to a custodial sentence imposed for the new offence. Because of this, it is wrong to increase the length of the sentence for the new offence because it was committed during the currency of a suspended sentence (*Levesconte* [2011] EWCA Crim 2754).

It is important when deciding whether to activate the suspended sentence, or whether to **3.48** activate it in full or in part, to have regard to the successful completion (or part completion) by the offender of one or more community requirements in the order. It will also be relevant whether the breach has occurred near the start, or near the end of the operational period, and whether any new offence is serious or trivial. Usually, if the offender has completed a significant part of the order, that is a good reason for not activating the suspended sentence in full (*Zeca* [2009] 2 Cr App R (S) 460). However, in a number of recent decisions the Court of Appeal has stressed that the offender should fully comply with the suspended sentence requirements. In *Finn* [2012] 2 Cr Ap R (S) 96 (p. 569) the Court of Appeal upheld the judge's decision to activate the suspended sentence in full despite the offender completing 140 hours of unpaid work, because he had breached the order on six occasions in what was described as a 'wholesale failure' to comply with the supervision requirement. Another example is *Sheppard* [2008] 2 Cr App R (S) 524.

Amendment of suspended sentence

A range of possible amendments to the requirements in a suspended sentence may be made **3.49** in accordance with schedule 12 by the court on application to it by the offender or the responsible officer. These include amendments prompted by change of the circumstances of the offender or change of residence from one local justice area to another.

F EXTENDED SENTENCES OF IMPRISONMENT AND DETENTION IN A YOUNG OFFENDER INSTITUTION

The provisions relating to the imposition of extended sentences of imprisonment and deten- **3.50** tion in a young offender institution have been amended several times since their creation by the CJA 2003, most recently by the LASPOA 2012.

Extended sentences

Section 226A of the CJA 2003 applies where: **3.51**

    (1) (a) a person aged 18 or over is convicted of a 'specified offence' (whether the offence was committed before or after this section comes into force), and

          (b) the court considers that there is a significant risk to members of the public of serious harm occasioned by the commission by him of further specified offences;

          (c) the court is not required by section 224A or 225(2) to impose a sentence of imprisonment for life, and

          (d) Condition A or B is met.

    (2) Condition A is that, at the time the offence was committed, the offender had been convicted of an offence listed in Schedule 15B.

    (3) Condition B is that, if the court were to impose an extended sentence of imprisonment, the term that it would specify as the appropriate custodial term would be at least 4 years.

'Specified offences' are those sexual offences or violent offences which are listed in schedule **3.52** 15 to the CJA 2003. Schedule 15 is in two parts. Part 1 contains specified violent offences and includes the following; manslaughter, kidnapping, false imprisonment, soliciting murder, threats to kill, wounding (OAPA 1861, section 18 and section 20), other offences against the person (OAPA 1861, sections 21, 22, 23, 27, 28, 29, 30, 31, 32, 37, 38), certain offences involving explosives, firearms offences (FA 1968, sections 16, 16A, 17(1) and (2), 18), cruelty to children, certain Theft Act offences (robbery, burglary with intent and aggravated burglary), arson, certain aviation offences, certain public order offences (riot, violent disorder and affray), racially or religiously aggravated assaults and harassment, death by dangerous driving and death by careless driving under the influence of drink or drugs, certain maritime and shipping offences, certain terrorist offences, offences relating to female genital mutilation, aiding, abetting, counselling, procuring or inciting the commission of, or conspiring, or attempting, to commit any of the offences listed.

Part 2 contains specified sexual offences and includes the following: most offences under the SOA 1956 (sections 1–7, 9–17, 19–29, 32, 33) indecency with a child, burglary with intent to commit rape, offences concerning indecent photographs of children, most offences under the SOA 2003 (sections 1–19, 25, 26, 30–41, 47–50, 52, 53, 57–59, 61-67, 69, 70), aiding, abetting, counselling, procuring or inciting the commission of, or conspiring, or attempting, to commit any of the offences listed.

In contrast with the requirements for the passing of a discretionary life sentence it is not necessary for the purpose of eligibility for an extended sentence that the 'specified offence' be a 'serious' specified offence. The offences set out in schedule 15B are listed in paragraph 3.58 of this Chapter. The 'dangerousness test' set out section 226A(1)(b) has been the subject of extensive case law, which applies equally to circumstances in which the court is considering whether to apply a discretionary life sentence. The ramifications of the test, as explored in the case law, are considered at paragraph 3.64 of this Chapter.

3.53   An extended sentence of imprisonment (or in the case of a person aged eighteen, nineteen, or twenty, an extended sentence of detention in a young offender institution), is a sentence of imprisonment or detention in a young offender institution (not exceeding the maximum for the offence) the term of which is equal to the aggregate of

(a)   the appropriate custodial term, and
(b)   a further period (the extension period) on licence, of such length as the court considers necessary to protect members of the public from serious harm occasioned by the commission by the offender of further specified offences (section 226A(7)).

The custodial term of the extended sentence is the commensurate sentence appropriate to the offence. The extension period must not exceed five years in the case of a specified violent offence and must not exceed eight years in the case of a specified sexual offence (section 226A(8)).

The total term of the extended sentence must in no case exceed the maximum penalty for the offence for which the extended sentence is imposed. In *Oldfield* [2012] 1 Cr App R (S) 211 an extended sentence of eight years was quashed on appeal as an unlawful sentence where the maximum penalty for the offence (unlawful wounding under section 20 of the Offences Against the Person Act 1861) was five years.

3.54   If the offender is convicted of more than one offence, at least one of which is a specified offence, and the question is whether the specified offence is serious enough to bring the case within Condition B above (that if the court were to impose an extended sentence of imprisonment the term that it would specify would be at least four years), then if the specified offence standing alone could not justify such a sentence the seriousness of the aggregate offending must be considered. If a four-year sentence results from aggregating the sentences, then that four-year term can be imposed for the specified offence. If appropriate, a concurrent determinate sentence (or sentences) may be passed for the other offence(s). These were the conclusions of the Court of Appeal in *Pinnell* [2011] 2 Cr App (S) 168.

Extended sentences: release on licence

Prior to amendment of these provisions by the LASPOA 2012, an offender sentenced to **3.55** an extended sentence of imprisonment or detention in a young offender institution would be released on licence halfway through the custodial term. For the extended sentence as amended by the 2012 Act, however, release is now normally at the two-thirds points of the custodial term, unless the custodial term of the extended sentence is ten years or more, or the sentence is imposed for an offence listed in schedule 15B, when the case must be referred at the two-thirds point to the Parole Board, who will consider whether it is no longer necessary for the protection of the public for the offender to be detained. Clearly the involvement of the Parole Board in making a risk assessment at this point is consistent with the rationale of the extended sentence—that the offender is dangerous, and should only be released when it is safe to do so, and subject to an extended licence period and with a clear supervision plan on release. The Court of Appeal in *Saunders* [2013] EWCA Crim 1027 said that the 'new' version of the extended sentence is therefore 'much more onerous' than the former version.

At the time when release from an extended sentence took place by law at the halfway point **3.56** of the custodial term, the Court of Appeal in *Pinnell* held that generally courts should avoid using consecutive sentences in this context, and it was preferable where possible to adjust the length of the custodial term within concurrent sentences to reflect the totality of the overall offending, but if otherwise appropriate, an extended sentence could be added to a determinate custodial sentence (or if necessary vice versa), and that two extended sentences could in principle be ordered to run consecutively to each other. Given the 2012 Act changes, and the new discretionary element in the date of release from the custodial term, it seems that the latter aspect of the decision in *Pinnell* will have to be revisited. The Court of Appeal in *Saunders* noted this problem but since the actual appeal did not raise the issue directly, declined to make any ruling on the matter.

G LIFE SENTENCE FOR THE SECOND LISTED OFFENCE

Section 122 of the Legal Aid, Sentencing and Punishment of Offenders Act 2012 Act cre- **3.57** ated a sentence of the 'life sentence for second listed offence' by inserting a new section 224A into the CJA 2003. The sentence (which is one of life imprisonment if the offender is aged twenty-one or over, or custody for life if he is aged eighteen, nineteen, or twenty) is available by section 224A where:

(a) a person aged eighteen or over is convicted of an offence listed in part 1 of schedule 15B to the 2003 Act,

(b) the offence is such that the court would have imposed a determinate sentence of ten years or more (including an extended sentence where the *custodial* term would have been ten years or more), and

(c) that the offender has a previous conviction for an offence listed in schedule 15B (not just in Part 1) for which he received a 'life sentence' (with a minimum term of at least five years) or a determinate sentence of ten years or more (including an extended sentence where the *custodial* term was ten years or more).

(d) The court must impose a sentence of imprisonment for life under this section unless the court is of the opinion that there are particular circumstances which—

(i) relate to the offence, to the previous offence or to the offender, and

(ii) would make it unjust to do so in all the circumstances.

It should be noted that the new offence must be listed in *Part 1* of schedule 15B, while the **3.58** previous offence can be listed anywhere in that schedule. This is to allow for the inclusion within the range of qualifying previous convictions the offence of murder and certain repealed offences (such as under the Sexual Offences Act 1956) which have been replaced with broadly equivalent offences. Schedule 15B contains the relevant offences.

Part 1 includes the following: manslaughter, soliciting murder, OAPA 1861, section 18, FA 1968, sections 16, 17(1), 18, robbery where, at some time during the commission of the offence, the offender had in his possession a firearm or an imitation firearm, Protection of Children Act 1978, sections 1, Terrorism Act 2000, sections 56, 57, 59, Anti-Terrorism, Crime and Security Act 2001, sections 47, 50, 113, Terrorism Act 2006, sections 5, 9, 10, 11, SOA 2003, sections 1, 2, 4, 5, 7, 8, 9, 10, 11, 12, 14, 15, 25, 30, 31, 34, 48, 49, 50, 62, the DVCVA 2004, section 5, any attempt, conspiracy or incitement to commit a listed offence or murder or aiding, abetting, counselling, or procuring a listed offence.

Part 2 includes murder and any offence that was abolished before the coming into force of schedule 15A but would, if committed on the relevant day, have constituted an offence listed in Part 1. Oddly, some of these offences are not punishable with life imprisonment. Many of the sexual offences listed carry maximum sentences of ten to fourteen years. The offence under the Protection of Children Act 1978, section 1, is included which has a maximum of ten years, and so is causing the death of a child or vulnerable adult under the Domestic Violence Crime and Victims Act (DVCVA) 2004, section 5, which has a maximum of fourteen years. The offence of robbery (which does carry life) is included, but only if the offender had with him a firearm or imitation firearm. This formulation has caused problems under earlier provisions (see in particular *Gore* [2010] 2 Cr App R (S) 590).

The reference in (c) above to a previous 'life sentence' incorporates the definition of that term in the Crime (Sentences) Act 1997, section 34, which defines 'life sentence' to include imprisonment for public protection. That sentence was repealed by LASPOA 2012.

The wording in (d)(i) and (ii) above is the same as that which applies in the prescribed sentence provisions such as the three-strikes domestic burglary provisions.

3.59 Since this is a new sentence there are no appellate authorities in relation to it. It is clear that it is not intended to be a replacement for the repealed sentence of imprisonment for public protection. There are probably very few examples of offenders who would fall within the criteria set out earlier and not attract a discretionary life sentence for the new offence in any event. It should be noted that to qualify for a discretionary life sentence (or an extended sentence for that matter) the offender must pass the 'dangerousness test'. This is not a requirement for the sentence of life for the second listed offence. It caters for cases where an offender has one very serious offence on his record (say, an armed robbery, or manslaughter) which attracted a ten-year sentence, and who now commits a second equally serious offence. Such an offender would be likely to fulfil the criteria for assessment as a dangerous offender, but that is not strictly a requirement here. Despite the wording of section 224A ('the court must impose a sentence of imprisonment for life unless...') the Court of Appeal in *Burinskas* [2014] EWA Crim 334 said that the court should decide whether the offender passes the 'dangerousness test' before turning its mind to section 224A.

H DISCRETIONARY LIFE SENTENCE

3.60 By section 225 of the CJA 2003, where a person aged eighteen or over is convicted of a serious specified offence and the court is of the opinion that there is a significant risk to members of the public of serious harm occasioned by the commission by him of further specified offences, the offence is punishable with life imprisonment and the court considers that the seriousness of the offence, or of the offence and one or more offences associated with it, is such as to justify a sentence of imprisonment for life, the court must impose a sentence of imprisonment for life. A 'specified offence' is an offence listed in schedule 15 to the 2003 Act (section 224(1)). A 'serious specified offence' is any of those offences which is punishable with imprisonment for life or imprisonment for ten years or more (section 224(2)). Clearly in respect of this sentence we are just interested in offences which carry life as the maximum sentence. The offender must pass the 'dangerousness test'. The judge must decide whether the offender poses the 'significant risk etc' so as to fall within the terms of the discretionary life sentence at the time of sentencing, but clearly the indeterminate sentence is directed to the uncertainty of the period of time for which that risk may endure. This principle is expressed in clear terms by Lord Judge CJ In *MJ* [2012] 2 Cr App R (S) 416. It should also be remembered that in any case where the sentence for the offence would otherwise fall within the provisions for the sentencing of dangerous offenders, nothing prevents the sentencing court from imposing a hospital or guardianship order under the Mental Health Act 1983 instead.

Before passing such a sentence the court must of course comply with all the general criteria **3.61** for the imposition of custodial sentences in sections 152 and 153 of the CJA 2003. These were dealt with in Chapter 2. If the court decides that the seriousness of the case cannot be met by the passing of a determinate sentence, whether of imprisonment, detention in a young offender institution, or detention under section 91 of the PCC(S)A 2000, and that an indeterminate sentence is required, it must fix an appropriate minimum term under the PCC(S)A 2000, section 82A. That section is dealt with at paragraph 3.67, this Chapter. If the offender is aged eighteen, nineteen, or twenty years old, the equivalent sentence is custody for life under section 225. If the offender is aged under eighteen the equivalent sentence is detention for life under the CJA 2003, section 226. In *Lang* [2006] 2 All ER 410 the Court of Appeal said that when sentencing young offenders it must be remembered that they may change and develop in a shorter time than an adult. This, together with their level of maturity, may be highly relevant when assessing future risk. Discretionary life sentences are very rare indeed in relation to young offenders.

What are the criteria which govern the choice between a very long determinate sentence **3.62** and an indeterminate (life) sentence? The criteria for imposing discretionary life sentences of different descriptions have been essentially the same. The Court of Appeal has said that such sentences should be reserved for cases of the utmost gravity where the culpability of the offender is particularly high or the offence itself is particularly grave. It is almost always reserved for offenders whose mental state makes them dangerous in accordance with the statutory test, but who cannot be dealt with under the provisions of the Mental Health Act 1983. Often in such cases the courts have identified a degree of mental instability on the part of the offender which means that he will remain a danger to the public for a very long time requiring constant supervision and reassessment in a custodial setting. There were several Court of Appeal decisions to guide the choice between a discretionary life sentence and the sentence of imprisonment for public protection, given that the two sentences were very similar in their practical effect. These cases have had the effect of restricting the appropriate use of the discretionary life sentence to the most serious and grave cases where a life sentence would have 'denunciatory value' over and above imprisonment for public protection. The main authorities were *Kehoe* [2009] 1 Cr App R (S) 41, *Wood* [2010] 1 Cr App R 6, and *Wilkinson* [2010] 1 Cr App R (S) 628. The sentence of imprisonment for public protection was abolished by the LASPOA 2012. Given that the new form of life sentence (life for the second serious offence) is likely to be used quite rarely, the border between the discretionary life sentence and the extended sentence (as amended by

LASPOA 2012) will require re-drawing by the Court of Appeal. The Court of Appeal has not addressed this issue in detail, but guidance was given in *Saunders* [2013] EWCA Crim 1027 and *Burinskas* [2014] EWCA Crim 224. In the former case Lord Judge CJ said that in cases in which, prior to the enactment of the LASPOA, the court would have been driven to the conclusion that imprisonment for public protection was required for public protection the discretionary life sentence will now arise for consideration. Where appropriate, if the necessary level of public protection cannot be achieved by the new extended sentence, a discretionary life sentence will be ordered. The 'denunciatory' ingredient identified to distinguish between the circumstances in which the discretionary life sentence rather than imprisonment for public protection should be imposed is no longer apposite. By that His Lordship meant that although the 'denunciatory' element of the sentencing decision may continue to justify the discretionary life sentence, its absence does not preclude such an order. As every judge appreciates, however, the life sentence remains the sentence of last resort.

3.63 Not all offences which carry life imprisonment as their maximum sentence are serious specified offences as defined in section 224. The offence of importation of Class A drugs, for example, carries that sentence, but because it is not a violent or sexual offence it does not appear in schedule 15 to the 2003 Act. The Court of Appeal in *Saunders* [2013] EWCA Crim 1027 has confirmed that courts do retain power to pass a discretionary life sentence in respect of such offences, although the occasions on which a court might impose a life sentence on an offender who did not fall within the dangerousness provisions of the CJA 2003 would be rare. By section 94 of the PCC(S)A 2000, where an offender is aged eighteen, nineteen, or twenty years old, and has been convicted of an offence which is punishable with life imprisonment in the case of an offender aged twenty-one or over, the court may, if it considers that a sentence for life would be appropriate, sentence him to custody for life.

The dangerousness test

3.64 As explained earlier, before a discretionary life sentence under section 225 or 226 or an extended sentence under section 226A or 226B can be imposed the court must be of the opinion that there is a significant risk to members of the public of serious harm occasioned by the commission by him of further specified offences. The Act defines 'serious harm' as 'death or serious personal injury, whether physical or psychological'. The Court of Appeal in *Pedley* [2009] 1 WLR 2517 said that there was no justification for trying to redefine the 'significant risk of serious harm' test in terms of numerical probability. Each case must be determined on its own facts, but that did not mean that the sentence was too uncertain to comply with Article 5(1) of the ECHR. Section 229 of the CJA 2003 is concerned with the criteria for the assessment of dangerousness. It states that in making that assessment, the court *must* take into account all information about the nature and circumstances of the offence, and *may* take into account all information about the nature and circumstances of any other offences committed by the offender and any information about the offender. Importance guidance on the dangerousness test was given by the Court of Appeal in *Lang* [2006] 1 WLR 2509 and in *AG's Reference (No 55 of 2008)* [2008] 2 Cr App R (S) 22. These decisions have been superseded in some respects by later statutory changes, but the following key parts of the guidance remain valuable.

3.65 'Significant risk' must be shown in relation to the commission of further specified (but not necessarily serious specified) offences, of causing thereby serious harm to members of the public. The requirement that a risk be 'significant' means more than a possibility—it must be 'noteworthy, of considerable amount or importance'. A wide variety of information will need to be considered before the assessment of dangerousness is made by the court. The court will rely upon the detailed facts of the offence before it, the pre-sentence report (which will focus on a risk assessment of the offender), and the details of the offender's previous convictions, where relevant. A psychiatric report will be appropriate in some cases. Reports before the courts are not binding on the sentencer but, if the judge was minded to depart from the conclusion set out in a report, counsel should be warned in advance. As far as the previous convictions are concerned, the prosecution should be in a position to describe to the court the facts of any previous specified offences on the record. If there is doubt over the accuracy of the facts or circumstances of previous convictions of the offender, it may be necessary to adjourn to investigate the context of an earlier offence. It is clear that in the assessment of dangerousness it is *not* just previous specified offences which are relevant. The court may have regard to offences on the record which are not specified offences, especially where they indicate an escalating pattern of seriousness. Indeed, it is not a prerequisite to a finding of dangerousness that the offender has any previous convictions. A first offender might qualify. Nor is it necessary that serious harm (or indeed any harm) has been caused by the offender in the course of past offences, since that may have been simply a matter of good fortune. The Court of Appeal in *Lang* confirmed that risk to 'members of the public' was a general term, and should not be construed so as to exclude any particular group, such as prison officers or staff in mental hospitals. It seems safe to assume that such a risk could properly be made out where the risk is specific to a small group of individuals, or just to one potential victim. In *Considine* [2008] 1 WLR 414 the Court of Appeal confirmed that the word 'information' in section 229 was not restricted in its meaning to 'evidence', and that relevant information bearing on the offender's dangerousness in a particular case might include material which had not been proved by criminal conviction.

The judge, in accordance with the CJA 2003, section 174, should give reasons for his conclusions on the issue of dangerousness, especially whether there is or is not a significant risk of further offences or serious harm, and whether the nature of the offence is such that a discretionary life sentence (rather than an extended sentence or a determinate sentence) must be imposed. **3.66**

I SETTING MINIMUM TERM UNDER PCC(S)A 2000, SECTION 82A

Section 82A applies in every case where the court is imposing a life sentence other than a mandatory sentence for murder. It extends to life sentences imposed on offenders aged under eighteen as well as to those aged eighteen and over. The section empowers the judge imposing such a sentence to set a minimum term which must be served by the offender before he can first be considered for early release by the Parole Board. The imposition of a life sentence is of course designed to protect the public from the offender who has been found to be dangerous, whereas the period specified under section 82A is meant to reflect the degree of punishment and deterrence appropriate for the offence, aside from the question of public protection (*Wheaton* [2005] 1 Cr App R (S) 425). The specified period should not be lengthened with a view to protecting the public (*Adams* [2000] 2 Cr App R (S) 274). **3.67**

The effect of specifying the minimum term of the sentence under section 82A is that the life sentence prisoner will not become eligible to be considered for early release until the expiry of that period. The *Criminal Practice Directions*, paragraph L.1 to L.5, which provides guidance on the imposition of a discretionary life sentence, says that although the judge is not strictly obliged to make use of the provisions of section 82A the judge should in **3.68** practice always do so, save in the very exceptional case where he considers that the offence is so serious that imprisonment for life is justified by the seriousness of the offence alone, irrespective of the risk to the public. In that case, he should state this in open court when passing sentence. If the court is of that view it should make an order under section 82A(4) to the effect that the early release provisions shall not apply at all to the offender. In *Oakes* [2013] HRLR 9 the Court of Appeal said that such an order (referred to in the judgment as a 'whole life order') must be reserved for the most exceptional discretionary life sentence cases. While stopping just short of saying that a whole life order was limited to cases of murder, the Court said that whole life orders outside the context of murder would be 'very rare indeed'. Despite the decision of the Grand Chamber of the European Court of Human Rights in *Vinter v UK* [2013] ECHR 645 which stated that a life sentence without the possibility of review was unlawful because it violated Article 3 of the ECHR, the Court of Appeal in *Attorney General's Ref (No 69 of 2013)* [2014] EWCA Crim 188 has held that English law is compliant with the ECHR because a prisoner serving a whole life term may still be released in exceptional circumstances on compassionate grounds by virtue of the Crime (Sentences) Act 1997, section 30.

3.69   When specifying the relevant period, the judge should have regard to the specific terms of the section, and should always indicate clearly the reasons for the decision. Before specifying the relevant period, the sentencer should permit counsel for the defence to address the court on the appropriate length of the relevant part. If appropriate the judge may have regard to the provisions of schedule 21 to the CJA 2003, which set out principles for selecting the starting point for sentencing in a murder case (*McNee* [2008] 1 Cr App R (S) 24). When announcing the minimum term the judge should indicate what would be the appropriate determinate sentence in the case, explain that the minimum term is set at one-half of that determinate sentence, and further explain that if the offender is at some point after the expiry of the minimum term released on licence the offender will remain on licence for the rest of his life and be subject to recall to prison if he does not comply with the terms of that licence. A decision on the part of the judge not to specify a minimum term under section 82A can be the subject of an appeal (*Hollies* (1995) 16 Cr App R (S) 463). An order under section 82A specifying the length of the minimum term may be the subject of an appeal by the offender (*McBean* [2002] 1 Cr App R (S) 430) or might be referred to the Court of Appeal by the Attorney General as constituting an unduly lenient sentence (*A-G's Ref (No 82 of 2000)* [2001] 2 Cr App R (S) 289).

3.70   Section 82A is set out in full below:

(1) This section applies if a court passes a life sentence in circumstances where the sentence is not fixed by law.

(2) The court shall, unless it makes an order under subsection (4) below, order that the provisions of section 28(5) to (8) of the Crime (Sentences) Act 1997 (referred to in this section as the 'early release provisions') shall apply to the offender as soon as he has served the part of his sentence which is specified in the order.

(3) The part of his sentence shall be such as the court considers appropriate taking into account—

    (a) the seriousness of the offence, or of the combination of the offence and one or more offences associated with it;

    (b) the effect of any direction which it would have given under section 240ZA of the Criminal Justice Act 2003 (crediting periods of remand in custody) or under section 246 of the Armed Forces Act 2006 (equivalent provision for service courts) or under section 240A of that Act of 2003 (crediting periods of remand on bail subject to certain types of condition) if it had sentenced him to a term of imprisonment; and

(c) the early release provisions as compared with section 244(1) of the Criminal Justice Act 2003.

(4) If the offender was aged 21 or over when he committed the offence and the court is of the opinion that, because of the seriousness of the offence or of the combination of the offence and one or more offences associated with it, no order should be made under subsection (2) above, the court shall order that the early release provisions shall not apply to the offender.

Section 82A(3)(b) is prospectively amended by the Criminal Justice and Immigration Act 2008, section 19 (which will insert new subsections (3A) to (3C)). These provisions have not been brought into force and are omitted from the section as set out here.

Turning to consider section 82A(3)(a), in *A-G's Ref (No 3 of 2004)* [2005] 1 Cr App R (S) 230, the Court of Appeal emphasized that, when having regard to the seriousness of the offence (or the combination of the offence and other offences associated with it), the section permitted the judge to consider the totality of the associated offences, rather than just the offence for which the indeterminate sentence was being passed. In a case where the offender falls to be sentenced on the same occasion for more than one serious specified offence, or for one or more serious specified offence and one or more specified offence, such sentences should take effect concurrently rather than consecutively but the seriousness of the totality of the offences should be reflected in the length of the period selected by the judge under section 82A (*Edwards* [2007] 1 Cr App R (S) 646, and *Meade* [2007] 1 Cr App R (S) 762). **3.71**

Section 82A(3)(b) deals with the relevance to the minimum term of time spent on remand by the offender (under section 240ZA) and of time spent under a qualifying curfew (under section 240A). These matters are considered at paragraphs 3.15 and 3.20, this Chapter, respectively. It will be recalled that as a result of legislative change in LASPOA 2012 the former position where the judge had to make adjustment to sentence to take account of time spent by the offender on remand under section 240 was changed, and by section 240ZA (which replaced section 240) such time is now deducted automatically. Section 82A(3)(b) is now rather oddly worded, given that a court (following the implementation of section 240ZA) can no longer 'give a direction' under that section, but it is submitted that section 82A(3)(b) must be taken to mean that the court when setting the period under section 82A should make an appropriate adjustment for both of the matters referred to in section 82A(3)(b). According to the Court of Appeal in *Marklew* [1999] 1 WLR 485, the sentencer should normally give full credit under section 82(3)(b) for any period spent by the defendant on remand. *Marklew* also indicates, however, that there may be some circumstances in which the giving of full credit to the offender would not be appropriate. It is not entirely clear whether a judge retains any discretion in this regard. **3.72**

A sentencer setting the minimum term under this section is required by section 82A(3) (c) to take into account the fact that under the CJA 2003, section 244, a prisoner who has received a determinate sentence is entitled to be released after serving one-half of his sentence. In *Marklew* the Court of Appeal issued guidance on the setting of the period to be specified under section 82A. Thomas J stated that henceforth sentencers should make clear what the determinate sentence would have been and should then normally fix the specified period at one-half of the notional term. The principle of setting the specified period at one-half of the notional determinate sentence has been followed and applied in many subsequent cases. The rationale, according to Pill LJ in *West* [2001] 1 Cr App R (S) 103, is that an indeterminate sentence prisoner should be in no worse a position on an application for early release than a determinate sentence prisoner. If subsections (3A) to (3C) referred to earlier are brought into force they will permit the sentencer to reduce the notional determinate **3.73** sentence by some lesser period than one-half when fixing the specified period. Since they are not in force they are not consider further here.

3.74 In fixing the notional determinate sentence, allowance should be made for a guilty plea (*Meek* (1995) 16 Cr App R (S) 1003). Where the court is passing a discretionary life sentence (as opposed to the mandatory one for murder), under section 82A the court is required to determine first what the notional equivalent determinate sentence would have been for the offence, and then to adjust it to reflect the guilty plea. The judge will do that in exactly the same way as he would when adjusting a determinate sentence, with the normal recommended maximum reduction of one-third if the plea of guilty was tendered at the first reasonable opportunity. Once that figure has been arrived it, it then has to be converted to the appropriate minimum term, which is done by dividing it in two.

KEY DOCUMENTS[1]

Sentencing Guidelines Council, Definitive Guideline, *New Sentences: CJA 2003* (December 2004).

Sentencing Guidelines Council, Definitive Guideline, *Reduction in Sentence for a Guilty Plea* (effective from 23 July 2007).

Sentencing Guidelines Council, Definitive Guideline, *Attempted Murder* (effective 27 July 2009).

Sentencing Guidelines Council, Definitive Guideline, *Sentencing Youths* (effective 30 November 2009).

Criminal Practice Directions [2013] EWCA Crim 1631 (effective 7 October 2013), amended by [2013] EWCA Crim 2328 (effective 10 December 2013).

European Convention on Human Rights, Articles 3 and 7.

---

[1] All sentencing guidelines can be found on the Sentencing Council website: <http://sentencing council.judiciary.gov.uk/>.

4

CUSTODIAL SENTENCES: OFFENDERS UNDER 18

A AVAILABLE CUSTODIAL SENTENCES

4.01 The great bulk of sentencing of offenders aged under eighteen takes place in the youth court. For a discussion of the jurisdiction of the youth court, and the circumstances in which, exceptionally, young offenders may (or must) be sentenced in the Crown Court, see paragraph 1.19 in this book. The aims of sentencing applicable to the sentencing of youths are different from those applicable to the sentencing of adults, and are subject to the SGC guideline, *Sentencing of Youths*, which is considered further below. Because the custodial sentences for those under eighteen are different from those applicable to adults, and because different sentencing aims apply, the offence-based sentencing guidelines do not in general apply to young offenders. The sentencing guidelines which do, exceptionally, contain separate starting points and ranges for young offenders are the SGC guidelines on *Robbery* and on *Breach of an Anti-social Behaviour Order*.

4.02 The imposition of custodial sentences, whether by a youth court or the Crown Court, is governed by the general statutory sentencing framework consolidated in the PCC(S)A 2000 and the CJA 2003, together with a range of specific statutory provisions and case law dealing with particular forms of custodial sentences. The general restrictions which apply in relation to imposing any discretionary custodial sentence and in determining the length of such sentence (to be found in sections 152 and 153 of the CJA 2003) were considered at paragraphs 2.22 and 2.30, earlier in this book. These are important, and should be borne in mind throughout this Chapter. The SGC guideline, *Sentencing Youths* points out (at paragraph 11.13);

> A court imposing a custodial sentence is required to set the shortest term commensurate with the seriousness of the offence(s)—CJA 2003, s.153(2). Offence specific guidelines do not generally provide starting points or ranges for offenders aged under 18 because of the

wide range of issues that are likely to arise, and the marked differences in the sentencing framework depending on the age of the offender. Where they are provided, they are for offenders aged 17 with a provision that, for younger offenders, a court should consider whether a lower starting point is justified in recognition of the offender's age and maturity.

4.03 By the PCC(S)A 2000, section 76(1), the term 'custodial sentence' means:

(a) a sentence of imprisonment,
(b) a sentence of detention under the PCC(S)A 2000, section 90 or 91,
(c) a sentence of custody for life under the PCC(S)A 2000, section 94,
(d) a sentence of detention in a young offender institution, or
(e) a detention and training order.

The term 'sentence of imprisonment' does not include a committal for contempt of court or any kindred offence (section 76(2)).

4.04 Of the sentences listed in section 76(1) only (b) and (e) are applicable to offenders under eighteen years old. The detention and training is the 'standard' determinate custodial sentence for young offenders, with detention under section 91 being employed only in special circumstances. The mandatory sentence in cases of murder committed by an offender who was aged under eighteen at the time of the offence is detention during Her Majesty's pleasure. The age of criminal responsibility in England and Wales is ten. For offenders aged ten and eleven years old the detention and training order is not available, and for offenders aged twelve, thirteen, or fourteen it is available only where the offender qualifies as a 'persistent offender'.

4.05 Before a custodial sentence can be passed on an offender aged under eighteen, the following conditions must all be complied with:

(a) the offence must be imprisonable (see paragraph 3.04 in the previous Chapter).
(b) the offender must be legally represented, or otherwise fall within one of the exceptions set out in the PCC(S)A 2000, section 83. When dealing with an offender aged under eighteen years of age section 83 must be complied with whenever the court is considering the imposition of a custodial sentence rather than (as is the case with an adult offender) when considering the imposition of such a sentence for the first time (see paragraph 3.05 of this book).
(c) The offender must have been aged under eighteen at the date of conviction. If the offender is seventeen at the time of the offence but turns eighteen before he is convicted then he is sentenced as an eighteen-year-old and the appropriate custodial sentence is detention in a young offender institution. In such a case, however, where the offender has crossed a legally significant age threshold between the date of the offence and the date of conviction the court 'should take as its starting point the sentence likely to have been imposed on the date on which the offence was committed' (see paragraph 3.09, this book).

B DETENTION AND TRAINING ORDER

4.06 Sections 100 to 107 of the PCC(S)A 2000 provide for the detention and training order. The detention and training order is available to youth courts and to the Crown Court in respect of offenders aged under eighteen who have been convicted of an offence punishable with imprisonment in the case of an adult. As we have seen, if the offender is aged seventeen at the date of conviction but is aged eighteen when sentenced, the sentence takes effect as a detention and training order rather than a sentence of detention in a young offender institution (*Danga* (1992) 13 Cr App R (S) 408). Ordinarily, the period of detention and training shall be one-half of the full term of the order, although the Secretary of State retains a discretion to release a person under such an order at a somewhat earlier date (PCC(S)A 2000, section 102). This power is in effect delegated to the governor of the institution, who may release certain categories of young offender early on home detention curfew. The second half of the order is the period of supervision, although again the Secretary of State retains power to provide by order that the period of supervision shall be curtailed (section 103). The supervision will be carried out by an officer of a local probation board, an officer of a provider of probation services, a social worker of a local authority, or a member of a youth offending team. There is no power in the court to order an extension of the supervision period (see *B* [2005] 2 Cr App R (S) 535).

The PCC(S)A 2000, section 100(2) provides that a court shall not make a detention and **4.07** training order (a) in the case of an offender under the age of fifteen at the time of the conviction, unless it is of the opinion that he is a 'persistent offender' or (b) in the case of an offender under the age of twelve at that time, unless (i) it is of the opinion that only a custodial sentence would be adequate to protect the public from further offending by him; and (ii) the offence was committed on or after such date as the Secretary of State may by order appoint. The meaning of 'persistent offender' is considered later in this Chapter. No order has so far been made by the Secretary of State under section 100(2)(b), so this means that the minimum age for a detention and training order is twelve years old. A young offender aged ten or eleven may in some circumstances be given a custodial sentence under the PCC(S)A 2000, section 91, but they cannot receive a detention and training order (see paragraph 4.24 this Chapter). Section 100(4) states that, where the court makes a detention and training order on an offender aged under fifteen, it must state in open court that it is of the opinion mentioned in section 100(2)(a). This is in addition to the normal obligations on the sentencer under section 79(4), to give reasons for imposing a custodial sentence.

A detention and training order cannot be suspended.   **4.08**

Persistent offender

The question whether a young offender aged twelve, thirteen, or fourteen qualifies as a **4.09** persistent offender and hence is eligible for a detention and training order has caused some difficulty. Unhelpfully, the statute does not provide a definition of 'persistent offender', and not all the cases are agreed on the best approach. The case law is now subject to guidance on the matter in the SGC guideline, *Sentencing Youths*, but this has sometimes been overlooked. The resulting picture is not as clear at it might be.

The first issue is the relevance of out-of-court disposals. In *AD* [2001] 1 Cr App R (S) 202, **4.10** it was held that formal cautions recorded against the young offender were relevant in determining persistence. Formal cautions for those under eighteen years old were replaced by reprimands and warnings (the latter sometimes also known as 'final' warnings) by the Crime and Disorder Act 1998, but it is clear that these are to be regarded as relevant in the same way. Reprimands and warnings are now in their turn replaced by youth cautions since 2013 when the relevant provisions of the LASPOA 2012 came into force. These continue to be relevant in same way. The SGC guideline, *Sentencing Youths* states that a finding of persistence may be derived from previous convictions and from orders which 'require an admission or finding of guilt, such as reprimands and final warnings, but not penalty notices for disorder'. This seems right given that although warnings, reprimands etc are not criminal convictions, official records of them are retained and they will appear on the offender's antecedents in any subsequent court appearance. The guideline goes on to propose that a young offender is likely to be found to be persistent 'if he has been so dealt with in relation to imprisonable offences on at least three occasions in the past 12 months'. This aspect of the guideline has not so far been specifically endorsed by the Court of Appeal, and so it is necessary to consider some of the relevant case law.

4.11   Some of the earlier cases took a very broad approach to 'persistence', and in *S (A)* [2001] 1 Cr App R (S) 62, the Court of Appeal found that a fourteen-year-old who had no previous convictions was a persistent offender for the purposes of section 100(2)(a). S had pleaded guilty to three counts of robbery, two of possession of an offensive weapon (a kitchen knife), and one count of false imprisonment. The offences were committed in the company of two other youths, and the victims were boys of fourteen and twelve years of age. The offences were committed over a total period of two days. The Court of Appeal upheld the maximum sentence of twenty-four months. A similar approach was adopted by the Court of Appeal in *C* [2001] 1 Cr App R (S) 415, where a fourteen-year-old who had committed a burglary and an offence of allowing himself to be carried in a vehicle taken without consent, committed two further burglaries and an offence of aggravated vehicle-taking while on bail for the earlier offences. Astill J said that this criminal behaviour demonstrated a sufficient degree of persistence to satisfy the terms of the section. A detention and training order for twelve months was upheld.

4.12   It is important to remember that the 'persistent offender' provision applies only to twelve-, thirteen-, and fourteen-year-old offenders where the court is considering imposing a detention and training order. It does not apply to the sentence of detention under the PCC(S)A 2000, section 91. See paragraph 4.24, this Chapter.

Duration of the order

4.13   By section 101(3) a detention and training order is an order that the offender in respect of whom it is made shall be subject, for the term specified in the order, to a period of detention and training followed by a period of supervision. Normally the sentence falls into two equal halves. According to the SGC guideline on *Sentencing Youths*, when a court is considering the duration of a detention and training order where the offender is aged fifteen, sixteen, or seventeen, and there is no specific offence guideline, it may be appropriate, depending on the young offender's maturity as well as actual age, to consider a starting point from one-half to three-quarters of that which would have been identified for an adult offender. For offenders younger than fifteen-years old greater flexibility will be required to reflect the wide range of culpability that may be encountered.

4.14   For this sentence, unlike any other custodial sentence on the statute book, the legislation requires that the youth court or Crown Court must select a detention and training order for one of the terms specified in section 101(1). These are four, six, eight, ten, twelve, eighteen, or twenty-four months. No other sentence lengths are possible. A sentence of fourteen months would be an unlawful sentence. The statute does not say what would be the effect of passing such a sentence—whether it would be a nullity or whether it could be adjusted to a lawful period on an appeal. The selection of even-numbered terms may be designed to make calculation of the two distinct parts of the sentence easy to do and, more importantly, easy for the young offender to understand at the point of sentence. It is not clear on this rationale, however, why sentences of fourteen months or twenty months are impermissible. It may have something to do with the traditional predilection of sentencers for the terms listed in section 101(1). Historically sentences of twelve or eighteen months custody have been common, but terms of fourteen or sixteen months relatively rare. The formal restriction to the seven terms listed in the subjection has, however, given rise to practical problems. If the appropriate duration of a detention and training order would otherwise be, say, eighteen months, but the offender enters a timely guilty plea and/or there is significant mitigation, or the offender has spent time in custody on remand, in principle the court should reduce the term, at least to twelve months, to take such matters into account. There is no stopping point between eighteen and twelve months. The most anomalous effects of this, at least in relation to time spent on remand, have been alleviated by decisions of the Court of Appeal considered below.

It can be seen that four months is the minimum term for a detention and training order. **4.15** It was noted by the Divisional Court in *Inner London Crown Court, ex parte N and S* [2001] 1 Cr App R (S) 343, that one effect of the introduction of detention and training orders had been to raise the custody threshold for young offenders. Obviously this means that if the maximum penalty for the offence is three months (such as for the offence of interference with a motor vehicle under the Criminal Attempts Act 1981, section 9), then a detention and training order cannot be imposed at all. In a case where the proportionate sentence would have been four months but there has been a guilty plea or there is significant personal mitigation (including the youth of the offender) which would take the sentence below that figure, then again a detention and training order cannot be passed. In these situations a youth rehabilitation order is likely to be the appropriate sentence. It is clear that the four-month minimum cannot be reached by passing shorter consecutive detention and training orders because the shorter terms would themselves be unlawful, a point confirmed in *Ganley* [2001] 1 Cr App R (S) 60.

The youth court is not restricted, like the magistrates' court when dealing with an adult of- **4.16** fender, to a maximum sentence of six months for a single offence—the youth court can pass a detention and training order of up to twenty-four months. This is of course subject to the court not exceeding the maximum sentence for the offence concerned, and if the offence is a summary offence the maximum detention and training order would be six months (section 101(2A)). Youth court magistrates are given much greater powers to impose custody than magistrates sitting in the adult court. At first sight this looks odd given the policy of passing shorter sentences on youths, but it is designed to ensure that as many cases as possible involving young offenders are heard and sentenced in the youth court. Raising the upper sentencing limit for the youth court powers means that very few cases involving offenders under eighteen will find their way into the Crown Court. If the youth court or a Crown Court makes a mistake and passes a detention and training order for more than twenty-four months, the effect of section 101(5) is that the 'excess shall be treated as remitted'. This is an automatic effect of the statute—any surplus length simply disappears. This leads on to the question of the circumstances in which a maximum sentence of a twenty-four-months' detention and training order might be appropriate. In accordance with the general principles relating to reduction for a plea of guilty, and the SGC guideline on *Reduction of Sentence for a Guilty Plea*, it is clear that a twenty-four-month sentence could hardly ever be justified following a plea of guilty, or where there was other significant mitigation. Sentences of two years were quashed on these grounds in *Kelly* [2002] 1 Cr App R (S) 41 and *Dalby* [2006] 1 Cr App R (S) 216. One exceptional situation can arise, however, where the Crown Court takes the view that the offender deserves a sentence in excess of two years, and the offence is one which qualifies the offender for a sentence in excess of that amount under the PCC(S)A 2000, section 91. In such a case the final sentence, allowance having been made for a guilty plea and any other relevant matters, may turn out to be exactly two years, thereby justifying the maximum detention and training order. The SGC guideline specifically allows for that possibility, at paragraph 5.9. Clearly, if that is the route by which a two-year detention and training order has been arrived at, is essential for the judge to explain his reasoning. The judge did so 'impeccably' in *Fieldhouse* [2001] 1 Cr App R (S) 361, and the Court of Appeal upheld the two-year sentence even though the offender had pleaded guilty and spent time in custody on remand.

Concurrent and consecutive sentences

4.17 Concurrent and consecutive terms of detention and training may be ordered, and the principles applicable seem to be the same as those for sentences of imprisonment or detention in a young offender institution. The offender may be made subject to consecutive orders on a single sentencing occasion, or a second detention and training order may be passed on an offender who is already serving one (section 101(3)). In either case, however, the consecutive detention and training orders must not exceed twenty-four months in total (section 101(4)). If this happens, once again, any excess over that period will be automatically remitted (section 101(5)). In the case of an offender who is already serving a detention and training order, a consecutive order cannot be passed once the offender has completed the custodial part of the original order and has been released (section 101(6)). This is similar, but not identical to, to the rule in the CJA 2003, section 265, which operates in relation to sentences of imprisonment and detention in a young offender institution. If this has happened in the present context the old order is left out of account when determining whether the total detention and training order exceeds twenty-four months (section 101(7)). Section 101(13) states that, where consecutive detention and training orders are ordered, these 'shall be treated as a single term'. This might be construed as meaning 'a single term which is one of those set out in section 101(1)'. The Court of Appeal in *Norris* [2001] 1 Cr App R (S) 401, however, held that the statute should not be construed in that way and, provided that each of the individual detention and training order terms is lawful in itself, the terms need not add up to one of the terms listed. Thus consecutive terms of eight months may be imposed, giving sixteen months in all, despite the fact that sixteen months would not be lawful as a single term. It must also follow that two unlawful terms (say, five months each) cannot be run consecutively to reach a sentence of ten months, which is on the list. The sentence would be unlawful because its constituent terms are unlawful.

4.18 Section 106 of the PCC(S)A 2000 deals with the unusual situation where a young offender is serving a detention and training order and is then sentenced to a term of detention in a young offender institution, his eighteenth birthday having passed before conviction for the second offence. The section provides that if the offender has already been released from the custodial part of the order, the new sentence takes effect from the date on which it is passed, but if the offender is still serving the custodial part of the order the new sentence may at the court's discretion start from the date on which it is passed or on the date when the offender would have been released from the detention and training order. Section 106A of the PCC(S)A 2000, which was inserted by the CJA 2003, makes similar provision to deal with a sentence of detention under section 91 passed on an offender already serving a detention and training order, and vice versa. Earlier decisions in *Hayward* [2001] 2 Cr App R (S) 149 and *Lang* [2001] 2 Cr App R (S) 175 to the effect that these sentences could not run consecutively must now be read in light of section 106A. The section also envisages that an offender might be subject to concurrent sentences under section 91 and a detention and training order, but it is submitted that such combinations are best avoided. Section 106A does not appear to have been the subject of appellate consideration.

Time served on remand in custody or under qualifying curfew

4.19 Section 101 states that in determining the length of a detention and training order the court shall take account of any period for which the offender has been remanded (a) in custody, or

(b) on bail subject to a qualifying curfew condition and an electronic monitoring condition (within the meaning of section 240A of the Criminal Justice Act 2003), in connection with the offence, or any other offence the charge for which was founded on the same facts of evidence.

The requirement for the sentencer to make adjustment for time spent on remand is similar **4.20** to the rule which until recently existed under the CJA 20003, section 240 in relation to sentences of imprisonment and detention in a young offender institution, but which has been repealed by the LASPOA 2012 (see paragraph 3.15 in this book). Neither section 240, nor the 2012 Act, apply to detention and training orders, and so when passing a detention and training order the sentencer must continue to make appropriate adjustment in accordance with the PCC(S)A 2000, section 101. The requirement to take account of time spent under a qualifying curfew is identical to that which applies to the sentences of imprisonment and detention in a young offender institution, and was fully considered at paragraph 3.20 in this book.

In *Eagles* [2007] 1 Cr App R (S) 612 the seventeen-year-old offender, who pleaded guilty **4.21** to assault occasioning actual bodily harm had spent eighty-eight days in custody on remand. The judge decided that the appropriate sentence following a plea of guilty was a detention and training order for twelve months, reduced to ten months to take into account the eighty-eight days. The Court of Appeal said that this approach was wrong, and since a detention and training order fell into two parts, the first half served in custody and second half in the community, the number of days served on remand had to be doubled (to 178 days) before settling on the length of the order. The requirement on the court to make such reduction has caused difficulty in relation to the specified duration of a detention and training order, which must be for one of the seven periods set out in the PCC(S)A 2000, section 101(1). In *Inner London Crown Court, ex parte I* (2000) *The Times*, 12 May 2000, the Divisional Court stated that the duty imposed by section 101(8) was to 'take account' of the time spent on remand in custody, but this did not require the sentencer to make a 'one-for-one discount'. This general approach was confirmed by the Court of Appeal in *B* [2001] 1 Cr App R (S) 89 and by the Divisional Court in *Inner London Crown Court, ex parte N and S* [2001] 1 Cr App R (S) 343. In the last of these cases, where the young offender had spent just three days in custody on remand, the Court said that it was impossible to fine-tune a detention and training order by reference to a few days. Returning to the case of *Eagles*, the Court in that case said that if the judge had taken a starting point of twelve months and given proper allowance for the 178 days served on remand, which was equivalent to six days short of a six-month custodial sentence, the nearest permissible period was a detention and training order for six months. The final reflection on this matter is provided by Rose LJ in *Fieldhouse* [2001] 1 Cr App R (S) 361. His Lordship noted: '[i]f a defendant has spent four weeks in custody on remand that is the equivalent of a two month term. The court is likely to take such a period into account in different ways according to the length of the detention and training order...If that period is four months the court may conclude that a non-custodial sentence is appropriate. If that period is six, eight, 10 or 12 months, the court is likely to impose a period of four, six, 8 or 10 months respectively. If that period is 18 or 24 months, the court may well conclude that no reduction can properly be made...'.

Breach of detention and training order

Section 104 of the PCC(S)A 2000 provides powers in relation to breach of the supervi- **4.22** sion requirements in a detention and training order. If it is proved to the satisfaction of a youth court acting for the relevant local justice area that the offender has failed to comply with supervision requirements specified in the order, the court may order the offender to be detained in 'youth detention accommodation' for a period of three months, or the remainder of the term of the order, whichever is the shorter, or it may impose on the offender a fine not exceeding level 3 on the standard scale. 'Youth detention accommodation' means a secure training centre, a young offender institution, or local authority accommodation (section 107). If a fine is imposed it will normally be appropriate to order that the parent or guardian of the young offender should pay (PCC(S)A 2000, section 137(2)). Since December 2012, when the LASPOA 2012 section 80 was brought into effect the court also has power to order a period of supervision for three months, or the remainder of the term of the order, whichever is the shorter. In *H v Doncaster Youth Court* (2009) 173 JP 162 the Divisional Court held that the 'remainder of the term' of the order meant the period of the order which was outstanding at the date when the court dealt with the breach, and not the period outstanding from the date of the breach itself. The court felt that the wording of the provision was ambiguous, and chose to interpret it in the way which benefited the defendant. This decision is reversed by section 80, which makes it clear that the 'remainder of the term' is to be measured from the date of the offender's breach. This brings the practical effect of section 104 into line with section 105, discussed in the next paragraph. An offender may appeal against an order made under section 104 to the Crown Court.

4.23 Section 105 relates to the commission of a further imprisonable offence by the offender during the term of a detention and training order. The court, whether or not it passes any other sentence on the offender, may order him to be detained in 'youth detention accommodation' from the date of the new order for the whole or part of the period between the date of commission of the new offence and the date at which the full term of the original order would have come to an end. Such an order may be made even where the offender is convicted of the new offence after the full term of the original order has come to an end, as long as the offence was committed during the order. The reinstated part of the sentence may be served before any sentence imposed for the new offence, or it may be served concurrently with that sentence, but the reinstated period should be disregarded in determining the appropriate length of the new sentence. This course was taken in *Eagles* [2007] 1 Cr App R (S) 612 (see paragraph 4.21) where the Court of Appeal, having reduced the new detention and training order to six months, upheld the order of the judge that it should run consecutively to a term of seventy-six days which was unexpired from the previous order.

C   DETENTION UNDER THE PCC(S)A 2000, SECTION 91

4.24 Section 91 of the PCC(S)A 2000 gives the Crown Court (but not a youth court) power to sentence a young offender convicted of one of a list of certain 'grave crimes' to detention for a term not exceeding the maximum prison sentence carried by the offence in question. Set against the detention and training order, it will be seen that the section 91 power can be used in the Crown Court, where appropriate, to impose much longer sentences than the two years permitted under a detention and training order. An offence of domestic burglary, which falls within section 91, attracts a maximum sentence of two years under a detention and training order but (at least in theory) a maximum of fourteen years under section 91. A sentence under section 91 may also be for life, where the crime falling within section 91 carries life imprisonment as its maximum sentence. Robbery is an important example. Because the 'standard' custodial sentence for young offenders is the detention and training order, sentences under section 91 are normally for longer (sometimes much longer) than two years, but there are some circumstances in which a sentence under section 91 for less than two years is permissible and appropriate.

4.25 A sentence under the PCC(S)A 2000, section 91 cannot be suspended.

Committal with a view to sentence under section 91

The power under section 91 is reserved to the Crown Court after the offender has been **4.26** convicted on indictment. A youth court cannot pass this sentence in any circumstances, nor may the Crown Court do so if the young offender is sent there after a finding of guilt in a youth court (*McKenna* (1985) 7 Cr App R (S) 348). In a case where the offender has committed an offence which falls within section 91, and the circumstances are so serious that a sentence in excess of two years is likely to be required, the magistrates in the youth court should commit the young offender for trial to the Crown Court. The magistrates (or their clerk) should also be alert to the possibility of committing a case where the offender is aged ten or eleven, or is aged twelve, thirteen, or fourteen but is not a persistent offender. In these instances the young offender is not eligible to receive a detention and training order, but the statutory restrictions do not apply to the sentence under section 91, which can be passed on a young offender aged ten or eleven, and where there is no equivalent constraint in relation to persistence. Whether, or in what circumstances these cases should be committed to the Crown Court has been controversial.

In *AM* [1998] 1 WLR 363, the Court of Appeal forcefully reminded magistrates of the **4.27** need to commit for trial any case which might merit detention under section 91. In *J-R and G* [2001] 1 Cr App R (S) 109 the Court of Appeal upheld a sentence of detention under section 91 in respect of an offender aged fourteen who was not a persistent offender and so could not have received a detention and training order. In *R (D) v Manchester City Youth Court* [2002] 1 Cr App R (S) 573, however, the Divisional Court quashed a committal for a trial of a boy aged thirteen who was charged with indecent assault. Again, the boy was not a 'persistent offender', and so a detention and training order could not have been imposed. In this case Gage J said that committal with a view to sentence under section 91 should normally be ordered only where a custodial sentence in excess of two years was envisaged by the youth court. That approach was endorsed by the Divisional Court in the leading case of *R (W) v Southampton Youth Court* [2003] 1 Cr App R (S) 455, where Lord Woolf CJ said that the general policy of the legislation was that young offenders should, wherever possible, be tried by a youth court. If an offender did not qualify for a detention and training order because he was under fifteen and not a persistent offender, the most likely outcome was a non-custodial penalty. Only exceptionally, if the appropriate sentence would be twenty-four months or thereabouts, would committal to Crown Court with a view to sentence under section 91 be appropriate. *J-R and G* was not followed in *R(M), Waltham Forest Youth Court* [2003] 1 Cr App R (S) 67, where Sedley LJ went so far as to say that detention under section 91 simply cannot be used in a case where Parliament had ruled out the use of a detention and training order. The SGC guideline, *Sentencing Youths* says (at paragraph 12.11) that a young person aged ten or eleven (or aged twelve, thirteen, or fourteen, but not a persistent offender) should be committed to Crown Court only where charged with an offence of such gravity that a sentence exceeding two years is a realistic possibility. That seems to settle the matter in principle, but the sentencing statistics show some cases each year where orders under section 91 for less than two years have been passed.

Sentencing under section 91

The young offender must have been convicted of an offence falling within section 91. The **4.28** basic principle is that an offence falls within section 91 if it is punishable in the case of an adult with imprisonment for fourteen years or more, but section 91 has been amended over time and some other offences have been included where the maximum penalty is less than fourteen years. It is therefore necessary to set out the section in more detail:

4.29 By section 91(1), the power to sentence under section 91 applies

> where a person aged under eighteen is convicted on indictment of—
>
> (a) an offence punishable in the case of a person aged 21 or over with imprisonment for 14 years or more, not being an offence the sentence for which is fixed by law; or
>
> (b) an offence under section 3 of the Sexual Offences Act 2003 (sexual assault); or
>
> (c) an offence under section 13 of the SOA (child sex offences committed by children or young persons); or
>
> (d) an offence under section 25 of the SOA (sexual activity with a child family member); or
>
> (e) an offence under section 26 of the SOA (inciting a child family member to engage in sexual activity).

4.30 Sections 91(1A) to 91(1C) extend the scope of the section 91 power to certain offences under Firearms Act 1968, and under the Violent Crime Reduction Act 2006, where Parliament has laid down prescribed minimum sentences. Section 91(5) explains that where these provisions apply the court should pass a sentence of detention under this section for a term of at least the term provided for in that section, but not exceeding the maximum term of imprisonment with which the offence is punishable. If a young person is charged with such an offence and the criteria for that sentence would be likely to be satisfied if the young person was convicted, there is an exception to the normal presumption that young offenders should be tried in the youth court and a sentence of detention under section 91 may be passed in the Crown Court where the provisions apply. There can be a departure from the minimum prescribed sentence if the Crown Court finds that there are 'exceptional circumstances'.

4.31 Section 91(3) says that if the court is of the opinion that neither a youth rehabilitation order nor a detention and training order is suitable, the court may sentence the offender to be detained for such period, not exceeding the maximum term of imprisonment with which the offence is punishable in the case of a person aged twenty-one years or over, as may be specified in the sentence. Section 91(4) states that subsection (3) is subject (in particular) to sections 152 and 153 of the CJA 2003.

4.32 The general approach of fixing eligibility for sentence under section 91 to offences which carry a maximum sentence of fourteen years or more creates some apparent anomalies, given the lack of any clear rationale for the setting of maximum penalties generally. Offences falling within section 91 include manslaughter, arson, wounding with intent, robbery, domestic burglary, racially aggravated criminal damage, possessing cannabis with intent to supply, and handling stolen goods. Offences falling outside the scope of section 91 include riot, violent disorder, sexual assault, unlawful wounding (even if racially aggravated), assault occasioning actual bodily harm (even if racially aggravated), non-domestic burglary, and aggravated vehicle taking (unless it results in a death). It should be noted, however, that some of the offences falling outside the scope of section 91 are 'specified offences' and the young offender may thereby be eligible for an extended sentence (see paragraph 4.39 later in this Chapter). Mistakes have been made in the past by assuming that a commercial burglary is included within section 91, when it is not (see *Brown* (1995) 16 Cr App R (S) 932).

4.33 The Court of Appeal has said on numerous occasions that the power to order detention under section 91 should be used sparingly, as a last resort, reflecting the language of section 91(3) and (4). General guidance on the use of section 91 was provided by Lord Lane CJ in *Fairhurst* [1986] 1 WLR 1374, in which his Lordship commented that it was not necessary, in order to invoke the provisions of section 91, that the crime committed should be one of exceptional gravity, such as attempted murder, manslaughter, wounding with intent, armed robbery or the like but, on the other hand, that it was not good sentencing practice to pass a sentence of detention under section 91 simply because the maximum available sentence of youth custody (now a detention and training order) appeared to be on the low side for the particular offence committed. These comments were endorsed by Lord Bingham CJ in *AM* [1998] 1 WLR 363. Lord Bingham also stated that, while a Crown Court sentencer should not exceed the twenty-four-month limit without much careful thought, if it was concluded that a longer (even if not much longer) sentence was called for then the court should impose whatever it considered the appropriate period of detention under section 91 to be. Traditionally the sentence has been used in offences involving grave violence or where there is a significant danger to the public. A sentence of detention under section 91 was upheld in principle, but reduced from seven years to six years, in *Taylor* (1995) 16 Cr App R (S) 570, where the seventeen-year-old offender had committed a robbery with great violence on a seventy-year-old man. The circumstances in which section 91 detention is appropriate for non-violent but serous property offences is less clear. In *Oakes* (1983) 5 Cr App R (S) 389 the Court of Appeal quashed a sentence of thirty-months' detention under section 91 where a sixteen-year-old offender had burgled the homes of several elderly people by tricking his way in and stealing items while his accomplice kept the victim occupied. The Court of Appeal said that section 91 was not meant to be used for simple offences of dishonesty, however despicable they might be. In contrast in *Simmons* (1995) 16 Cr App R (S) 801, five years' detention under section 91 was upheld on a sixteen-year-old who pleaded guilty to seven counts of house burglary and asked for sixty-seven similar offences to be taken into consideration.

If the Crown Court is dealing with a case in which the young offender has been convicted **4.34** of several offences, one or more of which fall within section 91 and one or more of which do not, the Court of Appeal in *Mills* [1998] 2 Cr App R (S) 128 has said that it will normally be appropriate to pass a sentence under section 91 for the eligible offences but to take into account the other offences by way of the length of the term imposed under section 91. It may then be appropriate to pass 'no separate penalty' for the lesser offences. This approach was followed in *Reynolds* [2007] 2 Cr App R (S) 553, where the young offender was sentenced for wounding with intent and assault occasioning actual bodily harm, offences committed against the same victim. The judge imposed detention under section 91 for six years for the former offence and one year for the latter, concurrently. The Court of Appeal said that a total of six years was appropriate, but that the latter offence did not qualify for a sentence under section 91. Accordingly that sentence was quashed, and no separate penalty substituted.

An offender serving a sentence of detention under section 91 will be released automatically **4.35** on licence after he has served one-half of the appropriate custodial term.

Concurrent and consecutive sentences

Section 106A of the PCC(S)A 2000, which was inserted by the CJA 2003, makes provi- **4.36** sion to deal with a sentence of detention under section 91 passed on an offender already serving a detention and training order, and vice versa. Earlier decisions in *Hayward* [2001] 2 Cr App R (S) 149 and *Lang* [2001] 2 Cr App R (S) 175 to the effect that these sentences could not run consecutively must now be read in light of section 106A. The section also envisages that an offender might be subject to concurrent sentences under section 91 and a detention and training order, but it is submitted that such combinations are best avoided. Section 106A does not appear to have been the subject of appellate consideration.

D DETENTION FOR LIFE

4.37 An offender aged under eighteen years old who is convicted of an offence which is punishable in the case of an adult with a maximum sentence of life imprisonment may be sentenced to detention for life under section 91. In many respects the sentence of detention for life is parallel to the discretionary life sentence for adult offenders and the sentence of custody for life under section 93 for offenders aged eighteen, nineteen, or twenty years. All the limitations on the imposition of a determinate sentence under section 91 apply here too, so that, in particular, the offence must have been sent by the youth court for trial in the Crown Court. This is in contrast to the sentence of detention for life where it is imposed under the CJA 2003, section 226, where it is possible for the youth court to deal with the case and then commit the young offender to the Crown Court for sentence. By section 226 an offender aged under eighteen who is convicted of a 'specified offence' (which means a violent offence or a sexual offence listed in schedule 15 to the CJA 2003) which is also a 'serious offence' (which means in this context an offence punishable with life imprisonment in the case of adult) may attract a sentence of detention for life, provided that the court considers that there is 'a significant risk to members of the public of serious harm occasioned by the commission by him or further specified offences' (the 'dangerousness test', as to which see paragraph 3.64, this book) (section 226(1)). If all these criteria are fulfilled the court may impose a sentence of detention for life under the CJA 2003, section 226 (section 226(2)). If the young offender has been convicted by a youth court, and it appears to that court that the above criteria are met, the court must commit the young offender to the Crown Court for sentence. Whether detention for life is imposed under the PCC(S)A 2000, section 91 or the CJA 2003, section 226, the Crown Court must fix a minimum period under the PCC(S)A 2000, section 82A (see paragraph 3.67 in this book). A person sentenced to detention for life will remain on licence after release from custody for the rest of his life.

4.38 Detention for life is, understandably, rarely imposed. The following examples were all imposed under section 91 (or an equivalently worded predecessor to that section). In *Carr* [1996] 1 Cr App R (S) 191, the offender was a fifteen-year-old girl who pleaded guilty to causing grievous bodily harm with intent, having stabbed another schoolgirl in the back with a knife. She asked for two other offences, in which she had tried to strangle other schoolgirls, to be taken into consideration. Reports revealed other instances of disturbed and aggressive behaviour and indicated that the defendant was 'exceptionally dangerous'. An indeterminate sentence under section 91 was imposed. A court which passes a sentence of detention under section 91 for life must specify a period to be served in accordance with the PCC(S)A 2000, section 82A (see paragraph 3.67, this book). In *JM* [2003] 1 Cr App R (S) 245, a sentence of detention for life was upheld in the case of a boy of fourteen convicted of causing grievous bodily harm with intent, who had a history of violent and disturbed behaviour. He had struck a man on the back of the head with a wooden stake, fracturing his skull, and causing long-lasting injuries. It was accepted that the offender was likely to remain a serious danger to the community for the foreseeable future, and no confident prediction of improvement could be made. Taking a notional determinate sentence of seven years, a period of three-and-a-half years was specified under the PCC(S)A 2000, section 82A. This was reduced by the Court of Appeal by four months, to take account of time spent in custody on remand.

E EXTENDED SENTENCE OF DETENTION

4.39 The Crown Court may impose an extended sentence of detention on a person aged under eighteen at the date of conviction if the offence is a 'specified offence' (which means an offence listed in schedule 15 to the CJA 2003, irrespective of the maximum penalty for the offence), the court considers that there is 'a significant risk to members of the public of serious harm occasioned by the commission by him or further specified offences' (the 'dangerousness test', as to which see paragraph 3.64, this book), and the case is not one where the court is required under section 226(2) to impose a sentence of detention for life (section 228(1)). The extended sentence of detention may be imposed only if the appropriate determinate custodial term would be at least four years (section 228(2A)). If the young offender has been convicted by a youth court, and it appears to that court that the above criteria are met, the court must commit the young offender to the Crown Court for sentence. In the leading case of *Lang* [2006] 2 Cr App R (S) 3, and again in *JW* [2009] 2 Cr App R (S) 94, the Court of Appeal has said that when a court is considering whether a young offender poses a significant risk of serious harm in the future it is important to bear in mind that, within a shorter time than adults, they may change and develop. This, together with their maturity, may be highly pertinent when assessing what their future conduct may be. An extended sentence of detention is a sentence of detention the total term of which is equal to the aggregate of the appropriate custodial term and a further period (the extension period) for which the offender is to be subject to licence and is of such length as the court considers necessary for the propose of protecting members of the public from serious harm occasioned by the commission by him of further specified offences. The appropriate custodial term must not exceed the maximum penalty for the offence and must never be less than four years. The extension period must not exceed five years in the case of a specified violent offence or eight years in the case of a specified sexual offence (section 228(4)). The young offender will be on licence until the conclusion of the whole term of the sentence (see *S; Burt* [2006] 2 Cr App R (S) 35). The total term of the extended sentence must not exceed the maximum penalty for the offence (section 228(5)).

4.40 For concurrent and consecutive extended sentences see paragraphs 3.54 to 3.56 in the previous Chapter in this book.

4.41 An offender serving an extended sentence of detention will be released automatically on licence after he has served one-half of the appropriate custodial term.

KEY DOCUMENTS[1]

Sentencing Guidelines Council, Definitive Guideline, *Robbery* (effective 1 August 2006).

Sentencing Guidelines Council, *Breach of an Anti-Social Behaviour Order* (effective 5 January 2009).

Sentencing Guidelines Council, Definitive Guideline, *Sentencing Youths* (effective 30 November 2009).

Sentencing Council, Definitive Guideline, *Sexual Offences* (effective 1 April 2014).

---

[1] All sentencing guidelines can be found on the Sentencing Council website: <http://sentencingcouncil.judiciary.gov.uk/>.

5

CUSTODIAL SENTENCES: MANDATORY AND PRESCRIBED SENTENCES

A MANDATORY LIFE IMPRISONMENT FOR MURDER

5.01 Life imprisonment is the mandatory sentence for murder when committed by an offender aged 21 or over (Murder (Abolition of Death Penalty) Act 1965, section 1(1)). The sentence for an offender under the age of twenty-one who is convicted of murder is custody for life under section 93 of the PCC(S)A 2000 (see paragraph 5.07, this Chapter), unless the offender was aged under eighteen at the date of the offence, in which case the sentence is detention during Her Majesty's pleasure, under section 90 of that Act (see paragraph 5.09, this Chapter). These three sentences are all mandatory sentences, so that the Crown Court judge has no discretion whatever over the choice of the sentence. Murder is the only crime in English law which has a mandatory sentence. There are numerous references in the sentencing legislation to a sentence which is 'fixed by law'. The only offence the sentence for which is fixed by law is murder, which includes participation in the murder as a secondary party: *A-G's Reference (No 24 of 2008)(Sanchez)* [2009] 2 Cr App R (S) 41. The mandatory sentence does not apply to offences which are closely related to murder, such as attempted murder, conspiracy to murder, or to manslaughter.

5.02 The existence of the fixed penalty for murder is clearly anomalous in our sentencing system, and it has been the subject of considerable criticism from the judiciary and from commentators over the years. The sentence can be attacked on the basis that, at least on the face of it, it permits no judicial discretion in the sentencing of a crime where offender culpability can vary considerably, and where that ought to be reflected in the sentence passed by the court. However, the Crown Court judge has a very important task in every murder case of setting the minimum term which the offender must serve in custody before being considered for early release. This task is carried out subject to guidelines established directly by Parliament and set out in schedule 21 to the CJA 2003. These guidelines are the only ones to be issued directly in this way, rather than via the Court of Appeal, the Sentencing Guidelines Council or the Sentencing Council. Indeed they are properly not called 'guidelines' at all, but rather 'general principles'. One point to note is that a judge imposing a sentence for murder is, by section 269(5) required to 'have regard to' the general principles in schedule 21, rather than being required to 'follow' them, as has been the case for all true sentencing guidelines since 2010. Schedule 21 is structured much like other sentencing guidelines, however, and was clearly modelled on guidelines issued by the Lord Chief Justice in a Practice Statement issued in 2002. That Statement was superseded by the 2003 Act provisions. The Lord Chancellor retains power to amend schedule 21 by order, but must consult with the Sentencing Council before doing so. The scheme, as set out in schedule 21, provides for ranges and starting points for the setting of minimum terms which are substantially higher than those which existed prior to the 2003 Act and in the 2002 Practice Direction. This has led to very significant increases in minimum terms imposed for murder cases since 2003, and there have inevitably been knock-on effects in relation to more severe sentencing for related offences such as attempted murder and manslaughter. Apart from that the schedule 21 scheme has attracted a good deal of judicial criticism. Schedule 21 is set out and considered in more detail at paragraph 14.04 later in this book.

Minimum terms in murder

By the CJA 2003, section 269(2), the court must normally make an order that the early re- **5.03** lease provisions of the Crime (Sentences) Act 1997, section 28(5) to (8), are to apply to the offender as soon as he has served the part of his sentence which is specified in the order. This exercise was once known as fixing the tariff, but has now become known as fixing the minimum term in a murder case. The part of the sentence which must be so served in full (the minimum term) is such as the court considers appropriate, taking into account (a) the seriousness of the offence, or the combination of the offence and any one or more offences associated with it, and (b) the effect of any direction which it would have given under section 240ZA of the CJA 2003 (crediting periods of remand in custody) or under section 240A (crediting periods of remand on bail spent under qualifying curfew), if it had sentenced him to a determinate term of imprisonment (section 269(3)). Notwithstanding the replacement of section 240 by section 240ZA, in a murder case the judge fixing the minimum term will still need to know the number of days spent by the offender on remand in custody in order to make appropriate adjustment to the minimum term.

If the offender was aged twenty-one or over when he committed the offence, the court **5.04** may, however, because of the seriousness of the offence, order that the early release provisions are not to apply to the offender (section 269(4)). An order under section 269(4) has the effect of imposing a 'whole life' minimum term, which means that the offender must remain in prison for the rest of their life, with no possibility of obtaining release. It was held in *Secretary of State for the Home Department, ex parte Hindley* [2001] 1 AC 410, before the 2003 Act, that a 'whole life tariff' did not infringe the ECHR Article 3 (no-one shall be subjected to torture or to inhuman or degrading treatment or punishment). This was confirmed by the Court of Appeal in *Bieber* [2009] 1 WLR 223, the Court noting that even in such a case the Secretary of State has power to release the offender on compassionate grounds under the Crime (Sentences) Act 1997, section 30(1). The compatibility of the 'whole life minimum term' provision when sentencing for murder with Article 3 of the ECHR is currently a matter of dispute. In *Oakes* [2013] HRLR 9 a five-strong Court of Appeal, confirmed earlier decisions including *Bieber* [2009] 1 WLR 223, and having regard to the decision of the European Court of Human Rights in *Vinter v UK* (2012) 55 EHRR 34, found that a whole life order is *not* incompatible with Article 3. It was stressed that a whole life order was a sentence of last resort for cases of the most extreme gravity and there was always the residual possibility that the Home Secretary could order the release of any offender on grounds of compassion. However, there was a further appeal in *Vinter* to the Grand Chamber of the European Court, and in *Vinter v UK* [2013] ECHR 645 it was decided that for any sentence of life imprisonment to be compatible with Article 3 there had to be a provision which allowed for the possibility of review of the prisoner's case and the possibility of release. Despite this decision, the Court of Appeal in *Attorney-General's Ref (No 69 of 2013)* [2014] EWCA Crim 188 has confirmed the line which it took in *Oakes*, that the possibility of release on compassionate grounds under section 30 of the 1997 Act means that English law is compliant with the ECHR.

5.05 It is important to appreciate that a judge fixing the minimum term to be served as part of the mandatory life sentence for murder is concerned with the seriousness of the offence, and not with the dangerousness of the offender. There is no 'dangerousness test' to be passed, as there is in the case of a discretionary life sentence, or an extended sentence of imprisonment. In murder cases the necessary element of public protection is provided by the indeterminate nature of the life sentence itself, and becomes the responsibility of the Parole Board once the minimum term has been served in full by the offender (*Leigers* [2005] 2 Cr App R (S) 654). Schedule 21 provides that the obligation to have regard to any guilty plea applies to the fixing of the minimum term. Clearly a life sentence is an unknowable period of time and the guilty plea discount cannot attach to it. The guilty plea discount does, however, impact on all minimum terms, except the rare cases where a whole life order is passed, where there can be no reduction for a guilty plea. The most important difference between a determinate sentence and a minimum term set in a case of murder is that in the former the offender will (in most circumstances) be released from prison at the halfway point of the sentence, whereas a minimum term must be served in full. So, the reduction for a plea of guilty in the case of a minimum term needs to be halved in order to achieve the same effect (a one-third reduction for plea in the case of a determinate sentence of, say, ten years, equates to a one-sixth reduction for plea in the case of a minimum term of ten years). Even so, the whole question of reducing sentence for a plea of guilty in a murder case is a very sensitive issue, and the SGC in its guideline on *Reduction in Sentence for a Guilty Plea* decided that (in murder cases only) in addition to the percentage reduction it was necessary to have a cap on the total number of years which could be deducted. So, the formula is that the reduction for a plea of guilty cannot exceed one-sixth and will never exceed five years. One-sixth is of course appropriate only where the plea of guilty was tendered at the first reasonable opportunity, with a recommended 5 per cent reduction for a late plea.

Appeal

5.06 Since the sentence for murder is a mandatory sentence, there is no appeal against it. By section 9(1A) of the Criminal Appeal Act 1968, however, an offender may appeal against an order specifying a minimum term, or an order under section 269(4) that the early release provisions are not to apply. Also, the Attorney General may refer an order specifying a minimum term under section 269(2) to the Court of Appeal under the CJA 1988, section 36(3A), on the basis that the minimum term was unduly lenient. Section 36(3A) states that the Court of Appeal 'shall not, in deciding what order under that section is appropriate for the case, make any allowance for the fact that the person to whom it relates is being sentenced for a second time'. This is a reference to the normal approach on an Attorney General's reference for review of a sentence on the basis that it was unduly lenient, that some reduction from the increased sentence is appropriate to reflect the fact that the offender has had to face the prospect of being sentenced twice over. Subsection (3A) creates an important exception to that so-called 'double jeopardy' principle.

B CUSTODY FOR LIFE

5.07 Section 93 of the PCC(S)A 2000 states that where a person under twenty-one is convicted of murder the court shall sentence him to custody for life unless he is liable to receive a sentence of detention during Her Majesty's pleasure (murder committed by a person aged under eighteen at the time of the offence). Custody for life under section 93 is a mandatory sentence and should be distinguished from custody life as a discretionary sentence available for eighteen-, nineteen-, and twenty-year-old offenders as the maximum penalty for offences punishable with life imprisonment in the case of an adult. Sections 269 to 277 and schedule 21 apply to the mandatory sentence of custody for life as they do to the mandatory sentence of life imprisonment.

5.08 The various starting points in schedule 21 in principle apply to offenders aged eighteen, nineteen, or twenty as they do to those aged twenty-one and over, save that no offender aged under twenty-one can receive a whole life minimum term (paragraph 4(1)). Of course the age of the offender (both in terms of actual age and level of maturity) are always relevant matters. In *Peters* [2005] 2 Cr App R (S) 627 it was said that although eighteenth and twenty-first birthdays represented significant moments in the life of an individual, they are not necessarily indicative of the individual's true level of maturity, insight, and understanding. There are no sudden changes in growing up. The Court added that a judge should always employ a flexible starting point for an offender aged between eighteen and twenty-one, to take account of the mitigation which would normally arise from an offender's youth, and contribute to a desirable sentencing consistency. It is not the case that, as soon as an offender turns eighteen, the minimum term will automatically move from twelve years to fifteen years.

C DETENTION DURING HER MAJESTY'S PLEASURE

5.09 Section 90 of the PCC(S)A 2000 provides that where a person convicted of murder appears to the court to have been under eighteen at the time the offence was committed the court shall sentence him to be detained during Her Majesty's pleasure. The cross-heading to the section refers to 'detention *at* Her Majesty's pleasure' rather than *during* Her Majesty's pleasure, so there is a little uncertainty about the actual name of this sentence. More importantly, it will be seen that eligibility for the sentence turns upon the age of the offender at the time the offence was committed, not (as is the normal rule) his age at the date of conviction. Of course most young offenders will still be under eighteen at the date of conviction, but the rule can operate oddly where an individual is not brought to justice until years after the event. In January 2012, the two offenders Dobson and Norris were convicted of the murder of Stephen Lawrence. They had been aged sixteen and fifteen at the time of the murder, but were aged thirty-six and thirty-five when convicted and sentenced. The correct sentence in each case was detention during Her Majesty's pleasure. As with the other mandatory sentences, detention during Her Majesty's pleasure applies only to cases of murder (see *Abbott*

[1964] 1 QB 489). A person so sentenced will be detained in such place and under such conditions as the Secretary of State may direct or arrange (PCC(S)A 2000, section 92).

5.10 Sections 269 to 277 and schedule 21 apply to the mandatory sentence of detention during Her Majesty's pleasure as they do to the mandatory sentence of life imprisonment. However, no offender aged under twenty-one can receive a whole life minimum term (paragraph 4(1)), and the starting point for sentence for murder committed by a person aged under eighteen is always twelve years. Of course the age of the offender (both in terms of actual age and level of maturity) are always important considerations which the judge must bear in mind when fixing the minimum period to be served. The House of Lords in *Secretary of State for the Home Department ex parte Venables* [1998] AC 407 stressed that when passing such a sentence on a very young offender the welfare of that child or young person was of great importance, and there should be flexibility in the early release arrangements so that the executive authorities could review the case promptly in the light of progress during the period of detention.

D PRESCRIBED MINIMUM SENTENCE FOR THIRD CLASS A DRUG TRAFFICKING OFFENCE

5.11 Section 110 of the PCC(S)A 2000 states that where:

(a) a person is convicted of a Class A drug trafficking offence,

(b) at the time when that offence was committed he was aged 18 or over and had been convicted in any part of the UK of two other Class A drug trafficking offences (or equivalent offence in another EU Member State), and

(c) one of those offences was committed after he had been convicted of the other,

the Crown Court must impose a custodial sentence of at least seven years, unless the court is of the opinion that there are particular circumstances which relate to any of the offences or to the offender which would make it unjust to do so in all the circumstances (section 110(2) and (2A)).

For the purposes of section 110, section 110(5) defines 'drug trafficking offence' by reference to the Proceeds of Crime Act 2002, schedule 2, and 'custodial sentence' means imprisonment or detention in a young offender institution (section 110(6)). Nothing in section 110 prevents a hospital order being imposed on an offender in an appropriate case (Mental Health Act 1983, section 37(1A)). If a person is charged with a drug trafficking offence which is normally triable either way and the circumstances are that if he was convicted of that offence he could be sentenced for it under section 110, then the offence is triable only on indictment. In a case where either of the earlier Class A drug trafficking offences was dealt with by way of an absolute or conditional discharge, and the offender was not subsequently sentenced for the offence, the conviction for that offence is a conviction for limited purposes only (by virtue of section 14 of the PCC(S)A 2000), and does not count as a qualifying conviction for the purposes of section 110.

5.12 In *Harvey* [2000] 1 Cr App R (S) 368, the Court of Appeal upheld a sentence of seven years' imprisonment on an offender imposed under this section. Lord Bingham CJ said that the object of the provision plainly was to require courts to impose a sentence of at least seven years in cases where otherwise they would not, or might not, otherwise have done so. This provision is not mandatory, however, since the court may impose a lesser sentence if it finds that there are 'particular circumstances' relating to the offences or to the offender which would make the seven-year sentence unjust. If the court takes this line it must explain in open court why it is of that opinion and what the particular circumstances are which would make the sentence unjust (section 110(3)). In *McDonagh* [2006] 1 Cr App R (S) 647 Gage LJ in the Court of Appeal contrasted this phrase with 'exceptional circumstances', which applies in relation to the minimum sentences for firearms offences and may perhaps be taken to imply a somewhat stricter test. Lord Bingham in *Harvey* declined to indicate what might amount to particular circumstances 'which would make it unjust' to impose the prescribed sentence, but a number of later cases provide some illustration. The cases are fact-specific, however, and it is difficult to identify any clear principles. In *Pearce* [2005] 1 Cr App R (S) 364 it was held that the offender fell squarely within the provision and the seven-year sentence was upheld despite the fact that the latest offence involved only a small quantity of cocaine and there was no question of commercial supply, but in *Turner* [2006] 1 Cr App R (S) 565 the prescribed sentence was reduced because the offender had acted as an intermediary between drug users and was not involved in commercial supply. In *Lucas* [2012] 2 Cr App R (S) 57 a three-strikes drug trafficking sentence was upheld despite the offender being eighteen at the time of the offence and previous offences committed when he was fifteen and seventeen. Court must 'loyally apply' the section—the facts fell 'fairly and squarely within the provision'. In *McDonough* [2006] 1 Cr App R (S) 647 the Court reduced the prescribed sentence to four-and-a-half years, this time for the more principled reason that the previous convictions were very old, dating from 1990 and 1993.

Guilty plea

Where the offender has pleaded guilty, the sentencing court is required to take into account **5.13** the stage at which he indicated his intention to plead guilty and the circumstances in which this indication was given (CJA 2003, section 144). Section 144(2) states that in the case of an offence coming within section 110 the court may not impose a sentence which would be less than 80 per cent of the minimum sentence specified. Eighty per cent of seven years produces a sentence slightly less than five years and eight months. The 'not less than 80 per cent rule' is potentially misleading. It does not necessarily mean that the maximum reduction for a guilty plea under section 110 is 20 per cent (although practitioners sometimes have referred to it in that way). If the sentencer deals with the case by taking a starting point above the seven years' minimum sentence, a sentence reduction to reflect the guilty plea of, say, one third, may be perfectly appropriate on the facts provided that the final sentence is not less than 80 per cent of the minimum sentence. This was clearly explained in the decision in *Gray*, a case under section 111, but the principle is equally applicable here. In *Darling* [2010] 1 Cr App R (S) 420 the Court of Appeal held that, where the sentencing judge is of the opinion that there are particular circumstances which would make it unjust to impose the minimum sentence, and adopts a starting point which is less than seven years, then the limited reduction permissible for a guilty plea no longer applies and the judge may in an appropriate case reduce sentence to reflect a guilty plea to a sentence which is less than 80 per cent of the minimum sentence specified. For these reasons it is highly desirable for the judge to explain how the final sentence has been arrived at, as the Court of Appeal pointed out in *Brown* [2000] 2 Cr App R (S) 435.

E PRESCRIBED MINIMUM SENTENCE FOR THIRD DOMESTIC BURGLARY

Section 111 of the PCC(S)A 2000 provides that where: **5.14**

(a) a person is convicted of a domestic burglary;
(b) at the time when the domestic burglary was committed he was aged 18 or over and had been convicted in England and Wales of two other domestic burglaries; and

(c) one of those other burglaries was committed after he had been convicted of the other, and both of them were committed after 30 November 1999,

the Crown Court shall impose a custodial term of at least three years except where the court is of the opinion that there are particular circumstances which relate to any of the offences or the offender which would make it unjust to do so in all the circumstances.

For the purposes of section 111, 'domestic burglary' means a burglary committed in respect of a building or part of a building which is a dwelling (section 111(5)), and it must always be established that each of the relevant burglaries was in fact a domestic burglary (*Miller* [2011] 1 Cr App R (S) 7). This should now always be specified on the indictment. It is not appropriate to leave it to a *Newton* hearing at the sentencing stage to decide whether the property was a person's home or not (*Flack* [2013] EWCA Crim 115). An attempt to commit a domestic burglary is not a qualifying offence (see *Maguire* [2003] 2 Cr App R (S) 40). 'Custodial sentence' means imprisonment or detention in a young offender institution (section 110(6)). Nothing in section 111 prevents a hospital order being imposed on an offender in an appropriate case (Mental Health Act 1983, section 37(1A)). If a person is charged with a domestic burglary offence which would normally be triable either way and the circumstances are that if he was convicted of that offence he could be sentenced for it under section 111, then the offence is triable only on indictment.

5.15 In a case where either of the earlier domestic burglaries was dealt with by way of an absolute or conditional discharge, and the offender was not subsequently sentenced for the offence, the conviction for that offence is a conviction for limited purposes only (by virtue of section 14 of the PCC(S)A 2000), and does not count as a qualifying conviction for the purposes of section 111. A finding of guilt in a youth court is equivalent to a conviction, and counts for these purposes (*Frost* [2001] 2 Cr App R (S) 124). It is unclear whether an earlier spent conviction for domestic burglary counts as a qualifying conviction. It is submitted that such a conviction does count, but that the fact that the conviction was spent may be a particular circumstance relating to that offence making the imposition of the prescribed sentence unjust in all the circumstances.

5.16 The key considerations in the PCC(S)A 2000, section 111, are the dates on which the qualifying offences were committed and the dates on which the defendant was convicted. The sequence must be (a) commission, then conviction, (b) commission, then conviction, (c) commission, then conviction. The section would not bite in a case where the offender commits a third domestic burglary before being convicted of the second (*Hoare* [2004] 2 Cr App R (S) 261). 'Convicted' must be distinguished from 'sentenced'. So, commission of a third domestic burglary at a time when the offender is on bail awaiting sentence for a second domestic burglary does trigger the operation of the section (*Webster* [2004] 2 Cr App R (S) 126). Section 111 can certainly operate in an uneven way, so that one offender will infringe the provision after having been convicted of just three domestic burglaries, while another might have been convicted of (or had taken into consideration) many more such offences without yet having infringed it.

5.17 The court may impose a lesser sentence if it finds that there are 'particular circumstances' relating to the offences or to the offender which would make the minimum three-year sentence unjust. If the court takes this line it must explain in open court why it is of that opinion and what the particular circumstances are which would make the sentence unjust (section 111(2)). In *McDonagh* [2006] 1 Cr App R (S) 647, a case decided under section 110 but equally applicable here, Gage LJ in the Court of Appeal contrasted this phrase with 'exceptional circumstances', which applies in relation to the minimum sentences for firearms offences (see paragraph 5.26 later in this Chapter) and may perhaps be taken to imply a somewhat stricter test. There is little useful authority on what might constitute such 'particular circumstances'. In *McInerney* [2003] 1 All ER 1089, Lord Woolf CJ said:

> It may be helpful to give examples of the type of situation where a three year sentence may be unjust. The sentence could be unjust if two of the offences were committed many years earlier than the third offence, or if the offender has made real efforts to reform or conquer his drug addiction, but some personal tragedy triggers the third offence, or if the first two offences were committed when the offender was not yet 16. As we read section 111 it gives the sentencer a fairly substantial degree of discretion as to the categories of situations where the presumption can be rebutted.

An example of a three-strikes domestic burglary sentence which was held to be unjust on appeal is *Stone* [2012] 2 Cr App R (S) 50, where the offender reached through an open window and stole a box containing items worth £60. He had two previous convictions for domestic burglary, committed eleven years and six years earlier, and there was personal mitigation. Sentence was reduced to eight months, to permit his immediate release. In *Gibson* [2004] 2 Cr App R (S) 451, the Court of Appeal held that, where the judge had adjourned sentence to obtain an assessment of the offender's suitability for a community penalty in circumstances where that gave rise to an expectation on the offender's part that, if the report was positive, he would receive such a sentence, it was unjust then to impose the prescribed sentence under section 111.

5.18 It was held in *Sparkes* [2011] EWCA Crim 880 that where the offender is sentenced for several offences and consecutive sentences are appropriate, but one of those offences attracts a prescribed sentence, the principle of totality still needs to be applied, but in a manner which does not undermine the policy of the prescribed sentence. It is not entirely clear how this should best be achieved, whether by adjustment of the prescribed sentence or the consecutive sentence. See also *Raza* [2010] 1 Cr App R (S) 354.

Guilty plea

5.19 See paragraph 5.13, earlier this Chapter. The same principles apply. Eighty per cent of three years produces a sentence of just less than two years and five months.

F PRESCRIBED MINIMUM SENTENCE FOR FIREARMS OFFENCES

5.20 Section 51A of the FA 1968 provides for minimum custodial sentences for certain firearms offences. By section 51A(1) the section applies where a person is convicted of:

(i)   an offence under section 5(1)(a), (ab), (aba), (ac), (ad), (ae), (af), or (c) of this Act, or
(ii) an offence under section 5(1A)(a) of this Act, or
(iii) an offence under any of the provisions of this Act listed in subsection (1A) in respect of a firearm or ammunition specified in section 5(1)(a), (ab), (aba), (ac), (ad), (ae), (af), or (c) or section 5(1A)(a) of this Act,

and the offence was committed at a time when he was aged 16 or over.

By section 51A(1A) (which must be one of the clumsiest-named subsections in the statute book), the provisions referred to in (iii) above are:

(a) section 16 (possession of firearm with intent to injure);
(b) section 16A (possession of firearm with intent to cause fear of violence);
(c) section 17 (use of firearm to resist arrest);
(d) section 18 (carrying firearm with criminal intent);

(e)   section 19 (carrying a firearm in a public place);

(f)   section 20(1) (trespassing in a building with firearm).

Where these provisions apply the court must impose an appropriate sentence of imprisonment or order for detention for a term of at least the required minimum, unless the court is of the opinion that there are exceptional circumstances relating to the offence or to the offender who justify its not doing so (section 51A(2)). The minimum sentences specified in the section are five years' imprisonment or detention in a young offender institution in the case of an offender aged eighteen or over when convicted, and three years' detention under the PCC(S)A 2000, section 91 for any offender aged at least sixteen but under eighteen at the time he committed the offence (section 51A(4)). Nothing in section 51A prevents a hospital order being imposed on an offender in an appropriate case (Mental Health Act 1983, section 37(1A)). In *Rehman* [2006] 1 Cr App R (S) 404 Lord Woolf CJ said that the weapons with which the section was concerned were ones in relation to which Parliament had signalled the importance of imposing deterrent sentences which paid less attention to the personal circumstances of the offender, not necessarily because the offender would pose a danger in the future, but to send out a message that an offender convicted of such an offence would be dealt with more severely so as to deter others.

5.21   In *A-G's Ref (No 114 of 2004)* [2005] 2 Cr App R (S) 24, the Court of Appeal made it clear that section 51A applies only where one of the specific offences listed there is proved or admitted. Although the offender in the case considered by the court might properly have been charged with an offence under section 5 of the Firearms Act 1968, no such count had been included on the indictment and so the minimum sentence could not apply. In *A-G's Ref (Nos 48 and 49 of 2010)* [2011] 1 Cr App R (S) 706 it was held that, although section 51A did not extend to a conspiracy or an attempt to commit any of the offences there set out, the specified minimum sentence was clearly relevant when sentencing for an inchoate offence and it was difficult to imagine a case where there had been a deliberate attempt to create a working handgun which would not require a sentence of at least five years.

5.22   In *Raza* [2010] 1 Cr App R (S) 354 the Court of Appeal said that, where an offender was being sentenced for a number of offences, one of which is subject to a prescribed minimum custodial sentence, the principle of totality applies and the sentencer must pass an overall term which is proportionate to the overall offending, but that principle must not be applied in such a way that it undermines the intention of Parliament. In that case the Court approved the reduction by two years of an otherwise appropriate consecutive sentence of ten years.

Guilty plea

5.23   In contrast to the PCC(S)A 2000, sections 110(2) and 111(2), there is no provision in section 51A of the Firearms Act 1968 limiting the extent to which the offender's guilty plea can affect the sentence imposed. The Court of Appeal in *Jordan* [2005] 2 Cr App R (S) 266 held that, in respect of section 51A, its terms were plain and unambiguous and Parliament must have intended to exclude the normal principles of reduction of sentence to reflect a guilty plea. No discount was therefore available for plea. It should be noted that this is the only determinate sentence in English law which does not allow for a reduction in light of a plea of guilty. The Court said that the rigour of section 51A in this respect was mitigated by the possibility of 'exceptional circumstances' being found. Such cases would be rare but, if the judge had properly identified exceptional circumstances, the sentence would then be at large. The question of what might amount to 'exceptional circumstances' is considered next.

Exceptional circumstances

The 'exceptional circumstances' proviso in the Firearms Act 1968, section 51A(2), brings **5.24**
the minimum sentence provision on firearms offences broadly into line with the three
strikes provisions under sections 110 and 111 of the PCC(S)A 2000. The provisions are differently worded, however, in that they permit the sentencer to avoid the prescribed sentence
if there are 'particular circumstances...which would make it unjust' to impose the minimum sentence. Here, however, the section refers to 'exceptional circumstances relating
to the offence or to the offender which justify' the court is not imposing the prescribed
sentence. Guidance was given on this issue by Lord Woolf CJ in the Court of Appeal in
Rehman [2006] 1 Cr App R (S) 404. His Lordship said that firearms offences under section
5 are absolute offences, and an offender might commit such an offence without even realizing that he had done so. That was a matter of great significance, since if an offender has
no idea that he is doing anything wrong, a deterrent sentence will have no deterrent effect
upon him. The reference in the section to the circumstances of the offender is important.
If the offender is unfit to serve a sentence of five years, or he is of very advanced years, that
may be relevant. These matters should be read into the words used in the section, otherwise
a sentence may be inappropriately harsh and perhaps fall foul of Article 3 of the ECHR.
His Lordship also said that it is important not to divide circumstances into those which are
capable of being exceptional, and those which are not. Sometimes there would be a single
isolated factor that would amount to an exceptional circumstance, but in other cases it
would be the collective impact of all the relevant circumstances. His Lordship said that the
circumstances would be 'exceptional' if it would mean that to impose the minimum sentence would result in an arbitrary and disproportionate sentence. Unless a judge was clearly
wrong in not identifying exceptional circumstances when they were present, the Court of
Appeal would not readily interfere with the trial judge's decision. It may be that the formulation of the test in *Rehman* permits greater discretion for the trial judge than exists in
relation to the three strikes sentences.

In *Rehman* itself, the Court of Appeal found that the judge had erred in not finding excep-   **5.25**
tional circumstances in the case, where the offender's background (in particular his previous
good character), his early plea of guilty, his ignorance of the unlawfulness of the weapon
(he had purchased it as a collector's model), and the fact that there was just one weapon, all
taken together, amounted to exceptional circumstances. The sentence was reduced from
five years to one year, allowing the offender's immediate release. While *Rehman* remains
the leading authority in this area, in *Wilkinson* [2010] 1 Cr App R (S) 628, where the Court
reconsidered sentencing for the most serious firearms offences, Lord Judge CJ said that
exceptional circumstances 'must indeed be *exceptional*' (emphasis in the original). All the
other cases on section 51A are highly fact-specific, but the general approach has been to up-
hold what is clearly the intention of Parliament—to impose very heavy sentences on anyone
associated with these weapons. In *Blackall* [2006] 1 Cr App R (S) 131, the exceptional
circumstances rejected by the judge but accepted on appeal were that the offender was para-
plegic as a result of having been shot by a man who was never apprehended. The offender's
physical disability would mean that the impact of any sentence of imprisonment on him
would be very severe. It was said, however, that the fact that the offender was keeping a re-
volver for his own protection could not amount to an exceptional circumstance, since that
was a common feature of such cases. In *McEneaney* [2005] 2 Cr App R (S) 531, the offender
suffered from schizophrenia following a head injury incurred in his youth. The illness was
controlled by medication and a hospital order was not recommended. The Court of Appeal
said that the offender's psychiatric history did not amount to exceptional circumstances.
In *Ocran* [2011] 1 Cr App R (S) 223 the prescribed sentence of five years was upheld on a
young woman aged twenty-four, who was a single mother with no previous convictions,

who pleaded guilty at the first opportunity and admitted that she had known for several weeks about the presence a semi-automatic pistol, a sawn-off shotgun, and a silencer in her flat, which had apparently been put there by other persons who had keys to the flat. The Court of Appeal said that the judge 'was not clearly wrong' and upheld the sentence. In contrast is the case of *Jones* [2012] 1 Cr App R (S) 149 where the defendant, twenty-two-years old and of positive good character, was convicted of harbouring a pistol and ammunition for two to three weeks following threats from a stranger. She ran a defence of duress which failed. The judge accepted that she had been very frightened, but that she had ample time to contact the police. There was very strong personal mitigation. Court of Appeal said 'if ever there was a case of exceptional circumstances this is it'. Sentence was dramatically reduced, from five years to six months.

Prescribed minimum sentence for using someone to mind a weapon

5.26   The Violent Crime Reduction Act 2006, section 28, creates an offence where the offender uses another person to look after, hide, or transport a dangerous weapon for him under arrangements or in circumstances that facilitate, or are intended to facilitate, that weapon being available to the offender for an unlawful purpose. By section 29 of that Act, where at the time of the offence the offender was aged eighteen or over and the dangerous weapon in respect of which the offence was committed was a firearm mentioned in section 5(1)(a) to (af) or (c) or section 5(1A)(a) of the Firearms Act 1968 (firearms possession of which attracts a minimum sentence), the court must impose a term of imprisonment (or detention in a young offender institution) of not less than five years, unless it is of the opinion that there are exceptional circumstances relating to the offence or to the offender which justify its not doing so. If the offender is aged under eighteen at the time of conviction, the court must impose a sentence of detention under section 91 of the PCC(S)A 2000, of not less than three years, unless it is of the opinion that there are exceptional circumstances relating to the offence or to the offender which justify its not doing so.

5.27   Where a court is considering the seriousness of an offence under section 28 of the 2006 Act, the fact that the offender was aged eighteen or over and the person used to look after the weapon was not, the court must treat that fact as increasing the seriousness of the offence (section 29(11)). The judge should state in open court that the offence was so aggravated.

G PRESCRIBED MINIMUM SENTENCES FOR CERTAIN OFFENSIVE WEAPONS OFFENCES

Threatening with offensive weapon in public and threatening with article with blade or point or offensive weapon

5.28   By the Prevention of Crime Act 1953, section 1A(1) a person is guilty of an offence if he (a) has an offensive weapon with him or her in a public place, (b) unlawfully and intentionally threatens another person with the weapon, and (c) does so in such a way that there is an immediate risk of serious physical harm to that other person. By section 1A(4) the maximum penalty for the offence is four years on indictment and six months summarily. Section 139AA(1) of the CJA 1988 provides that a person is guilty of an offence if that person (a) has an offensive weapon with him or her in a public place or on school premises, (b) unlawfully and intentionally threatens another person with the weapon, and (c) does so in such a way that there is an immediate risk of serious physical harm to that other person.

By section 139AA(6) the maximum penalty for the offence is four years on indictment and six months summarily. In respect of each of these offences there is also a minimum sentence which applies as follows. If the offender is aged eighteen or over the court must impose a sentence of at least six months' imprisonment or detention in a young offender institution unless the court is of the opinion that there are particular circumstances which relate to the offence or to the offender, and would make it unjust to do so in all the circumstances. If the offender is aged sixteen or seventeen the minimum sentence is a detention and training order of four months. These provisions were inserted by the LASPOA 2012, and there is so far no appellate authority in relation to them.

Guilty plea

Where sentence is imposed under either of these sections and the offender has pleaded **5.29** guilty, the sentencing court is required to take into account the stage at which he indicated his intention to plead guilty and the circumstances in which this indication was given (CJA 2003, section 144). Section 144(3) states that in the case of an offence coming within section 1A(6)(a) of the 1953 Act or section 139AA(8)(a) of the 1988 Act the court may not impose a sentence which would be less than 80 per cent of the minimum sentence specified. See the discussion at paragraph 5.13, earlier. If the offence comes within section 1A(6)(b) of the 1953 Act or section 139AA(8)(b) of the 1988 Act, however, there is no such limitation on reduction for a guilty plea and the normal principles apply.

KEY DOCUMENTS[1]

Criminal Justice Act 2003, schedule 21.

Sentencing Guidelines Council, Definitive Guideline, *Reduction in Sentence for a Guilty Plea* (effective from 23 July 2007).

European Convention on Human Rights, Article 3.

---

[1] All sentencing guidelines can be found on the Sentencing Council website: <http://sentencingcouncil.judiciary.gov.uk/>.

6

COMMUNITY SENTENCES

6.01 Community sentences lie within a central band of sentencing options appropriate in cases where the offender has committed an offence of an intermediate degree of seriousness. By the CJA, section 147, a 'community sentence' means a sentence that consists of or includes a 'community order' (as defined by section 177) or 'a youth rehabilitation order'. By section 177, a community order is an order imposed on an offender aged eighteen or over.

The order will contain one or more requirements imposed by the court. These requirements are considered further later in this Chapter. The youth rehabilitation order is broadly equivalent to a community order, but imposed on a young offender. The youth rehabilitation order is considered at paragraph 6.45 later in this Chapter. Some general sentencing provisions apply to the imposition of all community sentences. These were outlined at paragraph 2.27 this book (the community sentence threshold) and are now dealt with more fully. Care should be taken when reading what follows to distinguish provisions which apply to the 'community sentence' (irrespective of the age of the offender) from those which apply to the 'community order' (limited to offenders aged eighteen and over).

A PASSING A COMMUNITY SENTENCE

The maximum duration of a community sentence (whether a community order or a youth **6.02** rehabilitation order) is three years. Section 148(2) says that where a court passes a community sentence

    (a) the particular requirement or requirements forming part of the community order, or, as the case may be, youth rehabilitation order, comprised in the sentence must be such as, in the opinion of the court, is, or taken together are, the most suitable for the offender, and

    (b) the restrictions on liberty imposed by the order must be such as in the opinion of the court are commensurate with the seriousness of the offence, or the combination of the offence and one or more offences associated with it.

So, at this point the court has to consider seriousness again, but now also suitability. The question of offence seriousness relates primarily to the onerousness of the community order or youth rehabilitation order—both as to its length and the number and nature of the requirements inserted by the court. While all community sentence requirements involve some degree of limitation upon the offender's freedom and can be regarded as restrictions on their liberty, some requirements are more overtly about punishment than others. Since the Crime and Courts Act 2013 came into force, section 148(2) is made subject to section 177(2A), which says that when the court imposes a community order (but not a youth rehabilitation order) it must include in the order at least one requirement imposed for the purpose of punishment, or impose a fine in addition to the community order, or do both of those things, unless there are 'exceptional circumstances' relating to the offence or the offender which would make it unjust to do so. This provision can be seen as an attempt to 'toughen up' the community sentence for offenders aged eighteen and over. It may give rise to problems in the future, however, since it may be a matter of dispute whether a particular requirement imposed by the judge was 'imposed for the purpose of punishment' or not. Most of the requirements which can be included within a community sentence may properly serve more than one purpose. Is a night-time curfew with electronic monitoring 'imposed for the purpose of punishment'? Some might regard it as a punishment, certainly, but others would see it more as a means of keeping the offender away from trouble, and thereby protecting the public.

The Court of Appeal in *Hemmings* [2008] 1 Cr App R (S) 623 said that a community order, **6.03** especially one which includes requirements which will have a real impact on an offender's liberty, is clearly a form of punishment. A requirement to perform unpaid work in the community for a specified number of hours is certainly intended to be punitive, although it may have beneficial rehabilitative side-effects through introducing a structure of work into a previously chaotic lifestyle, and it will also have reparative value within the community in which the work is done. In principle, though, it is intended to be a punishment, and the greater the number of hours the more onerous the punitive element is intended to be. On the other hand a supervision requirement is designed primarily to be supportive and rehabilitative of the offender, while no doubt at times challenging. The duration of a supervision requirement will reflect the duration of support and guidance which is appropriate to that offender rather than the seriousness of the offence. Of course any one community sentence may contain more than one requirement, designed to achieve a combination of purposes. It is common, for example, for a community sentence to include both a supervision requirement and an unpaid work requirement. The issue of suitability may be relevant in a different way, such as where there is evidence that the offender is physically unfit to perform manual labour under an unpaid work requirement. Unless a less physically demanding work assignment can be found by the probation service (or social worker in the case of a youth rehabilitation order), this particular requirement will not be suitable, and a different one will have to be found.

6.04 The SGC guideline, *New Sentences: CJA 2003* provides the following guidance on the balance to be struck between seriousness and suitability. It should be noted that although the SGC refers throughout to 'community sentences' it is clear from the context that the guideline is confined to community orders.

> In community sentences the guiding principles are proportionality and suitability. Once a court has decided that the offence has crossed the community sentence threshold and that a community sentence is justified, the initial factors in defining which requirements to include in a community sentence should be the seriousness of the offence committed. If a court is to reflect the seriousness of an offence there is little value in setting requirements as part of a community sentence which are not demanding enough for an offender. On the other hand, there is equally little value on imposing requirements that would 'set an offender up to fail' and almost inevitably lead to sanctions for breach. Sentencing ranges must remain flexible enough to take account of the suitability of the offender, his or her ability to comply with particular requirements and their availability in the local area. (paragraphs 1.13 and 1.1.14)

The guideline goes on to advocate the idea that once a sentencer has reached the provisional view that a community order is the right disposal, a pre-sentence report should be requested and a steer should be given to the probation service on whether the sentencer thinks that the case should fall within the low, medium, or high range of the community order and the purpose(s) of sentencing which the court is seeking to achieve. It is not known how often courts adhere to this approach in practice. There seems to be a more general tendency to avoid specifics when ordering a pre-sentence report, lest the offender's hopes be raised that a community disposal will result, only for those hopes later to be dashed. More recently the Sentencing Council has said that '[a] community sentence combines punishment with activities carried out in the community, Overall, the requirements aim to change offenders' behaviour so they don't commit crime in the future, and to make amends to the victim of the crime or the local community'. (See <http://www.sentencingcouncil.judiciary.gov.uk/sentencing/community-sentences.htm>.)

6.05 There are a number of situations in which a community order or a youth rehabilitation order cannot be imposed. These are set out in the CJA 2003, section 150(1), and include cases where the sentence is fixed by law (murder), or where the dangerous offender provisions apply, or where the case falls under one of provisions which creates a prescribed custodial sentence (such as the three-strikes rule in cases of domestic burglary). Section 150A also restricts the power to make a community order (but not a youth rehabilitation order), by limiting it to cases where the offence is punishable with imprisonment. One reason for the removal of the power to pass a community order for an non-imprisonable offence is that it removes the risk of the offender being sent to prison for failure to comply with the order. In addition to what is set out in section 150(1), it is clear that a community sentence cannot be combined with a custodial sentence (whether immediate or suspended) or with a hospital order (Mental Health Act 1983, section 37(8)).

B TIME SPENT ON REMAND BEFORE COMMUNITY SENTENCE PASSED

As was explained in Chapter 2, if an offender has spent time in custody on remand before **6.06** being given a sentence of imprisonment or detention in a young offender institution, that period is automatically deducted from the length of the sentence which is passed. Section 149 of the CJA 2003 deals with the situation where an offender has been remanded in custody before being dealt with for the offence by way of a community sentence. It states that the sentencing court 'may have regard' to any such period of remand when determining the restrictions on liberty to be imposed by a community order or youth rehabilitation order. This section confers discretion, rather than requiring the court to take that period into account. The SGC guideline, *New Sentences: CJA 2003*, says (at paragraph 1.1.37) that 'the court should seek to give credit for time spent on remand in all cases, and should make clear, when announcing sentence, whether or not it has been given'. If the court does not give credit the SGC says that it should explain why this is not justified, or would not be practicable, or would not be in the best interests of the offender. The same position applies in relation to time spent by the offender under a qualifying curfew. The judge is required to take those days into account by adjusting the sentence in accordance with section 240A.

There have a number of appellate decisions in relation to section 149, and they do not **6.07** all sit happily together. In *Hemmings* [2008] 1 Cr App R (S) 623 the offender had spent ninety-nine days on remand. He pleaded guilty to battery and criminal damage. The maximum penalty for the offences was six months, and the offender had spent the equivalent of that time on remand (ninety-nine days is three months, and an offender will serve one-half of a six-month sentence). The Court of Appeal quashed the community order in this case, saying that a community order was a form of punishment and, given the period spent on remand, further punishment was inappropriate. A conditional discharge was substituted. One difficulty with this case is that section 149 says that time served on remand may be relevant to the 'restrictions on liberty' imposed within the community sentence. It does not say that time served on remand can make the difference between a custodial sentence and a community sentence. Later, in *Rakib* [2012] 1 Cr App R (S) 1, the Court of Appeal doubted whether *Hemmings* was right on this point. This time the Court said that there were circumstances where a judge might properly make a community order on an offender who had spent perhaps a substantial period of time on remand (173 days in that case), because there might be strong rehabilitative or public protection reasons for a community disposal. This decision reflects the different purposes which can underlie the requirements within a community sentence. As explained above, community sentences are restrictions on liberty, but they are not all about punishment. Another significant case is *Bodman* [2011] 2 Cr App R (S) 249. Here the offender pleaded guilty to burglary and was given a community order. The judge said, when passing sentence, that one reason for passing that sentence was that the offender had already spent 114 days on remand. Otherwise, one assumes, the offender would have gone to prison. The judge also said that if the offender had to be re-sentenced for the burglary (following breach of the order) then the remand time would not count. The offender committed a further burglary while under the community order, and the judge passed a prison sentence with no credit for the 114 days. The Court of Appeal upheld the sentence and said that, looking at the case in the round, where the judge had made the position clear from that start, he had not been wrong to withhold credit on re-sentencing.

C REPORTS

6.08 The CJA 2003, section 156 deals with pre-sentence reports, in relation to community sentences. It was considered in paragraph 1.74 in Chapter 1 of this book. Whenever a court is considering whether to impose a community sentence, and what restrictions to put on the offender's liberty as part of that sentence, the court must take into account all the information available to it, including information about the offence and about the offender. Before imposing a community sentence, the sentencing court must normally obtain a pre-sentence report but the court need not obtain such a report if it considers it 'unnecessary' to do so. Given the information and specialist advice contained in pre-sentence reports, it would be rare for a court to impose a community sentence without first considering such a report. The SGC guideline, *New Sentences: CJA 2003* says that, in many cases, the pre-sentence report 'will be pivotal in helping a sentencer decide whether to impose a custodial sentence or whether to impose a community sentence and, if so, whether particular requirements, or combinations of requirements, are suitable for an individual offender'. The guideline also says that the court must always ensure (especially where there are multiple requirements) that the restriction on liberty placed on the offender is proportionate to the seriousness of the offence committed. The court must also consider the likely effect of one requirement on another, and that they do not place conflicting demands upon the offender (paragraph 1.1.15). Having come to a provisional view that a community sentence is the most appropriate disposal, the sentencer should request a pre-sentence report, indicating the purpose(s) of sentencing that the package of requirements is designed to fulfil (paragraph 1.1.16).

6.09 Section 159 deals with disclosure of pre-sentence reports to the defence and the prosecution. Section 160 applies where a report (other than a pre-sentence report) is made by an officer of a local probation board with a view to assisting any court in deciding how best to deal with an offender. This section provides for disclosure of the contents of that report to the defence (but not the prosecution).

D COMMUNITY ORDER REQUIREMENTS

6.10 A wide range of requirements may be inserted by the court into a community order (offender aged eighteen or over). Initially these are listed in the CJA 2003, section 177, and further details of each requirements is provided in subsequent sections of the Act as indicated. The available requirements are:

(a) an unpaid work requirement
(b) an activity requirement
(c) a programme requirement
(d) a prohibited activity requirement
(e) a curfew requirement
(f) an exclusion requirement
(g) a residence requirement
(ga) a foreign travel prohibition requirement
(h) a mental health treatment requirement

(i) a drug rehabilitation requirement

(j) an alcohol treatment requirement

(ja) an alcohol abstinence and monitoring requirement

(k) a supervision requirement

(l) in a case where the offender is aged under twenty-five, an attendance centre requirement, and

(m) an electronic monitoring requirement

In the list in section 177 the clumsy numbering of (ga) and (ja) reflects the creation of new forms of requirements, inserted by LASPOA 2012. As we shall see, (m) is also new, at least as a free-standing requirement, and was inserted by the Crime and Courts Act 2013.

General matters

There are some general provisions which apply across the list of requirements. These are dealt with next, before examining the details of the individual requirements. **6.11**

(a) Any community order must specify the local justice area in which the offender resides or will reside (section 216(1)).

(b) The court must ensure, so far as practicable, that any requirement imposed in a community order is such as to avoid any conflict with the offender's religious beliefs, or with the requirements of any other relevant order to which the offender may be subject, and any interference with the times, if any, at which the offender normally works, attends school or any other educational establishment (section 217(1)).

(c) The court which makes the relevant order must forthwith provide copies of the order to the offender, to the appropriate responsible officer (section 219(1)), to those responsible for the relevant programme etc which forms a requirement of the order, and to certain other persons affected by the order (section 219(2) and schedule 14). The details which the court officer should provide persons affected: the offender, an appropriate adult if the offender is aged under fourteen, the responsible officer or supervisor, and any person affected where the court imposes a requirement for the protection of that person or requiring the offender to reside with that person, are set out in the CPR 2012, regulation 42.2.

(d) Where two or more requirements are imposed in a community order the court must ensure that they are compatible with each other (section 177(6)). It is submitted that this includes not only logical incompatibility, such as where the requirements require the offender to be in two places at the same time, but also where (in the words of the SGC in the *New Sentences: CJA 2003* guidelines, paragraph 1.1.15) two requirements place conflicting demands on the offender. Requirements should always add up to make a coherent package.

(e) There is a general duty on the offender made subject to a community order to keep in touch with the responsible officer in accordance with such instructions as he may from time to time be given by that officer, and the offender must notify the officer of any change of address (section 220). The 'responsible officer' is usually an officer of a local probation board or a member. It seems that this obligation is enforceable as if it were a requirement in the order, so that a failure to keep in touch would constitute a failure to comply with the order. The responsible officer is entitled to insist that the offender notify the officer in advance if he is going to miss an appointment, and why (*Richards v National Probation Service* [2007] EWHC 3108 (Admin)).

(f) A community order must specify a date (the 'end date'), not more than three years after the date of the order, by which all the requirements in it must have been complied with, but if a community order imposes two or more different requirements the order may specify a date by which each of those requirements must have been complied with.

The last of those days must be the same as the end date (section 177(5) and (5A)). This is designed to ensure that at least one requirement continues to be in place until the community sentence is complete. There should not be a 'gap' with no operative requirement. A community order ceases to be in force on the end date, but that is subject to section 200(3) (duration of community order imposing unpaid work requirement: see paragraph 6.12, this Chapter). Before making a community sentence which contains two or more requirements, the court must consider whether, in the circumstances of the case, the requirements are compatible with each other (section 177(6)).

(g) Section 177(2A) requires that where the court makes a community order the court must (a) include in the order at least one requirement imposed for the purpose of punishment, or (b) impose a fine for the offence in respect of the community order is made, or (c) do both of those things unless, by section 177(2B), there are exceptional circumstances which relate to the offence or to the offender which would make it unjust in all the circumstances for the court to comply with subsection (2A)(a) in the particular case and would make it unjust in all the circumstances to impose a fine for the offence concerned.

The various requirements are now considered in turn.

Unpaid work requirement

6.12 Section 199 of the CJA 2003 states that the number of hours of unpaid work which may be ordered by the court must not be less than forty, nor more than 300. Usually the court will be passing a single community order on the offender, but it is open to the court dealing with an offender convicted of two or more offences to make separate orders each containing an unpaid work requirement. The number of hours specified in the two orders may run concurrently or consecutively, but in no case may they exceed a maximum of 300 hours (section 199(5)). Before inserting an unpaid work requirement into a community order the court must (if it thinks necessary) hear from an appropriate officer that the offender is a suitable person to perform work under the requirement (section 199(3)) and that local arrangements are in place for the unpaid work requirement to be carried out (section 218(1)). The appropriate officer in this case is a probation officer or an officer of a provider of probation services. The work required under the order should normally be completed within twelve months (section 200(2)) but a community order for twelve months containing an unpaid work requirement remains in force beyond the twelve-month limit until such time as the offender has completed the number of hours required, unless the order is revoked for some reason (section 200(3)). If, under a community order for twelve months containing a single requirement of unpaid work, the offender completes the hours in a shorter time, the order is still a 'community sentence of at least 12 months' for the purposes of the 'sex offender register' (notification requirements under the Sexual Offences Act 2003): *Davison* [2009] 2 Cr App R (S) 76. Work must be carried out as directed by the responsible officer.

Activity requirement

6.13 Section 201(1) of the CJA 2003 states that an activity requirement requires the offender to present himself to a person specified in the order at such approved place and on a set number of days as specified in the order, to participate in activities specified and comply with instructions given by the person in charge. These activities may include reparation, such as those involving contact between the offender and persons affected by his offence(s) (see section 201(2)). The aggregate number of days must not exceed sixty (section 201(5)). Before inserting an activity requirement into a community order the court must consult an officer of a local probation board or an officer of a provider of probation services, be satisfied that it is feasible to secure compliance with the requirement, and be satisfied that local arrangements exist for persons to participate in such activities. If the activity requirement would require the involvement of some other person apart from the offender and the responsible officer (such as the victim), the consent of that other person must be obtained before the requirement can be inserted into the order.

Programme requirement

Section 202(1) of the CJA 2003 defines programme requirement as one which requires **6.14** the offender to participate in an accredited programme (a 'systematic set of activities') at a place approved for the purpose on a specified number of days. These programmes are designed and approved to address particular forms of offending behaviour, such as anger management, sexual behaviour, substance misuse, domestic violence, and so on. The offender must follow instructions given by the responsible officer and the person in charge of the programme. The Court of Appeal in *Price* [2013] EWCA Crim 1283 held that the judge must decide whether to order the programme requirement or not—this task could not be delegated to the supervising officer.

Prohibited activity requirement

Section 203(1) of the CJA 2003 defines a prohibited activity requirement. The court can **6.15** require the offender to refrain from taking part in certain specified activities on a specified day or days or over a specified period of time. The requirement may include forbidding him to contact a named person or persons, and may be that the offender does not possess, use, or carry a firearm (section 203(3)). Before inserting such a requirement into a community order the court must consult an officer of a local probation board or an officer of a provider of probation services. It has been held that since the primary purpose of a prohibited activity requirement is to prevent, or reduce the risk of, future offending, any such requirement should be proportionate to that risk (*J* (2008) 172 JP 513).

Curfew requirement

By the CJA 2003, section 204 a curfew requirement is a requirement that the offender **6.16** remain at a specified place (usually his home address) for certain periods of time. These periods must be not less than two hours and nor more than sixteen hours in any one day. The maximum number of hours was increased from twelve to sixteen in 2012. An order might, therefore, require the offender to remain indoors from 5 o'clock in the evening until 9 o'clock in the morning. A curfew order must not last for more than twelve months from the day on which it is made (section 204(3)). The maximum was increased from six months to twelve months in 2012. Before inserting a curfew requirement into a community order the court must obtain and consider information about the place proposed to be included in the order, including information as to the attitude of persons likely to be affected by the presence of the offender there (section 204(6)). When the court makes a community order which includes a curfew requirement it must normally also impose an electronic monitoring requirement unless the court thinks it is inappropriate to do so (section 177(3)).

This requirement is usually imposed together with electronic monitoring as a means of **6.17** preventing re-offending. The curfew period is usually (but not always) set during the evening and night-time, but it is not confined to offenders who have committed their offence(s) at night (see *Henry* [2011] EWCA Crim 630). It is sometimes simply imposed as an additional measure of punishment, being an unwelcome restriction of the offender's leisure time.

Exclusion requirement

6.18 The CJA 2003, section 205 provides that an exclusion requirement is one which prohibits the offender from entering a specified place, places, or area (such as a particular town centre) during a period specified in the order. The period specified must not be more than two years (section 205(2)). The order can exclude the offender from different places for different periods of time. It can also be used as a way of keeping the offender away from a specified person, in which the person for whose benefit the order is made should be given a copy of the requirement (section 219 and schedule 14). A different way of achieving a similar protection would be for the court to make a restraining order under the Prevention of Harassment Act 1997, section 5. Such an order can now be made whatever the offence of conviction and whatever the sentence imposed, for the purpose of protecting the victim of the offence or another person mentioned in the order form, further conduct which amounts to harassment or will cause a fear of violence. It may last for any specified period, or until further order. An order made under section 5 must be drafted in clear and precise terms and will often include a map setting out specific roads or addresses where the offender is not permitted to go. It is submitted that this procedure is also appropriate for an exclusion re-quirement. If the court makes a community order which includes an exclusion requirement it must normally also impose an electronic monitoring requirement unless the court thinks it is inappropriate to do so (section 177(3)). It has been held that since the primary purpose of an exclusion requirement is to prevent, or reduce the risk of, future offending, any such requirement should be proportionate to that risk (*J* (2008) 172 JP 513).

Residence requirement

6.19 By the CJA 2003, section 206 a residence requirement is a requirement that the offender lives at a place which is specified in the order for a specified period of time. Before making this requirement the court must consider the home surroundings of the offender. The court cannot specify residence at a hostel except on the recommendation of an officer of a local probation board or an officer of a provider of probation services.

Foreign travel prohibition requirement

6.20 This requirement is relatively new, having been introduced in 2012. By section 206A of the CJA 2003 the court may prohibit an offender from travelling, on a day or days specified in the order, or for a period so specified, to any country outside Britain, or any country spe-cified in the order, or any country other than one specified in the order (section 206A(1)). A day specified must not fall outside the period of twelve months starting with the date of the order, and a period specified cannot exceed twelve months, starting with the day of the order.

Mental health treatment requirement

6.21 This requirement is dealt with in Chapter 13, at paragraph 13.03.

Drug rehabilitation requirement

6.22 By the CJA 2003, section 209 the court may insert into a community order a drug rehabili-tation requirement, which includes drug treatment and testing. It requires that during a period of time specified in the order (the 'treatment and testing period') the offender must submit to treatment by or under the direction of a specified person having the necessary qualifications or experience, and must provide samples at such times and in such circumstances as are requested to determine whether he has any drug in his body during that period (section 209(1)). Before imposing a drug rehabilitation requirement the court must be satisfied that the offender is dependent on, or has a propensity to misuse, any controlled drug (as defined by the Misuse of Drugs Act 1971, section 2) and that his dependency or propensity is such as requires and may be susceptible to treatment (section 209(2)(a)). The court must also be satisfied that arrangements have been made for the proposed treatment to take place (section 209(2)(b)), and that the drug rehabilitation requirement has been recommended to the court as being suitable for the offender by an officer of the local probation board or an officer of a provider of probation services (section 209(2)(c)). The offender must express his willingness to comply with the requirement (section 209(2)(d)). There is no minimum testing period, and the order may be carried out in a residential setting or as a non-resident (section 209(4)).

6.23 A community order which includes a drug rehabilitation requirement may (and must if the treatment and testing period is more than twelve months) provide for the requirement to be reviewed periodically by the court which imposed it at intervals of not less than one month (review hearings). The offender is required to attend each review hearing and the responsible officer is required to produce before each review a report in writing on the offender's progress under the requirement. Such report must include the test results and the views of the treatment provider as to the treatment and testing of the offender (section 210(1)).

6.24 At a review hearing the court may, after considering the report, amend the drug rehabilitation requirement (section 211(1)). The offender must agree to that amendment. If the offender does not consent to the proposed amendment then the court may revoke the community order and re-sentence the offender as if he had just been convicted (section 211(3)). If it dies so the court must take into account the extent to which the offender had complied with the requirements of the order. If at a review hearing the court, after considering the report, may in light of good progress amend the order so that subsequent reviews may be made by the court without a hearing (section 211(6)). Conversely, if at a review without a hearing the court finds that the offender's progress is no longer satisfactory it may require the offender to attend a review hearing, and perhaps subsequent hearings.

6.25 While there is little appellate authority on the appropriate use of drug treatment and testing orders some assistance can be derived from earlier case law on the similar (but now repealed) drug treatment and testing orders. The general approach of the Court of Appeal in *AG's Reference (No 64 of 2003)* [2004] 2 Cr App R (S) 1096 was that courts should be alert to pass sentences which had a prospect of reducing drug addiction whenever it was realistic to do so. It was essential that there was evidence that the offender was now determined to free his life from drugs. Typically the order might be used in the case of an offender convicted of property offences, but very rare in cases where serious offences of violence had been committed. Excessive weight should not be given to the prospect, or mere hope, of rehabilitation.

Alcohol treatment requirement

6.26 By the CJA 2003, section 212 the court may insert into a community order an alcohol treatment requirement. It requires that, during a period specified in the order the offender must submit to treatment by or under the direction of a specified person having the necessary qualifications or experience, with a view to the reduction or elimination of the offender's dependency on alcohol. Before imposing an alcohol treatment requirement the court must be satisfied that the offender is dependent on alcohol and that his dependency is such as requires and may be susceptible to treatment (section 212(2)) and that arrangements have been made for the proposed treatment to take place. The offender must express his willingness to comply with the requirement (section 212(3)). The order may be carried out in a residential setting or as a non-resident (section 212(5)).

Alcohol abstinence and monitoring requirement

6.27 This requirement is relatively new, having been introduced in 2012. At the time of writing it is being piloted and is available only in certain trial areas and not nationally. A court imposing a community order may insert an alcohol abstinence and monitoring requirement only where the consumption of alcohol by the offender is an element of the offence for which the order is to be imposed (or an associated offence), or the court is satisfied that the consumption of alcohol by the offender was a factor that contributed to the commission of that offence (or an associated offence): section 212A(9). The court must be satisfied that the offender is *not* dependent on alcohol (section 212A(10)) and the court must not include an alcohol treatment requirement in the order (section 212A(11)). The offender is required either to abstain entirely from consuming alcohol throughout a specified period, or not to consume alcohol such that at any time during a specified period there is more than a specified level of alcohol in his body. In neither case can the specified period exceed 120 days. In either case the offender must agree to testing and monitoring to see whether he is complying with the requirement or not.

Supervision requirement

6.28 A 'supervision requirement', inserted in accordance with the CJA 2003, section 213, is a requirement that during the relevant period the offender must attend appointments with the responsible officer, or another person specified by the responsible officer, at such time and place as may be determined by the officer (section 213(1)). The purpose of a supervision requirement is promoting the rehabilitation of the offender (section 213(2)). The 'relevant period' is the whole of the period for which the community order remains in force.

Attendance centre requirement

6.29 By the CJA 2003, section 214 an attendance centre requirement is a requirement that the offender must attend at an attendance centre specified in the order for such number of hours as may be specified. The cross-heading in the statute (although not the section itself) states that the attendance centre requirement is available 'only in case of offenders aged under 25' and it is clear that the requirement is so limited. Section 177, which lists the available requirements, also includes this limitation. The aggregate number of hours must not be less than twelve or more than thirty-six (section 214(2)). An offender cannot be required to attend at an attendance centre on more than one occasion on any day and for not more than three hours on any occasion (section 214(6)). Before making such a requirement the court must be satisfied that the attendance centre which has been specified is reasonably accessible to the offender (section 214(3)). The responsible officer will inform the offender of the date and time required for the first attendance and subsequent hours are fixed by the officer in charge of the attendance centre. The attendance centre requirement has the effect that the offender must engage in occupation or receive instruction under the supervision of and in accordance with instructions given by the officer in charge of the centre (section 214(7)).

Electronic monitoring requirement

By section 215 of the CJA 2003 the court may insert into a community order an elec- **6.30**
tronic monitoring requirement, which is designed to 'secur[e]...the offender's compliance with other requirements imposed by the order'. So, currently electronic monitoring
can only be used as a means of backing up and ensuring compliance with another requirement. This position is about to change, and electronic monitoring will, in due
course, also become available as a free-standing requirement, as is explained later in
this Chapter.

Where the court makes a community order which includes a curfew requirement or an **6.31**
exclusion requirement, it *must* also impose an electronic monitoring requirement, unless
the court considers it inappropriate to do so (section 177(3)), and it *may* do so in respect
of any other requirement (section 177(4)). The periods of electronic monitoring can be
specified by the court in the order, or set by the responsible officer (section 215(1)). If the
court is proposing to include such a requirement but there is a person, other than the offender, without whose cooperation it will not be practicable to secure that monitoring, the
requirement cannot be included without that person's consent (section 215(2)). The court
must ensure that electronic monitoring arrangements are available in the local area by a
person approved by the Secretary of State, and that the necessary provision can be made
under those arrangements (section 215(4)). An electronic monitoring requirement may not
be included in the order for the purposes of monitoring compliance with an alcohol absti-
ence and monitoring requirement, unless the electronic monitoring requirement is in place
for the purpose of monitoring compliance with a different requirement in the order (section
215(5) and (6)).

When section 33 and schedule 16 part 4 of the Crime and Courts Act 2013 is brought into **6.32**
force section 215 will also provide for the use of an electronic monitoring requirement for
monitoring the offender's whereabouts, other than for the purpose of monitoring his compliance with other requirements in the order, during a period specified in the order. This
will in effect allow the electronic monitoring requirement to be used as a free-standing
requirement.

E BREACH OF COMMUNITY ORDER REQUIREMENT

The relevant provisions which deal with breach of a community order requirement are set **6.33**
out in the CJA 2003, schedule 8. These are considered next. They are distinct from the powers of the court when faced with an offender subject to a community order who has now
committed a further offence. These are dealt with in paragraph 6.41, this Chapter.

Duty to give warning

If the responsible officer is of the opinion that the offender has failed without reasonable **6.34**
excuse to comply with any of the requirements of a community order the officer must give
the offender a warning under schedule 8, paragraph 5(1). The warning must describe the
circumstances of the failure and state that the failure is unacceptable. If a warning has
already been given at any time within the preceding twelve months, a second failure will
require the officer to bring the matter before the court. In *West Yorkshire Probation Board
v Robinson* [2010] 4 All ER 1110 the Divisional Court confirmed that the clear purpose of
this provision was to provide the probation officer with a discretion which could be exercised once only.

Powers of court on breach

6.35 Paragraph 6(1) deals with the process by which the officer should bring the matter before a magistrates' court or the Crown Court. The alleged breach will come before a magistrates' court unless the community order was imposed by the Crown Court and no direction was given by that court that any breach was to be dealt with by the magistrates. In practice this is hardly ever done, and the Crown Court deals with its own alleged breaches and the magistrates deal with theirs. In most cases the breach is admitted by the offender. If it is not admitted then it must be proved by the probation service which brings the action for breach. In the Crown Court any question of whether the offender has failed to comply with any requirement is determined by the court and not by the verdict of a jury (schedule 8, paragraph 10(6)). The issue will usually be whether the offender has failed 'without reasonable excuse', which is a matter of fact for the relevant court to decide. It was held in *West Midlands Probation Board v Sadler* [2008] 1 WLR 918 that the mere fact that the offender has lodged an appeal against his conviction is not a reasonable excuse for non-compliance with the community order. It was held in *Clarke* [1997] 2 Cr App R (S) 163, a case under earlier provisions which still seems to be applicable, that the probation service must be in a position when presenting the alleged breach to provide details of the alleged breach, any earlier breach for which a warning was given, and the circumstances of the offence for which the community order was given. This may require some investigation into the role played by the offender in the original offence, as compared to that of any co-defendants, and how they were sentenced. The probation service should liaise with the Crown Prosecution Service to ensure that this information is available to assist the judge.

6.36 By the CJA 2003, schedule 8, paragraph 9(1), where it is proved that the offender has failed without reasonable excuse to comply with any of the community requirements of the community order the *magistrates' court* must deal with the offender in one of the following ways:

    (a) by amending the terms of the community order, so as to impose more onerous requirements which the court could include if it were then making the order;

    (aa) by ordering the offender to pay a fine of an amount not exceeding £2500;

    (b) where the community order was made by a magistrates' court, by dealing with him, for the offence in respect of which the order was made, in any way in which the court could deal with him if he had just been convicted by it of the offence;

    (c) where the community order was made by a magistrates' court, the offence was not an offence punishable with imprisonment, the offender is aged 18 or over, and the offender has wilfully and persistently failed to comply with the requirements of the order, by dealing with him in respect of that offence by imposing a sentence of imprisonment (or detention in a young offender institution) for a term not exceeding six months.

If the community order was made by the Crown Court, the magistrates' court may commit the offender in custody or release him on bail to appear before the Crown Court (paragraph 9(7)).

It is important to note that the court *must* take one of these courses of action. It is not open to the court to 'take no action' and simply allow the order to continue. The LASPOA 2012 contained provision to relax this requirement, but the relevant section was repealed without being brought into force.

6.37 When dealing with the offender under paragraph 9(1), the magistrates' court must take into account the extent to which the offender has already complied with the requirements of the community order (paragraph 9(2)). It would, for example, always be relevant when dealing with an offender for a failure to comply with the supervision requirement that he had been complying with his unpaid work requirement. Such partial compliance, depending on the circumstances, might still result in the court revoking the order and re-sentencing the offender to a custodial sentence. The court should make it clear, however, that it has taken the relevant matter into account and explain why one of the other options permitting the order to continue is not feasible in that case. If the court deals with an offender under paragraph 9(1)(a), it may extend the duration of particular requirements (subject to any statutory limitation on the maximum duration of a particular requirement). This can include extending the duration of the community order for up to six months beyond its original end date even if that involves the total duration of the order exceeding three years. Such an extension may be exercised only once. Again, if dealing with the offender under paragraph 9(1)(a) and the community order does not contain an unpaid work requirement, the court may insert one on breach of between twenty and 300 hours. The lower limit is twenty rather than forty.

By the CJA 2003, schedule 8, paragraph 10(1), where it is proved that the offender has failed **6.38** without reasonable excuse to comply with any of the community requirements of the community order the *Crown Court* must deal with the offender in one of the following ways:

(a) by amending the terms of the community order, so as to impose more onerous requirements which the Crown Court could impose if it were then making the order;

(aa) by ordering the offender to pay a fine of an amount not exceeding £2500;

(b) by dealing with him, for the offence in respect of which the order was made, in any way in which he could have been dealt with for that offence by the court which made the order if the order had not been made; or

(c) where the offence was not an offence punishable with imprisonment, the offender is aged 18 or over, and the offender has wilfully and persistently failed to comply with the requirements of the order, by dealing with him in respect of that offence by imposing a sentence of imprisonment (or detention in a young offender institution) for a term not exceeding six months.

When dealing with an offender who appears or is brought before the *Crown Court*, by **6.39** paragraph 10(1) the Crown Court must take into account the extent to which the offender has already complied with the requirements of the community order (paragraph 10(2)). It would, for example, always be relevant when dealing with an offender for a failure to comply with the supervision requirement that he had been complying with his unpaid work requirement. Such partial compliance, depending on the circumstances, might still result in the court revoking the order and re-sentencing the offender to a custodial sentence. The court should make it clear, however, that it has taken the relevant matter into account and explain why one of the other options permitting the order to continue is not feasible in that case. If the court deals with an offender under paragraph 10(1)(a), the court may extend the duration of particular requirements (subject to any statutory limitation on the maximum duration of a particular requirement). This can include extending the duration of the community order for up to six months beyond its original end date even if that involves the total duration of the order exceeding three years. Such an extension may be exercised only once. Again, if dealing with the offender under paragraph 9(1)(a) and the community order does not contain an unpaid work requirement, the court may insert one on breach, of between twenty and 300 hours. The lower limit is twenty rather than forty. Where the Crown Court deals with an offender under sub-paragraph (1)(a), (b), or (c) it must revoke the community order if it is still in force.

It is important to note that the Crown Court *must* take one of these courses of action. It is not open to the court to 'take no action' and simply allow the order to continue. The LASPOA 2012 contained provision to relax this requirement, but the relevant section was repealed without being brought into force.

6.40 The SGC guideline, *New Sentences: CJA 2003* states (at paragraph 1.1.44) that if the court on dealing with breach decides to increase the onerousness of the requirements in the order, 'the court must consider the impact on the offender's ability to comply and the possibility of precipitating a custodial sentence for further breach'. Further (at paragraph 1.1.45) the SGC notes that '[t]he court dealing with breach of a community sentence should have as its primary objective ensuring that the requirements of the sentence are finished . . . A court that imposes a custodial sentence for breach without giving adequate consideration to alternatives is in danger of imposing a sentence that is not commensurate with the seriousness of the original offence and is solely a punishment for breach'. It should be noted that, where the court does choose to revoke the community order and re-sentence the offender, its power to impose custody following breach is greater than that available if the offender is in breach of a suspended sentence, where the court cannot impose a custodial sentence which is longer than the term originally suspended. This point was considered by the Court of Appeal in *Phipps* [2008] 2 Cr App R (S) 114.

F REVOCATION OF COMMUNITY ORDER FOLLOWING FURTHER OFFENCE

6.41 To deal first with the powers of a magistrates' court, schedule 8, paragraph 21 provides that where an offender in respect of whom a community order made by a magistrates' court is convicted of a further offence by a magistrates' court and it appears to the court that it would be in the interests of justice to exercise its powers under this paragraph, having regard to circumstances which have arisen since the community order was made, the magistrates may:

(a) revoke the order, and
(b) deal with the offender for the offence in respect of which the order was made, in any way in which he could have been dealt with for that offence by the court which made the order if the order had not been made.

In dealing with the offender under (b) above the court must take into account the extent to which the offender has complied with the requirements of the community order (paragraph 21(3)). A person sentenced under (b) may appeal to Crown Court against the sentence (paragraph 21(4)).

6.42 By paragraph 23, where the Crown Court is dealing with an offender in respect of whom a community order is in force is convicted of a further offence by the Crown Court, or is brought or appears before the Crown Court, or is committed to that court by a magistrates' court for sentence, and it appears to the court that it would be in the interests of justice to exercise its powers under this paragraph having regard to circumstances which have arisen since the community order was made, the Crown Court's powers are identical to (a) and (b) in paragraph 6.41 of this Chapter. In dealing with the offender under (b) the court must take into account the extent to which the offender has complied with the requirements of the community order (paragraph 23(3)).

G REVOCATION AND AMENDMENT OF COMMUNITY ORDER

6.43 Schedule 8, paragraphs 13 and 14 deal with applications to the court seeking revocation of a community order where, having regard to changed circumstances since the order was made, it is in the interests of justice to revoke the order, or to revoke it and deal with the offender in some other way. These circumstances include the offender achieving good progress under the order.

Schedule 8, paragraphs 16 to 20 deal with applications to the court seeking amendment of a **6.44** community order relating to matters such as change of residence, change of circumstances, extending the overall duration of the order, and so on.

H YOUTH REHABILITATION ORDER

The sentence equivalent to a community order when the offender is aged under eighteen is **6.45** the youth rehabilitation order. For the general provisions relating to the imposition of a 'community sentence', which includes a youth rehabilitation order (see paragraphs 6.01 to 6.09 earlier). The SGC guideline, *Sentencing Youths* states that the court (which will normally be a youth court, but may also be the Crown Court in those situations where it falls to that court to sentence an offender aged under eighteen) must (as with the community order) be satisfied that the offence is 'serious enough' to justify the order, but even where the offence crosses that threshold, a court is not obliged to make a youth rehabilitation order. Again, as with a community order, the guiding principles are proportionality and suitability, and the maximum length of the order is three years. The youth rehabilitation order is a generic community sentence within which the court must include one or more requirements. It is not available to the court in cases where the sentence is fixed by law (murder), or where the dangerous offender provisions apply, or where the case falls under one of the provisions which create a prescribed custodial sentence. In addition, the youth rehabilitation order is not available where the youth court is obliged to impose a referral order on a first-time offender who has pleaded guilty to an imprisonable offence. Finally, a court must not make a youth rehabilitation order on an offender who is already subject to one, or on an offender who is subject to a reparation order, without first revoking the earlier order (schedule 1, paragraph 30).

It should be remembered that when sentencing a young offender the aims of sentencing are **6.46** different from those applicable when sentencing an offender aged eighteen or over. The relevant statutory aims were considered at paragraph 2.04, this book. The relevant provisions for young offenders are the Crime and Disorder Act 1998, section 37, which states that the principal purpose of the whole of the youth justice system including the sentencing of young offenders, 'is to prevent offending by children and young persons', and there is also a duty under the Children and Young Persons Act 1933, section 44, to 'have regard to the welfare of the child or young person'. According to the SGC guideline, *Sentencing Youths*, paragraph 2.2, young offenders require a different, individualistic, sentencing approach from adults, and the guideline stresses that even within the category of 'youth' the response to an offence is likely to be very different depending on whether the offender is at the lower end of the ten-to-seventeen-year-old age bracket, in the middle, or towards the top. In many instances the maturity of the offender will be just as important as the chronological age.

Before making a youth rehabilitation order the court will almost invariably consider a **6.47** pre-sentence report. The circumstances in which a court can proceed to sentence an offender under eighteen without a report are more limited than those in which it may sentence an adult. The legal provisions on ordering pre-sentence reports were considered at paragraph 1.74, this book. The pre-sentence report will be prepared by a member of the local youth offending team, probably a local authority social worker. The report writer will seek to identify the appropriate balance in pursuit of the statutory aims set out earlier in this Chapter. In most cases an assessment of the risk of the young offender's re-offending will be undertaken by use of *Asset*, a multifactorial tool designed to extrapolate from the range of factors and circumstances that form the background to the offending to the likelihood of re-offending and the risk of serious harm in any such further offending. In addition, before making a youth rehabilitation order the court must obtain and consider information about the offender's family circumstances and the likely effect of such an order on those circumstances (CJIA 2008, schedule 1, paragraph 28).

6.48   A youth rehabilitation order generally takes effect on the day on which it is imposed, but the court does have discretion to order that it should start on a later date. The CJIA 2008, schedule 1 paragraph 30 states that this may, in particular, arise if the offender is currently serving a detention and training order. The court may direct that the youth rehabilitation order should start either when the period of supervision of the detention and training order begins, or when it is completed. The wording of the paragraph suggests that there must be other circumstances in which the court may order a youth rehabilitation order to start at a later date but these are not described.

6.49   In addition to what might be described as the 'standard' youth rehabilitation order, two special forms of the order are available: the youth rehabilitation order with intensive supervision and surveillance, and the youth rehabilitation order with fostering. These are dealt with at paragraphs 6.71 and 6.75 of this Chapter.

6.50   In contrast to a community order, a court may pass impose a youth rehabilitation order (other than one with intensive supervision and surveillance or fostering) for an offence which is not imprisonable.

I YOUTH REHABILITATION ORDER REQUIREMENTS

6.51   By the Criminal Justice and Immigration Act 2008, section 1, where a person under eighteen is convicted of an offence, the court by or before which the person is convicted may in accordance with schedule 1 to the 2008 Act make a youth rehabilitation order imposing on the person one or more of the following requirements:

(a)   an activity requirement
(b)   a supervision requirement
(c)   in a case where the offender is aged sixteen or seventeen at the time of the conviction, an unpaid work requirement
(d)   a programme requirement
(e)   an attendance centre requirement
(f)   a prohibited activity requirement
(g)   a curfew requirement
(h)   an exclusion requirement
(i)   a residence requirement
(j)   a local authority residence requirement
(k)   a mental health treatment requirement,
(l)   a drug treatment requirement
(m)   a drug testing requirement
(n)   an intoxicating substance treatment requirement, and
(o)   an education requirement

Every youth rehabilitation order must specify an end date, which cannot be more than three years after the date on which it was made. All requirements in the order must have been complied with by that date, and at least one requirement must remain in place until that end date. It is common for a supervision requirement to last for the full duration of the order.

General matters

The following matters are relevant in relation to all youth rehabilitation orders: **6.52**

(a) In any case before inserting two or more requirements into a youth rehabilitation order the court must consider whether the requirements to be imposed are compatible with each other (schedule 1, paragraph 29). The court must also ensure, so far as is practicable, that any requirement is such as to avoid any conflict with the young offender's religious beliefs, any interference with the times at which he normally works or attends school, and any conflict with the requirements of any other youth rehabilitation order to which the young offender may be subject (schedule 1, paragraph 29).

(b) Where a youth rehabilitation order has effect, it is the duty of the responsible officer to make any arrangements that are necessary in connection with the requirements imposed by the order, to promote the offender's compliance with those requirements, and where appropriate to take steps to enforce those requirements (section 5). The 'responsible officer' for these purposes means a member of the local youth offending team, an officer of a local probation board, an officer of a provider of probation services and, where appropriate, the person responsible for electronic monitoring of the offender or the person in charge of the attendance centre (section 4).

(c) In giving instructions in pursuance of a youth rehabilitation order the responsible officer must ensure that, as far as practicable, any instruction should avoid conflict with the offender's religious beliefs, any interference with the times, if any, at which the offender normally works or attends school or any other educational establishment, and avoids any conflict with the requirement of any other youth rehabilitation order to which the offender may be subject (section 5(3)).

(d) An offender under a youth rehabilitation order must keep in touch with the responsible officer in accordance with the instructions which he may from time to time be given by the officer and must notify the responsible officer of any change of address (section 5(5)). This obligation is enforceable as if it were a requirement imposed by the order (section 5(6)).

According to the SGC guideline, *Sentencing Youths*, at paragraphs 10.9 to 10.10:   **6.53**

> In determining the nature and extent of requirements to be included within an order and the length of that order, the key factors are the assessment of the seriousness of the offence, the objective(s) the court wishes to achieve, the risk of re-offending, the ability of the offender to comply, and the availability of requirements in the local area. Since a court must determine that the offence (or combination of offences) is 'serious enough' to justify such an order, a court will be able to determine the nature and extent of the requirements within the order primarily by reference to the likelihood of the young person re-offending and of the risk of the young person causing serious harm. This is in accordance with the principal aim of the youth justice system and the welfare principle.

Activity requirement

By the CJIA 2008, schedule 1, paragraphs 6 to 8, an activity requirement is a requirement   **6.54**
to take part in activities or residential exercises, as specified in the order, for such number of days as is specified. The maximum number of days is ninety. The offender must comply with instructions given by the person in charge of the place or the activity in question. A court may include an activity requirement only if it has consulted an appropriate officer and is satisfied both that it is feasible to secure compliance and that provision for the activities can be made. Where compliance with an activity requirement would involve the cooperation of a person other than the offender and the responsible officer, the court may not include such a requirement unless that other person consents.

6.55 There is power to impose an activity requirement which lasts for more than ninety but not more than 180 days, but this can only be done within a youth rehabilitation order with intensive supervision and surveillance.

Supervision requirement

6.56 By schedule 1, paragraph 9, a supervision requirement is a requirement to attend appointments at such times and places as required by the responsible officer. This requirement always lasts for the duration of the order.

Unpaid work requirement

6.57 Schedule 1, paragraph 10 provides that an unpaid work requirement is a requirement, available only for offenders aged sixteen and seventeen on the date of conviction of the offence, to work for a specified number of hours between forty and 240. The work should normally be completed within twelve months. The court must not impose an unpaid work requirement unless, after hearing (in the court thinks necessary) from an appropriate officer that the offender is a suitable person to be made to perform work under such a requirement in the local area. Unless revoked the order remains in force until the offender has worked the specified number of hours.

Programme requirement

6.58 By schedule 1, paragraph 11, a programme requirement is a requirement to participate in a programme (a 'systematic set of activities') at a specified place for a specified number of days. Where appropriate this may include a requirement to reside at a specified place for a specified period. A court may include a programme requirement only if it is recommended by the appropriate officer, and the court is satisfied that the programme in question is available locally. Where compliance with the requirement would involve the cooperation of a person other than the offender and the responsible officer, the court may not include such a requirement unless that other person consents.

Attendance centre requirement

6.59 Schedule 1, paragraph 12 provides that the offender may be required to attend at an attendance centre for a specified period, and to engage in occupation or receive instruction as directed. For a young person aged sixteen or over at the date of conviction, the minimum duration is twelve hours and the maximum is thirty-six hours. At age fourteen or fifteen the minimum is twelve hours and the maximum is twenty-four hours. At age thirteen or below the maximum is twelve hours. Attendance cannot be for more than one occasion on any one day and not for more than three hours on any one occasion. A court may include an attendance centre requirement only where it is notified that a place at a centre is available, and that centre is reasonably accessible to the offender. The first time at which the offender is to attend is fixed by the responsible officer, and subsequent hours are fixed by the officer in charge of the attendance centre, having regard to the offender's circumstances.

Prohibited activity requirement

6.60 By schedule 1, paragraph 13 a prohibited activity requirement is a requirement to refrain from specified activities on a specified day, or days, or during a specified period. A court may include a prohibited activity requirement only if it has consulted an appropriate officer.

The requirements that may be included include a requirement that the offender does not possess, use, or carry a firearm.

Curfew requirement

6.61 A curfew requirement is a requirement that the young offender must remain at a specified location for specified periods of between two hours and sixteen hours per day. The periods may not fall outside twelve months beginning with the day on which the order is made. Before making a curfew requirement a court must obtain and consider information about the place to be specified, and this must include information about the attitude of people likely to be affected by the enforced presence there of the offender. The court must include an electronic monitoring requirement as well, unless the court considers it to be inappropriate.

Exclusion requirement

6.62 By schedule 1, paragraph 15 an exclusion requirement is a prohibition placed upon the offender from entering a specified place or area (such as a named road or a town centre clearly marked on a map) during a specified period that must not exceed three months. The court must include an electronic monitoring requirement as well, unless the court considers it to be inappropriate.

Residence requirement

6.63 A residence requirement is a requirement that the young offender must live with a specified person or in a specified place (schedule 1, paragraph 16). The person named in the order must consent to this. If the court specifies a place where the young offender must live, this is referred to as a 'place of residence requirement', and may be imposed only if the offender is aged sixteen or over at the time of conviction. Before making a place of residence requirement the court must consider the home surroundings of the young offender. It may not specify a hostel or institution as a place where the young offender must reside except on the recommendation of the appropriate officer. If the order requires residence at a specified place, it may also provide that it does not permit residence anywhere else without the prior approval of the responsible officer.

Local authority residence requirement

6.64 By schedule 1, paragraph 17 a local authority residence requirement is a requirement to reside in accommodation provided by the local authority for a specified period. This period must not exceed six months, nor may it apply to a young offender once they attain the age of eighteen. The requirement may also state that the young person must reside with a named person. This requirement cannot be included in a youth rehabilitation order unless the court is satisfied that the behaviour which constituted the offence was due to a significant extent to the circumstances in which the young offender was living at the time and that the requirement will assist in his rehabilitation. Further, the young offender must be legally represented when the court is considering whether to include this requirement and there must be consultation with the parent or guardian, unless that is impracticable, and the relevant local authority.

Mental health treatment requirement

6.65 This requirement is dealt with in Chapter 13, at paragraph 13.07.

Drug treatment requirement

6.66   A drug treatment requirement is a requirement that the young offender must attend for residential or non-residential treatment with a view to reducing or eliminating the offender's
dependency on, or propensity to misuse, controlled drugs as defined by the Misuse of Drugs
Act 1971, section 2. This requirement may be included only if arrangements can be made
for the treatment, it has been recommended to the court by an appropriate officer, and the
young person has expressed willingness to comply with it. The court must be satisfied that
the young person is dependent on (or has a tendency to misuse) controlled drugs and that
the dependency is susceptible to treatment (schedule 1, paragraph 22).

Drug testing requirement

6.67   A drug testing requirement is a requirement to provide samples as directed, in order to
find out whether there is a controlled drug in the young offender's body during any treatment period. This requirement will operate alongside the drug treatment requirement, (see
paragraph 6.66 earlier). The court must specify the minimum number if samples in each
month, and may specify when, how, and what type of sample must be provided. As with
the drug treatment requirement, it may be included only where the court has been notified
that arrangements are in place to enable the testing to take place and the young offender has
expressed willingness to comply with it (schedule 1, paragraph 23).

Intoxicating substance treatment requirement

6.68   An intoxicating substance treatment requirement is a requirement that the young offender
attend for residential or non-residential treatment with a view to reducing or eliminating
the offender's dependency on, or propensity to misuse, intoxicating substances (alcohol
and any other substance or product, but not a controlled drug, capable of being inhaled or
otherwise used for the purpose of causing intoxication). This requirement may be included
only if arrangements can be made for the treatment, the treatment has been recommended
to the court by an appropriate officer, and the young person has expressed willingness to
comply with it. The court must be satisfied that the young person is dependent on (or has a
tendency to misuse) intoxicating substances and that the dependency is susceptible to treatment (schedule 1, paragraph 24).

Education requirement

6.69   By schedule 1, paragraph 25 an education requirement is a requirement to comply during
a period or periods specified in the youth rehabilitation order, with 'approved education
arrangements'. This means arrangements for the education of the offender which are made
by the parent or guardian of the young offender and approved by the local authority specified in the order. The court must consult the local authority and must be satisfied both that
(i) in the view of the authority suitable arrangements exist to provide full-time education
suited to the young offender, and that (ii) such a requirement is necessary to secure the good
conduct of the young offender or to prevent further offending.

Electronic monitoring requirement

6.70   An electronic monitoring requirement is a requirement for electronic monitoring to ensure
compliance with another requirement in a youth rehabilitation order. The court must have
been notified that arrangements are in place in the area and that provision can be made

for the monitoring being proposed. Where compliance with the electronic monitoring requirement would involve the cooperation of a person other than the young offender and the responsible officer the court may not include an electronic monitoring requirement unless that other person consents (schedule 1, paragraph 26). A youth rehabilitation order may impose an electronic monitoring requirement in any case, and must do so where the order includes a curfew requirement or an exclusion requirement unless in the particular circumstances of the case the court considers it inappropriate to do so (CJIA, section 1 (2)). It should be noted that when the relevant provisions of the Crime and Courts Act 2013 are brought into force an electronic monitoring requirement will become available for inclusion as a free-standing requirement in a community order. This change will not extend to the youth rehabilitation order and an electronic monitoring requirement will continue to be available solely as a means of ensuring compliance with another requirement.

J YOUTH REHABILITATION ORDER WITH INTENSIVE SUPERVISION AND SURVEILLANCE

As mentioned earlier, in addition to what might be described as the 'standard' youth re- **6.71** habilitation order, two special forms of the order are available: the youth rehabilitation order with intensive supervision and surveillance, and the youth rehabilitation order with fostering. These are considered now.

The CJIA 2008, section 1(3), states that a youth rehabilitation order may be with intensive **6.72** supervision and surveillance, but only if (by section 1(4)):

(a) the court is dealing with an offender for an offence which is punishable with imprisonment in the case of an adult, and

(b) the court is of the opinion that the offence, or the combination of the offence and one or more offences associated with it was so serious that a custodial sentence would be appropriate (or if the offender was aged under 12 at the time of conviction, would have been appropriate if the offender had been aged 12), and

(c) if the offender was aged under 15 at the time of conviction, the court is of the opinion that the offender is a persistent offender.

It should perhaps be explained, in relation to section 1(4)(b) and (c), that the relevant custodial sentence for an offender under the age of eighteen is a detention and training order. This sentence is currently not available for young offenders aged ten or eleven, and for offenders aged twelve, thirteen, or fourteen, only available if the young offender is found to be a 'persistent offender'. When imposing a youth rehabilitation order with intensive supervision and surveillance the court must give reasons for concluding that the offence crosses the custody threshold, and that the other requirements set out here have all been met (CJA 2003, section 174(8)).

By schedule 1, paragraph 3, a youth rehabilitation order with intensive supervision and **6.73** surveillance may include an activity requirement for a maximum number of days at least ninety but not more than 180, rather than the maximum for the standard order, which is ninety days. This is described an 'extended activity requirement'. If it imposes such a requirement the court must then also include a supervision requirement and a curfew requirement. The curfew must be accompanied by electronic monitoring unless the exceptions apply. Where appropriate other requirements (but not the fostering requirement) may also be included, but always subject to the overall duty that the requirements must be the most suitable for the offender and the restrictions on liberty must be commensurate with the seriousness of the offence(s). The SGC guideline, *Sentencing Youths* adds at paragraph

10.27 that when imposing such an order a court must ensure that the requirements are not so onerous as to make the likelihood of breach almost inevitable.

6.74 There is relatively little case law on the youth rehabilitation order, no doubt because cases involving young offenders which reach the appellate courts are generally concerned with the most serious cases attracting custodial sentences. In *L* [2012] EWCA Crim 1336, however, the fourteen-year-old defendant pleaded guilty to three offences of robbery and one of attempted robbery, and was sentenced as follows: on counts one, two, and three (robbery), a ten-month detention and training order on each count concurrently. There was no separate penalty for the attempted robbery. There were two other accused who were slightly older, and they were sentenced to detention and training orders of twenty-four months and sixteen months. L had no previous convictions but did have two reprimands, one for the theft of a bicycle and the second for the possession of an imitation firearm in public (the prosecution was unable to provide any details). The re-sentence report described L's genuine remorse and unfortunate family background, and it seems that he had been influenced by older and more entrenched offenders. L presented as 'frightened and vulnerable' and Court of Appeal asked to consider a youth rehabilitation order for twelve months. The Court of Appeal noted that it had been assumed by all parties that a detention and training order was open to the court. However, such a sentence may only be passed on an offender aged fourteen if he can be described as a 'persistent offender'. The offences in the instant case were serious and would normally attract a custodial sentence. Having considered the authorities, the Court came to the view that the two reprimands and the three robberies committed on a single occasion within a minute or so of each other could not be characterized as 'persistent offending'. The pre-sentence report recommended a youth rehabilitation order for twelve months with a supervision requirement, an extended activity requirement, enforced by electronic monitoring for three months monitored from 7 o'clock in the evening to 7 o'clock in the morning. This amounted to a youth rehabilitation order with intensive supervision and surveillance, which could only be made if dealing with a person under fifteen who is 'a persistent offender'. Accordingly, that approach was inappropriate since the Court had found that the young offender not to be a persistent offender. The Court, after discussion with the appropriate officer, said that 'within a supervision requirement a significant number of the activities which would form part of the extended activity requirement could be part of the supervision'. Accordingly, the detention and training order was quashed and replaced with a youth rehabilitation order for twelve months with the requirements of supervision for twelve months and a three-month curfew to be electronically monitored from 7 o'clock in the evening to 7 o'clock in the morning.

K YOUTH REHABILITATION ORDER WITH FOSTERING

6.75 A youth rehabilitation order with fostering may be ordered only if all the conditions set out in the CJIA 2008, section 1(4) are satisfied (see paragraph 6.10, earlier this Chapter). In addition, by schedule 1, paragraph 4, the court must be satisfied that the behaviour which constituted the offence was due to a significant extent to the circumstances in which the young person was living, and that the imposition of a fostering requirement would assist in the rehabilitation of the young person. The requirement may be included only where the court has been notified that arrangements are available in the area of the relevant local authority. A youth rehabilitation order with a fostering requirement cannot also include intensive supervision and surveillance. It must include a supervision requirement. Where appropriate, other requirements may also be included, but always subject to the overall duty that the requirements must be the most suitable for the offender and the restrictions on liberty must be commensurate with the seriousness of the offence(s).

Before a fostering requirement can be made the court must consult a parent or guardian of **6.76** the offender (unless this is impracticable), and the local authority which is to receive the offender (schedule 1, paragraph 17). A supervision requirement must also be made. The court must specify the period during which the young person must reside with a foster parent, which must not exceed twelve months (schedule 1, paragraph 18) nor operate after the young person has attained the age of eighteen. Further, by schedule 1, paragraph 19, the young person must be legally represented when the court is considering whether to include this requirement, or representation was made available for the purposes of the proceedings under the LASPOA 2012 but was withdrawn because of the offender's conduct, or the offender has been informed of his right to apply for representation but has refused or failed to apply.

The SGC guideline, *Sentencing Youths* notes at paragraph 10.28 that the imposition of **6.77** a youth rehabilitation order with fostering may well engage Article 8 of the European Convention on Human Rights (right to respect for family and private life) and any such interference must be proportionate. Further, by paragraph 10.31, '[i]t is unlikely that the statutory criteria will be met in many cases; where they are met and the court is considering making an order care should be taken to ensure that there is a well-developed plan for the care and support of the young person throughout the period of the order and following the conclusion of the order. A court will need to be provided with sufficient information, including proposals for education and training during the order and plans for the offender on completion of the order'.

L BREACH OF YOUTH REHABILITATION ORDER REQUIREMENT

The relevant provisions which deal with breach of a youth rehabilitation order requirement **6.78** are set out in the CJIA 2008, schedule 2. These are considered next. They are distinct from the powers of the court when faced with an offender subject to a youth rehabilitation order who has now committed a further offence. These are dealt with in paragraph 6.87, this Chapter.

Duty to give warning

If the responsible officer is of the opinion that the offender has failed without reasonable **6.79** excuse to comply with any of the requirements of a youth rehabilitation order, the officer must give the offender a warning under schedule 2, paragraph 3. The warning must describe the circumstances of the failure, and state that the failure is unacceptable. If a warning has already been given at any time within the preceding twelve months, a second failure may lead to the order being referred back to the court. The position here allows more flexibility than the equivalent provisions in relation to breach of a community order on adult offender. According to the SGC guideline, *Sentencing Youths*, paragraph 10.34, '[t]here is a presumption in favour of referring the matter back to court after the third failure to comply and a discretionary power to do so after the second failure to comply'.

Powers of court on breach

Paragraph 5(1) deals with the process by which the officer should bring the matter before a **6.80** youth court or the Crown Court. The alleged breach will come before a youth court unless the youth rehabilitation order community order was imposed by the Crown Court and no direction was given by that court that any breach was to be dealt with by the youth court. In most cases the breach is admitted by the young offender. If it is not admitted then it must be proved by the responsible officer who brings the action for breach. In the Crown Court any question of whether the offender has failed to comply with any requirement is determined by the court and not by the verdict of a jury (schedule 2, paragraph 7(15)). The issue will usually be whether the offender has failed 'without reasonable excuse', which is a matter of fact for the relevant court to decide. It was held in *West Midlands Probation Board v Sadler* [2008] 1 WLR 918 that the mere fact that the offender has lodged an appeal against his conviction is not a reasonable excuse for non-compliance with the community order. It was held in *Clarke* [1997] 2 Cr App R (S) 163, a case under earlier provisions which still seems to be applicable, that the probation service must be in a position when presenting the alleged breach to provide details of the alleged breach, any earlier breach for which a warning was given, and the circumstances of the offence for which the community order was given. This may require some investigation into the role played by the offender in the original offence, as compared to that of any co-defendants, and how they were sentenced. The probation service should liaise with the Crown Prosecution Service to ensure that this information is available to assist the judge. It is submitted that these authorities are equally applicable to breach of a youth rehabilitation order.

6.81 By the CJIA 2008, schedule 2, paragraph 6(2), where it is proved that the offender has failed without reasonable excuse to comply with any of the community requirements of the community order the *youth court* may deal with the offender in one of the following ways:

    (a) by ordering the offender to pay a fine of an amount not exceeding £2500,
    (b) by amending the terms of the youth rehabilitation order, so as to impose any requirement which could have been included in the order when it was made—
        (i) in addition to, or
        (ii) in substitution for,
    any requirement or requirements already imposed by the order;
    (c) by dealing with the offender, for the offence in respect of which the order was made, in any way in which the court could deal with the offender for that offence (had the offender been before that court to be dealt with for it).

The court may not amend the terms of a 'standard' youth rehabilitation order by making it a youth rehabilitation order with intensive supervision and surveillance or a youth rehabilitation order with fostering. Should one of these forms of the order be considered appropriate following breach of the standard order the offender must be re-sentenced and the original order revoked (paragraph 6(8)).

If the youth rehabilitation order was made by the Crown Court, the youth court may commit the offender in custody or release him on bail to appear before the Crown Court (paragraph 7).

It is important to note that, in contrast to the position in relation to breach of a community order on an adult offender, the court *may* take one of these courses of action, but is not required to do so. It is open to the court to 'take no action' and allow the youth rehabilitation order to continue.

6.82 When dealing with the offender under paragraph 6, the youth court must take into account the extent to which the offender has already complied with the youth rehabilitation order (paragraph 6(4)). If the court deals with an offender under paragraph 6(2)(b), the youth court may extend the duration of particular requirements (subject to any statutory limitation on the maximum duration of a particular requirement). This can include extending the duration of the youth rehabilitation order for up to six months beyond its original end date even if that involves the total duration of the order exceeding three years. Such an extension may be exercised only once. Again, if dealing with the offender under paragraph 6(2)(b), the young offender is aged sixteen or seventeen and the youth rehabilitation order does not contain an unpaid work requirement, the court may insert one on breach, of between twenty and 240 hours. The lower limit is twenty rather than forty hours.

If the court is dealing with an offender under paragraph 6(2)(c) and it finds that the offender **6.83** has 'wilfully and persistently failed to comply with a youth rehabilitation order', the court may impose a youth rehabilitation order with intensive supervision and surveillance. If the original order was a youth rehabilitation order with intensive supervision and surveillance and the offence was punishable with imprisonment, the court may impose a custodial sentence (paragraph 6(12), (13), and (14)).

By the CJIA 2008, schedule 2, paragraph 8(1), where it is proved that the offender has failed **6.84** without reasonable excuse to comply with any of the community requirements of the community order the *Crown Court* may deal with the offender in one of the following ways (paragraph 8(2)):

    (a) by ordering the offender to pay a fine of an amount not exceeding £2500,
    (b) by amending the terms of the youth rehabilitation order, so as to impose any requirement which could have been included in the order when it was made—
        (i) in addition to, or
        (ii) in substitution for,
    any requirement or requirements already imposed by the order;
    (c) by dealing with the offender, for the offence in respect of which the order was made, in any way in the Crown Court could have dealt with the offender for that offence.

When dealing with a young offender who appears or is brought before the *Crown Court*, **6.85** by paragraph 8(4) the Crown Court must take into account the extent to which the offender has complied with the youth rehabilitation. If the Court deals with the matter under paragraph 8(2)(c) it must revoke the youth rehabilitation order if it is still in force. If the court deals with an offender under paragraph 8(2)(b), the court may extend the duration of particular requirements (subject to any statutory limitation on the maximum duration of a particular requirement). This can include extending the duration of the youth rehabilitation order for up to six months beyond its original end date even if that involves the total duration of the order exceeding three years. Such an extension may be exercised only once. Again, if dealing with the offender under paragraph 8(2)(b) and the youth rehabilitation order does not contain an unpaid work requirement, the court may insert one on breach, of between twenty and 240 hours. The lower limit is twenty rather than forty hours.

If the court is dealing with an offender under paragraph 6(2)(c) and it finds that the offender **6.86** has 'wilfully and persistently failed to comply with a youth rehabilitation order', the court may impose a youth rehabilitation order with intensive supervision and surveillance. If the original order was a youth rehabilitation order with intensive supervision and surveillance and the offence was punishable with imprisonment, the court may impose a custodial sentence (paragraph 6(12), (13), and (14)).

The court may not amend the terms of a 'standard' youth rehabilitation order by making it a youth rehabilitation order with intensive supervision and surveillance or a youth rehabilitation order with fostering. Should one of these forms of the order be considered appropriate following breach of the standard order the offender must be re-sentenced and the original order revoked (paragraph 8(8)).

It is important to note that, in contrast to the position in relation to breach of a community order on an adult offender, the Crown Court *may* take one of these courses of action, but it is not required to do so. It is open to the court to 'take no action' and allow the youth rehabilitation order to continue.

M REVOCATION OF YOUTH REHABILITATION ORDER FOLLOWING FURTHER OFFENCE

6.87   To deal first with the powers of a *youth court*, schedule 2, paragraph 18 provides that where an offender in respect of whom a youth rehabilitation order made by a youth court is convicted of a further offence by a youth court and it appears to the court that it would be in the interests of justice to exercise its powers under this paragraph having regard to circumstances which have arisen since the community order was made, the court may:

      (a) revoke the order, and

      (b) deal with the offender for the offence in respect of which the order was made, in any way in which he could have been dealt with for that offence.

In dealing with the offender under (b), the court must take into account the extent to which the offender has complied with the order (paragraph 18(6)). A person sentenced under (b) may appeal to Crown Court against the sentence (paragraph 18(7)).

6.88   By paragraph 19, where the *Crown Court* is dealing with an offender in respect of whom a youth rehabilitation order is in force is convicted of a further offence by the Crown Court, or is brought or appears before the Crown Court, or is committed to that court by a youth court for sentence, and it appears to the court that it would be in the interests of justice to exercise its powers under this paragraph having regard to circumstances which have arisen since the community order was made, the Crown Court's powers are identical to (a) and (b) in paragraph 6.87. In dealing with the offender under (b) the court must take into account the extent to which the offender has complied with the requirements of the community order (paragraph 19(5)).

N REVOCATION AND AMENDMENT OF YOUTH REHABILITATION ORDER

6.89   Schedule 2, paragraphs 11 and 12 deal with applications to the court seeking revocation of a youth rehabilitation order where, having regard to changed circumstances since the order was made, it is in the interests of justice to revoke the order, or to revoke it and deal with the offender in some other way. These circumstances include the offender achieving good progress under the order.

6.90   Schedule 2, paragraphs 13 to 17 deal with applications to the court seeking amendment of a youth rehabilitation order relating to matters such as change of residence, change of circumstances, extending the overall duration of the order, and so on.

KEY DOCUMENTS[1]

Sentencing Guidelines Council, Definitive Guideline, *New Sentences: CJA 2003* (December 2004).

Sentencing Guidelines Council, Definitive Guideline, *Sentencing Youths* (effective 30 November 2009).

Criminal Procedure Rules (SI 2013, No 1554) (effective 7 October 2013).

---

[1] All sentencing guidelines can be found on the Sentencing Council website: <http://sentencing council.judiciary.gov.uk/>.

7

REFERRAL ORDERS AND REPARATION ORDERS

This short Chapter deals with two non-custodial sentencing measures which are only **7.01** available for young offenders. The referral order and the reparation order fall outside the definition of 'community sentence', and so were not covered in the last Chapter. By their very nature both orders are almost exclusively relevant to the youth court. A key feature in both orders is the making of requirements which involve the offender in making reparation, either directly to a person who is a victim of the offence or to the community more generally.

A REFERRAL ORDER

Making a referral order

The relevant statutory provisions are sections 16 and 17 of the PCC(S)A 2000. A court which **7.02** is dealing with an offender under the age of eighteen for whom this is his first conviction is in certain circumstances required to sentence that young offender by ordering him to be referred to a youth offender panel. In other circumstances the court has discretion to deal with the young offender in that way. The relevant court is almost always the youth court, but might occasionally be an adult magistrates' court such as where that court is dealing with co-defendants one of whom is over eighteen and one of whom is under eighteen. Normally an adult magistrates' court would remit a juvenile to the youth court for sentence, but in the case of a referral order the adult court may deal with the matter itself (PCC(S)A 2000, section 8(7)). The Crown Court does not have power to make a referral order.

The referral order is a unique form of sentence. It in effect transfers (or 'refers') respon- **7.03** sibility for the setting of conditions to govern the young offender's future behaviour to a youth offender panel established by the local youth offending team. The youth court simply sets the duration of the order, technically known as the 'compliance period'. The young offender must attend meetings of the panel. The panel consists of members of the local community, steered by a member of the youth offending team. Meetings will normally also be attended by the parent or guardian of the young offender and, wherever this can be arranged, the victim of the offence. Of course the attendance of the victim always requires their agreement. The panel will during the first meeting draw up an agreement, called a 'youth offender contract' in which the young offender agrees a programme of activity, usually including a strong reparative element, designed to prevent re-offending in the future. The SGC guideline, *Sentencing Youths* states that when fixing the duration of the order the primary consideration is the seriousness of the offence, and that orders of ten to twelve months should be reserved for the more serious cases.

7.04 A referral order must specify the youth offending team which will be responsible for implementing the order, require the offender to attend meetings of the youth offender panel, and specify the period during which the contract to be drawn up is to have effect. The minimum period is three months and the maximum period is twelve months. The court may also order the offender's parent or (where appropriate) a representative of the local authority to attend meetings of the panel.

Duty to make a referral order

7.05 The circumstances which must exist before the court is required to make a referral order are set out in the two sections indicated. By section 16 they are as follows:

(a) that the youth court is dealing with an offender under the age of 18 where neither the offence not any connected offence is one for which the sentence is fixed by law;

(b) the court is not proposing to pass a custodial sentence or make a hospital order in respect of the offence or any connected offence;

(c) the court is not proposing to grant an absolute or conditional discharge in respect of the offence.

The compulsory referral conditions set out in section 17 must also be satisfied.

7.06 The compulsory referral conditions in section 17 are satisfied in relation to an offence if:

(a) the offence is punishable with imprisonment in the case of an adult;

(b) the offender pleaded guilty to the offence and to any connected offence; and

(c) the offender has never been convicted by or before a court in the UK of any offence other than the offence and any connected offence, nor convicted by or before a court in another Member State of any offence.

Power to make a referral order

7.07 The circumstances which must exist before a court has power to make a referral order but is not required to do so are (a) to (c) of section 16, as set out in paragraph 7.05 earlier, together with the following additional matters (which are set out in section 17(2)). These are:

(a) that the offender is being dealt with by the court for the offence and one or more connected offences, whether or not any of them are punishable with imprisonment; and

(b) the offender pleaded guilty to at least one of the offences mentioned in (a) above.

It follows that the power to make a referral order is available to the court in circumstances where this is not the young offender's first conviction, or where the young offender has not pleaded guilty to all matters, or where the offence is not punishable with imprisonment.

Referral orders and other orders

7.08 It will be apparent from the above provisions that, whether the court is making a referral order because it is required to do so or because it opts to do so, it is very limited in what else it can do. It cannot impose a custodial sentence or a hospital order. Nor can the court deal with the young offender in any of the other prohibited ways, so that it must not at the same time make a youth rehabilitation order, impose a fine, grant an absolute or conditional discharge, or make a reparation order, It may not bind over the young offender to keep the peace, or order his parent or guardian to be bound over. Also, where the court is required to do so rather than having power to do so, it may not defer sentence. It would seem that where the court is dealing with the offender for more than one offence and passes a referral order for one of those offences, the other matters must either be dealt with by a concurrent referral order or a discharge. The court may make a parenting order after considering a report from the appropriate officer. A compensation order, restitution order, or a deprivation order may be added to a referral order.

Referral back to court

A young offender may be referred back to the youth court by the youth offender panel for **7.09** one of a number of reasons, including the young offender's failure to agree a contract with the panel within a reasonable period of time, his failure to sign the contract, his failure to comply with the terms of the contract, or where there is a change in the young offender's circumstances. Where the offender has now had his eighteenth birthday the appropriate court to deal with referral back is the adult magistrates' court. If there is a referral back and the court is satisfied that the youth offender panel was entitled to make the findings of fact that it did and that the panel has exercised its discretion in the matter reasonably, the court may revoke the order and deal with the young offender in any manner in which the court which made the order could have dealt with him (PCC(S)A 2000, schedule 1, paragraph 5(5)(a)). The court which deals with the offender in this way must have regard to the circumstances in which the matter was referred back to court, and the extent to which the young offender has complied with any part of the contract if indeed such contract was made (paragraph 5(5)(b)). The court may decline to revoke the referral order or it may discharge it.

Commission of further offence

If the young offender commits a further offence during the compliance period of the re- **7.10** ferral order the court dealing with the new offence may revoke the referral order and deal with the young offender in any manner in which the court which made the order could have dealt with him (paragraph 14(3)). The court must have regard to the extent to which the young offender has complied with any part of the contract (paragraph 14(4)). Alternatively, if the court finds that there are exceptional circumstances which indicate that extending the compliance period is likely to help prevent further re-offending by him, the court may decide to extend that period, but cannot extend it beyond the maximum of twelve months (PCC(S)A 2000, schedule 1, paragraph 12).

B REPARATION ORDER

Making a reparation order

The statutory provisions are sections 73 and 74 of the PCC(S)A 2000. The relevant court **7.11** will almost always be a youth court, but the Crown Court also has power to make a reparation order. The order is not available to an adult magistrates' court dealing with a juvenile. Where the court is dealing with a young offender convicted of any offence other than one the sentence for which is fixed by law the court may make an order 'requiring him to make reparation specified in the order

(a) to a person or persons so specified; or
(b) to the community at large,

and the person so specified must be a person identified by the court as a victim of the offence or a person otherwise affected by it' (section 73(1)).

7.12 Reparation in this context means making reparation for the offence in some form other than paying compensation (section 73(3)). Any reparation required under the reparation order must be made under the supervision of the responsible officer (a probation officer, social worker, or member of a local youth offending team) and must be made within a period of three months from the date of making the order (section 74(8)). Before making the order the court must obtain and consider a written report by a probation officer, a social worker, or a member of the local offending team, indicating the type of work that is suitable for the offender and the attitude of the victim or victims to the requirements proposed to be included in the reparation order (section 73(5)). The court must give reasons if it does not make a reparation order in any case in which it has power to do so (section 73(8)). A reparation order cannot require the young offender to work for more than twenty-four hours in total or to make reparation to any person without that person's agreement (section 74(1)). Subject to that, the requirements specified in the order shall be such as, in the opinion of the court, are commensurate with the seriousness of the offence. Requirements so specified shall, so far as practicable, be such as to avoid any conflict with the offender's religious beliefs or with the requirements of any community order to which he may be subject, and any interference with the times, if any, at which he normally works or attends school. When making a reparation order the court is required to explain to the young offender in ordinary language the effect of the order and the requirements proposed to be included in it and the consequences of any failure to comply with its terms. The consent of the young offender is not required.

7.13 The wording of section 73(2) indicates that the court may require reparation to a person who is a victim or to someone 'otherwise affected' by the offence. There is no case law on the meaning of this phrase, but it might extend to include a bystander who suffers shock at witnessing an assault as well as the injured party himself. The reparation seems mainly to be designed to achieve a form of direct reparation to the victim of the offence, but section 73(1) also allows for reparation to the community at large. In this form the reparation order runs very close to an unpaid work requirement in a youth rehabilitation order, but under the former the maximum number of hours is twenty-four whilst under the latter it is ten times that figure.

Reparation orders and other orders

7.14 A reparation order cannot be combined with a custodial sentence or a youth rehabilitation order (section 73(4)) or a referral order. A court cannot make a reparation order on a young offender who is already subject to a youth rehabilitation order unless it first revokes the earlier order. A compensation order, restitution order, or a deprivation order may be added to a reparation order.

Breach of requirement of reparation order

7.15 By the PCC(S)A 2000, schedule 8, paragraph 2(2), if it is proved to the satisfaction of the relevant youth court on application of the responsible officer that the young offender has failed to comply with any requirement specified in the reparation order, the court

(a) whether or not it also revokes or amends the order may order the young offender to pay a fine not exceeding £1000, or

(b) if the order was made by a youth court, revoke the order and deal with the offender for the offence in any way in which he could have been dealt with for that offence by the court which made the order.

The young offender may appeal to the Crown Court against any order made under paragraph 2(2). If the reparation order was made by the Crown Court the youth court may commit him in custody or on bail to appear before that court. Where the matter does come before the Crown Court in that way the court must revoke the reparation order and deal with the young offender in any way in which that court could have dealt with him for the offence (paragraph 2(4)).

When dealing with a young offender for breach of a requirement in a reparation order the court must always take into account the extent to which he has complied with the requirements in the order (paragraph 2(7)).

Revocation and amendment of reparation order

The PCC(S)A 2000, schedule 8, paragraph 5 provides for a range of circumstances in **7.16** which, during the period a reparation order is in force, on application to the court by the young offender or by the relevant officer, the court may revoke the order, or amend it. There is no provision in schedule 8 which deals with the power of the court to deal with a reparation order following the young offender's conviction of a further offence during the period of the order.

KEY DOCUMENTS[1]

Sentencing Guidelines Council, Definitive Guideline, *Sentencing Youths* (effective 30 November 2009).

---

[1] All sentencing guidelines can be found on the Sentencing Council website: <http://sentencing council.judiciary.gov.uk/>.

8

DEFERMENT, BINDING OVER, AND DISCHARGE

A DEFERMENT OF SENTENCE

8.01 Both magistrates' courts and the Crown Court have power to adjourn before passing sentence (see paragraph 1.39 in this book). A comparable, though distinct, power to defer sentence is provided for both courts by the Powers of Criminal Courts (Sentencing) Act 2000, sections 1 to 1D. The court should always make it clear which power it is exercising, and avoid using the word 'defer' if it is actually adjourning or exercising a power to bind the offender over (*Fairhead* [1975] 2 All 737).

8.02 Section 1(1) provides that a court may defer passing sentence on an offender for the purpose of enabling it 'to have regard to his conduct after conviction (including, where appropriate, the making by him of reparation for his offence), or any change in his circumstances'. The exercise of this power is subject to the offender giving his consent (section 1(2)). This must be addressed properly, and in open court, and the defendant must agree both to the deferral and to any requirements which the court proposes to include (*McQuaide* (1974) 60 Cr App R 239). Consent will usually be forthcoming, as the offender may reasonably expect that, if he complies with all the requirements, the court will then refrain from imposing custody. Sometimes, however, an offender will not wish to put off matters any more, and will prefer to be sentenced there and then. In any case the deferment must not exceed six months (section 1(4)) and, subject to one unusual exception mentioned at paragraph 8.07, sentence may be deferred just once. The date to which sentence is deferred should be set at the time of deferment. Given that the maximum period of deferment is six months, it may be prudent for the court to defer for a lesser period, say four or five months, to ensure that the matter can be dealt with in the relevant time period, making allowance for any slippage. This is not essential, however, since it was held in *Ingle* [1974] 3 All ER 811 that, in exceptional circumstances, the court may adjourn to a later date, even if that is more than six months after the original deferment. The Court of Appeal in *Anderson* (1983) 78 Cr App R 251 said that the Crown Court is not deprived of its jurisdiction by reason of a delay beyond six months, but if that happens the sentence eventually passed should reflect how stale the offence has then become. The court must always be satisfied that exercise of the power to defer would be in the interests of justice (section 1(3)). When deferring sentence, the court does not bail the offender; he is released subject to the requirements of the deferred sentence. If he should fail to appear on the deferment date, however, a warrant may be issued for his arrest (section 1(7)). It appears that since deferment of sentence is not a final disposal of the case the court cannot impose any punishment or ancillary order at the time of deferral, save for a restitution order or a disqualification from driving (*Dwyer* (1974) 60 Cr App R 39).

Use of deferment of sentence

The requirements imposed by the court when deferring sentence may include reparative **8.03** and other activity to be undertaken during the period of deferment. Deferment is often used where there is information in the pre-sentence report, or otherwise before the court, that important circumstances in the offender's life are about to change for the better, and that it may be prudent to wait to see whether the offender can make good use of his opportunity. A solid and substantiated offer of employment might offer such an opportunity. Requirements may include one as to residence (section 1A). The court may also impose a requirement that the offender participate in a restorative justice programme (section 1ZA). The SGC guideline, *New Sentences: CJA 2003*, indicates that '[t]he use of deferred sentences should be predominantly for a small group of cases close to a significant threshold where, should the defendant be prepared to adapt his behaviour in a way clearly specified by the sentencer, the court may be prepared to impose a lesser sentence' (paragraph 1.2.7). When the court comes to impose sentence at the end of the period of deferment, it will consider the conduct of the offender during the intervening period. In this context, 'conduct' of course relates to how well the offender has complied with any requirements imposed by the court. It is important, then, that the requirements imposed on deferment are clear, appropriate, and achievable within the time frame of the deferral. A requirement that the offender must make an effort to resolve problems in his marriage, as was imposed in *Aquilina* (1989) 11 Cr App R (S) 431, might be thought defective on this ground.

The requirements should always be reduced to writing, so that there can be no later misun- **8.04** derstanding. A copy should be kept on the court file, and a copy given to the offender (section 1(5)). The court may appoint a supervisor, who may be a probation officer, to monitor the offender's compliance with the requirements imposed. It will usually be appropriate to do this, so then the court can be alerted of any failure of the offender to comply with the requirements during the deferral period. The court may require the officer to produce an addendum to the pre-sentence report in order to update the court which deals with the case at the end of the period of deferment. Before deferring sentence the court will need to consider carefully whether some other order, such a community sentence or a suspended sentence with appropriate community requirements, would meet the needs of the case. If so, deferral is probably best avoided. In *Skelton* [1983] Crim LR 686 the Court of Appeal said that a requirement that the offender should go into hospital for mental treatment during the deferment period was not appropriate, and a community order with an appropriate treatment requirement should have been used. The SGC guideline, *New Sentences: CJA 2003* says that '[s]entencers should impose specific measurable conditions that do not involve a serious restriction on liberty'. It goes without saying that a court should not defer sentence just because it does not know what to do, or simply as a means of putting off the decision. According to Lord Lane CJ in the leading case of *George* [1984] 1 WLR 1082, it makes sense for the judge who deferred sentence also to deal with the matter at the end of the deferral period or in the event of the matter being brought back early in light of the offender's failure under the order. A circuit judge or a district judge will generally reserve a deferred sentence to himself to deal with, but it may be more difficult to achieve this in practice where sentence has been deferred by a recorder or by a lay bench. In such a case it would be prudent for the court if possible to leave a note on the file to explain the reasoning which led to the deferral (*Jacobs* (1976) 62 Cr App R 116). Often, compliance with the requirements in a deferred sentence is partial rather than complete, and the judge who deferred sentence in the first place is best placed to assess the level of compliance and deal with the matter accordingly. It is also desirable for defence counsel who appeared in the original matter also to appear when the case returns.

8.05 It is possible for a deferred sentence to be referred by the Attorney General to the Court of Appeal for review if he considers that the deferral constitutes an unduly lenient sentence (see *A-G's Ref (No 22 of 1992)* [1993] 14 Cr App R (S) 435).

Sentencing after deferment

8.06 If the court is satisfied that the offender has failed to comply with one or more requirements, it may deal with him *before* the end of the period of deferment (section 1B). He may also be dealt with *before* the end of the period of deferment if he is convicted of another offence (section 1C). If the offender is convicted of a new offence, the court passing sentence on him for the subsequent offence may also sentence for the offence for which sentence was deferred (section 1C(3)). If the Crown Court is sentencing for the subsequent offence, and sentence was deferred by a magistrates' court, the Crown Court's powers in respect of the offence for which sentence was deferred are limited to those of a magistrates' court.

8.07 If the offender reaches the end of the period of deferment without further mishap, the court dealing with the offender at that point may deal with him in any way the deferring court could have done (section 1D(2)(a)). By section 1D(2)(b), that includes, where sentence was deferred by a magistrates' court, a decision to commit the offender to the Crown Court for sentence. If a magistrates' court does take this course the Crown Court may also defer sentence, that being only the exception to the rule that sentence may be deferred only once (section 1D(3)). In practice, a 'double deferral' such as this is very unlikely to happen. If the offender has substantially complied with the requirements in the deferred sentence, or has made substantial efforts to comply, he can properly expect a non-custodial sentence to be passed. Failure to do so may lead to any custodial sentence being quashed because it may appear that the sentencing court has simply taken a different view from the judge who deferred sentence (*Glossop* (1981) 3 Cr App R (S) 347). If, in the view of the court dealing with the deferred sentence, the offender has failed to comply, wholly or substantially with the specified requirements, the nature and extent of that failure should be explained in open court. Just because the offender has 'kept out of trouble' during the deferment period is not enough to ensure a non-custodial sentence if in other respects the offender has failed to comply with the specific requirements imposed. An example is *Smith* (1979) 1 Cr App R (S) 339.

B BINDING OVER TO KEEP THE PEACE

8.08 There is a range of powers available to English courts which are conveniently grouped together under the heading of 'binding over'. All these powers take the form of a suspended financial penalty, on the basis of an undertaking by the person bound over to comply with the requirements of the court. Powers of a magistrates' court to bind over a person to keep the peace arise either on complaint (under the Magistrates' Courts Act 1980, section 115) or of the court's own motion under common law powers and pursuant to various statutes, most importantly the Justices of the Peace Act 1361. While an order under section 115 can be made only after a full hearing of the complaint, where the court binds over of its own motion it may do so at any time before the conclusion of criminal proceedings, on withdrawal of the case by the prosecution, on a decision by the prosecution to offer no evidence, on an adjournment, or upon acquittal of the defendant, where a justice considers that the person's conduct is such that there might be a breach of peace in the future, whether committed by him or by others. These powers, which are exercisable 'as a measure of preventive justice' (*Veater v Glennon* [1981] 1 WLR 567), can be used in a wide variety of situations, including as a sentencing option against a convicted offender. By the Justices of the Peace Act 1968, section 1(7), any 'court of record having a criminal jurisdiction' has the power to bind over a person who or whose case is before the court, by requiring him to enter into his own recognizances or to find sureties or both, and committing him to prison if he does not comply. The Crown Court is a court of record (Senior Courts Act 1981, section 45), so that both magistrates' courts and the Crown Court have powers to bind over offenders and others who are before the court. The Court of Appeal (Criminal Division) also possesses these powers (*Sharp* [1957] 1 QB 552). *The Criminal Practice Directions* states at paragraph J2, that the court must in any case be satisfied to the criminal standard of the matters complained of before binding over. If the procedure has been commenced on complaint the burden rests on the complainant; in other cases it rests on the prosecution. The appropriate test is whether the court is 'satisfied so that it is sure that a breach of the peace involving violence, or an imminent threat of violence has occurred, or there is a real risk of violence in the future', whether committed by the person to be bound over or by a third party as a natural consequence of that person's conduct. The *Practice Directions* further require that rather than binding over a person to keep the peace in general terms, the court should identify the specific conduct or activity from which the individual must refrain (paragraph J3). Reasons should be given by the court, and a written order should be drawn up and served on all relevant parties (paragraph J4).

8.09 Formerly, there was power to bind over a person 'to be of good behaviour' where that person's behaviour did not amount to a breach of the peace but was found to be contrary to good order and morality. In *Hashman and Harrup v UK* (2000) 30 EHRR 241, however, the European Court of Human Rights said that the nature of requirements imposed on a person bound over to be of good behaviour was insufficiently precise to qualify as a 'restriction...prescribed by law' under Article 10 of the ECHR. The power to bind over to be of good behaviour is no longer available.

8.10 The power to bind over a parent or guardian of a young offender is considered at paragraph 10.02 later in this book.

Use of the power to bind over to keep the peace

8.11 The power to bind over is frequently used as a method of disposal in cases involving minor assaults or minor incidents of public disorder, where the prosecution are prepared not to proceed, provided that the defendant agrees to be bound over. The person bound over is required to enter into a recognizance in an amount which will be forfeited if he fails to keep the peace for a specified period. The court must be satisfied on the merits of the case that an order for binding over is appropriate, and should announce that decision before considering the amount of the recognizance. Those who may in principle be bound over include not only a convicted defendant, but also an acquitted one (*Inner London Crown Court, ex* *parte Benjamin* (1986) 85 Cr App R 267), a defendant before the court in respect of whom the prosecution has been unable to proceed (*Lincoln Crown Court, ex parte Jude* [1998] 1 WLR 24), a witness before the court (*Sheldon v Bromfield Justices* [1964] 2 QB 573), and a complainant (*Wilkins* [1907] 2 KB 380). On the other hand, the person must be before the court, and so the victim of an assault who was never called to give evidence against his assailant, who has pleaded guilty, could not be bound over (*Swindon Crown Court, ex parte Pawitter Singh* [1984] 1 WLR 449). The Practice Direction includes the reminder that an order should not appear in the list of a person's criminal convictions unless it has been imposed on a conviction (paragraph J16).

8.12 The period for which the order may run is entirely within the discretion of the court. A period must be specified, and it is common to bind over for twelve months. The *Practice Directions* say that the length of the order should be proportionate to the harm sought to be avoided and should not generally exceed twelve months (paragraph J4). Although an order to bind over may name a person or persons for whose special protection it is made, there is no general power to insert conditions in an order binding a person over to keep the peace (*Randall* (1986) 8 Cr App R (S) 433). In that case a condition that the person bound over did not teach, or try to teach, anyone under the age of eighteen was held to be invalid. There is no power to bind over a person on condition that they leave the jurisdiction and do not return (*Ayu* [1958] 1 WLR 1264). One condition which can be imposed, however, is that the person bound over shall not possess, use, or carry a firearm (Firearms Act 1968, section 52(1)). The sum of money to be forfeited upon breach of the bind over is also within the discretion of the court. There is no limit, save that the sum should be reasonable in all the circumstances. There is authority that a person may be bound over in a sum which exceeds the maximum fine which could have been imposed for the offence (*Sandbach Justices, ex parte Williams* [1935] 2 KB 192). The court should fix the period of the recognizance and the sum of money to be forfeited upon breach at the time when it orders the bind over. Where the court proposes to bind over a person who has been convicted in anything other than a trivial sum, his means should be investigated and representations allowed. It was held in *Lincoln Crown Court, ex parte Jude* [1998] 1 WLR 24 that a sum of £500 was not so trivial an amount as to dispense with the requirement of a means inquiry. The *Criminal Practice Directions*, paragraph J11 says that when fixing the recognizance the court must have regard to the defendant's means and should hear representations from that person or his lawyer regarding ability to pay.

8.13 Where a court contemplates exercising its power to bind over, especially against a person who has not been charged with an offence, it should ensure that the person concerned understands what the court has in mind and give him the opportunity to make representations (*Hendon Justices, ex parte Gorchein* [1973] 1 WLR 1502 and the *Practice Directions* paragraphs J5 and J6). It is also good practice to allow an acquitted defendant, upon whom the court proposes to make a bind over, an opportunity to address the court on the matter (*Woking Justices, ex parte Gossage* [1973] QB 448). A mere belief that the acquitted person might pose a threat of violence was not enough. The power to bind over an acquitted defendant may usefully be compared with the power to make a restraining order on an acquitted defendant under the Prevention of Harassment Act 1997, s.5A.

8.14 Under the Magistrates' Courts (Appeals from Binding Over Orders) Act 1956, there is a right of appeal to the Crown Court against an binding over order made by a magistrates' court. Where the bind over is made by the Crown Court on sentence, an appeal lies to the Court of Appeal by virtue of Criminal Appeal Act 1968, section 50(1).

Refusal or failure to enter into recognizance

Whenever the court requires a person to be bound over to keep the peace that person must **8.15** consent to being so dealt with. The sanction for failure or a refusal to enter into a recognizance is imprisonment. There seems to be no limit to the duration of the term of custody which may be imposed where the court acts under its common law powers, but the matter comes before the magistrates' court on complaint imprisonment may be for a maximum period of six months, or until the person complies with the order, if sooner (MCA 1980, section 115(3)). Of course imprisonment cannot be imposed on a person who is under the age of twenty-one (PCC(S)A 2000, section 89). It has been held that such a person may properly consent to be bound over even though his refusal to consent could not lead to imprisonment (*Conlan v Oxford* (1983) 5 Cr App R (S) 237). A person aged between eighteen and twenty years inclusive who refuses to consent to be bound over may be detained under the PCC(S)A 2000, section 108 (see *Howley v Oxford* (1985) 81 Cr App R 246). It seems that the Crown Court may deal with a refusal to be bound over as a contempt of court.

The *Criminal Practice Directions*, paragraph J13 says that if there is any possibility that an **8.16** individual will refuse to enter into a recognizance the court should consider whether there are any appropriate alternatives to binding over, such as continuing with the prosecution. Before the court exercises a power to commit the individual to custody for a refusal to enter into a recognizance that individual should be given the opportunity to obtain legal advice. Public funding should generally be granted to cover the cost of representation.

Failure to comply with bind over

If a person who has been bound over by the Crown Court is adjudged to have failed to **8.17** comply with the conditions of the order, the court may forfeit the whole or part of the recognizance in its discretion. It may also allow time for payment, direct payment by instalments, or it may reduce or discharge the recognizance (PCC(S)A 2000, section 139(1)). It is not empowered to impose a prison term (*Finch* (1962) 47 Cr App R 58), which stands in contrast to the court's power to impose imprisonment for a refusal to be bound over. The Crown Court, when forfeiting a recognizance, must fix a term of imprisonment or detention, to be served in default (PCC(S)A 2000, section 139(2)). In the magistrates' court, a recognizance can be declared to be forfeit only by way of an order on complaint (MCA 1980, section 120), by virtue of whichever power originally imposed the bind over. Such proceedings are civil in character, and require only the civil standard of proof (*Marlow Justices, ex parte O'Sullivan* [1984] QB 381) but the person concerned should be told the nature of the breach alleged and be given an opportunity to present evidence, call witnesses or give an explanation. There appears to be no right of appeal against an adjudication of forfeiture (*Durham Justices, ex par ex parte Laurent* [1945] KB 33).

C BINDING OVER TO COME UP FOR JUDGMENT

A common law power enjoyed by the Crown Court (but not a magistrates' court or a youth **8.18** court) is to bind over a person to come up for judgment to be sentenced on a certain later day, on recognizance of certain specified conditions. If the offender breaks one or more of those conditions he will be brought back before the court for sentencing for the original offence but if he does not break any of the conditions within the specified period he will either not be sentenced for it at all or will receive a nominal penalty for it. An offender should agree to be bound over in this way, although it was held in *Williams* [1982] 1 WLR 1398 that the offender's fear that he might otherwise be sent to prison does not vitiate consent. This kind of bind over has always been made instead of sentence and it should not be added to another sentence (*Ayu* [1958] 1 WLR 1264). On the other hand, it qualifies as a 'sentence' made on conviction on indictment, and so there is an appeal available to the Court of Appeal under the Criminal Appeal Act 1968, section 50(1). The *Criminal Practice Directions*, paragraph J17 says that the court should specify the conditions with which the individual is to comply in the meantime, and not specify that the individual is to be of good behaviour.

8.19 This power is anomalous, and it appears now hardly ever to be used. It has a long history, and pre-dates all the modern non-custodial disposals and the power to defer sentence. Given that these are all now statutory in form, there is a strong argument that the bind over to come up for judgment should no longer be used, whether instead of an existing statutory power or as a way of stepping outside the limits set by Parliament on one of those powers. A contrary argument, however, is that when Parliament by schedule 23 of the CJA 2003 recast the powers to defer sentence in the PCC(S)A 2000 it did not repeal the bind over to come up for judgment but specifically preserved it (see section 1(8) of the 2000 Act).

D ABSOLUTE AND CONDITIONAL DISCHARGE

8.20 The power of any criminal court to pass an absolute or a conditional discharge may be found in section 12 of the Powers of Criminal Courts (Sentencing) Act 2000, a section which re-enacts several earlier provisions, a history which is helpfully reviewed by the Court of Appeal in *Clarke* [2010] 1 Cr App R (S) 296. The power to discharge is, in general terms, available whatever the age of the offender and whatever the offence committed, subject only to the crime of murder and cases where the prescribed sentences apply, although in theory a discharge could be passed in a case where the court held that there were 'particular circumstances' or 'exceptional circumstances' as the case may be, for not passing the prescribed sentence. There are restrictions on a youth court combining a discharge with a referral order. There are also a few other special situations in which a conditional discharge cannot be imposed, and those are dealt with at paragraph 8.26.

8.21 A discharge is not a community sentence within the meaning of the CJA 2003, section 147, so none of the conditions which apply before a community sentence can be passed apply here. There is no requirement that a court obtain a pre-sentence report before obtaining one, although it is true that a court might decide to pass a discharge after considering the contents of such a report. A discharge is not, technically a 'punishment', since section 12(1) requires the court, having considered the circumstances, including the nature of the offence and the character of the offender, to rule that 'it is inexpedient to inflict punishment' although in practice a conditional discharge can be regarded as a mild penalty. There is little reported judicial consideration of the phrase 'inexpedient to inflict punishment', but one effect of it is to restrict the other sentences or orders with which a discharge can lawfully be combined. Having reached the view that it is inexpedient to inflict punishment the court may discharge the offender absolutely, or subject to the condition that he commits no offence during such period, not exceeding three years from the date of the order, as may be specified in the order. This is the only sort of 'condition' which can be specified in a conditional discharge. If the court wants the offender to do certain things, or to engage in certain activities, or to keep away from certain places, or refrain from doing certain things (apart from committing crimes), it must make an order of a different sort.

Use of the absolute discharge

8.22 When a court grants an absolute discharge as the penalty for a single offence the offender leaves court with no effective penalty at all. The absolute discharge must, of course, be distinguished from an acquittal, since in the case of a discharge a conviction has been returned and will appear for the future on the offender's record. Three further points should be noted. First, an absolute discharge may be granted by a criminal court in a case where the person has been charged with an offence and has not been convicted but has either been found unfit to plead or not guilty by reason of insanity. Second, by section 14 of the PCC(S)A 2000, whenever a conviction is followed by a discharge (whether absolute or conditional) that conviction counts as a conviction for a limited range of purposes only (see paragraph 8.30, this chapter). Third, where an offender has been sentenced for more than one offence, and one of those offences was more serious than the others or the others were part and parcel of the main offence, some sentencers are in the habit of passing a substantive sentence (such as a fine) for the main offence and absolute discharges for the others. This is an alternative to using 'no separate penalty' for the other offences.

It is tempting simply to assume that the absolute discharge is just used in the most trivial of **8.23** cases. This is true to some extent, but there are perhaps two main types of case in which an absolute discharge has been seen as the proper sentence.

(a) In cases where the offender is virtually blameless for what has occurred, or the public interest does not require that the offender should suffer any penalty beyond the stress of a court appearance and the recording of guilt. In the old case of *Surrey County Council v Battersby* [1965] 2 QB 194 the Divisional Court recommended that magistrates should absolutely discharge a woman who had been convicted of the offence of failing to register a fostering arrangement. The facts were that before entering into the arrangement she had sought, and received, official advice that no registration was required in her case. That advice turned out to be wrong. This was a mistake about the criminal law, which cannot found a defence, but it pointed to little if any culpability. Hence an absolute discharge was the right sentence. A more recent example is *Jackson* [2007] 1 Cr App R 28, where at a Court Martial the offender pleaded guilty to flying his plane at a height of under 100 feet, forbidden by service regulations. The Court of Appeal said that if a person infringes the law with no fault then it may well be that the proper penalty is an absolute discharge.

(b) Sometimes the absolute discharge may be used by the court to register its disapproval of the police or prosecution's inappropriate handling of the case. An old case example is *Willcock v Muckle* [1951] 2 KB 844, where an absolute discharge was 'emphatically approved' by the appeal court where the police had exercised emergency powers to demand identity documents from the offender in inappropriate circumstances. Criticism may be directed at prosecuting authorities if a charge for a very trivial, stale, or technical offence has been brought. In this context the Code for Crown Prosecutors, paragraph 4.17 says that a prosecution is less likely to be required if the court is likely to impose a nominal penalty. The public interest would be better served by dropping the prosecution. In trivial cases out of court disposals such as a caution (for an adult) or a reprimand or warning (for a juvenile) will almost always be a better option than taking the matter to court.

There are one or two situations in which statute allows the court to use a conditional dis- **8.24** charge but not an absolute discharge. A football banning order cannot be made where the offence has been dealt with by an absolute discharge (Football Spectators Act 1989, section 14A(5)). The same limitation applies where a drinking banning order is made (Violent Crime Reduction Act 2006, section 7(3)).

Use of the conditional discharge

When a discharge is conditional the sole condition is that the offender must commit no **8.25** further offence during the period of the discharge. No other condition or requirement may be inserted. By section 12(6) the court may, on making an order for conditional discharge, allow any person who consents to do so to give security for the good behaviour of the offender, but this seems very rarely to happen in practice. The *Criminal Practice Directions* state that if the court does exercise this power it should specify the type of conduct from which the offender is to refrain (paragraph J20). The period of the conditional discharge is fixed by the court, up to a maximum of three years. In practice they are usually set for periods of twelve months, eighteen months, or two years. There appears to be no appellate guidance on how the court should fix the length of the period. If the offender commits a further offence (of any kind) within that period then he is in breach of the conditional discharge and will fall to be sentenced for that as well as for the new offence. Those two matters will inevitable be dealt with at the same time. The court has a complete discretion as to how deal with the breach of the conditional discharge. However it is then dealt with, it ceases to have effect.

8.26 There are some limited circumstances in which a conditional discharge cannot be used as the sentence for the offence. Obviously it cannot be used where the sentence is fixed by law or where the prescribed sentence provisions apply. Apart from those, a conditional discharge cannot be passed:

(a) where the offender has been convicted of doing something without reasonable excuse which he is prohibited from doing by an anti-social behaviour order (Crime and Disorder Act (CDA) 1998, section 1(1)), or an anti-social behaviour order made on conviction (Crime and Disorder Act 1998, section 1(11)); or

(b) except where there are exceptional circumstances relating to the offence or the offender which justify its doing so, where the offender is convicted of an offence within two years of receiving a warning (CDA 1998, section 66(4)), or within two years of having received two youth cautions (section 66ZB(5) and (6)); or

(c) where an offender is in breach of a drinking banning order (Violent Crime Reduction Act 2006, section 11(3)); or

(d) where the offender is in breach of a sexual offences prevention order (Sexual Offences Act 2003, section 113).

In none of these situations is the court prevented from using an absolute discharge.

8.27 The conditional discharge is widely used by the courts, but there is little appellate authority on its use, no doubt because a convicted person is unlikely to appeal in a case where they have been so dealt with. An offender who has been discharged by the Crown Court or a magistrates' court may appeal against his conviction, or sentence or any other ancillary order made in conjunction with the discharge (section 14(6)). It is always possible that on appeal a conditional discharge may be substituted for some greater penalty. If so, and made on appeal from a magistrates' court, it is deemed that the conditional discharge was imposed by that court and, if made on appeal from the Crown Court or the Court of Appeal, to have been made by the Crown Court (PCC(S)A 2000, section15(2)).

Combining a discharge with other sentences or orders

8.28 By the PCC(S)A 2000, section12(1) a discharge can only be imposed where 'it is inexpedient to inflict punishment'. It has therefore been held that a discharge cannot be combined with a punitive measure for the same offence (*Savage* (1983) 5 Cr App R (S) 216) except where that is expressly permitted by statute. Thus a discharge cannot be combined with a custodial sentence, a community order, or a fine (*Sanck* (1990) 12 Cr App R (S) 155). If, however, an offender is given a discharge for one of a number of offences, the court is free to exercise its normal powers of sentence with respect to the other offences (*Bainbridge* (1979) 1 Cr App

R (S) 36). Section 12(7), however, states that '[n]othing in this section shall be construed as preventing a court, on discharging an offender absolutely or conditionally in respect of any offence, from making an order for costs against the offender or imposing any disqualification on him or from making in respect of the offence an order under section 130, 143 or 148 below (compensation orders, deprivation orders and restitution orders)'. This subsection has given rise to some difficulty over the years. It is now clear that since it permits the combination of a discharge with 'any disqualification', a discharge may be combined with an order for disqualification from driving, whether imposed under the Road Traffic Acts or the PCC(S)A 2000, section 146 or 147. A discharge may be combined with an order to disqualify a person from acting as a company director or with a recommendation for deportation. Section 12(7) makes no mention of confiscation orders. The Supreme Court in *Varma* [2012] UKSC 42 held that a confiscation order can lawfully be passed on an offender who has been sentenced by way of a discharge.

Breach of conditional discharge

A conditional discharge can be breached only by the conviction of the offender of a further **8.29** offence committed during the period of the discharge. In every case the alleged breach must be clearly admitted by the offender or be proved (*Devine* (1956) 40 Cr App R 45). This will normally present no problem since the period of the discharge and the date of the subsequent offence are matters of record. Breach must always be dealt with by sentencing for the original offence. In general terms, a court dealing with the breach (the Crown Court if it made the conditional discharge, or the magistrates' court if it made it) may sentence the offender for the original offence in any manner in which it could have dealt with him if he had just been convicted before the court for that offence (section 13(6)). If, however, the Crown Court is dealing with a person conditionally discharged by a magistrates' court, it is limited to the lower court's powers (section 13(7)). One magistrates' court may deal with breach of a conditional discharge imposed by a different magistrates' court, but only with the consent of the original magistrates' court (section 13(8)). Sentencing for the original offence always terminates the conditional discharge itself, but any order for compensation or costs made at the time of the discharge remains valid (*Evans* [1963] 1 QB 979).

Limited effect of conviction on the grant of absolute or conditional discharge

By the Powers of Criminal Courts (Sentencing) Act 2000, section14(1), '...a conviction **8.30** of an offence for which an order is made under section 12 above discharging the offender absolutely or conditionally shall be deemed not to be a conviction for any purpose other than the purposes of the proceedings in which the order is made and of any subsequent proceedings which may be taken against the offender under section 13 above'. The section goes on to explain that if the offender was aged eighteen or over at the time of his conviction of the offence, and was subsequently dealt with for breach of the conditional discharge, subsection (1) will cease to apply. By section 14(3), without prejudice to subsections (1) and (2), 'the conviction of an offender who is discharged absolutely or conditionally under section 12 above shall in any event be disregarded for the purposes of any enactment or instrument which—

(a) imposes any disqualification or disability upon convicted persons; or
(b) authorises or requires the imposition of any such disqualification or disability'.

The main purpose of section 14 is to ensure that a person granted a discharge for a particular offence would not be debarred from holding an employment from which convicted persons are normally barred. The section also has a number of (perhaps unexpected) consequences. One is that a 'conviction' in respect of which a discharge was granted does not count for the purpose of the prescribed sentences, so that a previous conviction for domestic burglary which was dealt with by way of an absolute or conditional discharge is not a qualifying conviction for the purposes of the 'three strikes' rule in section 110 or 111 of the 2000 Act. It was held in *Moore* [1995] QB 353 that an offence sentenced by way of a discharge did not count as a 'conviction' for a new offence committed within the operational period so as to justify activation of an 'old-style' suspended sentence under the 2000 Act. It is unclear whether the position is the same for the current form of suspended sentence under the CJA 2003.

KEY DOCUMENTS[1]

Sentencing Guidelines Council, Definitive Guideline, *New Sentences: CJA 2003* (December 2004).

Criminal Practice Directions [2013] EWCA Crim 1631 (effective 7 October 2013), amended by [2013] EWCA Crim 2328 (effective 10 December 2013).

European Convention on Human Rights, Article 10.

---

[1] All sentencing guidelines can be found on the Sentencing Council website: <http://sentencing council.judiciary.gov.uk/>.

9

COMPENSATION, RESTITUTION, AND SURCHARGE

A COMPENSATION ORDERS

Since most criminal offences are also civil wrongs, victims, at least in theory, will often be **9.01** able to sue their offender in a civil court for damages. In reality, however, this is rarely done. In a case where the perpetrator has been caught, prosecuted, and convicted, and the facts of the matter are before the criminal court, it would seem to be an unnecessary duplication to require in addition that the victim must sue the offender in respect of their losses. It makes good sense, at least in cases which are factually clear and straightforward, for the criminal court to make an award of compensation to the victim at the same time as it imposes an appropriate punishment on the offender. The power to make compensation orders is contained in the PCC(S)A 2000, sections 130 to 134.

The central aim of making a compensation order was explained by Scarman LJ in *Inwood* **9.02** (1975) 60 Cr App R 70, when he said that it was to provide victims of crime with 'a convenient and rapid means of avoiding the expense of resorting to civil litigation, when the criminal clearly has the means which would enable the compensation to be paid'. Since the compensation order is ancillary to sentence, it should not be regarded as part of the punishment for the offence (even though the offender who is required to pay may not appreciate the difference between a compensation order and a fine), and hence its imposition does not require any adjustment in the punishment for the offence. In particular, compensation orders should not provide an escape route by which wealthy offenders may buy their way out of the normal consequences of their offending. Compensation orders are not an appropriate route for depriving an offender of the proceeds of his crime. In a case where the court has this aim in mind, a confiscation order is the appropriate option to pursue.

Power to make a compensation order

Compensation may be ordered for 'any personal injury, loss or damage' resulting from the **9.03** offence. This phrase has been quite liberally construed by the courts. Although, as already mentioned, one of the aims of making a compensation order is to save the victim from the inconvenience of making a civil claim, it was held in *Chappell* (1984) 80 Cr App R 31 that it is not a prerequisite of making a compensation order that the offender would be liable in civil law. A compensation order can be made in respect of any offence of which the offender has been convicted, to which he has pleaded guilty, or which he has asked to have taken into consideration. A table of suggested awards for different types of physical and mental injury, and physical and sexual abuse, is set out in the *Magistrates' Courts Sentencing Guidelines*. The figures given for 'physical injury' are set out at paragraph 9.04. These figures are said to be 'starting points' for compensating a range of injuries commonly encountered in a magistrates' court.

Clearly when assessing personal injury the severity of the injury including any long-lasting effects, needs to be taken into account. If this is in dispute, it may be necessary for the court to make an order for an agreed lesser sum, or to make no order at all. 'Personal injury, loss or damage' has been taken to include distress and anxiety, as well as physical injury and property damage. In *Bond v Chief Constable of Kent* (1982) 4 Cr App R (S) 314 a compensation order was upheld where an occupier suffered distress when the offender threw a stone through his window. There must in every case, however, be an acceptable level of evidence that the loss has occurred, so that in *Vaughan* (1990) 12 Cr App R (S) 46 the Court of Appeal said that the court should not simply assume from the facts of the case that the person concerned did suffer shock or distress. The other problem in *Vaughan* was that an award of compensation in that case was made to a bystander who had witnessed the victim's property being damaged. The Court quashed that order on grounds of lack of proof of shock or distress, merely querying in the process whether a bystander could properly be the recipient of a compensation order. A further important point is made in the *Magistrates' Courts Sentencing Guidelines*, which is that '[c]ompensation should benefit, not inflict further harm on, the victim'. What is meant here is that a victim may not want compensation from the victim, and it should not be assumed that they do unless there is evidence to that effect. Particular care should be taken when the injury has been the result of a sexual offence. The victim's views are properly ascertained through sensitive discussion with the police or witness liaison service at the court.

9.04 Section 130(4) states that compensation shall be of such amount as the court considers appropriate 'having regard to any evidence and to any representations that are made by or on behalf of the accused or the prosecutor'. Thus the amount of the victim's loss should either be agreed by the defence or be established by the evidence. In *Horsham Justices, ex parte Richards* (1985) 7 Cr App R (S) 158, Neill LJ said that the court must not make a compensation order 'where there are real issues raised as to whether the claimant has suffered any, and if so, what, loss'. A compensation order can be made wherever it can fairly be said that a particular loss results from the offence (*Rowlston v Kenny* (1982) 4 Cr App R (S) 85). A common sense test should be applied to this, without having regard to technical issues of causation. Thus, in *Taylor* (1993) 14 Cr App R (S) 276 it was held to be appropriate to require the offender to pay £50 compensation to a man who had been kicked in the course of an affray in which the offender and four others had taken part. It could not be established that Taylor had kicked the victim, but it was said to be 'artificial and unjust to look narrowly at the physical acts of each defendant'. A case which fell on the other side of the line was *Derby* (1990) 12 Cr App R (S) 502 where the offender had threatened the victim with a knife and his co-defendant had seriously injured the victim by attacking him with a piece of wood. It was held that a compensation order in the sum of £4000 made against the offender was improper since the offender had clearly not been responsible for inflicting those injuries. In a case where no injury, loss, or damage can be established (such as where a stolen article has

Type of injury	Description	Starting Point
Graze	Depending on size	Up to £375
Bruise	Depending on size	Up to £100
Cut: no permanent scar	Depending on size and whether stitched	£100–£500
Black Eye		£125
Eye	Blurred or double vision lasting for up to six weeks	Up to £1000
	Blurred or double vision lasting for six to thirteen weeks	£1000
	Blurred or double vision lasting for more than thirteen weeks (recovery expected)	£1750
Brain	Concussion lasting one week	£1500
Nose	Undisplaced fracture of nasal bone	£1000
	Displaced fracture requiring manipulation	£2000
	Deviated nasal septum requiring septoplasty	£2000
Loss of non-front tooth	Depending on cosmetic effect	£1250
Loss of front tooth		£1750
Facial scar	Minor disfigurement (permanent)	£1500
Arm	Fractured humerous, radius, ulna (substantial recovery)	£3300
Shoulder	Dislocated (substantial recovery)	£1750
Wrist	Dislocated/fractured—including scaphoid fracture (substantial recovery)	£3300
	Fractured—colles type (substantial recovery)	£4400
Sprained wrist, ankle	Disabling for up to six weeks	Up to £1000
	Disabling for six to thirteen weeks	£1000
	Disabling for more than thirteen weeks	£2500
Finger	Fractured finger other than index finger (substantial recovery)	£1000
	Fractured index finger (substantial recovery)	£1750
	Fractured thumb (substantial recovery)	£2000
Leg	Fractured femur, tibia (substantial recovery)	£3800
Abdomen	Injury requiring laparotomy	£3800

been recovered undamaged, and is of no less value to the owner than before it was taken) no compensation order can be made (*Hier* (1976) 62 Cr App R 233). Conversely, if there has been damage or loss to the victim, a compensation order is not precluded by the fact that the offender has made no profit from the offence.

9.05 The victim does not have to apply to the court before a compensation order can be made, and in practice victims rarely do so. The court is required by section 130(2A) to consider making a compensation order in any case where the section empowers it to do so, and section 130(3) requires the court, if it does not do so, to give reasons why no order has been made. Such reasons might well include the incompatibility of the sentence imposed for the offence (in particular, an immediate custodial sentence), or the offender's lack of means to satisfy the compensation order, or the complexity of the case. Occasionally a victim may make it known to the court that they do not wish to receive compensation from the offender and, if so, that view ought to be respected. In *R(Faithfull) v Crown Court at Ipswich* [2008] 1 WLR 1636 it was held that an action for judicial review is not available in respect of the Crown Court's failure to make a compensation order. The court should make clear in each case which amounts of compensation relate to which offence. Thus, the fixing of a global figure for compensation is not appropriate. Where there are co-defendants, it is preferable to make separate orders against each of them. It may be appropriate in a case of assault to reduce compensation to reflect a degree of provocation by the victim (*Flinton* [2008] 1 Cr App R (S) 575). When considering whether to make a compensation order the criminal court should not concern itself with whether the victim might be able to recover the relevant sum via an insurance policy or from the Criminal Injuries Compensation Scheme.

9.06   There is no limit to the amount of compensation which the Crown Court may order, although it is an important principle of sentencing that the sentencer must always have regard to the offender's ability to pay. In a magistrates' court, as a result of a change introduced by the Crime and Courts Act 2013, there is now no limit in respect of an adult offender, but for an offender aged under eighteen the PCC(S)A 2000, section 131(1) provides that the maximum sum which may be ordered by way of compensation for any offence is £5000. In *Crutchley* (1994) 15 Cr App R (S) 627, followed in *Hose* (1995) 16 Cr App R (S) 682, the Court of Appeal held that where an offender pleads guilty on the basis of specimen counts, the amount of compensation is limited to the losses shown to have resulted from the offences charged. *Crutchley* was distinguished in *Revenue and Customs Prosecutions Office v Duffy* [2008] 2 Cr App R (S) 593, where the Court of Appeal found that on the facts the relevant counts were not specimen charges.

9.07   A compensation order in respect of bereavement may only be made for the benefit of a person who could claim damages for bereavement under the Fatal Accidents Act 1976, section 1A (the spouse of the deceased or, in the case of a deceased minor, his parents). The amount of compensation shall not exceed the sum specified in the 1876 Act, section 1A(3) (£11,800 where the accident occurred after 1 January 2008) (section 130(10)). A compensation order in respect of funeral expenses can be made for the benefit of anyone who incurred these expenses (section 35(3B)).

9.08   A compensation order may only be made in respect of injury, loss, or damage (other than loss suffered by a person's dependants in consequence of his death) which was due to an accident arising out of the presence of a motor vehicle on a road, if it is damage which falls within section 130(5), or it is in respect of injury, loss, or damage for which the offender is uninsured in relation to the use of the vehicle, and compensation is not payable under any arrangements to which the Secretary of State is a party (the Motor Insurers' Bureau Agreement) (section 130(6)). In the case of property damage, the Agreement does not cover the first £300 of the damage (ie there is an 'excess' of £300), and a compensation order up to that amount may be made in an appropriate case (*DPP v Scott* (1995) 16 Cr App R (S) 292). If a compensation order is made in respect of such an accident, the compensation can include a sum representing the whole or part of any loss of or reduction in preferential rates of insurance attributable to the accident (a no-claims bonus) (section 130(7)). A vehicle which is exempted from insurance (Road Traffic Act 1988, section 144) is not uninsured for these purposes (section 130(8)).

9.09   Where a child or young person is convicted of an offence and the court makes an order for compensation, it may, under section 137 of the PCC(S)A 2000, order the parent or guardian to pay the compensation order. See paragraph 10.06, this book, for further information on this provision, which also operates in respect of fines and surcharges imposed on a child or young person.

Compensation orders not to be regarded as a punishment

As already explained, the making of a compensation order should not in principle affect **9.10** the punishment imposed for the offence. In particular, it would be quite wrong that the payment of compensation should 'permit the offender to buy his way out of a custodial sentence'. This principle has been stated on many occasions, and is well illustrated by the case of *Barney* (1991) 11 Cr App R (S) 448. In that case the judge said to the offender: '[w]ere you in a position to pay compensation I would reduce the sentence for that...'. The Court of Appeal said that the impression given by that remark was incorrect. The significance of an offer by the offender to pay compensation is that it may be treated as some indication of remorse, and to that extent may be relevant to the sentencing exercise, but it must never be thought that a convicted criminal can buy his way out of imprisonment or any part of it. This principle has not always been followed in the courts, and there have been cases where a prison sentence has been suspended because if the offender goes to prison he will not be able to pay compensation to his victim. The importance of the general principle was, however, re-emphasized by Lord Taylor CJ in *A-G's Ref (No 5 of 1993)* (1994) 15 Cr App R (S) 201.

Section 130(12) provides that where the court will sentence the offender by way of a fine, **9.11** and intends to make a compensation order as well, but the offender has limited means, the fine should be reduced or, if necessary, dispensed with altogether, to enable the compensation to be paid. The principle stated in the last paragraph is compromised to some degree by this subsection, since it permits the offender to 'buy his way out of the punishment'. Perhaps it is unobjectionable, however, since it simply requires that where an offender can only afford to pay a certain amount, it is preferable that the money should go to his victim than to the state.

Starting points for compensating physical and mental injuries commonly encountered in **9.12** a magistrates' court and developed to be consistent with the approach in the Criminal Injuries Compensation Authority tariff, are set out in the *Magistrates' Courts Sentencing Guidelines*. The relevant guidance is set out at paragraph 9.04 earlier.

Relevance of the means of the offender

It is the responsibility of the offender to inform the court of his resources, and not for the **9.13** sentencer to initiate inquiries into the matter (*Bolden* (1987) 9 Cr App R (S) 83). It is not the duty of the prosecutor to establish the offender's means (*Johnstone* (1982) 4 Cr App R (S) 141), but where the defence lawyer advances mitigation on the basis that the offender will pay substantial compensation, the lawyer is under an obligation to ensure that the necessary means exist (*Coughlin* (1984) 6 Cr App R (S) 102, *Bond* (1986) 8 Cr App R (S) 11). If the offender misleads the court into believing that he has the means to pay compensation, a subsequent appeal by the offender against the compensation order will not succeed (*Dando* [1996] 1 Cr App R (S) 155). He must pay the compensation, or serve the appropriate term in default of payment. It may also be that the offender has thereby committed an offence of perverting the course of justice.

It is generally wrong to make a compensation order which will require the sale of the **9.14** offender's home (*Harrison* (1980) 2 Cr App R (S) 313), but it is not unreasonable to expect the offender to sell other items to pay the compensation (*Workman* (1979) 1 Cr App R (S) 335).

Co-defendants may be required to pay different sums by way of compensation if their cap- **9.15** acity to pay is different. An illustrative case is *Beddow* (1987) 9 Cr App R (S) 235, where the offender was one of two defendants who pleaded guilty to being carried in a vehicle taken without consent by a third defendant, who had fallen asleep at the wheel, causing the van to crash. The offender was conditionally charged and ordered to pay £300 in compensation. The other two defendants received a suspended sentence and a conditional discharge respectively, but neither was required to pay compensation. The Court of Appeal approved the sentences on the basis that the offender was the only one of the defendants who was in work and could afford to pay. A compensation order should not be imposed on the assumption that persons other than the offender will pay, or contribute to, the order (*Hunt* [1983] Crim LR 270).

Period over which compensation may be paid

9.16   In *Webb* (1979) 1 Cr App R (S) 16, Cantley J observed that '[i]t is no use making a compensation order if there is no realistic possibility of the compensation order being complied with'. This may be because the offender has very limited means (as in *Webb*), or because the offender is serving a custodial sentence with no immediate prospect of work (eg Grafton (1979) 1 Cr App R (S) 305). By the PCC(S)A 2000, section 141 the Crown Court may allow time for payment of a compensation order, or direct that such payment shall be by instalments of such amounts and on such dates as the court may specify. A compensation order should not be made which involves payments by instalment over an unreasonable length of time. In *Bradburn* (1973) 57 Cr App R 948, Lord Widgery CJ said that, in general, compensation orders 'should be sharp in their effect, rather than protracted', and that an order which would take four years to complete was 'unreasonably long'. In *Olliver* (1989) 11 Cr App R (S) 10, the Court of Appeal indicated that a fine (or compensation order) might properly be repaid over a period of up to three years. Lord Lane CJ said that '[c]ertainly it seems to us that a two-year period will seldom be too long, and in an appropriate case three years will be unassailable'. *Olliver* still represents the law on this point.

Compensation order to be made only in clear cases

9.17   It has been a long-standing feature of the law on compensation orders that the criminal court should not make an order if to do so would involve entering into complex issues of law or fact. Compensation orders are intended to provide a straightforward remedy in a simple case. In *Donovan* (1981) 3 Cr App R (S) 192, for example, the offender pleaded guilty to taking a conveyance, having hired a car for two days and failed to return it. The car had suffered no damage. The offender was fined £250, with £100 costs and £1388 compensation, on the basis of the hire company's loss of use. Eveleigh LJ said that '[a] compensation order is designed for the simple, straightforward case where the amount of the compensation can be readily and easily ascertained'. Since the amount of damages in a civil case of loss of use 'is notoriously open to argument', the compensation order was quashed, and the hire company was left to pursue its civil remedy if it wished to do so. In *Hyde v Emery* (1984) 6 Cr App R (S) 206 the offender pleaded guilty to three charges of obtaining unemployment benefit by false representation. There was a dispute over whether the sum claimed in compensation by the relevant government department should be reduced by the amount of supplementary benefit which he could legitimately have claimed. Watkins LJ said in the Divisional Court that the magistrates should have declined to deal with the matter.

9.18   More recently, however, without abandoning the principle the courts have been more prepared to persist with a compensation inquiry. In *James* [2003] 2 Cr App R (S) 574, for example, the offender pleaded guilty to twenty counts of false accounting. The total sum involved was in dispute, but there was an agreed minimum loss of £8000 to the victim. The Court of Appeal said that it was proper for a compensation order in that sum to be ordered, bearing in mind that the only realistic chance for the victim to receive any compensation from the offender was through the criminal process. This seems a desirable approach in a case where a minimum loss can be agreed, in preference to the court declining to consider compensation altogether. In *Pola* [2010] 1 Cr App R (S) 32 the Court of Appeal upheld a compensation order in the sum of £90,000 made against a man convicted of an offence under the Health and Safety at Work Act 1974, where a workman had been severely injured by the collapse of a wall. The court noted that criminal courts had now developed more expertise in financial assessment from the experience of confiscation proceedings, and it might be that the very cautious approach adopted in the earlier authorities to the making of compensation orders needed some modification.

Combining compensation orders with other sentences or orders

Compensation orders may be imposed on an offender 'instead of or in addition to dealing with him in any other way' (PCC(S)A 2000, section 130(1)). This is very broadly expressed, and it is further provided that a compensation order may be combined with an absolute or conditional discharge (section 12(7)). While a compensation order may be combined with a sentence of immediate custody where the offender is clearly able to pay, or has good prospects of employment on his release from custody (*Love* [1999] 1 Cr App R (S) 484), it is often inappropriate to impose a compensation order as well as imprisonment. The compensation order may be 'counterproductive, and force him back into crime to find the money' (*Inwood* (1974) 60 Cr App R 70). See also *Jorge* [1999] 2 Cr App R (S) 1. While it is not wrong to combine a compensation order with a suspended sentence, regard should be had to the fact that if the offender is in breach of the suspended sentence, its activation may bring to an end any prospect of the payment of compensation (*McGee* [1978] Crim LR 370). **9.19**

As explained earlier, where it would be appropriate both to impose a fine and to make a compensation order but the offender has insufficient means to pay both, the court must give preference to compensation, although it may impose a fine as well (section 130(12)). It can be seen that in some circumstances that it is lawful for a compensation order to stand alone on sentence. This position is much more likely to arise in a magistrates' court than in Crown Court. In a case where the court makes a compensation order as well as the specified surcharge (see paragraph 9.32) and the offender is of limited means and unable to pay both sums the surcharge shall be reduced (if necessary, to nothing) in order for the compensation to be paid. **9.20**

Enforcement of compensation orders

An offender may appeal against a compensation order to the Crown Court if the order was made by a magistrates' court, or to the Court of Appeal if it was made by the Crown Court. **9.21**

The victim of the offence does not receive the compensation until there is no further possibility of an appeal on which the order could be varied or set aside (section 132(1)). **9.22**

Enforcement of compensation orders, as with fines, is a function of the magistrates' courts. The maximum terms of imprisonment which a magistrates' court may impose in default of payment of compensation orders are specified in the Magistrates' Courts Act 1980, schedule 4. These are the same periods which apply in the case of fines, and which are set out in the table at paragraph 11.14, this book, except that the magistrates have no power to specify a term in default in excess of twelve months. These are maximum terms, and the magistrates have discretion to fix a lower term. The Crown Court is not normally empowered to make an order fixing the term to be served in default of payment of a compensation order (in contrast to its duty to do so in respect of fines (*Komsta* **9.23**

(1990) 12 Cr App R (S) 63). The maximum terms indicated in schedule 4 will thus normally also apply in default of compensation orders imposed by the Crown Court. Exceptionally, however, if the Crown Court makes a compensation order for an amount in excess of £20,000 and considers that a maximum default term of twelve months is inadequate, it may fix a longer period, not exceeding the term specified for the equivalent amount in the PCC(S)A 2000, section 139(4). As with fines, part payment of the compensation order will result in a proportionate reduction in the term to be served in default. A court may make an order for sums payable in respect of a compensation order made by a magistrates' court or the Crown Court to be deducted from the offender's benefit payments.

9.24 By the PCC(S)A 2000, section 133, at any time before the offender has paid into court the whole of the money under the order, the magistrates' court having power to enforce the order may, on the application of the offender, discharge the order or reduce it, on the ground that:

(a) the injury, loss, or damage in respect of which the order was made has been held in civil proceedings to be less than it was taken to be for the purposes of the order;

(b) that property, the loss of which was the subject of the order, has now been recovered;

(c) the means of the offender are insufficient to satisfy both the compensation order and a confiscation order made against him in the same proceedings under the CJA 1988, part IV, or the Proceeds of Crime Act 2002, part 2; or

(d) the offender's means have suffered a substantial reduction, which was unexpected at the time of making the order.

Where a material change in the offender's circumstances has occurred, the proper course is to apply to the magistrates' court, and not to appeal to the Court of Appeal (*Palmer* (1994) 15 Cr App R (S) 550). Before the magistrates can act to discharge or reduce the order under (c) or (d), they must have the consent of the Crown Court if the Crown Court made the order. See further *Favell* [2010] EWCA Crim 2948 and the CPR 2011, rule 42.5.

B RESTITUTION ORDERS

9.25 The Crown Court and a magistrates' court may make a restitution order. The relevant law is set out in the PCC(S)A 2000, section 148. A restitution order is an order which is imposed by the court as ancillary to the sentence for the offence, and may be made in combination with any other sentence passed, including a deferment of sentence (section 148(1) and (2)). Its basic object is simple compensation—to return stolen property from the offender to the victim from whom it was stolen. The legal provisions are, however, rather more complex since they must allow for the possibility that the offender has disposed of the goods in the meantime. In many situations a compensation order may achieve the same effect in a different way, but restitution orders remain an effective way of returning the actual property (rather than its value) to the victim.

Power to make restitution order

9.26 Power to make a restitution order arises where goods have been 'stolen'. This term is construed widely, to include not just theft and offences where theft is a constituent element, such as robbery and burglary, but also where goods were obtained by blackmail or by fraud. A restitution order can be made where goods have been stolen and the offender has been convicted of an offence 'with reference to the theft', or where such an offence has been taken into consideration when sentencing the offender for a different offence. An offence 'with reference to' the theft of stolen goods includes handling them. Provided that it is sufficiently established that the goods were stolen, a restitution order may be made even though nobody has been convicted of the theft itself.

When the court is entitled to make a restitution order it can order the offender (or anyone **9.27** else who is in possession of the goods or has control over them) to restore them to any person who is entitled to them (section 148(2)(a)). It may well be that the police will have taken possession of the stolen goods on arresting the offender so the enforcement of the order will create no practical problems. Where the offender no longer has the stolen goods, but is in possession of goods which directly or indirectly represent them, he may be ordered to transfer to any person entitled to them the goods representing those which have been stolen (section 148(2)(b)). Thus, if an offender steals a television set, sells it, and buys a laptop computer with the proceeds, the victim of the theft may apply to the court for an order that the laptop be transferred to him. This form of order may be made only where the proposed beneficiary makes an application. For the required terms of that application see the CPR 2011, rule 42.7. Lastly the court may order that, out of any money taken from the offender at the time of his apprehension, a sum not exceeding the value of the stolen goods should be paid to any person who would have been entitled to them if they had still been in the offender's possession (section 148(2)(c)).

An order may be made of the court's own motion under section 148(2)(a) without an ap- **9.28** plication being made. If an order is made under section 148(2)(a), it will be inappropriate to order restitution under section 148(2)(b) or (c) in addition since the person will thereby recover more than the value of the goods (*Parsons* (1976) CSP J3-2F01). For an order under section 148(2)(a), the person in 'possession or control' need not be the offender, and might be an innocent purchaser of the goods. Where a person has, in good faith, bought the relevant goods from the person convicted, or has, in good faith, lent money to the convicted person on the security of the goods, the court may order payment of compensation to that person out of money taken from the offender under section 148(2)(c). Under section 148(2) (b) an application must be made by the person claiming, and may not relate to goods held by a third party. Where the offender is no longer in possession of the goods, orders may be made under both section 148(2)(b) and (c) with reference to the same goods, providing again that the person claiming does not thereby recover more than the value of the goods (section 148(3)). An order may be made under section 148(2)(c) with or without an application being made by the victim. The phrase 'taken out of his possession on his apprehension' in section 148(2)(c) has been generously construed to extend to money seized from the offender well after he has been arrested (*Ferguson* [1970] 1 WLR 1246). There is no need to show that the money is the proceeds of the relevant offence—all that is necessary is to show is that it is money belonging to the offender. It was held in *Lewis* [1975] Crim LR 353 that where the offenders had split the proceeds of a robbery between them, a restitution order under section 148(2)(c) may be made against one offender for a greater sum that he actually received under his share, provided that this is not for a sum greater than the total loss.

Restitution orders: procedure

The factual basis for making a restitution order may be established from evidence given at the **9.29** offender's trial, from witness statements before the court in a case where he pleads guilty, or from admissions made by the offender or by anyone else who would be adversely affected by the making of the order. Orders should, however, be made only in cases where the evidence is clear and has been given before sentence is imposed (section 148(5) and (6), and *Church* (1970) 55 Cr App R 65). In particular a restitution order should not be made where the question of title to the goods is unclear. This point has been made in several cases, and is well established. It is analogous to the similar rule in compensation orders. Under the Police (Property) Act 1897 the police or any person claiming property at the end of criminal proceedings may invoke that Act, and a magistrates' court can then make an order for the delivery of the property to the person who appears to the court to be the owner. If the owner cannot be ascertained the court may make such order in relation to the property as it thinks fit (section 1(1)). This includes its sale or destruction, in a case where no owner has been ascertained.

9.30 If a magistrates' court commits the offender for sentence to the Crown Court the power to make a restitution order passes to the Crown Court, and should not be exercised by the magistrates before the committal. An offender may appeal against the making of a restitution order, as against any other sentence. Such an order is, however, subject to a unique proviso. Where the order is passed on conviction on indictment it is subject to an automatic suspension for twenty-eight days from the date of the conviction (unless the trial judge specifically directs to the contrary on the grounds that 'the title to the property is not in dispute': Criminal Appeal Act 1968, section 30(1)) or, further, until the determination of any appeal. If the restitution order is made by a magistrates' court, it is subject to an automatic suspension for twenty-one days from the date of conviction (unless the court directs to the contrary as above: section 49(4) or, further, until the determination of any appeal).

9.31 As already mentioned, a restitution order is an ancillary order and it is clear that it may be combined with any other sentence. A restitution order and a compensation order might be made at the same time, such as where the goods which are subject of the restitution order are returned but have been damaged.

C SURCHARGES

9.32 A surcharge is a financial order which must be added to the sentence imposed by a magistrates' court or by the Crown Court. The level of the surcharge varies in accordance with the sentence passed. The sum specified by the court is recovered from the offender and is channelled by the government into various schemes established to assist the victims of crime. The surcharge has sometimes been referred to, therefore, as the 'victim surcharge' but that expression is probably best avoided in practice. That is because of the risk that a judge imposing a surcharge may be misunderstood by the public or by the press as having ordered a sum of money to be paid by the offender which somehow reflects the harm which was done to the victim in the particular case before the court. The Council of Circuit Judges therefore issued in December 2012 an agreed form of words for judges to use when imposing the surcharge, which is that '[t]he surcharge provisions apply to this case and the order can be drawn up accordingly'.

9.33 The law on the surcharge derives from the CJA 2003, sections 161A and 161B. These sections were inserted by the Domestic Violence, Crime and Victims Act 2004, section 14. Prior to October 2012 a surcharge only had to be ordered when a fine was imposed on sentence, and the surcharge was set at a flat rate of £15, irrespective of the level of the fine. From 1 October 2012, however, the scheme was substantially amended, such that a surcharge, set at the appropriate amount, must be imposed by the sentencing court in (almost) every case. The Secretary of State has made an order (the Criminal Justice Act 2003 (Surcharge) Order 2012 (SI 2012 No 1696)) applicable to offences committed on or after 1st October 2012. For an offence committed before that date (or, if the court is dealing with the offender for more than one offence, any of those offences) the former flat-rate surcharge would apply. This has caused a fair amount of transitional difficulty, with the Court of Appeal having to quash surcharges passed during 2013 where one or more of the offences being dealt with were committed prior to 1 October 2012. Examples are *Stone* [2013] EWCA Crim 723 and *Swallow* [2013] EWCA

Crim 719. As time moves on this particular problem will largely disappear. The 2012 Order states that a surcharge will be payable in cases where the offender is dealt with by way of a disposal set out in the schedule to the Order. No surcharge is payable in respect of an absolute discharge or a hospital order. Whether a surcharge is payable in respect of a reparation order or a bind over to keep the peace is unclear. In all other cases the surcharge *must* be ordered. There is no scope for reducing the surcharge or for waiving it as where, for example, the offender appears to have no means to pay. The only exception to the requirement to impose the surcharge is if the offender is of limited means, where the surcharge may be reduced (if necessary, to nothing) to enable payment of a compensation order. There is also the possibility of the court giving the offender time to pay, by virtue of the PCC(S)A 2000, section 141 and the Administration of Justice Act 1970, schedule 9, paragraph 13.

The payable amounts

The Order sets out the amounts which are payable. There are three tables. **9.34**

(1) If the offender was under eighteen when the offence was committed:
conditional discharge £10
fine, youth rehabilitation order, referral order, or community order £15;
suspended sentence £20;
custodial sentence imposed by the Crown Court £20

It will be seen that the important date is the age of the offender when the offence was committed, not (as is usually the case with sentencing powers) his or her age when convicted of the offence. For offenders aged under eighteen, the PCC(S)A 2000, section 137(1A) provides that any surcharge must be paid by the young offender's parent or guardian unless he cannot be found, or it is unreasonable to require him to pay. The community order and the suspended sentence (listed above) are not available in law for offenders aged under eighteen, so they must be included here in order to cater for an offender aged seventeen at the time of the offence but eighteen when convicted. The reparation order has for some reason been omitted from the list. It is not a community order (CJA 2003, section 147), and so presumably should have been included.

(2) If the offender was aged eighteen or over when the offence was committed:
conditional discharge, £15;
fine—10 per cent of the value of the fine, rounded up or down to the nearest pound, which must be no less than £20 and no more than £120;
community order, £60;
suspended sentence where the term suspended is six months or less, £80;
suspended sentence where the term suspended is more than six months, £100;
imprisonment or detention in a young offender institution imposed by the Crown Court of up to and including six months, £80;
imprisonment or detention in a young offender institution imposed by the Crown Court for more than 6 months and up to and including twenty-four months, £100;
imprisonment or detention in a young offender institution exceeding twenty-four months, £120;
imprisonment for public protection or detention for public protection, £120;
imprisonment or custody for life, £120.

It will be seen that, in contrast to the position before October 2012 the surcharge payable following the imposition of a fine is no longer flat-rate. It varies as a proportion of the fine, but with lower and upper limits. It will also be seen the surcharge is payable in respect of all custodial sentences *in the Crown Court but not in magistrates' courts*. There is no mention in the list of a bind over to keep the peace, so it must be assumed that no surcharge is payable if such an order stands alone as a disposal.

(3) If the offender is not an individual (ie a corporate offender)
     conditional discharge, £15;
     fine, 10 per cent of the value of the fine, rounded up or down to the nearest pound,
     which must be no less than £20 and no more than £120.

There are some further principles which apply in relation to all three of these tables. If the
offender is sentenced for more than one offence,

(i)   the offender is only subject to the under-eighteen surcharge rate if all the offences were
       committed when he was under eighteen;
(ii)   in any case where the offender is made subject to two or more disposals of the same
       form the surcharge is paid once;
(iii) if the offender is made subject to two or more different forms of disposal, the surcharge
       to be imposed is the higher or highest applicable amount.

Enforcement of surcharge

9.35 A surcharge is normally enforced as a fine imposed on summary conviction, so it is for the
magistrates' court to recover the appropriate sum from the offender. If an immediate custodial sentence is passed in the Crown Court, however, the surcharge is recovered from the
offender by removal from him of money paid to him as the prisoner's 'wage' during his term
of imprisonment. It follows that the Crown Court should not set a term of imprisonment in
default of payment of the surcharge, as it is required to do in relation to a fine. The Crown
Court should not fix a period of imprisonment in default of payment of the surcharge
(*Holden* [2013] EWCA Crim 2017). The PCC(S)A 2000, section 139, which empowers the
fixing of a default term for a fine, has therefore not been amended to include the surcharge.

Appeal

9.36 Since there is no discretion over the imposing of a surcharge there are very limited circumstances
in which an offender could appeal against a surcharge having been imposed. If the sentencing
court has made a mistake and imposed too high a surcharge then according to the Court of
Appeal in *Stone* [2013] EWCA Crim 723 a surcharge falls within the definition of a sentence in
the Criminal Appeal Act 1968, section 50(1), so the Court can amend the surcharge on appeal.
The matter is more complicated if the sentencing court has made a mistake in the other direction
and either imposed too low a surcharge or (perhaps more likely) forgotten to do so at all. In that
situation the Court will only be able to correct the surcharge order if the offender has appealed
against his sentence and the Court has allowed the appeal by reducing some other element of the
sentence. The surcharge can then be amended appropriately provided that the overall sentence
is not more severe than before (Criminal Appeal Act 1968, section 11(3)). This situation has
arisen once or twice already and the Court has managed to make the appropriate adjustment.
An example is *Taylor* [2013] EWCA Crim 1704. The far preferable course is for the court not to
forget to order the surcharge in the first place or, if the matter has been forgotten, to rectify the
sentence within fifty-six days under the slip rule.

KEY DOCUMENTS[1]

Sentencing Guidelines Council, Definitive Guideline, *Magistrates Sentencing Guidelines* (effective
   4 August 2008).

Criminal Injuries Compensation Scheme 2012 <http://www.justice.gov.uk/victims-and-witnesses/cica>.

Motor Insurers Bureau Scheme <http://www.mib.org.uk>.

---

[1] All sentencing guidelines can be found on the Sentencing Council website: <http://sentencing
council.judiciary.gov.uk/>.

10

ORDERS AGAINST PARENTS

The SGC guideline, *Sentencing Youths*, says that a significant difference arising from the **10.01** procedures for dealing with young offenders is the importance attached to the presence of a parent, carer, or appropriate adult at key stages, especially when sentence is imposed. In addition, specific provisions exist to enable a court to reinforce the responsibilities of a parent or guardian. The obligation that a parent should attend court at sentence reflects the principal aim of the youth justice system of reducing offending, recognizing that this is unlikely to be achieved by the young offender alone. A court must be aware of the risk that a young person will seek to avoid this requirement by urging the court to proceed to sentence in the absence of an adult. If the court proceeds in the absence of a responsible adult it should ensure that the outcome of the sentencing hearing is properly communicated.

A BINDING OVER OF PARENT OR GUARDIAN OF YOUNG OFFENDER

The PCC(S)A 2000, section 150(1) places an obligation upon the youth courts and the **10.02** Crown Court to bind over the parent or guardian of an offender who is under the age of sixteen, whenever the court is satisfied that to do so would be desirable in the interests of preventing the commission by the young offender of further offences. If the court is not so satisfied it should state that in open court and give reasons for its view. In contrast to the obligation in relation to offenders aged under sixteen, the court has a discretion to bind over the parent or guardian of a young offender aged sixteen or seventeen. According to the *Criminal Practice Directions*, paragraph J19, whenever a court is considering making an order under section 150 it should clearly specify the actions which the parent or guardian is to take (paragraph J19).

The bind over will normally be imposed on the parent or guardian at the same time as sen- **10.03** tence is imposed on the young offender. In such a case the court may include a requirement in the bind over that the parent or guardian should ensure that the young offender complies with the terms and requirements of the sentence imposed. A bind over may not be made where the court deals with the young offender by way of a referral order.

By section 150(3) the court is empowered to order the parent or guardian to enter into a **10.04** recognizance, in a sum on money not exceeding £1000, to take proper care of the young offender and to exercise proper control over him. The maximum duration of the order is until the young offender reaches the age of eighteen, or for a period of three years, whichever is the shorter period (section 150(4)). Entry into the recognizance requires the consent of the parent or guardian, but if consent is refused and the court considers that the refusal is unreasonable, the parent or guardian may be punished by a fine not exceeding level 3 on the standard scale (section 150(2)). In fixing the level of the recognizance the court should takes into account, among other things, the means of the parent or guardian, whether such consideration has the effect of increasing or reducing the level of the recognizance fixed upon (section 150(7)).

10.05　As far as forfeiture of the recognizance is concerned, section 150(5) states that the MCA 1980, section 120 shall apply in relation to a recognizance order under section 150 as it does to a recognizance to keep the peace. The court may therefore order forfeiture of the whole or part of the recognizance in its discretion. A right of appeal to the Crown Court against an order made under section 150 which is made by a magistrates' court is created by section 150(8). Where the order is made by the Crown Court there is a right of appeal to the Court of Appeal (section 150(9)).

B FINANCIAL ORDERS TO BE PAID BY PARENT ETC

10.06　By the PCC(S)A 2000, section 137, the parent or guardian of an offender aged under eighteen shall normally be ordered by the court to pay the fine, costs, or compensation order upon the young offender. This applies whether the fine or compensation stands alone on sentence or is imposed in combination with some other form of disposal. The court must make such an order unless satisfied either (i) that the parent or guardian cannot be found, or (ii) that it would be unreasonable to make an order for payment, having regard to the circumstances of the case (section 137(1)). Section 137(2) further provides that where a person under eighteen would otherwise be required to pay a fine in respect of breach of a youth rehabilitation order, or reparation order, or for breach of a supervision requirement in a detention and training order, the court must order the fine to be paid by the parent or guardian, subject to the same qualifications. Section 137(1A) provides that the required surcharge must be paid by the parent or guardian, again unless he cannot be found or it is unreasonable to require him to pay. Section 137(3) states that in the case of a young offender aged sixteen or seventeen, these subsections have effect as if, instead of imposing a duty, they conferred a power to make such an order. No order of this kind should be made against a parent or guardian without giving that person the opportunity to be heard (section 137(4)). The only exception to that would be where the parent or guardian has been required to attend, but has failed to do so (section 137(5)). The term 'guardian' has the same meaning as in the Children and Young Persons Act 1933, section 107.

10.07　For the purposes of any order made under section 137 the references in the statutory provisions relating to the fixing of the various financial orders shall be read as if they referred to the means of the parent or guardian rather than the means of the offender (section 138). The court should not make an order under section 137 against a parent or guardian without first considering the means of that parent or guardian (*Lenihan v West Yorkshire Metropolitan Police* (1981) 3 Cr App R (S) 42). Before exercising its powers under section 137 the court may make a financial circumstances order with respect to the parent or guardian (section 136). It may be 'unreasonable' for the court to make an order under section 137 in a case where the parent or guardian has done all that he or she reasonably could to prevent the offending (*Sheffield Crown Court, ex parte Clarkson* (1986) 8 Cr App R (S) 454). An example of an order being improperly made is *J-B* [2004] 2 Cr App R (S) 211, where the judge ordered the father of the sixteen-year-old offender to pay compensation of £1000 to the victim without making any proper inquiry into the parent's means and indeed shortly after commenting that both parents had done well in bringing up their son. If the child has been in local authority accommodation under a voluntary arrangement it may well be unreasonable to require the local authority to pay (*TA v DPP* [1997] 1 Cr App R (S) 1). Assessment of the means of the parent or guardian, or assessment of the extent to which the parent or guardian has been neglectful of the offender, should be made on the basis of properly admissible evidence and not simply assumed from the pre-sentence report prepared upon the young offender (*Lenihan*).

Section 137(8) provides that where a local authority has parental responsibility for a child **10.08** or young person, and the child or young person is in the care of a local authority, or is being provided with accommodation by them in the exercise of their social services functions, references in section 137 to 'parent or guardian' should be construed as references to that local authority. A local authority or company which provides residential accommodation for 'difficult to place' children does not fall within the meaning of 'guardian' in the CYPA 1933, section 107, and so no order could be made with respect to them under section 137 unless, in the case of a local authority, it fell within the terms of section 137(8) (*Leeds City Council v West Yorkshire Police* [1983] 1 AC; *Marlowe Child and Family Health Services v DPP* [1988] 2 Cr App R (S) 438). In *D v DPP* (1995) 16 Cr App R (S) 1040, the Divisional Court held that a court should not make an order against the local authority in a case where the authority had done all that it reasonably and properly could to protect the public from the young offender and to keep the young offender from criminal ways. Where the local authority so contends, it should be ready to provide evidence to the court of the steps which it has taken. In *Bedfordshire County Council v DPP* [1996] 1 Cr App R (S) 322, the Divisional Court further held that before an order for payment by a local authority could be made, a causative link should normally be established between any fault proved on the part of the council and the offences committed. If no such causative fault was shown to the satisfaction of the court, it would be unreasonable to order compensation. In these provisions 'local authority' and 'parental responsibility' have the same meaning as they do in the Children Act 1989.

When the Crown Court makes an order under section 139 in respect of a fine it should not **10.09** fix any period to be served in default. The order is enforced by the magistrates' court. An appeal against an order made by a magistrates' court under section 137 lies to the Crown Court (section 137(6)) and an appeal against an order made by the Crown Court under section 137 lies to the Court of Appeal (section 137(7)).

C PARENTING ORDERS

Under sections 8 to 10 of the Crime and Disorder Act 1998, the Crown Court and youth **10.10** courts have power to impose a parenting order on a parent or guardian of a child or young person where, amongst other things, that child or young person has been convicted of any offence (section 8(1)(c)). Section 8(1)(a), (b), and (d) allow for the imposing of parenting orders in other circumstances, in consequence of making a child safety order, or an anti-social behaviour order, or a sex offender order in the case of a child or young person, or where a parent is convicted of an offence involving failure to comply with a school attendance order or failure to secure the regular attendance at school of a registered pupil. These matters are not directly related to sentencing, and so are not considered further here. 'Guardian' includes any person who has for the time being charge of or control over the child or young person. Given that more than one person may qualify as parent or guardian in respect of the youth offender, the court has some discretion over who is to be the subject of the order. The reality may be that, where one parent takes an interest in the youngster and attends court and the other parent does not, it is the one who attends who is the more likely to be the subject of the order, not least because the court must explain the effect of the order to the person attending court. The consent of the parent or guardian is not required.

10.11 It should be understood that a parenting order follows conviction of the young offender, but it is not a conviction of the parent—nor is it meant to be a case of punishing the parent for the sins of the child. It is true that in some cases a parent may have contributed to the commission of the child's offence (whether by complicity, dereliction of duty, or neglect) but this will not generally have been investigated by the court or be known. The parenting order is designed to hold the parent responsible in the sense of instilling a duty to prevent their child's future law-breaking.

Power to make parenting order

10.12 Parenting orders are not available in all local areas, so the court must first make sure that such an order can be made in their area. By section 8(4) a parenting order is an order which requires the parent or guardian to comply, for a period not exceeding twelve months, with requirements set out in the order and to attend, within the same period but for not exceeding three months, counselling or parental guidance sessions specified by the responsible officer (who will be a probation officer, social worker, or member of the youth offending team). There cannot be more than one counselling or guidance session in any one week. The court must be of the view that the parenting order would be desirable in the interests of preventing the commission of any further offence by the child or young person. The counselling or guidance programme which the parent is required to attend can be a residential course if the court is satisfied that attendance on a residential basis is likely to be more effective in preventing re-offending than attendance at a non-residential course, and that the interference with family life which is likely to result from that attendance is proportionate in all the circumstances. The counselling or guidance programme must be included in the parenting order unless the parent has already been the subject of a parenting order and attended such sessions on that earlier occasion. Other requirements in the order commonly include that the parent must ensure that the child is accompanied to and from school each day, and is indoors by a certain hour in the evening. In any event, requirements specified in the parenting order shall, as far as practicable, be such as to avoid any conflict with the parent's religious beliefs and any interference with the times, if any, at which he normally works or attends an educational establishment. In *R (M) v Inner London Crown Court* (2003) *The Times*, 27 February 2003, the Divisional Court held that the making of parenting orders did not contravene Article 8 of the ECHR, which guarantees respect for private and family life.

10.13 While section 8 creates a *power* to make a parenting order where the child or young person who has committed the offence is aged under eighteen, section 9 goes further and places a *duty* on the court to make a parenting order where the young offender is aged under sixteen. If, however, the court is not satisfied that the making of a parenting order would be desirable in the interests of preventing re-offending then the court must state in open court that it is not so satisfied, and why it is not (section 9(1)). This is an important discretion for the court. The judge or youth court magistrates may take the view that the home circumstances are such that a parenting order is unnecessary (perhaps because the parents are coping as well as they reasonably can, or because the parents recognize the need for help but are willing to receive that on a voluntary basis without the need for a court order), or would be counter-productive (perhaps because the family is already dysfunctional or under such pressure that the making of a parenting order would only make matters worse). Before making a parenting order on the parent of a young offender under sixteen, although a pre-sentence report is not required, the court must take into account the family circumstances, and if the order is made its effect must be explained in ordinary language to the parent. So must the consequences which may flow from breach of the order. The SGC guideline on *Sentencing Youths* suggests that when considering whether to impose a parenting order the court should give careful consideration to the strength of familial relationships and to any diversity issues that might impact on the achievement of the purposes of the order. Particular issues may arise where an offender is, or runs the risk of, experiencing familial abuse.

A youth court has power to make a parenting order at the same time as sentencing the **10.14** young offender by way of a referral order. If, however, the offender is aged under sixteen, such that the youth court would normally be under a duty to impose a parenting order, that duty does not extend to cases where the youth court is considering whether to make a parenting order at the same time as making a referral order. If the court intends to make a referral order and a parenting order at the same time, it should obtain and consider a report by an appropriate officer. A parent can be ordered by the court to attend referral order meetings (PCC(S)A 2000, section 20(1)).

A person in respect of whom a parenting order has been made has the same right of appeal **10.15** against that order as if the offence that led to the making of the order were an offence committed by him, and the order were a sentence passed on him for the offence (section 10(4)). Appeal will lie to the Crown Court or Court of Appeal as appropriate.

Breach, variation, and discharge of parenting order

If, while a parenting order is in force, the parent without reasonable excuse fails to **10.16** comply with any requirement included in the order, he shall be liable on summary conviction to a fine not exceeding level 3 on the standard scale (section 9(7)). It would appear that in the absence of such failure to comply by the parent, commission of a further offence by the child does not constitute a breach of the parenting order. There are very few reported cases dealing with breach of parenting orders, but N [2007] EWCA Crim 2524 is an example of a fourteen-year-old offender who was sentenced for an offence of arson against a background of 'woefully inadequate' parenting, the child being allowed 'to run wild and roam around at all hours of the day and night with no significant control'. Her father had been given parenting orders but had failed to comply with them and was in breach.

If, while the parenting order is in force, application is made to the court either by the re- **10.17** sponsible officer or by the parent, the court may, if appropriate, make an order discharging the parenting order, or varying it by cancelling any provision in it or inserting in it any provision which could have been included from the start. This procedure seems most apt to deal with a significant change in the family circumstances, and it should not be seen as an alternative to an appeal against the order. If an application is made for discharge of a parenting order and that application is dismissed, no fresh application for discharge can be made without the consent of the court which made the order.

KEY DOCUMENTS[1]

Sentencing Guidelines Council, Definitive Guideline, *Sentencing Youths* (effective 30 November 2009).

Criminal Practice Directions [2013] EWCA Crim 1631 (effective 7 October 2013), amended by [2013] EWCA Crim 2328 (effective 10 December 2013).

European Convention on Human Rights, Article 8.

---

[1] All sentencing guidelines can be found on the Sentencing Council website: <http://sentencing council.judiciary.gov.uk/>.

11

FINES

A fine is an order that the offender shall pay a specified sum of money to the state, and it is **11.01** the most commonly imposed penalty in the criminal courts. This Chapter also deals with deprivation orders, which are aptly described as a form of fine. Rather than operating by removal from the offender of a sum of money, however, they operate by removal of one or more items of property belonging to the offender. Both fines and deprivation orders are properly regarded as straightforward punishments, but the sentencing principles applicable to each are not always straightforward.

What is the place of the fine within the sentencing framework? As we saw in Chapter 1, **11.02** an offence crosses the custodial sentence threshold if the offence committed is so serious 'that neither a fine alone nor a community sentence can be justified for the offence' (CJA 2003, section 152(2)). Where this subsection applies it would seem the fine (at least standing alone as a sentence) can be ruled out. However, the *Magistrates' Courts Sentencing Guidelines* do allow for the possibility of imposing a fine in lieu of a custodial sentence, as we will see paragraph 11.07, this Chapter. The community sentence threshold applies where the offence is 'serious enough' to warrant a community disposal, but that clearly does not require that the offence must be too serious to be dealt with by a fine. There is thus an overlap between the fine and the community sentence, so that the court will sometimes have to make a choice between them. It seems that in making that choice the main consideration will be whether a simple financial penalty ('hitting the offender in the pocket') is a proper and adequate response to the case, or whether the nature of the offence and the character and circumstances of the offender requires supervision or some other more intensive intervention. Again, the *Magistrates' Courts Sentencing Guidelines* allow for that situation.

The great majority of indictable offences are punishable by way of a fine. The only absolute **11.03** exception is murder, where the mandatory sentence of life imprisonment applies. There are also the various prescribed minimum custodial sentences where the use of a fine is effectively excluded. The CJA 2003, section 163 states that where a person is convicted on indictment the court may impose a fine instead of (save for the cases already mentioned) or in addition to dealing with him in any other way, 'if not precluded from sentencing the offender by its exercise of some other power'. This is a reference to certain impermissible combinations of sentence—a fine cannot be combined with a hospital order, or a discharge, for instance.

11.04   All summary offences are punishable by fine. If a statute mentions only imprisonment as a means of dealing with offenders for a summary offence, a fine not exceeding level 3 on the standard scale may none the less be imposed as an alternative (MCA 1980, section 34(3)). Statutes creating summary offences permit a fine up to a certain level on the 'standard scale' of fines, rather than each offence referring to a sum of money. The standard scale can be found in the CJA 1982, section 37(2). It applies to summary offences only, and is as follows:

Level on the scale	Amount of fine
1	£200
2	£500
3	£1000
4	£2500
5	£5000

An offence which is punishable at level 1 on the standard scale is generally known as a 'level 1' offence, and so on. A fine for a level 1 offence cannot exceed £200. The actual level of the fine will be determined in accordance with the normal sentencing principles. Of course the advantage of this approach is that changes over time in the value of money may be taken into account by adjustment to the standard scale rather than by having to amend all the individual provisions affected.

A   FINES IN THE MAGISTRATES' COURTS

11.05   When an offender has been summarily convicted of an offence triable either way which is listed in schedule 1 to the MCA 1980, the magistrates may fine him an amount not exceeding the 'prescribed sum' (MCA 1980, section 32(1)). By section 32(9) 'the prescribed sum' is £5000. Where, however, the offender has been summarily convicted of an offence triable either way, and the statute creating the offence prescribes a particular maximum penalty upon summary conviction, the magistrates may fine him an amount not exceeding the maximum penalty indicated in the statute creating the offence or the prescribed sum, whichever is the greater (section 32(2)), and subject to the exception of certain drug offences listed in section 32(5). Where the maximum penalty indicated in the statute creating the offence is expressed to be 'the statutory maximum', that maximum used to mean the 'prescribed sum' of £5000, but since section 85 of the LASPOA 2012 came into force, this rule has changed, so that an offence punishable by the statutory maximum will (provided the offender is aged eighteen or over) become punishable by a fine of any amount. For offenders aged under eighteen, see paragraph 11.10 later in this Chapter.

11.06   When a magistrates' court imposes a fine it should not normally fix a term of imprisonment in default of payment. This is in sharp contrast to the duty in the Crown Court to fix such a period in default. In the exceptional cases where a magistrates' court does fix a term in default, the same periods apply as are set out in the table at paragraph 11.14, this Chapter, except that the default term can in no case exceed twelve months (MCA 1980, schedule 4).

The sentencing principles applicable in relation to the use of the fine in magistrates' courts **11.07** are basically the same as those which apply in the Crown Court, and these are considered in paragraphs 11.15 to 11.25 of this Chapter. The level of fine in each case is calculated in accordance with the same principles of having regard to both the seriousness of the offence and the offender's ability to pay a fine, but the *Magistrates' Courts Sentencing Guidelines* provide assistance to sentencers in the lower court by providing guideline fines expressed as one of three fine bands (A, B, or C). The guidelines explain that the selection of the relevant fine band, and the position of the individual offence within that band, is determined by the seriousness of the individual offence. The fine bands are as follows:

	Starting Point	Range
Fine Band A	50 per cent of relevant weekly income	25–75 per cent of relevant weekly income
Fine Band B	100 per cent of relevant weekly income	75–125 per cent of relevant weekly income
Fine Band C	150 per cent of relevant weekly income	125–175 per cent of relevant weekly income

The seriousness of the offence determines the choice of fine band and the position of the offence within the range for that band. The offender's financial circumstances are taken into account by expressing that position as a proportion of the offender's relevant weekly income. Where an offender is in receipt of income from employment or is self-employed and that income is more than £110 per week after stoppages, the actual income is the relevant weekly income. Where an offender's only source of income is state benefit (including where there is relatively low additional income as permitted by the benefit regulations) or the offender is on receipt of income from employment or is self-employed but the amount of income after deduction of tax and national insurance is £110 or less, the relevant weekly income is deemed to be £110. In calculating relevant weekly income no account should be taken of tax credits, housing benefit, child benefit, or similar. While the initial consideration for the assessment of a fine is the offender's relevant weekly income the court should take account of the offender's financial circumstances more broadly. Where an offender has savings these will not normally be taken into account. If the household of which the offender is a part has more than one source of income the fine should normally be based on the income of the offender alone, unless the offender is wholly financially dependent on the income of another or the offender's part of the income is very small, in which case the court may have regard to the total household income which will be available to meet the fine imposed. The figure of £110 used in the guideline is expected to remain appropriate and in use at least until March 2015, when a future revision of the guideline will update the amount in accordance with current benefit and minimum wage levels.

Two further fine bands (D and E) are provided to assist a magistrates' court in calculating a fine where the offence would otherwise warrant a community sentence (Band D) or a custodial sentence (Band E):

	Starting Point	Range
Fine Band D	250 per cent of relevant weekly income	200–300 per cent of relevant weekly income
Fine Band E	400 per cent of relevant weekly income	300–500 per cent of relevant weekly income

In cases where these fine bands apply it may be appropriate for the fine to be set at an amount which will require a period longer than twelve months to repay. There are some difficulties of principle which arise when a fine is selected to deal with an offence which would otherwise justify a custodial sentence, and care needs to be taken in exercising that option. These issues are discussed at paragraph 11.15 of this Chapter.

11.08 Where an offender has failed to provide information (including cases where the offender has simply failed to appear at court), or the court is not satisfied that it has been given sufficient reliable information, it is entitled to make such determination as it thinks fit regarding the financial circumstances of the offender (CJA 2003, section 164(5)). Where there is no information on which a determination can be made the court should proceed on the basis of an assumed relevant weekly income of £400. Where there is some information that tends to suggest a significantly lower or higher income than the recommended £400 default sum, the court should make a determination based on that information. A court is empowered to remit a fine in whole or in part if the offender subsequently produces information as to means (CJA 2003, section 165(2)). Of course the original assessment of offence seriousness and the placing of the offence within the band is unaffected by the provision of this information.

11.09 A fine is payable in full on the day on which it is imposed. The offender should always be asked for immediate payment when present in court and some payment on the day should be required wherever possible. If that is not possible the magistrates' court may order the offender to be detained. This power is exercised under the MCA 1980, section 135. The court may order that the offender be detained for a specified period ending no later than 8 o'clock in the evening on the day the order is made. This power is available both as a sentencing power in its own right (see paragraph 3.14 earlier in this book) but more usually as an order in respect of unpaid fines where it is used as an alternative to remitting the fine. More commonly the court will allow payments to be made over a period of time set by the court. The total period should not normally exceed twelve months, and for some offenders of very limited means it may be unrealistic to maintain payment over such a long period. It is generally recognized that the maximum weekly payment by a person in receipt of state benefits should rarely exceed £5. When allowing payment by instalments by an offender in receipt of earned income, the *Magistrates' Courts Sentencing Guidelines* suggest the following rates of payment as a general guide:

New weekly income	Starting point for weekly payment
£60	£5
£120	£10
£200	£25
£250	£30
£300	£50
£400	£80

The payment terms must be included in any collection order made by the magistrates' court in respect of the amount imposed.

B FINING YOUNG OFFENDERS

11.10 There are special provisions relating to the appropriate level of fines for offenders aged under eighteen. Where a young offender pleads guilty or is convicted in a youth court to an offence in respect of which the court is empowered to impose a fine exceeding £1000, the amount of the fine imposed on the young offender must not exceed £100 (PCC(S)A 2000, section 135(1)). If the offender is under the age of fourteen and the court could otherwise have imposed a fine exceeding £250, the amount of the fine must not exceed £250 (section 135(2)). It should also be noted that where a young offender is convicted before a youth court the amount of any order for costs made against him must not exceed the amount of any fine imposed (Prosecution of Offences Act 1985, section 18(5)). There is in principle no limit on the fine which may be imposed by the Crown Court on a young offender convicted on indictment. The SGC guideline, *Sentencing Youths* points out that many young people who offend have few resources. Where a young person is in receipt of the Education Maintenance Allowance or similar, which is related to the means of the offender or his family, the court should consider to what extent making a deduction from the allowance would prejudice the young person's access to education or training.

In some circumstances the parent or guardian of a young offender may be ordered to pay **11.11** a fine imposed in respect of an offence committed by that young offender, including a fine imposed for breach of an order, such as a youth rehabilitation order. The power to order the parent or guardian to pay the fine is discussed at paragraph 10.06, this book.

C FINES IN THE CROWN COURT

There is no statutory limit to the amount of the fine which may be imposed by the Crown Court **11.12** (Criminal Law Act 1977, section 32(1)). Fines on corporations, for example, may amount to millions of pounds. The SGC guideline, *Corporate Manslaughter and Health and Safety Offences Causing Death* indicates that for the offence of corporate manslaughter, 'the appropriate fine will seldom be less than £500,000 and may be measured in millions of pounds'. Nor is there a limit to the level of fine if the offender has been committed to the Crown Court for sentence under the PCC(S)A 2000 section 3 or section 4 following summary conviction in a magistrates' court for an offence triable either way. In *North Essex JJ, ex parte Lloyd* [2001] 2 Cr App R (S) 15 committal under section 3 for the express reason that the magistrates' powers to fine were insufficient in that case was approved by the Divisional Court, Lord Woolf in that case observing that it would be very helpful if that reason could be clearly set out in the decision to commit. If, however the magistrates' court commits a person to the Crown Court for sentence under the PCC(S)A 2000, section 6, the Crown Court is restricted to the powers of the magistrates' court, including the maximum fine which is available to the lower court. Now that magistrates have unlimited powers to fine in a case which is triable either way, fresh consideration will have to be given as to the circumstances in which the lower court should commit an adult to the Crown Court for the purpose of imposing a fine.

The enforcement of any fine imposed in the Crown Court is always a matter for the appro- **11.13** priate magistrates' court. Fine enforcement lies outside the scope of this book.

Fixing term in default

A term of imprisonment or a term of detention to be served in the event of the offender's **11.14** default in payment of the fine must be fixed in every case where the Crown Court imposes a fine (PCC(S)A 2000, section 139(2)), unless the offender is under eighteen years of age. No term of detention in default can be imposed on a person under eighteen (*Basid* [1996] 1 Cr App R (S) 421). If the offender is aged eighteen, nineteen, or twenty the term in default takes the form of a term of detention under the PCC(S)A 2000, section 108. If such an offender eventually has to serve the term in default he may be detained in a prison or young offender institution as appropriate (section 108(5)). All this stands in stark contrast to the position in the magistrates' court, where there is no requirement to fix a term in default. If the Crown Court imposes a fine on committal for sentence from a magistrates' court in circumstances where the Crown Court is limited to the powers of the lower court, the Crown Court must nonetheless set a term in default (section 139(7)).

The maximum terms of imprisonment or detention under section 108 which may be ordered by the Crown Court are as follows:

Fine Value	Maximum Default Term
Not exceeding £200	7 days
Over £200, not exceeding £500	14 days
Over £500, not exceeding £1000	28 days
Over £1000, not exceeding £2500	45 days
Over £2500, not exceeding £5000	3 months
Over £5000, not exceeding £10,000	6 months
Over £10,000, not exceeding £20,000	12 months
Over £20,000, not exceeding £50,000	18 months
Over £50,000, not exceeding £100,000	2 years
Over £100,000, not exceeding £250,000	3 years
Over £250,000, not exceeding £1 million	5 years
Over £1 million	10 years

As is clear from the table, the periods in the second column are maximum periods, and the Crown Court has a discretion to fix the actual term at an appropriate place within the relevant bracket (*Szraber* (1994) 15 Cr App R (S) 821). Despite the apparently mandatory nature of the requirement to fix a term in default, it has been held that a failure to fix such a term does not invalidate the fine (*Hamilton* (1980) 2 Cr App R (S) 1). The court may order the term to be served in default to run concurrently with, or consecutively to, any term of imprisonment or detention in a young offender institution to which the offender is sentenced at that time by the court, or which he is already serving (PCC(S)A 2000, section 139(5)). A consecutive custodial sentence would normally be appropriate, but is, as usual, subject to the totality principle. If the fine is ordered to be paid in instalments over a period of time, the period in default should of course reflect the whole sum and not an individual instalment.

Fines in the Crown Court: seriousness of offence

11.15 It is clear that there are some offences where the degree of seriousness is so high that a fine (of any amount) would be an inappropriate sentence. An example is *AG's Reference (No 41 of 1994)* (1995) 16 Cr App R (S) 792, where fines totalling £350 had been imposed on an offender who had pleaded guilty to an offence of wounding with intent to cause grievous bodily harm. The Court of Appeal in that case said that the sentence was 'absurd', unduly lenient, and substituted a custodial sentence of thirty months. This was a case where the court simply misjudged the seriousness of the offence. But suppose the reason for preferring a fine to a sentence of imprisonment is that the offender is well-off and can afford to pay. This is clearly wrong in principle, and the law should not arrive at a position where, for the same offence, a rich man pays a fine and a poor man goes to prison (see *Markwick* (1953) 37 Cr App R 125). This approach would allow the rich man to 'buy his way out of the penalty of imprisonment'. On the other hand, it seems that there are some trivial offences where the imposition of a fine may constitute too great a punishment. In the old case of *Jamieson* (1975) 60 Cr App R (S) 318 the offender, a man with a clean record and substantial personal mitigation, was convicted of the theft of half a bottle of whisky from a supermarket. The Court of Appeal varied the sentence to a conditional discharge.

Where the offence being dealt with falls within the appropriate range to be sentenced by **11.16** way of a fine, section 164(2) of the CJA 2003 states that '[t]he amount of any fine fixed by a court must be such as, in the opinion of the court, reflects the seriousness of the offence'. Clearly the maximum available fine must be reserved for the very worst instance of the case which is likely to occur, in parallel to the principle which applies in relation to maximum custodial sentences. It follows that the presence of a guilty plea, or significant personal mitigation, should rule out the maximum fine as an option. The SGC guideline on *Reduction for a Guilty Plea* makes it clear that the principle of reduction for plea applies to a fine as well as to a custodial sentence. This principle applies in the magistrates' court as well as the Crown Court, so that in *Universal Salvage v Boothby* (1983) 5 Cr App R (S) 428 it was held by the Divisional Court that the magistrates had erred in imposing the maximum available fine on a company in breach of tachograph regulations. It was accepted that there was substantial mitigation in the case, the company having reasonably relied upon advice from the relevant government department that the regulations did not apply to their business.

The level of the fine is a different matter from any compensation payable to the victim, and **11.17** the fine should be calculated by reference to any sum which the victim might be entitled to receive (*Roberts* (1980) 2 Cr App R (S) 121). As explained at paragraph 11.20, this Chapter, however, where the offender is of limited means, the appropriate level of fine might be reduced in order to allow priority for compensation to be paid.

Where the court is sentencing an offender for a number of offences, all of which are to be **11.18** dealt with by fines, the Divisional Court in *Chelmsford Crown Court, ex parte Birchall* (1989) 11 Cr App R (S) 510 made it clear that the sentencer should not simply add up all the appropriate fines and impose that total sum. This makes it clear that the totality principle, which has its clearest application in relation to custodial sentences, also applies to fines. The sentencer must review the total sentence and ensure that it is proportionate to the totality of the offending as well as being within the offender's means to pay. The CJA 2003, section 166(3) says that the court may mitigate the overall sentence 'by applying any rule of law as to the totality of sentences'. This is an application of that principle.

Any period which the offender has spent on remand in custody may be relevant. In *Warden* **11.19** [1996] 2 Cr App R (S) 269 the Court of Appeal observed that where a fine was the proper penalty for an offence, the sentence might properly reduce the level of the fine to reflect any period spent on remand. A slightly different situation would be where the sentencer takes the view that a short prison sentence might well have been justified for the offence but the offender has already served much of the relevant period in custody and that a fine would now meet the justice of the case. Neither of these situations is covered by the statutory provisions which deal with the effect of time served on remand in relation to custodial or community sentences.

Fines in the Crown Court: means of the offender

As well as weighing the seriousness of the offence (or offences) to be dealt with by way **11.20** of the fine, the court must also take into account the ability of the offender to pay. The CJA 2003, section 164(3) says that '[i]n fixing the amount of any fine to be imposed on an offender (whether an individual or other person), a court must take into account the circumstances of the case, including, among other things the financial circumstances of the offender as far as they are known, or appear to the court', and in the case of an individual offender inquire into his financial circumstances. A fine is meant to be a punishment, and there is nothing wrong with a fine occasioning a degree of hardship for the offender since 'one of the objects of the fine is to remind the offender that what he has done is wrong' (*per* Lord Lane CJ in *Olliver* (1989) 11 Cr App R (S) 10). On the other hand, to impose a fine which is well beyond the offender's ability to pay is wrong in principle. An excessive fine will inevitably lead to default and ultimately may result in imprisonment, a penalty disproportionate to the original offence. A fine is imposed upon the offender, and it is generally wrong for the court to assume that another, better-off, friend or relative will pay the fine. In *Charambous* (1984) 6 Cr App R (S) 389 the Court of Appeal said that a fine imposed on a married woman who had limited income of her own should not be set at a level which assumed that her husband would pay. See, however, the somewhat different guidance on this issue offered in the *Magistrates' Courts Sentencing Guidelines*, at paragraph 11.07 earlier in this Chapter.

11.21 Where an individual offender has been convicted of an offence, the court has power before sentencing him to make a financial circumstances order, which requires him to provide within a specified period a statement of his financial resources (CJA 2003, section 162). Failure to comply with such an order is an offence punishable with a fine not exceeding level 3, and making a dishonest statement in respect of such an order is an offence punishable with a fine not exceeding level 4.

11.22 If the offender does not have the means to pay the appropriate fine, it is clearly wrong to pass a prison sentence (whether immediate or suspended) instead. The point was strongly made in *Reeves* (1972) 56 Cr App R 366, where the judge had made comments which the Court of Appeal took to mean that the particular offence of obtaining property by deception merited a substantial fine, but the offender was unable to pay that sum, so a prison sentence of nine months was imposed instead. Roskill LJ said that if that really was what had happened, it was 'of course, completely wrong'. In *Reeves* the fine should have been adjusted to a level that was within the offender's ability to pay. If the offender had no available means at all, then the sentence should have reduced, say to a conditional discharge, and not increased to a custodial sentence. Problems of impecunious offenders are very common in the criminal courts, and every day magistrates' courts deal with large numbers of such cases. The fine bands set out in the *Magistrates' Courts Sentencing Guidelines* and the guidance on fining offenders on very low incomes or on benefits were considered above. The same principle applies in the Crown Court, and although the guidelines are not directly applicable, they do provide a helpful steer when the problem arises in the higher court.

11.23 Less frequently encountered is the well-heeled offender for whom payment of the proportionate fine for the offence would occasion no difficulty at all. The first point is that it would be wrong in principle to respond to this by imposing a custodial sentence (*Gillies* [1965] Crim LR 64). We have seen that a fine should be reduced if the offender is impecunious; should it be increased if he is rich? Statute provides the answer. The CJA 2003, section 164(4) says that '[s]ubsection (3) above applies whether taking into account the financial circumstances of the offender has the effect of increasing or reducing the amount of the fine'. So it is right to increase the fine in this case to sharpen the impact on the offender. There must be a limit to this, however. As the Court of Appeal in *Jerome* [2001] 1 Cr App R (S) 316 has said, there must remain some proportionality between the offence and the fine imposed for it. In that case a fine for handling stolen goods worth £2739 was reduced from £10,000 to £6000.

11.24 Where the offender is a company rather than an individual the same general principles apply. If the company wishes to make representations as to its ability to pay the fine, it should submit copies of the accounts to the court. If no such information is forthcoming, the court may assume that the company can afford to pay (*F Howe & Sons (Engineers)* [1999] 2 All ER 249). The SGC guideline on *Corporate Manslaughter and Health and Safety Offences Causing Death* provides further guidance as to the content and form of financial information which should be provided by a corporate offender and the approach which should be taken by the court in fixing the level of the fine.

Payment within a reasonable time

Although in principle a fine should be paid straight away, it is common for a judge to **11.25** make an order either allowing time for the payment to be made (eg by the first day of the next month) or directing payment of the fine by instalments of such amounts and on such dates as are specified. When a fine is imposed, and an order is made that it is payable in instalments, the usual principle is that it should be capable of being paid off within twelve months. This is clear from the *Magistrates' Courts Sentencing Guidelines* and from a number of appellate decisions. In the case of *Olliver* (1989) 11 Cr App R (S) 10, however, Lord Lane CJ indicated that twelve months was not an absolute rule, and that there were cases where payment over two years, or even three years, might be appropriate, depending on the circumstances of the offender and the nature of the offence. Clearly, a corporate offender may be required to pay a fine over a much longer period than would be normal for an individual offender: *Rollco Screw & Rivet Co* [1999] 2 Cr App R (S) 436.

D COMBINING FINES WITH OTHER SENTENCES

The fine is a flexible penalty and may be combined with most other sentences. A small **11.26** number of combinations are, however, unlawful, and some other combinations will often be undesirable in practice.

Unlawful combinations are as follows: **11.27**

(a) A fine is not available where the sentence is fixed by law (murder), or one of the prescribed minimum sentence provisions applies, or the court is required to sentence the offender as a dangerous offender (CJA 2003, section 163).

(b) A fine may not be imposed for the same offence for which the court orders an absolute or conditional discharge, because a discharge is imposed 'where it is inexpedient to inflict punishment' (PCC(S)A 2000, section 12(1) and *Sanck* (1990) 12 Cr App R (S) 155). If an offender is being sentenced for more than one offence, there is no objection to him being fined for one offence and discharged in relation to another.

(c) A fine may not be combined with a hospital order or guardianship order (MHA 1983, section 37(8)). This appears to relate to both sentences being imposed for the same offence rather than to different offences sentenced on the same occasion.

(d) Where a youth court makes a referral order on a young offender it cannot at the same time impose a fine.

(e) If the court is commencing proceedings with a view to a confiscation order being made under the Proceeds of Crime Act 2002, the court cannot impose any financial order as part of the sentence for the offence until the issue of confiscation is resolved and any confiscation order is made (POCA 2002, section 13(2)).

Undesirable combinations include the following: **11.28**

(a) A fine imposed at the same time as an immediate custodial sentence, whether for the same offence or for different offences, is generally undesirable. That is because the prison sentence will often deprive the offender of the means to pay the fine or saddle him with a significant financial burden upon release from custody (*Maunde* (1980) 2 Cr App R (S) 289). In some past reported cases a hefty fine has been added to a prison sentence as a means of depriving the offender of the profit that he has made from his offending.

This kind of case is now better dealt with by commencing proceedings for confiscation under the Proceeds of Crime Act 2002.

(b) A fine may be imposed in addition to a suspended custodial sentence. This should only be done, however, where the seriousness of the offence justifies the passing of a custodial sentence, to which the sentencer adds an immediate penalty in the form of a fine. If the offence does not require imprisonment, then it is wrong in principle to add a suspended sentence as a form of special deterrence.

(c) A fine may be imposed alongside a community sentence, whether for the same offence or for different offences. It may be thought, however, that since a community sentence will contain the appropriate balance of punitive and rehabilitative measures tailored to suit the individual offender, the addition of a fine is unnecessary and might be counterproductive.

11.29 Where more than one form of financial order is imposed in the same case issues of priority arise between those orders:

(a) A fine and a compensation order may be imposed for the same offence, but the PCC(S)A 2000, section 130(12) provides that where the offender lacks the means to pay both, the court shall give preference to the compensation order by reducing the fine, if necessary to nothing. Logically this can mean that a compensation order may stand alone as the sentence for the offence. Section 130(12) is a limited exception to the principle that the making of a compensation order should not occasion a reduction in the sentence for the offence.

(b) The appropriate surcharge must be ordered by the court in every case. The amount of any fine may be reduced to allow for payment of the surcharge in any case where the offender lacks the mean to pay both (CJA 2003, section 164(4A)).

(c) In addition to imposing a fine for the offence the court may also make an order for payment of, or contribution towards, prosecution costs. The applicable principles were laid down in *Northallerton Magistrates' Court, ex parte Dove* [2001] 1 Cr App R (S) 136. The judge must always have regard to the means of the offender, and there should be a reasonable relationship between the two orders in that a small fine should not be coupled with a very large order for costs. Generally speaking the fine will be the larger of the two sums, but this is not an absolute rule: see for example *Splain* [2010] EWCA Crim 49, where a fine of £6000 coupled with an order for costs of £22,000 was upheld on appeal in view of 'the totality of the sentencing process'. If the offender lacks the means to pay both the fine and the order for costs, then the order for costs should be reduced, or not made at all, in order for the fine to be paid.

E DEPRIVATION ORDERS

11.30 The main power of the courts to order the forfeiture of property which has been connected with the commission of a crime is to be found in section 143 of the PCC(S)A 2000. There is also a whole host of other powers of forfeiture associated with conviction for certain offences. Some of the most commonly encountered are mentioned briefly at paragraph 11.38 of this Chapter. The power to make a deprivation order (also commonly referred to as a forfeiture order) under section 143 may be exercised by a magistrates' court or by the Crown Court in respect of any offence. It is important to understand that (unlike a compensation order or a restitution order) a deprivation order is part of the punishment for the offence and is not an ancillary order. It is best regarded as a form of fine, which takes the form of confiscation of an item of the offender's property (which was connected with the offence) rather than a sum of money. The order operates to deprive the offender of his rights in the property, and the property is required to be taken into the possession of the police if it is not already there. The secondary purpose of the order is to take out of public circulation an item, such as a weapon or a package of drugs, which the court will order to be forfeited and destroyed.

An offender in respect of whom a deprivation order has been made may appeal against the order in the same way as against any other order of sentence of the court, from a magistrates' court to the Crown Court, or from the Crown Court to the Court of Appeal. **11.31**

Power to make deprivation order

Power to make the order arises where a person has been convicted of any offence. It may be made in respect of any property which has lawfully been seized from the offender or was in his possession or under his control, either at the time he was apprehended for the offence or when a summons in respect of it was issued. The property must have been used for the purpose of committing, or facilitating the commission of, any offence, or must have been intended by the offender to be so used (section 143(1)). An example is forfeiture of the offender's computer in a case where he has used the computer to commit the offence. Another example is the offender's car, where that has been so used—an example considered further at paragraph 11.33 in this Chapter. The power of forfeiture is confined to tangible items of personal property and does not extend to real property, such as a house (*Khan* (1982) 4 Cr App R (S) 298). In a typical case the property will have been used for the purposes of the offence which has led to the offender's conviction, but the statute clearly contemplates the offender being deprived of property which he used for a quite different offence. The power does not extent, however, to property used by some other person in connection with an offence (*Neville* (1987) 9 Cr App R (S) 222). 'Facilitating the commission of an offence' includes taking steps after the offence to dispose of the proceeds or avoid detection (section 143(8)). When considering whether to make a deprivation order, the court must always consider the value of the property and the likely financial and other effects on the offender of making the order (section 143(5)). This is commonly an issue where the offender's motor vehicle has been the subject of the order, and that situation is considered next. **11.32**

Deprivation orders and motor vehicles

In several reported cases deprivation orders have been used to confiscate an offender's car. Under section 143(6) and (7), in any case where the offender has been convicted of an offence involving 'driving, attempting to drive, or being in charge of a vehicle', or failing to provide a specimen for analysis or failing to stop and give information or report an accident, the vehicle is to be regarded as having been used for the purpose of committing the offence. Subsections (6) and (7), however, in no way limit the courts' power to order forfeiture of the offender's car under the general provision in section 143. The main issue here is whether the use of the car was merely peripheral to the offence, in which case there is no power to order forfeiture, or whether it can fairly be said that it was used for the purpose of the offence. In *McDonald* (1990) 12 Cr App R (S) 408 the offender indecently assaulted a young woman in the street and then tried to drag her to his car. An order for forfeiture of the car was quashed on appeal, since there was no sufficient connection between the vehicle and the offence. By contrast in *Buddo* (1982) 4 Cr App R (S) 268 the offender had driven himself and his accomplice to a chemist's shop, with the intention of breaking in to steal drugs. The Court of Appeal found that the use of the vehicle was an integral part of the offence, although the order under section 143 was quashed for other reasons. **11.33**

Deprivation orders: sentencing principles

11.34 It is usual for the prosecution to apply for the deprivation order to be made, but it is also open to court to proceed on its own initiative. Either way, the court before making a deprivation order must always have regard to the value of the property involved and to the likely impact on the offender of making the order. A failure to make this inquiry may well lead to the order being quashed on appeal (*Highbury Corner Justices, ex parte Di Matteo* (1990) 12 Cr App R (S) 594, and *Trans Berckx v North Avon Magistrates' Court* (2012) 176 JP 28). The deprivation order forms part of the punishment for the offence. In *Buddo* (paragraph 11.33 earlier), although the Court of Appeal said that the order was correct in principle, its imposition in addition to a custodial sentence of two years was 'overdoing the punishment'. In *Priestley* [1996] 2 Cr App R (S) 144 the offender was convicted of a conspiracy to contravene trademarks. He was sentenced to four years' imprisonment, together with a substantial confiscation order and an order depriving him of various items associated with the offending, including a sewing machine and a computer. On appeal the Court of Appeal found that the judge had given insufficient attention to totality, and reduced the prison sentence to three years. As part of its inquiry the court must consider whether a disproportionate impact on the offender would result from deprivation of the property. A strong case is *Tavernor* [1976] RTR 242 where an order under section 143 imposed in addition to a suspended prison sentence and a fine was quashed in view of the offender's physical disability and the fact that the car had been specially adapted for his use. Since an order under section 143 is a punishment and not an ancillary order, in a case where several offenders are equally implicated in an offence and receive comparable sentences, it is wrong to impose a deprivation order on just one of them (*Ottey* (1984) 6 Cr App R (S) 163).

11.35 A number of authorities establish that deprivation orders should only be made in clear straightforward cases. As with compensation orders, the court should avoid making an order where there may be dispute over the ownership of the property, or its value. In *Troth* (1980) 71 Cr App R 1 it was held that an order should not have been made in respect of a jointly owned tipper lorry used to commit a theft of coal, where there was no suggestion that the offender's business partner had been involved in the offence. Another example is *Kearney* [2011] 2 Cr App R (S) 608, where the offender had committed offences of making off without payment by driving into the filling station, topping up with fuel, and then driving off without paying. An order for deprivation of the car was quashed in appeal, it having emerged that the car was being purchased on a credit agreement.

11.36 The effect of an order under section 143 is to deprive the offender of his rights in the property. It does not affect the rights of any other person, who may apply to the court for the recovery of the property. The normal avenue would be the Police (Property) Act 1897, but no such application can be made more than six months from the date of the forfeiture order. The claimant must satisfy the court that he had not consented to the offender having possession of the property or, alternatively, that he did not know and had no reason to suspect that the property was likely to be used for criminal purposes.

Combining deprivation orders with other sentences

11.37 A deprivation order can in principle be combined with any other form of punishment, although regard must always be had to the principle of proportionality explained in the previous paragraph, since the deprivation order itself constitutes part of the punishment for the offence. A deprivation order can be combined with an absolute or conditional discharge, even though a discharge may only be used where it is 'inexpedient to inflict punishment'. Section 12(7) of the PCC(S)A 2000 specifically permits this combination. A deprivation order and compensation order may be made as part of the same sentence, and indeed provision is made in the PCC(S)A 2000, section 145 to allow the sale of property connected with the offence to finance the compensation.

F DEPRIVATION AND FORFEITURE UNDER OTHER STATUTORY PROVISIONS

Many statures empower the criminal courts to make an order for the deprivation, or forfeiture and destruction, of a particular item associated with the particular offence. It would be pointless to try to list all these, so only the ones frequently encountered are dealt with here.   **11.38**

Misuse of drugs

By the Misuse of Drugs Act 1971, section 27(1) the court by or before which a person is convicted of an offence under the 1971 Act (or a drug trafficking offence) may order anything shown to relate to the offence to be forfeited, and either destroyed or dealt with in such manner as the court may order. In practice, this always means destruction. 'Anything', in this context, is limited to tangible items—the drugs themselves, associated paraphernalia, and money, of which physical possession can be taken by persons authorized to do so. The power does not extend to real property such as a house, and is distinct from the power to order confiscation of the drug offender's assets acquired through their offending, where a confiscation order under the Proceeds of Crime Act 2002 would be an appropriate avenue to pursue. The item to be forfeited must always be shown to be related to the offence of conviction. It is not enough to show that it relates to some other offence, whether planned or committed (*Boothe* (1987) 9 Cr App R (S) 8). The making of such an order is generally straightforward and is unlikely to be contested in court, but if the matter is in dispute the court must hear evidence (*Churcher* (1986) 8 Cr App R (S) 95). In any case where ownership of the item is contested any other person claiming ownership may apply to the court to be heard (section 27(2)). Unlike the general power of deprivation under the PCC(S)A 2000, section 143 (above), there is no power under section 27(1) to order compensation to be paid from any proceeds of property seized.   **11.39**

Firearms and other weapons

Section 52 of the Firearms Act 1968 applies where a person is: **11.40**

(a) convicted of an offence under the 1968 Act (other than an offence relating to air weapons) or is convicted of *any other offence* for which he is given a sentence of imprisonment, detention in a young offender institution, or a detention and training order, or
(b) has been ordered into a recognizance to keep the peace a condition of which is that he shall not possess, use or carry a firearm, or
(c) is subject to a community order or a youth rehabilitation order containing a requirement that he shall not possess, use, or carry a firearm.

Forfeiture and disposal of air weapons is separately provided for in schedule 6 to the 1968 Act. The Firearms Act 1982 extends the forfeiture and destruction provisions to apply to imitation firearms, and they are further extended to apply to weapons listed in the Firearms (Amendment) Acts 1988 and 1997. Various firearms offences have been created by legislation since the 1968 Act, such as the offence of using someone to mind a weapon under the Violent Crime Reduction Act 2006, section 29. Section 50(3) of the 2006 Act extends the provisions of section 52 of the Firearms Act 1968 to offences created by the later legislation. In any case where section 52 applies, the court may make an order as to the forfeiture or disposal of any firearm or ammunition found in the offender's possession, and may cancel any firearms certificate or shotgun certificate held by him. The wording of section 52 is very broad, and does not actually require that the offender was in possession of the firearm at the time of the offence. Nor, indeed, does it require that the firearm was in any way connected to the offence.

11.41   By the Prevention of Crime Act 1953, section 1(2) when any person is convicted of an offence under section 1(1) (possession of an offensive weapon in a public place without lawful authority or reasonable excuse) the court may make an order for the forfeiture and destruction of any weapon in respect of which the offence was committed. The forfeiture power is expressed to apply only to that offence, and on the face of it does not extend to the offence under section 1A of threatening with an offensive weapon in a public place. There is no specific forfeiture and destruction power in relation to the various offences involving articles with a blade or point in the Criminal Justice Act 1988, but the Knives Act 1997, section 6 provides a general power in the court to order forfeiture and destruction of a knife found in the offender's possession or under his control at the time of his arrest. As usual, the court is required to have regard to the value of the item before making the order but in reality this is hardly likely to give rise to a serious issue. A similar provision relates to conviction under the Crossbows Act 1987, section 6(3).

Other offences

11.42   In addition to the commonly encountered powers of forfeiture mentioned in the previous two paragraphs, there are other specific powers of forfeiture. These include powers in relation to counterfeit currency and anything associated with the production of such currency (Forgery and Counterfeiting Act 1981, section 24(1)); obscene material (Obscene Publications Act 1959, section 3); indecent photographs of children (Protection of Children Act 1978, schedule 1); revenue and customs offences (Customs and Excise Management Act 1979, schedule 3); forfeiture of vehicles, ships, and aircraft associated with immigration offences (Immigration Act 1971, section 25C), and materials relating to terrorism (Terrorism Act 2000, section 23A). In some of these examples, and subject to certain conditions specified in the statutes, the court is under a duty, rather than merely being given a power, to order forfeiture of the relevant property or material.

KEY DOCUMENTS[1]

Sentencing Guidelines Council, Definitive Guideline, *Magistrates Sentencing Guidelines* (effective 4 August 2008).

Sentencing Guidelines Council, Definitive Guideline, *Sentencing Youths* (effective 30 November 2009).

Sentencing Guidelines Council, Definitive Guideline, *Corporate Manslaughter and Health and Safety Offences Causing Death* (effective 15 February 2010).

---

[1] All sentencing guidelines can be found on the Sentencing Council website: <http://sentencing council.judiciary.gov.uk/>.

12

ORDERS OF DISQUALIFICATION AND EXCLUSION

12.01   In this Chapter we consider a wide range of ancillary orders, all of which may be imposed in addition to the main substantive sentence for the offence. While in some ways a miscellaneous collection, they have in common a shared concern with protecting the public from future law-breaking by the offender. While the punishment for the offence (fine, community sentence, or custodial sentence) essentially looks back to the seriousness of the offence or offences committed, orders of disqualification or exclusion are mainly designed to address future risk. It follows that the imposition of an ancillary order in addition to the punishment is not a reason for then revisiting the punishment and reducing it. Indeed, ancillary orders are not properly to be regarded as punishments at all, although given the restrictions on freedom involved they may feel to the offender no different from punishment. A fine for a driving offence is the punishment, but an associated driving disqualification is a measure designed to protect other road users from future similar law-breaking by the offender. Even so, the disqualification may well impact on the offender's life to a greater extent than the fine. As we shall see, the law does not always draw such a sharp distinction between punishments and risk-prevention measures as these comments may suggest. Indeed, in some circumstances a driving ban can be imposed as a punishment for an offence entirely unrelated to driving. This does seem counterintuitive.

12.02   The number and range of ancillary orders involving disqualification and exclusion has grown significantly in recent years. We are in this Chapter concerned with measures which may, in the proper exercise of the court's discretion, be imposed as part of the sentence passed. Some forms of disqualification come into effect automatically upon conviction and hence are not strictly part of the sentencing decision. These are considered in Chapter 15. Compensation orders, one of the most important forms of ancillary order, require separate treatment, and they are covered in Chapter 9. The CPR 2013, rule 50.2 says that the court must not make a 'behaviour order' (by which is meant an order imposed under a power that the court can exercise on sentence that requires someone to do, or not do, something) unless that person has had an opportunity to consider the order which is proposed, the evidence in support of that order, and to make representations.

A DISQUALIFICATION FROM DRIVING

12.03   An offender may be disqualified from driving a mechanically propelled vehicle and from holding or obtaining a driving licence. Since disqualification is an ancillary order, it must be attached to the main sentence for the offence and cannot stand alone. A slight exception to this is where sentence is deferred but a driving disqualification starts from the date of deferral. As we will see, disqualification from driving is mandatory in some cases and discretionary in others where the offender has been convicted of a driving-related offence. For the most part the disqualification is designed to provide public protection from a person who has been found to have driven dangerously, or who has accumulated over time a number of driving-related convictions which show that he lacks respect for the rules of the road. The driving disqualification also impacts on the offender as a punishment and is no doubt intended to act as a deterrent to others. The attraction of disqualification as a punishment (rather than a matter of public protection) is evidenced by powers which the courts have to disqualify offenders who have not driven badly, but who have used their vehicle for the purposes of crime or, indeed, to disqualify offenders where there was no link between their driving and the offence at all.

12.04   The particulars of all offences involving obligatory or discretionary disqualification must be endorsed on the offender's licence (where he holds one) unless there are special reasons for not doing so. If the offender does not have a driving licence the court ordering endorsement must send notice of the order to the Secretary of State (in practice the Driver and Vehicle Licensing Authority).

Obligatory disqualification—serious road traffic offences

If an offender is convicted of an offence involving obligatory disqualification (or aiding **12.05** and abetting such an offence) he must be disqualified under the Road Traffic Offenders Act (RTOA) 1988, section 34 for *at least* the period specified in the following table. This is normally one year, but for some offences it is two years. The stated period is the minimum period and is not the normal period to be imposed. Where the letter E appears next to the minimum period it signifies that the court must order that the offender must also pass the appropriate extended driving test, and he remains disqualified until such time as he does so. Where the letter C appears next to the minimum period it signifies that if the offender has been convicted of a like offence within the ten years immediately preceding the commission of the latest offence, the minimum period is increased to three years. Although these are all described as 'obligatory' disqualifications the court always has power, on the finding of 'special reasons', that the offender should be disqualified for a shorter period of time, or not at all. It will be apparent that 'obligatory' does not mean here what it normally means. Here it means 'obligatory in the absence of special reasons'. If the court does find special reasons and does not disqualify it must endorse the offender's licence with three to eleven points. What might count as special reasons is considered at paragraph 12.07 in this Chapter.

Offence	Minimum Period of Years
Manslaughter	2 E
Causing death by dangerous driving (Road Traffic Act (RTA) 1988, section 1)	2 E
Causing serious injury by dangerous driving (RTA 1988, section 1A)	2 E
Dangerous driving (RTA 1988, section 2)	1 E
Causing death by careless driving (RTA 1988, section 2B)	1
Causing death by careless driving while under the influence of drink or drugs (RTA 1988, section 3A)	2 C
Causing death by driving unlicensed, disqualified or uninsured (RTA 1988, section 3ZA)	1
Driving or attempting to drive while unfit through drink or drugs (RTA 1988, section 4(1))	1 C
Driving or attempting to drive with excess alcohol (RTA 1988, section 5(1)(a))	1
Failing to supply evidential specimen (RTA 1988, section 7(6))	1 C
Motor racing on public highway (RTA 1988, section 12)	1
Where the offender has had more than one disqualification for a fixed period of 56 days or more imposed within the three years immediately preceding the commission of the latest offence (RTOA 1988, section 34)	3

If an offender has been convicted of one of a range of motoring offences and the court makes an order under the RTOA 1988, section 34 disqualifying him for a period of not less than one year, it may order that the period of disqualification can be reduced if the offender completes satisfactorily an approved course. Some of the offences falling within this provision are drink-related offences, including the offences under the Road Traffic Act

1988, section 3A(1)(a) (causing death by careless driving while unfit to drive), section 3A(1)
(b) (causing death by careless driving with excess alcohol), and section 5(1) (driving with
excess alcohol). Other offences within the provision include section 3 (careless driving),
section 36 (failing to comply with a traffic sign), and the Road Traffic Regulation Act 1984,
section 89(1) (speeding).

Discretionary disqualification

12.06   Many road traffic offences which are not so serious as to carry obligatory disqualification
from driving nonetheless carry discretionary disqualification and obligatory licence endorsement, which means that they carry 'penalty points'. If the offender is convicted of an
offence which carries discretionary disqualification he may be disqualified on that ground
alone or, more likely, the latest offence also results in penalty points which, taken together
with those already endorsed on his licence, means that reaches a total of twelve or more
points accumulated within a three-year period (see paragraph 12.08). If the court decides
in all the circumstances not to disqualify in such cases it must still endorse the licence with
the appropriate number of penalty points, unless there are special reasons for not doing so.

A few examples of road traffic offences which carry discretionary disqualification are set
out in the following table, which also lists the penalty points. The last three examples in
the table are offences which do not carry penalty points at all, and so are described as not
endorsable.

Offence	Penalty Points
Exceeding speed limit (RTRA 1984, section 89)	3–6 or fixed penalty
Careless driving (RTA 1988, section 3)	3–9
Leaving vehicle in dangerous position (RTA 1988, section 22)	3
Defective brakes, steering or tyres (RTA 1988, section 41A)	3
Overweight vehicle (RTA 1988, section 41B)	3
Using hand-held mobile telephone while driving (RTA 1988, section 41D)	3
Driving otherwise than in accordance with licence (RTA 1988, section 87(1))	3
Driving while disqualified (RTA 1988, section 103(1)(b))	6
Uninsured (RTA 1988, section 143)	6–8
Failing to stop, report, after accident (RTA 1988, section 170(4))	5–10
Stealing or attempting to steal a motor vehicle (Theft Act 1968, section 1; CAA 1981, section 1)	
Taking conveyance without authority (TA 1968, section 12; CAA 1981, section 1)	
Going equipped *etc* committed with reference to the theft or unauthorised taking of a motor vehicle (TA 1968, section 25)	

Special reasons

12.07   The effect of a finding by the court that there are special reasons for not applying the provisions as to disqualification is to allow the court a discretion whether or not to disqualify
under section 34. In what is still the leading authority, Lord Goddard CJ said in *Whittal v
Kirby* [1947] KB 194 that:

A special reason within the exception is one which is special to the facts of the particular case, that is, special to the facts which constitute the case. It is, in other words, a mitigating or extenuating circumstance, not amounting in law to a defence to the charge, yet directly connected with the commission of the offence, and one which the court ought properly to take into consideration when imposing punishment. A circumstance peculiar to the offender as distinguished from the offence is not a special reason within the exception.

These principles have been reviewed and endorsed on many later occasions. The facts relied upon as constituting special reasons must be established by the defence on a balance of probabilities, unless they are admitted by the prosecution (*Pugsley v Hunter* [1973] 1 WLR 578). Where there has been a trial and the defendant has been convicted of the offence it is still open to the defence to provide further evidence of special reasons (*DPP v Kinnersley* [1993] RTR 105). If the court does exercise its discretion under these provisions not to disqualify or to disqualify for a shorter period it should clearly state its reasons for doing so and, in a magistrates' court, enter those reasons in the court register (RTOA 1988, section 47(1)), although there is authority that a failure to comply with this requirement does not provide a ground of appeal (*Brown v Dyerson* [1969] 1 QB 45). If the court does find special reasons it may then exercise its discretion in favour of the offender, and in many cases will choose to do so, but it is not bound to do so. The court may still properly decide to disqualify in light of all the evidence in the case (*Taylor v Rajan* [1974] QB 424).

Penalty points

When a person who is the holder of a licence is convicted of an offence which carries obligatory or discretionary disqualification or endorsement, his licence must be produced to the court (RTOA 1988, section 27). Failure to do so is an offence punishable by a fine up to level 3. The court orders the licence to be endorsed with particulars of the offence and the appropriate penalty points. The number of penalty points to be attributed in each case is to be derived from schedule 2 to the RTOA 1988. The court must determine the appropriate figure, and if a range of points is available the court must decide the appropriate number, given the relative degree of seriousness of the offence (section 28). If an offender commits a series of offences which carry either obligatory or discretionary disqualification within a period of three years and thereby amasses a total of twelve or more penalty points within that period, he must normally be disqualified from driving for the relevant minimum period whether or not the latest offence would justify disqualification (RTOA 1988, section 35). The minimum period of disqualification is six months if the offender has not been disqualified under section 34 or 35 within the last three years, and one year if one, and two years if more than one, such disqualification within the last three years is to be taken into account. Section 35 states that the court must order disqualification unless satisfied that, having regard to all the circumstances, there are grounds for mitigating the normal consequences of the conviction and the court decides to order disqualification for a lesser period or not at all. 'Mitigating grounds' are different from 'special reasons' and what may amount to mitigating grounds is considered at paragraph 12.10, this Chapter. **12.08**

If the offender is disqualified under section 35 for the latest offence, no penalty points are endorsed on his licence for that offence, and all penalty points accumulated up to the time of the disqualification are expunged. If the court decides not to disqualify the offender the penalty points are endorsed on the licence unless there are special reasons for not doing so. See further *Brentwood Justices, ex parte Richardson* (1992) 95 Cr App R 187. If the offender is convicted of two or more offences which carry obligatory endorsement and were committed on the same occasion (whether or not they were dealt with on the same sentencing occasion) the total number of penalty points which should be endorsed is the number of points appropriate for the most serious offence. **12.09**

Mitigating grounds

12.10 Section 35(4) specifically excludes from consideration by the court any circumstances which are alleged to make the offence or any of the offences not serious, hardship (other than exceptional hardship) or any circumstances which, within the last three years, have already been taken into account in ordering the offender to be disqualified for a shorter period or ordering him not to be disqualified. Apart from these exclusions it seems that the court may have regard to circumstances relating to the offence, to the offender, or to both. This may be contrasted with the relevant considerations for establishing special reasons, at paragraph 12.07 earlier. It is for the offender to establish, on the balance of probability, the grounds which are relied upon and it is also for him to show that these grounds have not previously been relied upon (*Sandbach Justices, ex parte Pescud* (1983) 5 Cr App R (S) 177). The ground of 'exceptional hardship' is the one most frequently relied upon here, often in the context of the offender needing his vehicle to retain his employment. Since there are many such cases involving hardship, something out of the ordinary is needed to amount to 'exceptional' hardship. In *Owen v Jones* (1987) 9 Cr App R (S) 34 the Divisional Court agreed with the magistrates that exceptional hardship would result from disqualification in the case of a police officer who had acquired a total of thirteen points and disqualification would have forced him to resign, thereby losing his job and his police house.

Disqualification from driving: general principles

12.11 The court should not impose a driving disqualification without warning counsel of that possibility, and inviting submissions. In a magistrates' court, the MCA 1980, section 11(4), whenever the court is considering disqualifying the offender and the offender is not present in court, they should adjourn to give notice of their intentions and to consider any representations that might be made.

12.12 Usually a driving disqualification takes effect immediately upon sentencing the offender, but the court does have power to deal with the main part of the sentence on the day but to adjourn consideration of ancillary matters such as disqualification from driving until a later date. This might be because the offender's driving licence and relevant driving record is not immediately to hand and the court wishes to consider it before making the order (*Annesley* (1976) 62 Cr App R 13). If the court adjourns after conviction but before sentence it may impose an interim driving disqualification until the offender is dealt with for the offence. An interim disqualification can last only for six months, and it seems that if for some reason that limit is exceeded the offender cannot then be disqualified further in respect of the same offence. A court which has disqualified an offender may, if it thinks fit, suspend a period of disqualification pending an appeal against that order (RTOA 1988, section 39). Alternatively the Crown Court or the Court of Appeal, which is to hear the appeal, may suspend the disqualification until the appeal is heard (RTOA 1988, section 40).

12.13 Any disqualification must be for a certain period of time, but disqualification for life has been held to amount to disqualification for a certain period, and so is lawful, although it should be imposed only in exceptional circumstances (*Tunde-Olarinde* [1967] 2 All ER 491) where the offender will represent a considerable danger to the public for an indeterminate period of time were he be allowed to drive. As we have seen, in the case of obligatory disqualification the stated period is the minimum period and is not the normal period. Consecutive periods of disqualification cannot be ordered (*Johnstone* (1972) 56 Cr App R 859). Nor can the court order the disqualification to start at a later date, although this is subject to the RTOA 1988, section 35A. If the court is imposing an immediate custodial sentence as well as disqualifying the offender from driving it is obvious that the length of the disqualification will have to take into account the period during which the offender will be in custody and unable to drive in any event. The Court has declined to lay down any rule on how much longer than the served part of the custodial sentence the disqualification should be. In *Playford* [2010] EWCA Crim 2171 it simply observed that each case should be decided on its own facts. When sections 35A and 35B of the RTOA 1988 are brought into effect, in a case where the court imposes an immediate custodial sentence on an offender for the offence and also imposes a disqualification from driving under any of the relevant powers to disqualify, the order will be for the appropriate disqualification period plus an appropriate extension period which will disqualify the offender for such period of time that he is serving the custodial part of his sentence. The effect of that will be that the appropriate disqualification period comes into play at the point when the offender is released from custody.

It is clear that the length of a period of disqualification is designed to be forward-looking **12.14** and to address the nature and extent of the risk to the public inherent in the offender's bad driving rather than being a punishment in itself (*Hussain* [2009] EWCA Crim 2582). The policy of the courts has been that very long periods of disqualification should be avoided as far as possible. For persistent offenders a long driving ban may have the unintended effect of inviting the offender to drive while disqualified (*Matthews* (1987) 9 Cr App R (S) 1) or severely hamper efforts to rehabilitate himself on release from prison (*Russell* [1993] RTR 249). Exceptionally, however, long periods of disqualification including disqualification for life may be appropriate where the offender has an appalling record and/ or constitutes a real and enduring threat to public safety. According to the SGC guideline, *Reduction in Sentence for a Guilty Plea*, a plea of guilty should not affect the duration of a disqualification from driving, since a driving ban is not (according to the guideline) a 'punitive element' in the sentence but a separate ancillary order. The guideline is very clear on this point, but constitutes a sharp departure from earlier practice. Also irrelevant to the length of the ban is the provision in the RTOA 1988, section 42, which enables the offender to apply for restoration of his licence before the end of the period of disqualification (*Lark* (1993) 14 Cr App R (S) 196 and paragraph 12.19, this Chapter). It is a common feature of ancillary orders involving disqualification of various kinds that the offender is able to apply at a later date for the relevant period to be reduced. It can be taken to be a general principle that the possibility of later reduction should not affect the original decision.

Disqualification pending passing of driving test

The RTOA 1988, section 36 provides that where an offender has been disqualified under **12.15** section 34 or section 35 as a result of having been convicted of manslaughter (by the driving of a motor vehicle), causing death by dangerous driving, causing serious injury by dangerous driving, dangerous driving, or causing death by careless driving while under the influence of drink or drugs, the court *must* disqualify him until he passes the appropriate driving test (section 36(1)). In the case of conviction for any other offence which carries obligatory endorsement the court *may* order him to be disqualified until he passes the appropriate driving test (section 36(4)). In any case where there is discretion in the matter the court should have regard to the safety of other road users (section 36(9)). An 'appropriate driving test' means an extended driving test, which is more detailed and thorough than a normal test of competence to drive. Once the test has been passed the period of disqualification comes to an end upon production of evidence by the offender that he has passed. The power extends to those who are disqualified under section 34 or section 35 but there is no power to order an extended driving test where an offender is disqualified under any other provisions of the court (*Patel* (1995) 16 Cr App R (S) 756). Nor is there power to order the offender to take such a test if he is already subject to such an order (*Abdullahi* [2010] EWCA Crim 1886). It has been stressed by the appellate courts in cases such as *Bannister* (1991) 12 Cr App R (S) 314 that such an order is not imposed as a punishment but as a means of affording additional protection for other road users. Unless the requirement is obligatory it should only be used where there is real reason to doubt the offender's competence to drive, whether through the circumstances of the offence, or through matters relating to the offender, such as age or serious illness.

Reduced disqualification for driver retraining

12.16 Sections 34A to 34C of the RTOA 1988 provide for driver retraining on a course specified for that purpose by the Secretary of State. It is available for offenders aged seventeen and over who are convicted of certain drink-driving related offences. These are causing death by careless driving when under the influence of drink or drugs, driving while under the influence of drink or drugs, driving or being in charge with excess alcohol, and failing to provide a specimen. The provisions are restricted to cases where the court has made an order under section 34 disqualifying the offender for a period of at least twelve months. They offer a strong incentive for drivers to attend such a course by allowing a reduction in the period of disqualification for those who do. The reduction must be for not less than three months and not more than one-quarter of the period of disqualification imposed by the court.

Combining disqualification from driving with other sentences or orders

12.17 Disqualification from driving is an ancillary order and may be combined with any other order of the court. For the avoidance of doubt, it may be combined with an absolute or conditional discharge, notwithstanding the PCC(S)A 2000, section 14.

Appeal against, and removal of, disqualification

12.18 Section 38 of the RTOA 1988 provides that a person disqualified by a magistrates' court under section 34 or section 35 may appeal against the order as against a conviction, and by the CAA 1968, section 9, a person disqualified by the Crown Court may appeal to the Court of Appeal.

12.19 Section 42 provides for an offender who has been disqualified from driving to apply to the court to have that disqualification removed early. The court, having regard to the character of the person disqualified and his conduct subsequent to the order, the nature of the offence and any other circumstances of the case, may remove the disqualification as from such date as may be specified in the order. No application under section 42 can be made before the expiration of the relevant period, which is:

(a) two years, if the disqualification is for less than four years;
(b) one half of the period of disqualification if it is for less than ten years but not less than four years; and
(c) five years in any other case.

If an application is refused a further application cannot be made within three months. A court dealing with an application should be somewhat less ready to remove an obligatory disqualification than a discretionary one (*Damer v Davison* [1976] RTR 45).

Disqualification where motor vehicle used in offence

Where an offender has been convicted on indictment of an offence punishable with impris- **12.20** onment for two years or more (or has been convicted summarily of such an offence and committed to the Crown Court for sentence) the Crown Court may, under the PCC(S)A 2000, section 147, disqualify the offender from driving if a motor vehicle was used to commit, or to facilitate the commission of the offence. As with disqualification under sections 34 or 35 of the RTA 1988, power to disqualify under section 147 extends to persons who have been convicted of a qualifying offence but discharged absolutely or conditionally.

The power in section 147 is widely drafted. It may be noted in particular that, providing **12.21** the above conditions are satisfied, the offender may be disqualified from driving by the Crown Court even though the offence with which he has been convicted is non-endorsable. If robbers make their getaway from the scene of the crime in a car, they are liable to disqualification under section 147 notwithstanding that robbery is not an offence attracting mandatory or discretionary disqualification. The fact that the offender did not drive the motor vehicle in the course of the offence does not protect him from disqualification. It is sufficient that the vehicle was used in the circumstances specified in section 147 (*Matthews* [1975] RTR 32). If one of several joint offenders used a vehicle for the purposes of the joint offence, any or all of the offenders may be disqualified. The phrase 'facilitating the commission of an offence' is defined by section 147(6) as including 'the taking of any steps after [the offence] has been committed for the purpose of disposing of any property to which it relates or of avoiding apprehension or detection'.

No disqualification under section 147 may be ordered unless the vehicle was actually used **12.22** to commit the offence of which the offender has been convicted. There must be a causal connection between the use of the vehicle and the offence of conviction (*Parrington* (1985) 7 Cr App R (S) 18). This is a matter of fact and degree and will require assessment in every case. In *Patel* (1995) 16 Cr App R (S) 756 the offender had pursued another motorist who had cut in front of him. When both vehicles stopped at traffic lights the offender got out and seriously assaulted a passenger in the other vehicle. It was held that the use of the car had facilitated the assault, and so an order under section 147 was upheld. Section 147 does not empower the Crown Court to order endorsement of the offender's licence. If disqualified under section 147 the offender simply surrenders his licence for the duration of the disqualification. There is no power for the court to order the offender to take an extended driving test under the RTOA 1988, section 36.

If the court is minded to make an order under section 147 counsel should be alerted as **12.23** to that possibility and be allowed to address the court on the issue. A failure to do so may result in the disqualification being quashed on appeal (*Bowling* [2009] 1 Cr App R (S) 122).

Disqualification on commission of any offence

By the PCC(S)A 2000, section 146 a magistrates' court or the Crown Court may, in add- **12.24** ition to dealing with the offender in any other way, order him to be disqualified from driving for such period as the court thinks fit. As with disqualification under sections 34 or 35 of the RTA 1988 and section 147 of the 2000 Act, power to disqualify under section 146 extends to persons who have been convicted of a qualifying offence but discharged absolutely or conditionally. It will be seen that the power to disqualify under section 146 is wider than that under section 147 since it is not confined to the Crown Court and because it applies *whatever* the offence, irrespective of whether a motor vehicle was used to commit or facilitate the commission of the offence. Disqualification can be ordered under this section where no vehicle was involved in the offence at all. On the face of it, then, this power is so wide as to render the other powers of disqualification discussed earlier virtually redundant. There is, however, no power under this section for the court to order the offender to take an extended driving test under the RTOA 1988, section 36.

12.25   The appellate decisions in relation to disqualification reflect the difficulty inherent in imposing a driving ban on an offender who has not been involved in driving dangerously, or even in driving at all. In *Cliff* [2005] 2 Cr App R (S) 118 the offender was convicted of affray. He was sentenced to imprisonment for fifteen months and disqualified from driving under section 146 for two years. The Court of Appeal upheld the disqualification, confirming that there was no requirement that the offence be connected to driving. The court added, however, that the order should not be used arbitrarily, and that there should be sufficient reason for its use. In *Sofekun* [2009] 1 Cr App R (S) 460, however, where the offender had been found with bags of cannabis concealed under the bonnet of his car, the Court upheld the disqualification and said that nothing in *Cliff* should be taken to have created any restrictions on the exercise of the power which were not apparent from the statutory provision itself.

12.26   It is not clear whether an order under section 146 disqualifying the offender from driving should be regarded as an ancillary order or as part of the punishment. If it is the latter (which appears to be the rationale) then its imposition must affect the totality of the sentence. This seems to have been the view taken in *Sofekun*, where the court said that the disqualification was 'part of an overall punitive sentence'.

12.27   By analogy with disqualification from driving under section 147, if the court is minded to make an order under section 147 counsel should be alerted as to that possibility and be allowed to address the court on the issue.

B   RECOMMENDATION FOR DEPORTATION

12.28   The criminal courts have long had power, when sentencing a foreign criminal, to add a recommendation that the offender be subject to deportation at the end of his sentence. The power is enjoyed by the magistrates' courts and by the Crown Court. By the Immigration Act 1971, section 3(6), a recommendation may be made in respect of any person who is not a British citizen, who is aged seventeen or over, and who is convicted of an offence punishable with imprisonment in the case of an adult. The court has never in this context had power to deport the offender; simply to make a recommendation that the Secretary of State should consider whether such a course ought to be taken. In the old case of *Nazari* [1980] 1 WLR 1366, Lawton LJ said that:

> This country has no use for criminals of other nationalities, particularly if they have committed serious crimes or have long criminal records. The more serious the crime and the longer the record the more obvious it is that there should be an order recommending deportation. In the other hand a minor offence would not merit an order.

In later cases including *Kluxen* [2011] 1 WLR 218 the Court affirmed what was said in *Nazari*, and has added that a recommendation for deportation would be appropriate where the offender's conduct constituted 'a genuine and sufficiently serious threat to the requirements of public policy affecting one of the fundamental interests of society'.

12.29   A 'British citizen' is, broadly, a person who has a right of abode in the UK. In addition a Commonwealth citizen or a citizen of the Irish Republic must not be recommended for deportation if that person was resident in the UK when the 1971 Act came into force (1 January 1973) and has been ordinarily resident in the UK for at least the five years immediately prior to the date of conviction (section 7(1)). If an offender's citizenship is in question for these purposes, the IA 1971, section 3(8) places the onus on the offender to prove citizenship or their entitlement to any other exemption (such as military personnel or persons having diplomatic immunity).

Recommendation for deportation following the UK Borders Act

There is much more that could be said about these provisions, but their practical importance has been greatly diminished by the UK Borders Act 2007. Sections 32 to 39 of that Act place the Secretary of State under a duty to make a deportation order in respect of a 'foreign criminal' unless certain exceptions apply. This has become known as 'automatic deportation', although the term overstates the position. In fact the offender is not necessarily deported—the matter is ultimately one for the Home Secretary—but deportation will automatically be considered. 'Foreign criminal' is defined in section 32 as a person who is not a British citizen, is convicted in the UK of an offence, and who has either: **12.30**

(a)   been sentenced to imprisonment for at least twelve months, or
(b)   who has committed an offence specified by the Secretary of State under the Nationality, Immigration and Asylum Act 2002 and is subject to a period of imprisonment.

The reference to 'imprisonment' includes detention in a young offender institution. 'Sentenced to imprisonment for at least twelve months' requires that the offender must have received a single term of imprisonment of such length. Consecutive shorter sentences which add up to more than twelve months do not qualify. A suspended sentence does not count for this purpose either, unless it is later activated and then amounts to an immediate term of imprisonment of at least twelve months.

The UK Borders Act does not abolish the power to make a recommendation for deportation, but it follows from the provisions of the Act that the circumstances in which it will now be appropriate for a court to make a recommendation are very limited. If the appropriate sentence will be a custodial one in excess of twelve months then there is nothing to be gained by making a recommendation. So, only in the case of a shorter sentence, or a non-custodial disposal, will this now arise in practice. Bearing in mind the test of a 'serious threat to one of the fundamentals interests of society' (earlier), which continues to be valid, it is unlikely that cases resulting in a non-custodial disposal will justify a recommendation for deportation. So we are left with short custodial sentences only. It was pointed out in *Kluxen* [2011] 1 WLR 218 that recommendations may well still be appropriate in cases of misuse of identity documents, which typically attract sentences in the range of six to nine months. See, for example, *Chirimimanga* [2007] EWCA Crim 1684, where recommendations were upheld in respect of three offenders who pleaded guilty to possession of false identity documents. **12.31**

It was held in *Mintchev* [2011] 2 Cr App R (S) 465 that a court should not shorten the appropriate sentence in order to avoid the provisions of the Act. That is clearly right in principle, although one earlier case did point out that an otherwise appropriate sentence might be structured by way of consecutive terms to avoid 'automatic deportation' of the offender (see *Hakimzadeh* [2010] 1 Cr App R (S) 49). Of course the Secretary of State may still consider deportation even if the sentence is below twelve months and no recommendation is made. It is also important to understand that there is no inevitability that an 'automatic deportation' case will actually result in deportation. The sentencing court should not simply assume that will be the case. Thus in *Gebreu* [2011] EWCA Crim 3321 the Court of Appeal said that **12.32** the judge had fallen into error in saying that there was no point in considering whether the offender was dangerous and qualified for an extended sentence, because the offender would be 'deported automatically'. Hallett LJ said that judges should continue to pass the appropriate sentence, and not make that assumption. The Secretary of State will have access to a wide range of information relating to the offender and his family, their ties in the UK, the possibility that they might be required a further sentence in the country to which they might be deported, and the prevailing political circumstances in that country. The Article 8 rights of the offender are clearly engaged by any decision of the Secretary of State over whether to deport them, but it is equally clear that these broader issues are not ones for the sentencing court to consider. In *Carmona* [2006] 1 WLR 2264, decided before the UK Borders Act came into force but equally relevant thereafter, the Court of Appeal confirmed that since the sentencing court was only making a recommendation, and the decision whether to deport the offender rested with the Secretary of State, the issue of engagement with Article 8, as well as any possible argument under Articles 2 and 3, were for the Secretary of State, and not the criminal court.

12.33   A recommendation for deportation is an ancillary order which may be made in addition to any sentence which is imposed. For the avoidance of doubt, it may be combined with an absolute or conditional discharge, notwithstanding the PCC(S)A 2000, section 14 (Immigration Act 1971, section 6(3), and *Akan* [1973] 1 QB 491).

Recommendation for deportation: procedure

12.34   In the relatively rare cases where it is still appropriate to consider whether a recommendation for deportation should be made, a number of important procedural steps must be followed. By section 6(2) of the Immigration Act 1971 the court must not make a recommendation unless the offender has been given at least seven days' written notice of the court's intention. A failure to do so will probably render any subsequent recommendation invalid (*Omojudi* (1992) 13 Cr App R (S) 346, though see *Abdi* [2007] EWCA Crim 1913). If the court is considering making a recommendation the defence should be given an opportunity to address the court on that matter (*Antypas* (1973) 57 Cr App R 207). There must always be a proper inquiry into the circumstances. In *Kibunyi* [2009] EWCA Crim 9 it was suggested that the offender had applied for asylum in the UK. The judge was then in two minds whether to recommend deportation but said that he would not want the recommendation to stand if asylum was granted. The Court of Appeal said that the judge should have embarked on a *Newton* style inquiry into the true position, after which a fully informed decision could have been made. The Court added that there was certainly no prohibition on a court making a recommendation in a case where an application for asylum had been made. Several of the authorities, including *Bozat* [1997] 1 Cr App R (S) 270 and *Rodney* [1996] 2 Cr App R (S) 230, stress the importance of the court always giving reasons for making a recommendation. *Frank* (1992) 13 Cr App R (S) 500 is a striking example of a recommendation being added on to sentence as an afterthought. It was quashed on appeal.

C EXCLUSION FROM LICENSED PREMISES

12.35   By section 1 of the Licensed Premises (Exclusion of Certain Persons) Act 1980, where a person is convicted of an offence committed on licensed premises and the court is satisfied that in committing the offence the offender resorted to violence, or offered or threatened to resort to violence, a magistrates' court or the Crown Court may make an exclusion order, which prohibits the offender from entering those premises, or any other specified premises, without the express consent of the licensee of the premises. The order can be made either on the court's own initiative, or on an application made to the prosecutor by the victim or an interested third party (*Penn* [1996] 2 Cr App R (S) 214).

Making an order to exclude

The court should specify the relevant premises by name and address in the order (section 4(1)). It follows that an order which purports to ban the offender from all licensed premises in Norfolk is unlawful (*Grady* (1990) 12 Cr App R (S) 152). An order banning the offender from 165 specified licensed premises within Crewe and Nantwich was upheld in *Arrowsmith* [2003] 2 Cr App R (S) 301, although the Court of Appeal said that the decision should not be seen as encouraging overly wide exclusion orders. An exclusion order takes effect for such period, being not less than three months and not more than two years, as is specified in the order. The expression 'licensed premises' means, in relation to England and Wales, premises in respect of which there is in force a justices' on-licence within the meaning of the Licensing Act 1964, section 1. When the court makes an exclusion order it should ensure that a copy is sent to the licensee(s) of the establishment(s) listed in the order (section 4(3)). **12.36**

An exclusion order is an ancillary order which may be made in addition to any sentence which is imposed. For the avoidance of doubt, it may be combined with an absolute or conditional discharge, notwithstanding the PCC(S)A 2000, section 14. **12.37**

Breach of order

Anyone who enters premises in breach of an exclusion order is guilty of an offence punishable on summary conviction with a fine not exceeding £200 or to imprisonment for one month, or to both (section 2). At the time of such conviction the court must consider whether the exclusion order should continue in force. It may terminate it, or vary it. There is, however, no power to extend the duration of the order. A copy of the order which terminates or varies the exclusion order must be sent to the licenses(s) of the premises concerned (section 4(3)). **12.38**

D DRINKING BANNING ORDERS

The Violent Crime Reduction Act 2006, sections 1 to 14 create three distinct forms of drinking banning orders. The first is in the form of a civil application under section 3 to a magistrates' court by the local council. The second form, dealt with in sections 6 to 8, follows a conviction, with which we are principally concerned in this book. The third is an order made in the county court, provided for in section 4. It was the legislative intention that the second form of drinking banning order, imposed on conviction and ancillary to sentence, should replace the exclusion from licensed premises order under the 1980 Act (see paragraph 12.35, this Chapter). At the time of writing the magistrates' courts civil powers and the county courts' powers are fully in force but the power to impose a drinking banning order after conviction is in force in certain specified areas of the country only. **12.39**

Making a banning order

The power to make a drinking banning order on conviction applies where an offender aged sixteen years or over is convicted of an offence, and at the relevant time he was under the **12.40** influence of alcohol (section 6(1)). The court must consider whether (by section 3(2)) the offender has engaged in criminal or disorderly behaviour while under the influence of alcohol and that a drinking banning order is necessary to protect other persons from conduct by him of that kind while he is under the influence of alcohol. If so, the court may make a drinking banning order. For these purposes the court will normally be a magistrates' court or a youth court, or the Crown Court if the offender is committed to that court for sentence. A drinking banning order prohibits the offender from doings the things specified in the order, which are limited to those which are necessary for the purpose of protecting other persons from criminal or disorderly conduct by the offender while he is under the influence of alcohol (section 1(2)). The prohibitions must include such as the court thinks necessary on the offender's entering premises in respect of which there is a premises licence authorizing the sale of alcohol. A drinking banning order has effect for a period specified in the order, of not less than two months and not more than two years (section 2(1)).

12.41 The procedural provisions of section 6 are prescriptive. If the court decides that the conditions in section 3(2) above are not made out it should say so and give reasons in open court (section 6(5) and CPR 2013, rule 50.2). If the court decides that the conditions are made out, but does not make a drinking banning order, it must give its reasons in open court for not doing so (section 6(4)). The drinking banning order may contain provision for the order, or a particular prohibition within it, to come to an end early if the offender completes satisfactorily an approved course (section 2(3)), but at least half of the term of the original order must have been completed before it can be brought to an end early in this way (section 2(5)). Provision for attendance on an approved course can only be included if a place on an approved course is available locally and if the offender agrees. The court must explain to the offender what the course will involve, and what fee he will have to pay if he undertakes it. By section 2(8), if the court does not include provision for the offender to attend an approved course, the court must give its reasons in open court for not including it. A drinking banning order made on conviction takes effect on the day on which it is made or, if the offender is in custody, on the day when he is released from that custody (section 7(7)).

12.42 A drinking banning order is an ancillary order and may be made in addition to any sentence imposed for the offence. This includes an offender dealt with by way of a conditional discharge but not, it seems, an absolute discharge (section 7(3)). This is an unusual distinction in sentencing terms.

12.43 By section 10(1), an appeal against the making of a drinking banning order by a magistrates' court lies to the Crown Court. If the order is made by the Crown Court any appeal must lie to the Court of Appeal. Although such authority does not explicitly appear in the 2006 Act, a drinking banning order clearly comes within the definition of 'sentence' within the CAA 1995, section 50(1). The offender or the DPP may subsequently apply to the court which made the order for the order to be varied or discharged (section 8(1)). No order can be varied so as to extend the overall period to more than two years (section 8(5)). No order can be discharged earlier than the halfway point of the order, unless the DPP has agreed to its earlier discharge (section 8(6)).

Breach of order

12.44 If a person subject to a drinking banning order does without reasonable excuse anything that he is prohibited from doing under the order he is guilty of an offence. The offence is punishable on summary conviction with a fine up to level 4 (£2500). A conditional discharge cannot be imposed as the sentence for breach of a drinking banning order (section 11(3)). Oddly enough, an absolute discharge is available in that situation.

E FOOTBALL BANNING ORDERS

The legislative scheme created to deal with those who commit offences in and around foot-   **12.45**
ball matches, whether at domestic or international fixtures, can be found in the Football
Spectators Act (FSA) 1989, as heavily amended by the Football (Disorder) Act 2000. The
resulting legislation is notoriously complex and has given rise to a disproportionate number
of appeals to the Court of Appeal.

Making a banning order

A magistrates' court or the Crown Court has power to make a football banning order,   **12.46**
following conviction for a football-related offence under the FSA 1989, section 14A. The
magistrates' court also has power under section 14B to make such an order on application
by a senior police officer. This form of the order is not dealt with here. The order takes effect
on the day when the order is made (FSA 1989, section 14F(1)).

By section 14A, where an offender is convicted of a 'relevant offence' (see paragraph 12.51,   **12.47**
this Chapter and the court is satisfied that there are reasonable grounds to believe that making a banning order would help to prevent violence or disorder at or in connection with any
'regulated football matches' it must make a banning order in respect of the offender (section
14A(2)). When deciding whether or not to make an order the court may consider evidence,
from the prosecution and the defence, irrespective of whether such evidence would have
been admissible at trial. If the court is not satisfied that a banning order would help to prevent such violence or disorder at or in connection with a football match or matches, then it
must state that fact in open court and give its reasons (section 14A(3) and CPR, rule 50.2).
The mandatory terms of these provisions are clear. When they are made out, there is no discretion to not make a banning order (*Allen* [2011] EWCA Crim 3076). A regulated football
match is an associated football match (whether to be played in the UK or elsewhere) which
is a prescribed match or a match of a prescribed description (section 14(2)). The description
is a compendious one, and incudes association football league matches of all descriptions
or in the football conference, and FA Cup matches, but does not extend to amateur football
matches.

The order prohibits the offender from attending regulated football matches in England   **12.48**
and Wales. The order applies to all such matches, and cannot be tailored to ban the offender from attending the matches of a particular club. It requires the offender to report
to a specific police station within five days of the order being made (section 14E(2)). The
order requires the offender to notify to the police any change of address or other details.
Additionally, the order also requires the offender (in connection with regulated football
matches taking place outside the UK) to surrender his passport (section 14E(3)) unless there
are exceptional circumstances for not doing so. This means that if a person who is banned
wishes to travel abroad during the period when relevant matches are taking place he will
have to obtain individual permission by demonstrating that the purpose of travel is other
than attendance at proscribed matches. There is power whereby the court may impose
additional requirements on the person subject to the order in relation to any regulated football matches (section 14G(1)). In particular, the court may make an order under the Public
Order Act 1986, section 35, requiring the offender to attend at a police station to have his
photograph taken. The Court of Appeal in *Boggild* [2012] 1 Cr App R (S) 457 noted the
'potentially far-reaching consequences' of the order but said that strong provisions were
necessary to achieve some control of football hooliganism and violence. In *Gough v Chief
Constable of Derbyshire* [2002] QB 459 (a case where the ban was imposed following application to the magistrates' court) the Divisional Court held that football banning orders

were a lawful and proportionate restriction on a citizen's freedom of movement under European law. The same court in *R (White) v Blackfriars Crown Court* [2008] 2 Cr App R (S) 542 (this time dealing with a ban imposed following conviction) agreed with what was said in *Gough*, although some question still remains about the validity of the travel restriction element within the order.

12.49　If the offender is sentenced to custody for the offence, the banning order must be for at least six years and not more than ten years. If the offender receives some other sentence the banning order must be for at least three years and not more than five years (section 14F(3) and (4)). There is very little authority on the question of how long a particular ban should be. In *Curtis* [2009] EWCA Crim 1225 the offender had been involved in shouting and swearing at police officers after a match. He pleaded guilty to an offence under section 4 of the Public Order 1986, and was fined. He was aged twenty-two and had no previous convictions. On appeal it was held that the banning order was appropriate but that it was too long and was reduced from five years to three years.

12.50　A banning order is an ancillary order and may be made in addition to the sentence for any offence including a conditional discharge notwithstanding the PCC(S)A 2000, section 14. A banning order cannot be imposed where the offence has been dealt with by an absolute discharge.

12.51　The 'relevant offences' are listed in schedule 1 to the FSA 1989. A wide range of offences is included, involving violence, possession of an offensive weapon, drunkenness, public disorder, damage to property, and road traffic offences. These are relevant offences if (but only if) they were committed at or in connection with a football match, or when travelling to or from a football match, whether or not that match was actually attended by the offender. The offences listed extend to any inchoate form of the offence and to secondary participation in the offence.

12.52　In respect to some but not all of the offences listed in schedule 1, before making a banning order the court is required to make a 'declaration of relevance', which ordinarily requires that the prosecutor must give notice to the defendant, at least five days before the first day of his trial, that it is proposed to show that the offence charged did indeed relate to a particular football match or matches. Exceptionally the court may make such a declaration in a case where the required notice has not been given, but only if the defendant consents to waiving the full period of notice, or if the court is satisfied that the interests of justice do not require further notice to be given (section 23). In *DPP v Beaumont* [2008] 2 Cr App R (S) 549 it was held that the failure of the magistrates formally to state a declaration of relevance was not necessarily fatal to the proper making of a banning order, so long as it is clear from the record that the court had the relevant considerations in mind. If the prosecution and defence differ on the facts of the offence, such that it is unclear whether a declaration of relevance can properly be made, the matter should be resolved by the court, by way of a *Newton* hearing if necessary. The Act does not define when an offence is related to a football match, and the court must make that assessment. The Court of Appeal in *Doyle* [2012] EWCA Crim 995 declined to offer a definition, but did say that it would not normally be enough that the offence would not have happened but for the offender being en route to or from a match. It could sometimes be helpful to ask whether the 'spark' for the violence had been football-related, but that was only an example and not a full test.

12.53　Some of the offences listed in schedule 1 specify that for the purposes of a football banning order the offence must have been committed during 'a period relevant to a regulated football match'. The period relevant is the period beginning twenty-four hours before the start of the match and ending twenty-four hours after the end of the match (or if the match does not take place, twenty-four hours before and twenty-four hours after the advertised starting time).

It was held in *Hughes* [2006] 1 Cr App R (S) 632 that a banning order may properly be made **12.54** on the basis of a single offence without evidence of relevant past offending. Indeed, as we have seen, where the relevant criteria are made out and the court is of the view that a ban would help to prevent violence or disorder, there is no discretion not to make an order even if that might seem, on the facts of the particular case, severe. The court may properly take into account the general deterrent value of making such an order (*Curtis* [2010] 1 Cr App R (S) 193). In *Boggild*, however, the Court said that a banning order was not the inevitable consequence of football-related violence, and on the facts of the case before them the judge had properly decided not to impose one. The offenders, who all pleaded guilty to affray, had not been looking for trouble; they had responded to aggression from a different and larger group, and they were all of good character or had minor convictions only. The judge said that a banning order was not a punishment but was a preventive measure designed to address the future risk of disorder, and that the offenders had learned their lessons so there was no risk such as to justify a long ban under the FSA. The judge had, instead, imposed suspended sentences of detention in a young offender institution, or youth rehabilitation orders, in each case containing a prohibited activity requirement. The Court of Appeal said that judges must think carefully before taking this approach as an alternative to a ban under the FSA. There was a sophisticated regime for coordinating intelligence relating to those subject to football banning orders. Disobedience to a banning order was an offence, whereas a failure to comply with a prohibited activity requirement would be dealt with by a different route. The Court in *Doyle* [2012] EWCA Crim 995, another case involving affray but in a much more serious context, took a similar approach to *Boggild*. Hughes LJ in *Doyle* said that the more the offence was linked to football grievances or group culture of a set of fans, and the more there was a history of football-related offending, the more likely it would that the condition in section 14A(2) would be met and an order required. The test of reasonable grounds to believe that a banning order would help to prevent violence or disorder at regulated matches did not set a high hurdle but it was not automatically justified just because the offence was football-related. The Court in *Doyle* also considered whether a different form of ancillary order might be more suitable in the circumstances than the ban under the FSA, but did not think so on the facts. In his commentary in the *Criminal Law Review* Dr David Thomas suggests that an anti-social behaviour order under section 1C of the Crime and Disorder Act, or a restraining order under section 5 of the Prevention of Harassment Act 1997. Each of these orders have greater flexibility in terms of their content and length, and the penalty for breach is a maximum of five years' imprisonment, rather than the six months available under the FSA.

On making a banning order the court must explain the effect of the order to the offender in **12.55** open court in ordinary language (section 14E(1)).

The defendant may appeal against the making of a banning order, since such an order **12.56** clearly falls within the definition of 'sentence' in the CAA 1968, section 50. The defendant may also appeal against a declaration of relevance made by the sentencing court (section 23(3)). The prosecution may appeal against the failure of a court to make a banning order. If the failure is by a magistrates' court the appeal lies to the Crown Court, and if it is by the Crown Court the appeal lies to the Court of Appeal (section 14A(5A)). In this context the appeal lies to the Civil rather than the Criminal Division of the Court of Appeal (*Boggild* [2012] 1 Cr App R (S) 457. This odd situation arises because, by oversight, no provision was made in the FSA 1989 for the Court of Appeal Criminal Division to make a banning order. The Civil Division, however, was vested with a general power to make any order which the original court could have made, and so only the Civil Division had jurisdiction to hear the prosecutor's appeal under section 14A(5A)).

12.57 The court, on application by the offender or the prosecutor, may vary an order by imposing, replacing, or omitting a requirement in that order. If a banning order has been in force for at least two-thirds of the period of the order, the person subject to it may apply to the court by which the order was made to terminate it early (section 14H). The court may terminate the order as from a specified date or refuse the application. In deciding whether to terminate the order the court must have regard to the offender's character, the nature of the offence, his conduct since the offence, and any other relevant circumstances.

Breach of order

12.58 A person subject to a football banning order who fails to comply with any requirements imposed by the order is guilty of an offence punishable on summary conviction with imprisonment for a term not exceeding six months, or a fine not exceeding level 5 (£5000), or both (section 14J).

F DISQUALIFICATION FROM ACTING AS COMPANY DIRECTOR

12.59 The Company Directors Disqualification Act (CDDA) 1986 specifies certain circumstances in which a court may make an order disqualifying the offender from acting as a director of a company. Some, but not all, of these circumstances relate to the commission of criminal offences by the person concerned. It is important to distinguish the power of a criminal court to disqualify under section 2 with other powers to disqualify under the Act, especially under section 6 (where disqualification is mandatory and for a minimum of two years). Disqualification under that section requires a finding that the person concerned has conducted himself in a manner which makes him unfit to be concerned in the management of a company. Such finding is not required under section 2. Only the provisions of the Act which are concerned with disqualification after conviction of an offence are considered here.

Making a disqualification order

12.60 By section 2(1) of the CDDA 1986 the Crown Court or a magistrates' court may make a disqualification order against an offender whenever he is convicted of an indictable offence in connection with the promotion, formation, management, or liquidation of a company, or in connection with the receivership or management of a company's property. A disqualification order has the effect that the offender must not, for a specified period beginning with the date of the order, without the leave of the court:

(a) be a director of a company;
(b) act as a receiver of a company's property; or
(c) in any way, whether directly or indirectly, be concerned or take part in the promotion, formation, or management of a company, and
(d) he shall not act as an insolvency practitioner (section 1(1)).

The order has all these effects. It is not possible for the court to specify one or more function from which the offender is now disqualified, nor to narrow the scope of the order, nor to limit the ban to a certain type of company. It has been held that 'management of a company' is a term to be construed widely, and is not limited to the internal affairs of the company. It is sufficient that the offence has some factual connection with the management of a company, so that an order may be justified where fraud or a similar offence has been committed in the course of the trading of the company (*Georgiou* (1988) 87 Cr App R 207; *Goodman* (1993) 14 Cr App R (S) 147).

If a magistrates' court makes the order the maximum duration is five years. If the Crown Court makes the order the maximum is fifteen years. In neither court is there a minimum period. Unless the court directs otherwise, the disqualification begins twenty-one days from the date of the order (section 1(2)). Where a disqualification order is made against a person who is already subject to one, the second period of disqualification must run concurrently with the first (section 1(3)). A disqualification order following conviction may be made on grounds which include matters other than criminal convictions (section 1(4)), so it is clear that the whole picture of the offender's dealings (incompetence as well as dishonesty) should be considered. In *Young* (1991) 12 Cr App R (S) 262 the Court of Appeal said that section 2 of the Act (as opposed to the civil powers under section 6) gave the criminal court a 'complete and unfettered discretion' to make the order for disqualification. The main purpose of disqualification is to protect the public from those who, for reasons of dishonesty, naïvety, or incompetence may use or abuse their role and status as director (according to Potter LJ in *Edwards* [1998] 2 Cr App R (S) 213). In *Millard* (1994) 15 Cr App R (S) 445 the Court of Appeal identified an 'upper bracket' of disqualification for more than ten years, which should be reserved for particularly serious cases (including those where the director has been disqualified before), a 'middle bracket' of six to ten years, and a lower bracket of two to five years for cases which are, relatively, not very serious. Of course a disqualification for less than two years could be imposed under section 2 of the Act (in contrast to section 6) but it may be that two years was regarded by the Court in *Millard* as being, for practical purposes, the shortest period which could be imposed. A large number of earlier authorities on the length of disqualification orders were reviewed by the Court of Appeal in *Cadman* [2012] 2 Cr App R (S) 525. The offender was convicted of conspiracy to defraud, having been involved in a conspiracy to obtain funds from a scheme intended to provide financial support for students. He issued documentation purporting to show that the claimants were registered students or trainees, which they were not. Companies operated by the offender obtained in excess of £500,000. He was initially sentenced to imprisonment for five years and disqualified from being a company director for ten years. The conviction was quashed on appeal, and at the re-trial he pleaded guilty on a narrower factual basis. The new sentence was thirty-five months plus a disqualification for six years. He appealed on the basis that the new disqualification was too long. The Court of Appeal said that, in light of the earlier cases, the original disqualification should have been seven years and, taking into account the four years that had been in place until the retrial, the subsequent disqualification should have been for three years. Important considerations in this case were the offender's guilty plea on the second occasion, the fact that the companies had been set up and traded legitimately for a considerable time before the fraud, the fact that the offending took place over a relatively short time (eight months), the offender's good character, and the amount obtained, which was less than several of the other cases to which the Court had been referred.

12.61

A company director disqualification order under section 2 is an ancillary order and may be made in addition to any sentence imposed for the offence. On the face of it this includes, notwithstanding the PCC(S)A 2000, section 14, an offender dealt with by way of an absolute or conditional discharge. In *Young*, however, the Court of Appeal struck down a company director disqualification which had been imposed in conjunction with a conditional discharge. The Court was puzzled by the sentence passed on the facts of the case, but said

12.62

that since the disqualification was 'unquestionably a punishment' it could not be combined with a discharge. This reasoning here is open to doubt since, according to *Edwards*, the qualification is a preventative rather than a punitive measure. Section 12(7) of the PCC(S)A 2000 says that a court discharging an offender absolutely or conditionally may make any order for disqualification, and the other forms of disqualification or exclusion considered in this Chapter can be combined with a discharge.

12.63 A company director disqualification order is a sentence within the meaning of the CAA 1968, section 50, and so the offender has a right of appeal. A disqualification order may be added in a case where the Attorney General refers the case to the Court. An example is *A-G's Reference (No 88 of 2006)* [2007] 2 Cr App R (S) 155.

Breach of order

12.64 A breach of a company director disqualification order is itself a criminal offence, punishable with up to two years' imprisonment (section 13).

G FINANCIAL REPORTING ORDERS

12.65 The purpose of a financial reporting order is to require the offender upon whom it is imposed to make a report, to a person specified in the order, as to such particulars of his financial affairs as may be specified in the order.

Making a financial reporting order

12.66 Under the Serious Organised Crime and Police Act 2005, section 76 a court sentencing an offender for an offence which is listed in section 76(3) of that Act may also make a financial reporting order in respect of that offender, provided that it is satisfied that the risk of the person's committing another offence of the kind mentioned in section 76(3) is sufficiently high to justify the making of the order (section 76(2)). The offences include fraud, conspiracy to defraud, false accounting, lifestyle offences under the Proceeds of Crime Act 2002, money-laundering offences, offences under the Drug Trafficking Act 1994, fraudulent evasion of duty, and offences under the Terrorism Act 2000.

12.67 The order requires the offender to make a report to a person specified in the order as to such particulars of his financial affairs as may be specified. The order comes into force on the day it is made and has effect for the period specified in the order. If made by a magistrates' court the period must not exceed five years (section 76(6)). If made by the Crown Court the period must not exceed twenty years where the person has been sentenced to imprisonment for life, or fifteen years in any other case (section 76(7)). The report may relate to a specified period of time beginning with the start of the order and to subsequent periods beginning immediately upon expiry of the last one (section 79(2)). Each report must be made within a specified number of days after the end of the period in question (section 79(5)). The offender must set out in each report, in the manner specified, such particulars of his financial affairs relating to the period in question as may be specified. Section 81 provides for verification and disclosure of such orders. This permits the person to whom the financial reporting order is to be made to disclose it to any person whom he reasonably believes may be able to check the accuracy of the report or discover the true position, or to any person for the purposes of the prevention, investigation, or prosecution of criminal offences. Any other person may disclose information to the person to whom the financial reporting order is to be made, for the purpose of checking the accuracy of the report or discovering the true position.

The Court of Appeal has considered the appropriate use of these orders in just a handful of **12.68** cases. In *Adams* [2009] 1 WLR 301 the Court held that a financial reporting order was not a 'penalty' for the purposes of the ECHR, Art 7, and so an order imposed on an offender whose offences had pre-dated the coming into force of the 2005 Act did not amount to a retrospective penalty. In *Wright* [2009] 2 Cr App R (S) 313 the Court of Appeal upheld a financial reporting order for ten years on an offender convicted of very serious offences of importing and supplying cocaine and described as a manipulative 'master criminal'. His benefit from drug trafficking was assessed at £45 million. The Court held that the judge had addressed his mind to the relevant tests. The offender had been convicted of a specified offence, and the judge was satisfied that the risk of his committing another specified offence (in this case, money laundering in an attempt to conceal his asserts from the investigators) was sufficiently high to justify the making of the order. This was despite the fact that the offender was currently serving a thirty-year custodial sentence. The Court observed that a judge should always consider carefully whether a financial reporting order should be made, and what purpose it would serve. In a case where the offender was already subject to a confiscation order, a financial reporting order might well add little to the investigatory powers available under the confiscation regime. In *Bell* [2012] 2 Cr App R (S) 15 two offenders pleaded guilty to conspiracy to supply cocaine on a substantial scale, and were sentenced to eleven-and-a-half years' and fifteen years' imprisonment. Financial reporting orders of twelve years and fifteen years were also imposed. These orders were upheld but the fifteen-year order was reduced to twelve years. Kenneth Parker J said that before making a financial reporting order a judge should clearly state how he has assessed the risk of further relevant offending, and how any expected advantage for crime detection and prevention is to be weighed against the assessed risk of re-offending and the burden of the order. In making this assessment, a court is clearly permitted to look at the whole picture, and is not confined to the facts of the instant offence (*Bagnall* [2012] EWCA Crim 677).

A financial reporting order is an ancillary order and may be made in addition to any sen- **12.69** tence imposed for the offence. Notwithstanding the PCC(S)A 2000, section 14, there is nothing in the SOCPA 2005 to prevent the order being imposed for an offence sentenced by way of a discharge.

A financial reporting order is a sentence within the meaning of the CAA 1968, section 50, **12.70** and so the offender has a right of appeal. This point was confirmed in *Adams*.

Section 80 provides for an application to be made by the person in respect of whom the **12.71** report has been made, or by the person to whom the report is to be made, for variation or revocation of a financial reporting order. Application is to the court which made the original order.

Breach of order

A person who without reasonable excuse includes false or misleading information in a report **12.72** or who otherwise fails to comply with any requirement of section 79 is guilty of an offence and liable on summary conviction to imprisonment for a term not exceeding six months, or a fine not exceeding level 5 on the standard scale (£5000) or to both (section 79(10)).

H SEXUAL OFFENCE PREVENTION ORDERS

The Sexual Offences Act 2003, sections 104 to 113 provides power for the courts to impose **12.73** a sexual offences prevention order (SOPO).

Making a sexual offences prevention order

12.74 A court may make a sexual offences prevention order (SOPO) under the SOA 2003, section 104 where the court deals with the offender in respect of a sexual offence listed in schedule 3 to the 2003 Act, or one of the offences listed in schedule 5 to that Act where the context of the offence gives rise to concern over the risk of future sexual offending. A SOPO may also be passed where the defendant has been found not guilty of a relevant offence on the ground of insanity. A SOPO may also be applied for by a chief police officer by complaint to a magistrates' court in respect of a qualifying offender (see *R (Chief Constable of Cleveland Police) v Haggas* [2010] 3 All ER 506). This form of the order is not further dealt with here.

12.75 A SOPO prohibits the offender from doing anything described in the order, and it has effect for a fixed period of time (which must not be less than five years) as specified in the order, or the order may be 'until further order', which means indeterminate (section 107(1)). An order for less than five years is clearly unlawful (*Roberts* [2010] EWCA Crim 907). Few appellate cases specifically consider the criteria for determining the length of a SOPO, but logic suggests that duration should be related to expected endurance of the anticipated risk rather than to seriousness of offence. Likelihood of re-offending may, for example, diminish with age. In *Rampley* [2006] EWCA Crim 2203 the Court replaced an indeterminate SOPO on a fifty-seven-year-old man with an order for seven years. On the other hand, in *Collard* [2005] 1 Cr App R (S) 155, given the depth of the offender's obsession with collecting indecent images of children there was nothing to indicate that his proclivities might cease in the foreseeable future, and so an indefinite order was upheld. Strictly speaking a SOPO can only contain prohibitions; it should not contain a mandatory requirement, such as one which required the offender to allow access to the police to his home at any time of the day or night (*Smith* [2009] 2 Cr App R (S) 718).

12.76 The court must always be satisfied that it is 'necessary' to make such an order, for the purpose of 'protecting the public or any particular members of the public from serious sexual harm from the defendant' (section 104(1) to (3)). This phrase is further defined as 'protecting the public in the UK or any particular members of the public from serious physical or psychological harm, caused by the offender committing one or more offences listed in schedule 3' (section 106(3)). The only prohibitions which may be included in a SOPO are those which are 'necessary' to achieve the above purpose. The statutory criteria must always be made out, and a SOPO should never be made as a matter of course or without giving careful thought (*Roberts*). A case in which a SOPO was quashed because it was not necessary to achieve the purpose of protecting the public is *Frew* [2009] 1 Cr App R (S) 92. The twenty-eight-year-old offender had sexual intercourse with a girl who he knew to be fifteen-and-a-half years of age. The intercourse was consensual but resulted in pregnancy and subsequently a late and traumatic abortion. A SOPO with wide and restrictive terms was quashed by the Court of Appeal. The single sexual offence committed and its consequences would make it less likely rather than more likely that he would re-offend. Another example, this time involving indecent images on a computer, is *Rollason* [2010] EWCA Crim 2146. In *Hemsley* [2010] 3 All ER 965 the Court of Appeal offered the general guidance that a SOPO should be clear on its face as to what was required of the offender, be capable of being complied with by the offender without unreasonable difficulty and/or the assistance of a third party, and free of the risk of unintentional breach. Bearing in mind that such orders are often made against persons of limited education, clarity and simplicity are desirable. Further, in the leading decision in *Smith* [2012] 1 WLR 1316 Hughes LJ said that while SOPOs offer flexibility in drafting which can be tailor-made to suit the particular case, those drafting the prohibitions in a SOPO should not be so inventive as to store up trouble for the future. Prohibitions must not be vague, must not conflict with other obligations applicable to the offender, and they must not impose an impermissible level of restriction on the ordinary activities of life. Every SOPO should meet the twin tests of necessity and clarity. The test of necessity brings with it the sub-test of proportionality. It was further noted in *Smith* that an offender made subject to a SOPO would probably also be subject to the automatic disqualifications applicable under the sex offender notification scheme in the 2003 Act and the arrangements under the Safeguarding Vulnerable Groups Act 2006 barring the offender from working in future with children or vulnerable adults. Both these sets of provisions are considered in Chapter 15. Hughes LJ said that judges being asked to impose a SOPO should make sure that prohibitions within the order did not duplicate, or interfere with, prohibitions placed on the offender as a result of these other schemes. The prosecution should be in a position to assist the judge on this issue.

A particular prohibition which has caused problems reported in several appellate cases is **12.77** one designed to prevent or limit the offender's access to the Internet. In *Mortimer* [2010] EWCA Crim 1303 the Court of Appeal deleted or amended a number of restrictions in a SOPO which were intended to restrict the offender's online access. The Court found these to be both disproportionate and almost impossible to enforce. Provisions were substituted which prohibited the offender from owning any device which allowed Internet access without first notifying the monitoring officer, and prohibiting the offender from deleting from that device its history of Internet use. In *Smith* the Court recognized the difficulties in this area but suggested that the best approach was one which required the preservation of the history of Internet access with a requirement that the offender must submit that history to inspection on request.

A sexual offences prevention order is an ancillary order and may be made in addition to any **12.78** sentence imposed for the offence. Notwithstanding the PCC(S)A 2000, section 14, there is nothing in the SOCPA 2005 to prevent the order being imposed for an offence sentenced by way of a discharge. The question whether or in what circumstances a SOPO should be added to an indeterminate custodial sentence imposed on a dangerous offender has been considered in several cases. The considered view now seems to be that expressed in *Smith*, which is that ordinarily an indeterminate sentence requires no SOPO. In this case the sentence in issue was imprisonment for public protection, which was abolished in 2012, so that the decision now only relates to the life sentence. In *Terrell* the Court noted that the possibility of passing a determinate custodial sentence together with a SOPO might in some cases avoid the need to pass an indeterminate sentence, since the threshold of dangerousness for a life sentence or an extended sentence (where 'serious harm' means 'death or serious personal injury') is higher than the threshold required for a SOPO.

There is a right of appeal against a SOPO. The defendant may appeal under section 110. **12.79** As usual, leave is required. It was said in *Hoath* [2011] 1 WLR 1656 that it was important that leave should be sought promptly if it was to be argued that the SOPO should not have been made at all, or that a prohibition or prohibitions within the SOPO should not have been inserted.

Provisions relating to the variation, renewal, and discharge of a SOPO are set out in section **12.80** 108. The offender, or a chief officer of police, may make an application to the Crown Court for an order to vary, renew, or discharge the SOPO. An order may be renewed or varied so as to impose additional prohibitions only if it is necessary to do so for the purpose of protecting the public or any particular members of the public from serious sexual harm from the offender. The court must not discharge the SOPO before the end of five years from the date of making the order without the agreement of the offender and the relevant chief police officer. The Court in *Hoath* said that where there was an issue in principle in relation to the terms of the SOPO the matter should be dealt with promptly on an appeal under section 110. Section 108 was appropriate where unanticipated difficulties had arisen, or there had been a change in circumstances which meant that the terms of the original order were no longer apposite. The Crown Court should not make other than minor adjustments to the order, at least to a recently imposed order.

Sexual offences prevention order: procedure

12.81 Procedural problems seemed to have beset the making of these orders. In several decisions of the Court of Appeal it has been stressed that the relevant procedural requirements should be complied with before a SOPO is made. In *Roberts* [2010] EWCA Crim 907 it was said that these orders should not be made 'on the hoof', or simply tagged on to the main sentence. In *Buchanan* [2010] EWCA Crim 1316 it was said that in a case where the judge takes the initiative in making a SOPO this should first be prepared in draft with counsel given time to consider it and make submissions. If necessary the hearing should be put back so that the terms of the SOPO can be properly considered. Alternatively the judge may request the prosecution to submit a draft SOPO to the court and to the defence in good time before the sentencing hearing. In *Smith* Hughes LJ said that a draft proposed order prepared by the prosecution should always be served on the court and on the offender not less than two days before the sentencing hearing and should be provided in electronic form to facilitate amendments. In *Pelletier* [2012] EWCA Crim 1060 it was further suggested that the final agreed version of the order should be initialled by the judge and a copy given to the offender for him to sign.

Breach of order

12.82 If an offender who is subject to a SOPO without reasonable excuse does anything which he is prohibited from doing by that order, he commits an offence which is punishable on indictment with imprisonment for a term not exceeding five years, or on summary conviction with imprisonment for a term not exceeding six months, or a fine not exceeding the statutory maximum (£5000), or both. It is not open to a court dealing with breach of a SOPO to make a conditional discharge for that offence (section 113).

I RESTRAINING ORDER (PROTECTION FROM HARASSMENT ACT)

12.83 The Crown Court and the magistrates' courts have power, in addition to sentencing for an offence, to make an order designed to deter the offender from future conduct which would amount to harassment. Harassing a person includes alarming them, or causing them distress. Typically, such an order will be made in a case where the offender has been convicted of domestic violence, and the order is intended to prevent unwanted contact with the injured party, but it is also available in much wider circumstances. Unusually, a restraining order can be made where the defendant has been acquitted of the offence charged but there is evidence on which the court is satisfied that the order is still necessary to protect the victim.

Making a restraining order on conviction

12.84 Where a court is sentencing an offender for any offence (not just an offence under the Protection from Harassment Act (PHA) 1997) the court may make an order prohibiting the offender from doing anything described in the order, for the purpose of protecting the victim of the offence, or any other persons mentioned in the order, from conduct which amounts to harassment, or will cause fear of violence (PHA 1997, section 5(1) and (2)). The order may be for a period specified in the order, or 'until further order', which means indeterminate (section 5(3)).

The purpose of a restraining order is to prohibit conduct with a view to protecting the **12.85** victim or victims and preventing further harassment (*Debnath* [2006] 2 Cr App R (S) 169). A restraining order may be made for the protection of an individual (who should be clearly identified by name in the order), or a group of individuals (provided that the group can be sufficiently clearly defined) or, in very limited circumstances, a limited company (*Buxton* [2011] 1 WLR 857). The order must be clear and precise so there can be no doubt as to the prohibitions which apply. In considering the terms of the order and the extent of the limitations imposed the court must have regard to proportionality with the seriousness of the offence. The order is a form of 'civil order', and so the civil rather than the criminal standard of proof applies (*Major* [2011] 1 Cr App R (S) 322).

A restraining order is an ancillary order and may be made in addition to any sentence **12.86** imposed for the offence. Notwithstanding the PCC(S)A 2000, section 14, there is nothing in the PHA 1997 to prevent the order being imposed for an offence sentenced by way of a discharge.

The offender, the prosecutor, or any person mentioned in the order (most likely the victim of **12.87** the offence) may apply to the court which made the order for it to be varied or discharged by a further order (section 5(4)). Application to vary the terms of a restraining order should be made where unanticipated difficulties had arisen, or there had been a change in circumstances which meant that the terms of the original order were no longer apposite (see *Debnath*). Any person mentioned in the order (most likely the victim of the offence) is entitled to be heard on an application to vary or discharge the order (section 5(4A)). A term in the order may be varied, or the duration of the order extended (including an alteration of the order from one for a fixed term to an indefinite term) if that was what was required to protect the victim or potential victim from harassment (*DPP v Hall* [2006] 1 WLR 1000).

The offender has a right of appeal against a restraining order. If there is an issue in principle **12.88** in relation to the terms of the order the matter should be dealt with promptly on an appeal, rather than by way of an application to vary the terms of the order under section 5(4) (*Debnath*).

Making a restraining order on acquittal

A court before which a person is *acquitted* of any offence (not just an offence under the **12.89** Protection from Harassment Act 1997) may make an order prohibiting the offender from doing anything described in the order, for the purpose of protecting the victim of the offence, or any other persons mentioned in the order, from conduct which amounts to harassment, or will cause fear of violence (PHA 1997, section 5A). The order may be for a period specified in the order, or 'until further order', which means indeterminate.

It is striking that such an order may be made upon an acquittal as well as a conviction. **12.90** The only precedent for an ancillary order operating in this way is the ancient power to bind over a person to keep the peace. This is a very general (and anomalous) power, which can be exercised against any person before the court, including a person acquitted of the offence (see Chapter 8 this book, paragraph 8.08). In contrast the power to make a restraining order on acquittal has only been available since 2009, a result of the delayed implementation of the Domestic Violence, Crime and Victims Act 2004, section 12(5). Some other ancillary orders, including the SOPO, may be exercised against a person who has been acquitted on the grounds of insanity. The rationale in each of these examples seems to be the prevention of future risk of offending ('preventive justice' as it has been called in the context of the bind over to keep the peace). Such orders are also 'civil' in character, and although they cannot be imposed without sufficient evidence to support them, the criminal standard of proof is not required. In the case of a restraining order there may be insufficient evidence to convict but sufficient evidence before the court on which to form the judgment that is necessary to protect the victim from future harassment by the offender. The appellate case law makes it clear that there is no presumption that such an order should be imposed only in rare cases. A restraining order following an acquittal was upheld in *Thompson* [2011] 2 Cr App R (S) 131, where the offender was acquitted of assaulting a woman with whom he had had a relationship but the judge formed the view, based on evidence given at the trial, that the order was necessary to protect the complainant from harassment. An interesting, though very unusual case is *Smith* [2012] EWCA Crim 2566. The defendant had been a passenger on an aircraft, and during the flight he became very disturbed and upset, saying 'I need to get off', and trying to open an exit door. Cabin staff restrained him but he was violent and abusive. At his trial for criminal damage and interfering with the performance of the crew of an aircraft he was acquitted on the ground of insanity. The medical evidence was that the defendant had suffered from a brief reactive psychosis, but it was not necessary for public safety that he be detained in a hospital. The judge ordered an absolute discharge but also made an order under section 5A. The order was quashed on appeal, on the twin grounds that no specific person or persons had been identified in the order, and that it could not truly be said that the order was necessary for the protection of such other person or persons. The judge had employed the section as a means of protecting the public from the possible effects of the possible recurrence of an illness. That was not the function of the section.

12.91 A number of the appellate cases relating to this power have been concerned with the necessary evidence base for exercising it. It is clear that there is no general principle that a restraining order should only be made if the facts are uncontested, but in *Major* [2011] 1 Cr App R (S) 322 it was confirmed that a restraining order might properly be made on an acquittal if the conduct alleged had not been proved to the criminal standard but had been proved to the civil standard, or the evidence had failed to establish that there actually had been harassment but the court was satisfied that it might well occur in the future, an order may be appropriate. The judge must, however, always identify the factual basis for making it. The order was quashed on appeal in *Major* because the judge had failed fully to articulate the reasons for making it. An order on acquittal was quashed on appeal in *K* [2012] 1 Cr App R (S) 523. In that case the prosecution had in the end offered no evidence against the defendant, and the judge had made the order on his own initiative, after hearing submissions from counsel. The Court of Appeal said that the case papers (which would have been the subject of factual disagreement if the matter had gone to trial) did not provide a sufficiently sound evidential basis for making a restraining order. Another example is *Brough* [2012] 2 Cr App R (S) 30, where again the prosecution chose in the end to offer no evidence, but this time they took the initiative and applied for an order under section 5A. The judge made the order, but without having the benefit of guidance from the two previously mentioned cases. In *Brough* the Court said that the proper approach would have been for the judge to discuss with counsel the factual issues, then to have heard evidence from the person proposed to be named in the order and the defendant, and then expressed his findings and explained how those findings led him to conclude that there was a necessity for a restraining order to be made. The Court also said that care must be taken to ensure that an restraining order which is made must be drafted in terms of section 5A of the PHA 1997, and not section 5.

The offender, the prosecutor, or any person mentioned in the order may apply to the court **12.92** which made the order for it to be varied or discharged by a further order. Any person mentioned in the order is entitled to be heard on the hearing of an application to vary or discharge the order. Where the Court of Appeal quashes a conviction it may remit the case to the Crown Court to consider whether to make a restraining order. Where the Crown Court allows an appeal against a conviction in the magistrates' court, the Crown Court may make a restraining order.

Breach of order

If without reasonable excuse the offender does anything which he is prohibited from doing **12.93** under the order, he is guilty of an offence, punishable on conviction on indictment with imprisonment for a term not exceeding five years, or a fine, or both, and on summary conviction to imprisonment for a term not exceeding six months, or a fine not exceeding the statutory maximum (£5000), or both. If the offender claims to have had a reasonable excuse for the alleged breach he must provide evidence of that, and then it is for the prosecution to prove that there was no reasonable excuse (*Evans* [2005] 1 Cr App R (S) 546). The SGC guideline, *Breach of a Protective Order* provides guidance in cases of sentencing for breach of a restraining order. The earlier decision of the Court of Appeal in *Liddle* [2000] 1 Cr App R (S) 131 is also still of assistance.

J TRAVEL RESTRICTION ORDERS

Travel restriction orders designed to target offenders convicted of drug trafficking offences, **12.94** so as to prevent their travelling abroad for a period of time, were introduced by the Criminal Justice and Police Act (CJPA) 2001.

Making a travel restriction order

Where a court convicts an offender of a drug trafficking offence, as defined in section 34 of **12.95** the CJPA 2001 and the court decides that it is appropriate to impose a prison sentence of at least four years, the court is required to consider whether it would be appropriate in addition to make a travel restriction order (section 33(1)). The effect of the order is to restrict the offender's freedom to leave the UK for a specified period and may, but not must, by section 33(4) require delivery up of his passport (or 'travel authorization' as it strictly should now be called: Identity Cards Act 2006, section 39(3)). If the court decides that it would be appropriate then it should make such an order, for the period which it thinks suitable in all the circumstances. If it decides that it is not appropriate to make a travel restriction order it must state its reasons for coming to that view in open court (section 33(2)). It is not a good enough reason to decline to make an order that the offence itself contained no foreign aspect (according to Leveson LJ in *Shaw* [2011] EWCA Crim 98).

'Drug trafficking offences' for this purpose are: offences under the Misuse of Drugs Act **12.96** 1971, sections 4(2), 4(3), 19, and 20; offences under the Customs and Excise Management Act 1979, sections 50(2), 50(3), 68(2), and 170 (in relation to prohibited drugs). The inchoate forms of all these offences are also included. This is a different, narrower definition than that which is used for other criminal justice purposes, such as confiscation of the proceeds of crime. Offences of possession with intent to supply, and money-laundering offences in relation to drugs, are not included in the list. This is somewhat surprising, and the Court of Appeal questioned the omission of possession with intent to supply a Class A drug in *Whittle* [2007] 2 Cr App R (S) 578, where the sentencing judge had made the mistake of thinking that it was included. The same mistake was made in *Boland* [2012] EWCA Crim 1953, and again the Court of Appeal questioned the omission. The latter case might seem particularly suitable for such an order. The offender was convicted of possession of a Class A drug with intent, having been responsible for bringing large quantities of drugs into the country. He received a prison sentence of twelve years together with the travel restriction order which was quashed on appeal. Collins J pointed out that had the offender been charged with and convicted of the Customs and Excise Management Office the travel restriction order would have been valid and appropriate. Amending legislation would not be required to remedy the omission, since the Secretary of State has power under section 34(1)(c) to designate offences as drug trafficking offences for the purposes of section 33.

12.97 A travel restriction order lasts for the period specified in the order, and must be for a minimum of two years. No maximum period is specified in the statute. It is important to note that the period of the order does not start to run until the date of the offender's release from the custodial sentence.

12.98 The Court of Appeal in *Mee* [2004] 2 Cr App R (S) 434 offered guidance on the appropriate use of travel restriction orders. The order is designed to prevent or reduce the risk of re-offending after release from prison. It was most likely to be appropriate in cases involving drug importation, but was not confined to such cases. The restriction on a person's freedom to travel abroad was a significant restriction and should not be taken away for a long period unless there were clear grounds for doing so. The duration of the order would depend upon what was required to protect the public in light of the assessment of the risk of re-offending, taking into account the offender's age, previous record, employment considerations, and other relevant matters.

12.99 The Court of Appeal in *Hall* [2013] EWCA Crim 82 noted that the Crown Court has power under section 19 of the Serious Crime Act to make a serious crime prevention order in whatever terms are appropriate to the perceived risk. A specific example of such an order, contemplated by section 5(3)(f) of the Act, is one restricting travel whether within the UK or abroad. That power is wider than the similar power conferred in the case of drug offenders by section 33 of the earlier CJPA 2001, because it is applies to a wider range of offences and is not limited to offenders upon whom sentences of four years or more have been imposed.

12.100 As usual with orders of this kind the offender may apply to the court after the passage of a period of time for the travel restriction order to be revoked. In the case of the travel restriction order, however, the relevant provisions are more complex than usual. An application for revocation may be made at any time after the end of the 'minimum period' (section 35(1)). The 'minimum period' is two years where the travel restriction order was for four years or less, four years where the order was for more than four but less than ten years, and in any other case the minimum period is five years (section 35(7)). In each case of course the minimum period runs from the effective start of the order (when the offender is released from prison), not the date on which the order was made. If an offender has made a previous unsuccessful application for revocation of the order a further application cannot be made within three months. A court must not revoke a travel restriction order unless it considers that it is appropriate to do so in all the circumstances of the case and having regard, in particular, to the offender's character, his conduct since the making of the order, and the offence(s) for which he was convicted (section 35(2)). A further option for the offender is to apply for suspension of the order to allow the offender to travel abroad during the period of that suspension. The same minimum periods apply. A court must not suspend a travel restriction order for any period unless it is satisfied that there are exceptional circumstances that justify the suspension on 'compassionate grounds' (section 35(3)). The court may take into account any circumstances of the case which it considers relevant in making that decision. If the order is suspended, any period of suspension is added to the total length of the order (section 35(6)). The offender must be back in the UK when the period of suspension ends, and must surrender his passport again (section 35(5)) if that it is a requirement of the order.

Breach of order

It is an offence under section 36 of the CJPA 2001 for a person subject to a travel restriction order to leave the country when prohibited by the order from doing so, or for that person not to be present in the UK when a period during which the order was suspended comes to an end, or for that person to fail to deliver up their passport if that is a requirement of the order. The first two of these offences are triable either way with a maximum penalty of five years' imprisonment on indictment, or six months' imprisonment, a fine not exceeding the statutory maximum (£5000) or both, summarily. The third offence is punishable summarily only, with a maximum penalty of six months' imprisonment, a fine not exceeding the statutory maximum (£5000), or both. **12.101**

K ANTI-SOCIAL BEHAVIOUR ORDERS

A court dealing with an offender, for any offence committed after 2 December 2002 (when the relevant legislation came into force), may make an anti-social behaviour order (ASBO) if it considers that the offender has acted in a manner that caused or was likely to cause harassment, alarm, or distress to one or more persons not of the same household as himself and that an order is necessary to protect persons in any place in England and Wales from further anti-social acts by him (section 1C(2)). An ASBO can be made in circumstances other than its imposition as an order ancillary to sentence. In particular, an ASBO can be made following an information laid before the magistrates' court by the police. This form of ASBO is not further dealt with in this book, but much of the applicable case law refers both to ASBOs made on information and those made following conviction under section 1C. **12.102**

Making an anti-social behaviour order

The initiative for making an ASBO may come from the prosecutor, or it may be upon the court's own initiative (section 1C(3)). The test for making an order under the Crime and Disorder Act (CDA) 1998, section 1C is that of necessity to protect the public from further anti-social acts by the offender. Since the order is designed to protect the wider public it is not appropriate to prohibit contact between cohabitees (*Gowan* [2008] 1 Cr App R (S) 50). A restraining order is a more appropriate order in those circumstances. When considering whether to make an ASBO the court may hear evidence from the prosecutor and from the defence (section 1C(3A)), and such evidence is admissible whether or not it would have been admissible in the criminal proceedings where the offender has just been convicted (section 1C(3B)). The proceedings are civil in character and hearsay evidence, for example, would be admissible. The order may be made for a specified period of not less than two years, as set out in the order, or until further order, which means indefinite (1(7)). An ASBO on conviction may take effect immediately, or the court may direct that some or all of the requirements in the order should be suspended during any period when the offender is detained in custody (section 1C(5)). **12.103**

An ASBO is an ancillary order and may be made in addition to the sentence for any offence including a conditional discharge notwithstanding the PCC(S)A 2000, section 14. An ASBO cannot be imposed where the offence has been dealt with by an absolute discharge (section 1C(4)). **12.104**

12.105 An ASBO can be made when sentencing for any offence, and it is not necessary to show that the offence itself involved anti-social behaviour, but the court must be satisfied that the offender has acted in an anti-social manner at some time since the relevant date (which is 1 April 1999).

12.106 An ASBO may prohibit the offender from doing anything described in the order. On the face of it this is extremely wide, but the 'necessity' test must always be made out—the prohibitions in the order must be 'necessary for the purpose of protecting persons from further anti-social acts by the offender' (section 1(6))—and, as with other ancillary orders such as the SOPO, the terms of the order must be precise and capable of being clearly understood by the offender. Often ASBOs are imposed on young offenders, whose age and educational ability should be taken into account (*P* [2004] 2 Cr App R (S) 232). The exact terms of the order must be pronounced in open court and the written form must accurately reflect the order as pronounced. In every case the prohibitions in the order should be tailor-made for the offender and the temptation must be resisted to create a standard off-the-peg set of prohibitions (*Boness* [2006] 1 Cr App R (S) 690). Although the ASBO must last for a minimum of two years it is not necessary for all the prohibitions to last for the full duration of the order. A prohibition should not be imposed so as prohibit conduct which is itself a criminal offence, such as driving while disqualified (*Boness*). The findings of fact made by the court which justify the making of the ASBO should be recorded, and the implications of the order must be explained to the offender. These important matters were made clear by the Divisional Court when granting an application for judicial review in *C v Sunderland Youth Court* [2004] 1 Cr App R (S) 443. The youth court bench had failed to explain why it had made the order under section 1C, when a month earlier another youth court had declined to do so on substantially the same facts. There was also confusion and a discrepancy between the terms of the order as announced and in its written form. The Court said that an ASBO should only be imposed fairly, reasonably, and with regard to all the relevant circumstances.

12.107 If the offender is being dealt with by way of a community sentence which includes requirements aimed at addressing his behaviour, careful consideration should be given to whether an ASBO would add anything to that order (*R (F) v Bolton Crown Court* [2009] EWHC 240 (Admin)). In the case of a young offender in particular, if a significant custodial sentence is being imposed, there are only limited circumstances in which it would be right to add an ASBO. One reason might be to impose a specific prohibition which is desirable but would not form part of the usual licence conditions on release from custody (*P*).

12.108 An interesting contrast of approach arose in two cases involving offenders responsible for spraying graffiti on railway property including train carriages. In *Dolan* [2008] 2 Cr App R (S) 67 the Court of Appeal reduced custodial sentences imposed on two men, aged eighteen and twenty, who pleaded guilty to criminal damage to the extent of over £10,000, and quashed an associated ASBO. The Court found that there was no evidence that this conduct had caused harassment, alarm, or distress to anybody, the material itself was not threatening or offensive, and there was insufficient evidence that either man would re-offend. It had been wrong in principle to make the ASBO. In *Brzezinkski* [2012] 2 Cr App R (S) 364, by contrast, the twenty-three-year-old offender pleaded guilty to eight counts of criminal damage to the extent of over £16,000, and was sentenced to eighteen months' imprisonment together with an ASBO which prohibited the offender for three years from entry on any railway property which was not expressly open to the public, or from being in possession of paints, spray cans, and similar devices except in specified circumstances. The prosecution had provided the sentencing court with a detailed report stating that graffiti has a lasting negative impact and can increase fear of crime in those who use the railway system. The Court of Appeal upheld the ASBO, saying that the offender's conduct was 'plainly and obviously anti-social'.

Again as with other ancillary orders an offender, the Director of Public Prosecutions, or the **12.109** relevant local authority, may apply to the court which made the order for it to be varied or discharged. An order cannot be varied or discharged within two years on application of the offender, unless the DPP consents (section 1CA).

Breach of ASBO

If without reasonable excuse a person does anything which he is prohibited from doing by **12.110** an ASBO, this is a criminal offence punishable on conviction on indictment to imprisonment for a term not exceeding five years, or to a fine, or both, or on conviction by a magistrates' court to imprisonment for six months, a fine not exceeding the statutory maximum (£5000), or both (section 1(10)). If a person is convicted of the offence under section 1(10), the sentencing court may not sentence it by way of a conditional discharge.

The burden of proving that the offender acted without reasonable excuse rests with the **12.111** prosecution (*Charles* [2010] 1 Cr App R 2), When considering whether the offender had a reasonable excuse for failing to comply with the ASBO, the court dealing with the alleged breach may consider any ambiguity or lack of clarity in the order itself.

The court will pass sentence for the offence of being in breach of the order. The sentence **12.112** must be proportionate to the gravity of the breach. If an offender is convicted of breach of an ASBO as a result of behaving in a way which would itself amount to the commission of a distinct criminal offence, it is right for the court to bear in mind the maximum sentence available for that offence. The point is illustrated by *Tripp* [2005] EWCA Crim 2253, where the ASBO was breached by conduct which amounted to being drunk and disorderly. There is, however, no rule which limits the court sentencing for the breach to the maximum sentence available for that further criminal offence (*H* [2006] 2 Cr App R (S) 453). The SGC guideline, *Breach of an Anti-Social Behaviour Order* considers in detail the approach to dealing with breach occasioned by an adult or a young offender. In common with its approach to sentencing for breach of other ancillary orders, such as breach of a restraining order, the SGC states that the main aim of sentencing for breach of the order is to achieve the purpose of the order. The sentence should be commensurate with the seriousness of the breach, which as normal is assessed by the culpability of the offender and the harm which the offence caused, was intended to cause, or might foreseeably have caused. The guideline suggests that for an adult offender acting with a high degree of culpability, the starting point where serious harassment, alarm, or distress has been caused and was intended, is twenty-six weeks' custody, within a range of 'custody threshold to two years'. For an equivalent case but with a lesser degree of harm the starting point is six weeks' custody within a range of 'community order (medium) to 26 weeks', and for an equivalent case but with no harm caused and none intended the starting point in a community order (low) and the range is 'fine band B to community order (medium)'. Aggravating factors include a history of disobedience to court orders, the breach being committed shortly after the ASBO was made, and targeting a person whom the order was designed to protect. Mitigating factors are the breach occurring after a long period of compliance, and the prohibition breached not being fully understood by the offender.

If proceedings for breach are brought against a young offender the normal restriction **12.113** imposed by section 49 of the Children and Young Persons Act 1933 on reporting the proceedings does not apply, but the court may exercise its power under section 45 of the Youth Justice and Criminal Evidence Act 1999 to restrict such reporting (s 1(10D)). If the court decides to exercise that power it must give its reasons for doing so (section 1(10E)). In other words, the court is normally expected to permit the press to name the young offender, unless the court orders otherwise—a reversal of the usual approach applicable to the trial of young offenders.

Making an individual support order

12.114 A court which makes an order under section 1C in respect of a young offender must make an individual support order (ISO) if the court considers that the conditions for making an ISO are made out (section 1AA(1) and (1B)). These conditions are that an ISO would be desirable in the interests of preventing any repetition of the kind of behaviour which led to the making of the ASBO. An ISO cannot be made on a person who is already subject to one. If the court is not satisfied that the ISO conditions are fulfilled, it must state in open court that it is not so satisfied, and explain why not. The ISO will require the young offender to comply, for a period not exceeding six months, with such requirements as are specified in the order, and to comply with directions given by the responsible officer (section 1AA(2)). The order may contain those requirements which the court considers desirable in the interests of preventing repetition of the anti-social behaviour which led to the order (section 1AA(5)). They may include requirements that the young offender should participate in specified activities (but not so as to require attendance on more than two days per week) or comply with specified arrangements for education (section 1AA(6) and (7)). Requirements must avoid any conflict with the offender's religious beliefs and any interference with his normal work or education (section 1AA(8)).

12.115 Before making an ISO the court must obtain from a social worker or members of the youth offending team any information which it considers necessary in order to determine whether the conditions for making an ISO are fulfilled, and what requirements should be imposed (section 1AA(9)). The court must explain to the young offender in ordinary language the effect of the order, the requirements proposed to be included in it, the consequences of failure to comply, and the power of the court to review the order on application of the offender or the responsible officer (section 1AB(1)).

12.116 If a young offender is subject to an ASBO and also subject to an ISO, then if the ASBO ceases to have effect then the ISO also ceases to have effect (section 1AB(5)). If the ASBO is varied following an application to do so the court which varies it may also vary or discharge the ISO (section 1AB(7)).

Breach of ISO

12.117 If the young offender in respect of whom the ISO is made fails without reasonable excuse to comply with any requirement in the order, he is guilty of an offence and liable on summary conviction to a fine not exceeding (if he is aged fourteen or over at the date of his conviction) £1000, or (if he is aged under fourteen) £250 (section 1AB(3)). When sentencing for the offence under section 1AB(3) the court may not sentence by way of a referral order (section 1AB(4)), but it seems that all other sentencing options, including a conditional or absolute discharge, are available.

KEY DOCUMENTS[1]

Sentencing Guidelines Council, *Breach of Protective Order* (effective 18 December 2006).

Sentencing Guidelines Council, *Breach of an Anti-Social Behaviour Order* (effective 5 January 2009).

Criminal Practice Directions [2013] EWCA Crim 1631 (effective 7 October 2013), amended by [2013] EWCA Crim 2328 (effective 10 December 2013).

Criminal Procedure Rules (SI 2013, No 1554) (effective 7 October 2013).

---

[1] All sentencing guidelines can be found on the Sentencing Council website: <http://sentencing council.judiciary.gov.uk/>.

13

MENTALLY DISORDERED OFFENDERS

While gathering material to inform the sentencing decision, if not before, it may become **13.01**
apparent that the convicted defendant is suffering from a degree of mental disorder.
Suspicions may be raised by the nature and circumstances of the offence (such as certain
forms of sexual offending, or arson), or information from the antecedents, the plea in mitigation, or the pre-sentence report. It may become necessary for the sentencer to adjourn
for a medical report, if one has not already been prepared. The CJA 2003, section 157(1)
states that in any case where an offender is, or appears to be, mentally disordered, the court
must obtain and consider a medical report before passing a custodial sentence other than
one fixed by law (murder) unless, in all the circumstances, the court considers that it is unnecessary to do so.

Where the evidence of mental disorder is clear, a sentence may well be selected with a **13.02**
view to ensuring that the offender receives appropriate treatment, whether in the community or in a secure setting. If the offender represents a danger to the public the sentencer will have to make the difficult choice between a hospital order (with or without
restrictions) and a custodial sentence. The CJA 2003, section 166(5) states that nothing
in the remainder of that section should be read as requiring a court to impose a custodial
sentence on a mentally disordered offender, or as restricting any power under the MHA
2003 which would enable the court to deal with a mentally disordered offender in the
most appropriate way.

A COMMUNITY ORDER WITH MENTAL HEALTH TREATMENT REQUIREMENT

Community orders containing a treatment requirement are the most frequent form of psy- **13.03**
chiatric disposal in criminal cases. The offender must first qualify for the imposition of a
community order as set out in section 148 of the CJA 2003. This provision was considered at
Chapter 6 of this book, paragraph 6.02. In short, it is limited to cases where the offender is
aged eighteen or over and is convicted by a magistrates' court or the Crown Court. The duration of the community order may not be for more than three years. No community order
can be imposed unless the offence (or one of the offences) is punishable with imprisonment,

and the court is satisfied that the offence (or offences) is (or are) serious enough to justify such an order. The court must then be satisfied that the community order (with the relevant requirement) is the most suitable disposal and that the restrictions on liberty imposed by the order are commensurate with the seriousness of the offending. A pre-sentence report would inevitably be required before a community order with a mental health treatment requirement could be made, and there would often be a psychiatric report as well.

13.04 Before the court can insert a mental health treatment requirement into a community order it must be satisfied that the mental condition of the offender is such as requires and may be susceptible to treatment, but is not such as to warrant the making of a hospital order or a guardianship order. The court will normally have evidence before it from a psychiatrist to form the basis for this decision, but sometimes the defendant may already be receiving psychiatric help and the need for that to continue is clear to all concerned. The court must also be satisfied that arrangements have been made or can be made for the treatment to be specified in the order. Finally, and importantly, the offender must express his willingness to comply with the order.

13.05 The mental health treatment requirement, as expressed in section 207 of the CJA 2003, is a requirement that the offender must, during a period or periods specified in the order, submit to mental health treatment, by or under the direction of a registered medical practitioner or a registered psychologist. The treatment may take the form of treatment as a resident patient in a hospital (but not a high-security hospital) or care home, treatment as a non-resident patient, or treatment under the direction of such a doctor or psychologist as may be specified. Since this is a disposal geared towards the medical treatment of the offender, the role of the officer supervising the community order is to supervise only to the extent necessary for revoking or amending the order if that should become necessary.

13.06 If the offender fails to comply with any of the requirements in the order, including the requirement as to mental health treatment, he may be dealt with for breach of the community order. For provisions relating to breach of community order see Chapter 6, paragraph 6.35. If the offender commits a further offence within the currency of the community order, he may be dealt with in respect of the original offence in the usual ways. For revocation of the community order see Chapter 6, paragraph 6.41. A community order with a requirement for mental health treatment may be amended on application to the court. This will be initiated by the relevant doctor or psychologist writing to the supervising officer, who will then apply to the court for a variation or cancellation of the requirement.

B YOUTH REHABILITATION ORDER WITH MENTAL HEALTH TREATMENT REQUIREMENT

13.07 If the offender is aged under eighteen, the equivalent disposal to the community order is the youth rehabilitation order, as set out in the CJIA 2008. For full discussion of the youth rehabilitation order provisions see Chapter 6, paragraph 6.45. Where a person of that age is convicted (usually by a youth court, but sometimes by the Crown Court) the court may include a requirement for mental health treatment within the order. The offender must first qualify for the imposition of a youth rehabilitation order as set out in section 148 of the CJA 2003. The duration of the order may not be for more than three years. No youth rehabilitation order can be imposed unless the court is satisfied that the offence (or offences) is (or are) serious enough to justify such an order. The court must then be satisfied that the order (with the relevant requirement) is the most suitable disposal and that the restrictions on liberty imposed by the order are commensurate with the seriousness of the offending.

Before making a youth rehabilitation order the court must obtain and consider information about the offender's family circumstances and the likely effect of the order on those circumstances. In the case of a youth rehabilitation order with a requirement of mental health treatment a psychiatric report may be required as well.

Before the court can insert a mental health treatment requirement, it must be satisfied that **13.08** the mental condition of the offender is such as requires and may be susceptible to treatment but is not such as to warrant the making of a hospital order or a guardianship order. The court will normally have evidence before it from a psychiatrist to form the basis for this decision, but sometimes the defendant may already be receiving psychiatric help and the need for that to continue is clear to all concerned. The court must also be satisfied that arrangements have been made or can be made for the treatment to be specified in the order. Finally, and importantly, the offender must express his willingness to comply with the order.

The mental health treatment requirement in the CJIA 2008, schedule 1, paragraph 22, **13.09** is a requirement that the offender must, during a period or periods specified in the order, submit to mental health treatment, by or under the direction of a registered medical practitioner or a registered psychologist. The treatment may take the form of treatment as a resident patient in a hospital (but not a high-security hospital) or care home, treatment as a non-resident patient, or treatment under the direction of such a doctor or psychologist as may be specified. Since this is a disposal geared towards the medical treatment of the offender, the role of the officer supervising the community order is to supervise only to the extent necessary for revoking or amending the order if that should become necessary.

If the offender fails to comply with any of the requirements in the order, including the **13.10** requirement as to mental health treatment, he may be dealt with for breach of the youth rehabilitation order. For provisions relating to breach of youth rehabilitation orders see Chapter 6, paragraph 6.80. If the offender commits a further offence within the currency of the youth rehabilitation order, he may be dealt with in respect of the original offence in the usual ways. For revocation of the youth rehabilitation order see Chapter 6, paragraph 6.87. A youth rehabilitation order with a requirement for mental health treatment may be amended on application to the court. This will be initiated by the relevant doctor or psychologist writing to the supervising officer, who will then apply to the court for a variation or cancellation of the requirement.

C HOSPITAL ORDER

Criminal courts are given powers under the MHA 1983 to make a hospital order on a **13.11** person of any age convicted of an offence punishable with imprisonment in the case of an adult. The effect of the hospital order is that a social worker or other suitable person is authorized to take the offender to the mental hospital which is specified in the order. The hospital named in the order may be an ordinary NHS Trust hospital or the psychiatric ward of such a hospital, or it may be one of the secure special hospitals (Broadmoor, Rampton, and Ashworth). These three hospitals are high-security institutions and are appropriate only where the patient is thought to represent a serious risk to the safety of the public, including other patients and hospital staff. An admission to hospital by means of a hospital order has the same effect for most purposes as a compulsory civil commitment, with the important exception that the patient's 'next relative' does not have the power to order the patient's discharge. The order in principle lapses after six months, but may be (and often is) renewed for a further six months and at yearly intervals thereafter, provided the responsible medical officer considers further detention necessary 'for the protection of the public or in the interests of the patient's health or safety' (MHA 1983, section 20 and schedule 1). There is no limit to the number of renewals which might subsequently be made, so that a hospital order is in principle an indeterminate sentence, but the patient may be discharged from hospital by way of various powers exercised by the doctors, the hospital managers, or a Mental Health Review Tribunal. Clearly this sentence, while therapeutic in objective, involves a substantial restriction on the liberty on the offender, or 'patient', as he or she should now be called. Accordingly, in the case of an offender who is suffering from a degree of mental disorder the sentencer must always consider whether compulsory hospital detention is appropriate. If not, a community order with mental health treatment requirement may well be a better alternative (*Birch* (1989) 11 Cr App R (S) 202).

13.12 The power to impose a hospital order is set out in the MHA 1983, section 37. By section 37(1) if a person is convicted before the Crown Court or a magistrates' court of an offence punishable with imprisonment, and the conditions set out in section 37(2) are satisfied, and the offence is not murder, the court may by order authorize his admission to and detention in such hospital as may be specified in the order or, as the case may be, place him under the guardianship of a local social services authority or of such other person approved by a local social services authority as may be so specified. Subsection (1A) makes it clear that the power to impose a hospital order is available even though otherwise the case would attract a minimum custodial sentence. The conditions referred to in subsection (1) are that:

(a) the court is satisfied, on the written or oral evidence of two registered medical practitioners, that the offender is suffering from mental disorder and that either—
   (i) the mental disorder from which the offender is suffering is of a nature or degree which makes it appropriate for him to be detained in a hospital for medical treatment and appropriate medical treatment is available for him; or
   (ii) in the case of an offender who has attained the age of 16 years, the mental disorder is of a nature or degree which warrants his reception into guardianship under this Act; and
(b) the court is of the opinion, having regard to all the circumstances including the nature of the offence and the character and antecedents of the offender, and to the other available methods of dealing with him, that the most suitable method of disposing of the case is by means of an order under this section.

13.13 At least one of the two medical practitioners referred to in section 37(2) must be approved, for the purposes of section 12, by the Secretary of State, as having special experience in the diagnosis or treatment of mental disorder (section 54(1)). A hospital order or guardianship order cannot be made unless the court is satisfied, on the written or oral evidence of the approved clinician who would be in charge of the offender's treatment, or of some other person representing the managers of the hospital, that arrangements have been made for the offender's admission to that hospital within twenty-eight days of the date of the order (section 37(4)). If the person named in the order is not admitted to the hospital named in the order within that time, the order lapses. The implications of this are considered in *R(DB) v Nottinghamshire Healthcare NHS Trust* [2009] 2 All ER 792. The health authorities are under no legal obligation to accept offenders from the courts (a point noted by Field J in *Barker* [2003] 1 Cr App R (S) 212). They are, however, under a legal obligation to supply information to the courts about the availability of beds in their regions for the admission of persons under hospital orders (section 39(1)). In an emergency or other special situation arising within the twenty-eight days, the Secretary of State may give directions for the admission of the offender to a hospital different from that specified in the order (section 37(5)).

13.14 In *Blackwood* (1974) 59 Cr App R 170, the Court of Appeal said that a court should not normally make a hospital order if the offender was not legally represented. The Crown

Court or a magistrates' court may make a hospital order, and normally a youth court in the case of a young offender. The decision whether to make a hospital order under section 37 or impose a sentence of imprisonment is always within the discretion of the court. In *Khelifi* [2006] 2 Cr App R (S) 650 the offender had been part of a well-organized and elaborate bank fraud, which had netted close to £1 million. It was accepted that the offender had for several years suffered episodes of paranoid schizophrenia and had a history of treatment for that condition. During proceedings he had been subject to an interim hospital order (see paragraph 13.16). He was confirmed by doctors as suffering from schizophrenia, but the judge found that justice could not be done by making a hospital order and he passed a prison sentence for five years instead, which was approved on principle on appeal although reduced to three-and-a-half years. It is clear that the fact that all the conditions in section 37(2) are all made out does not compel the making of a hospital order, or give rise to a presumption that one will be made. The welfare of the offender is always an important consideration, but must be assessed in light of the seriousness of the offence. While a hospital order may be imposed even though there is no clear causal connection between the illness and the commission of the offence, it was said in *Nafei* (2005) 2 Cr App R (S) 127, where an offence of drug trafficking had been committed by the offender 'knowingly, with his eyes open', that the discretion to pass a hospital order would rarely be exercised in such circumstances.

Guardianship order

By section 37(6) the court may, instead of ordering the offender's committal to hospital, **13.15** order that he be placed under the guardianship of a local authority or of a named person approved by that authority (known as a 'guardianship order') provided of course that the local authority or named person is willing to receive the offender into guardianship. Such an order confers on the local authority or person named the same powers as a guardianship application made and accepted under Part II of the 1983 Act. Section 39A empowers a court which is minded to make a guardianship order to request the local social services authority to inform the court whether it would be willing to comply with the order and, if so, to give information about how it would exercise its powers under section 40(2). A guardianship order lasts for six months, but may be renewed for a further six months and thereafter annually (section 20).

Interim hospital order

Section 38 of the MHA 1983 provides for the making of an interim hospital order. The **13.16** qualifying conditions are virtually the same as for making a hospital order under section 37, but the interim order is available to the court 'before making a hospital order or dealing with him in some other way'. Its purpose is to establish whether the offender is suitable to be the subject of a hospital order. One difference in the powers is that an interim order can only be made if one of the doctors who gives evidence is employed at the hospital where the person is to be detained. An interim hospital order is not a final disposal of the case, but in a case where there is some doubt it is an experiment to see if the case can properly be disposed of by way of a full order. An interim hospital order can also be used to discover whether a person should be made subject to a hospital direction or a limitation direction under section 45A of the 1983 Act (see paragraph 13.23, later in this Chapter). An interim order may last for up to twelve weeks, renewable for further periods of no more than twenty-eight days at a time, but in no case to last for more than a total of twelve months (section 38(5)). No minimum period is specified. At the end of the interim period the court must make a final disposal of the case, and the interim order comes to an end. In a case where a court renews an interim hospital order, or where it finally disposes of the case by making a hospital order under section 37, the offender need not appear before the court provided that he is legally represented, and his representative has an opportunity of being heard (section 38(2)).

13.17 The decision to make an interim hospital order does not commit the court ultimately to disposing of the case by way of a full hospital order. At the end of the interim order the court still has the full range of sentencing options at its disposal, although if it chooses to pass a sentence other than a hospital order the offender must be present for the hearing.

Combining a hospital order with other sentences or orders

13.18 If the court makes a hospital order or a guardianship order it is severely limited in which other orders may be made at the same time. By section 37(8), if a hospital order or a guardianship order is made, the court shall not pass a sentence of imprisonment or detention, impose a fine, make a community order or a youth rehabilitation order in respect of the offence, or require a parent of a juvenile so dealt with to enter into a recognizance. A hospital order cannot be combined with a referral order. The court may, however, 'make any other order which the court has power to make apart from this section'. This would allow ancillary orders, such as a compensation order, to be made, although this would of course be subject to the usual qualifications as to the offender's ability to pay, and so on.

D RESTRICTION ORDER

13.19 The Crown Court is given power by section 41 of the MHA 1983, when it makes a hospital order under section 37, to add to it a restriction order. A restriction order has no existence independent of the hospital order to which it relates, but it fundamentally affects the circumstances in which the patient is detained. The Crown Court should make such an order only where it appears to the court that, given the nature of the offence, the antecedents of the offender, and the risk of the offender's committing further offences is at large, the making of a restriction order is necessary to protect the public from serious harm (section 41(1) and *Courtney* (1987) 9 Cr App R (S) 404). This entails that the offender will probably require detention and treatment in one of the secure special hospitals rather than in an NHS hospital, and an order under section 41 affects the arrangements for discharge (see paragraph 13.22). A restriction order cannot be made unless at least of one of the two doctors, whose evidence is being taken into account by the court, has given oral evidence in court (section 41(2)).

13.20 Only the Crown Court may make a restriction order, although magistrates may commit the offender to Crown Court, provided the offender is aged fourteen years or over, with a view to such a disposal being made (section 43 and *Avbunudje* [1999] 2 Cr App R (S) 189). The magistrates must commit the offender to Crown Court in custody unless there is a place available for him in a hospital, in which case they can direct that he be detained in the hospital. If the criteria within section 41 are established the sentencer may, but is not obliged to, pass a restriction order. The likely alternatives are discretionary life imprisonment and custody for a fixed term. If an offender qualifies for a hospital order with restrictions and a place is available in a suitable hospital, the general rule is that a hospital order with restrictions should be made, and it is wrong for the sentencer to impose a life sentence simply to prevent the patient's possible premature release by order of the Mental Health Review Tribunal (MHRT) (*Mitchell* [1997] 1 Cr App R (S) 90; *Hutchinson* [1997] 2 Cr App R (S) 60). In the decision of the House of Lords in *Drew* [2004] 2 Cr App R (S) 65, however, it was noted that offenders subject to hospital orders (with or without restriction) are entitled to release when their medical condition has been successfully treated, while release from a life sentence is a matter for the Parole Board, which can take into account all relevant matters of risk rather than just mental health. A life sentence thereby provides a greater degree of control over the offender. The Court of Appeal in *A-G's Reference (No 54 of 2011)* [2011] EWCA Crim 2276 said that this was an 'absolutely crucial difference', and further noted that an offender may be recalled from his life licence if his behaviour showed that he was still a danger, but that a patient, once released, could only be recalled if his medical condition relapsed. If the sentencer considers that, notwithstanding the offender's mental disorder, there was an element of culpability in the offence which merited punishment, as where there was no connection between the disorder and the offence or where the offender's responsibility was diminished but far from extinguished at the time of the offence, the imposition of a prison sentence might be correct. This issue was considered by the Court of Appeal in the context of diminished responsibility manslaughter in *Welsh* [2011] EWCA Crim 73. There the Court preferred a life sentence to a restriction order to reflect the offender's 'substantial responsibility' for the offence and a finding that the offender would remain dangerous even if his schizophrenia was brought under control by medication. There will also be cases, however, where the offender presents a real risk to the public but a life sentence is not available or appropriate, and no place in a secure hospital is available. A proportionate determinate sentence would then be the only realistic option.

In this context the protection of the public from serious harm has been held not to be limited to personal injury, nor need it relate to the public in general. It is enough if a specific category of persons, or even one person, is adjudged to be at risk, although the category of persons at risk is taken to exclude the offender himself. The potential harm must be 'serious' (*Courtney* (1987) 9 Cr App R (S) 404; *Kearney* [2003] 2 Cr App R (S) 85). A high possibility of recurrence of minor offences will not suffice (*Birch* (1989) 11 Cr App R (S) 202). Clearly, medical evidence will be of great importance in making this assessment, but it is the court's decision and the court is not bound to accept the medical evidence it receives (*Birch*). A sentencer should not add a restriction order to a hospital order simply to mark the gravity of the offence, nor as a means of punishment. It would be a mistake simply to equate the seriousness of the offence with the likelihood of a restriction order being made. It is one factor, and the court would have to be sure of its ground to pass a restriction order where the commission of a serious offence was coupled with a low risk of re-offending. On the other hand it is not necessary to wait until someone has been seriously injured before a hospital order with restrictions can be passed (*Nwohia* [1996] 1 Cr App R (S) 170). There is no requirement that a causal connection be established between the disorder and the offence (*Hatt* [1962] Crim LR 647, approved in *Birch*), although in most cases this connection can safely be assumed. **13.21**

The main difference between an order under section 37 and an order under section 41 is that neither the doctors nor the hospital managers may discharge a restricted patient without the consent of the Secretary of State or a MHRT. Thus, in effect, the restriction order ensures that the criminal justice system retains an important degree of control over the offender once he becomes a patient. The Secretary of State or a MHRT may release a patient who is subject to a restriction order, either with or without the attachment of conditions to the release (section 42(1) and (2)). If the patient is discharged from hospital conditionally, the restriction order remains in force and the patient subsequently may be recalled to hospital if he comes to notice. Unlike a hospital order under section 37 a restriction order does not lapse in the ordinary way unless renewed, but continues for as long at the restriction order is in place. If the restriction order is for a fixed period, at the end of that period the restrictions no longer apply but the hospital order continues in effect (section 41(5)). The restrictions which may thus be added to a hospital order may be declared by the court to be **13.22** for a period of time which is specified in the order, or without limit of time. The Court of Appeal has said that it would be 'imprudent' in any but the most exceptional circumstances to impose a restriction for a fixed rather than an unlimited time (*Birch*; *Nwohia*).

E HOSPITAL AND LIMITATION DIRECTIONS

13.23 Sections 45A and 45B of the MHA 1983 are designed to apply where the court has heard evidence that the offender is suffering from a mental disorder and the making of a hospital order is appropriate, but the court wishes to ensure that the offender upon completion of his period of treatment will thence be transferred to prison for the remainder of the sentence rather than being released from hospital. The House of Lords in *Drew* [2004] 2 Cr App R (S) 65 said that where neither an order under the MHA nor a term of imprisonment was suitable in isolation an order under section 45A will often be appropriate. Such orders are often referred to as 'hybrid orders'.

13.24 Section 45A applies where a person is convicted before the Crown Court of an offence the sentence for which is not fixed by law and the court considers making a hospital order before deciding to impose a sentence of imprisonment (section 45A(1)). In this context, the term 'imprisonment' does not include the equivalent custodial sentences for offenders aged eighteen, nineteen, or twenty, and so the Court of Appeal in *Fort* [2013] EWCA Crim 2332 held that hospital and limitation directions were not available for offenders aged under twenty-one. The Court could see no good policy reason why the sections should be so limited. By section 45A(2), the court must be satisfied on the written or oral evidence of two registered medical practitioners (at least one of whom must give oral evidence) that the offender is suffering from a mental disorder, the mental disorder from which the offender is suffering is of a nature or degree which makes it appropriate for him to be detained in a hospital for medical treatment, and appropriate medical treatment is available for him. In these circumstances the court may make a 'hospital direction', which is a direction that, instead of being detained in prison, the offender be detained in a specified hospital. The court may also make a 'limitation direction', which is a direction that the offender also be made subject to the restrictions set out in section 41 of the 1983 Act (see paragraph 13.19, this book).

13.25 The court must also be satisfied on the written or oral evidence of the approved clinician who would have overall charge of his case, or of some other person representing the managers of the hospital, that arrangements have been made for the offender's admission to that hospital and for his admission within the period of twenty-eight days from the making of the order. The court may, pending admission within that period, give directions for the offender's detention in a place of safety (section 45A(5)). A hospital direction and a limitation direction given in respect of an offender have effect not only as regards the sentence of imprisonment imposed but also as regards any other sentence of imprisonment imposed on the same or a previous occasion (section 45A(9)).

13.26 Section 45B provides that with respect to any person a hospital direction shall have effect as a restriction direction. While a person is subject to a hospital direction and a limitation direction the responsible medical officer must supply to the Secretary of State a report on the offender at least every twelve months. In *Cooper* [2010] EWCA Crim 2335 the offender pleaded guilty to diminished responsibility manslaughter. Although he had no history of mental disorder he was substantially in the grip of a serious mental disorder at the time of the offence. The judge imposed imprisonment for public protection with a minimum term of six years together with a hospital and restriction order, directing that the offender was to remain at specified secure accommodation for treatment. The Court of Appeal upheld the sentence, noting that if and when the offender's treatment was successful the MHRT would make a recommendation to the Parole Board for release. The offender would remain in hospital until the Board made its decision. The offender on release would be subject to recall for breach of his life licence. See also *Staines* [2006] EWCA Crim 15.

F ORDERS CONSEQUENT UPON A FINDING OF INSANITY OR UNFITNESS TO PLEAD

The Criminal Procedure (Insanity) Act 1964, section 5 (as substituted by the Criminal **13.27** Procedure (Insanity and Unfitness to Plead) Act 1991) provides various powers of disposal after the Crown Court has either (a) returned a special verdict that the accused is not guilty by reason of insanity, or (b) recorded a finding that the defendant is under a disability (he is 'unfit to plead') and that he performed the act or made the omission charged against him. In neither of these situations, of course, has the defendant been convicted of the offence charged, but provisions is made for a range of disposals in such cases which are so closely similar to the sentencing options discussed elsewhere in this book that it is appropriate to consider them here.

The 1964 Act, by section 5 and schedule 1, formerly stated that on a finding that the de- **13.28** fendant was not guilty by reason of insanity or was unfit to plead the Crown Court judge was required to impose an order upon the defendant equivalent to an order under the MHA 1983, section 37 upon a person convicted, together with a restriction order under the MHA 1983, section 41. Thus a person who was found not guilty by reason of insanity faced mandatory commitment to a mental hospital with restrictions upon release. The 1991 Act broadened the options available to the Crown Court judge dealing with such cases, so that following options are now available:

(a) To make an order for admission to hospital. By schedule 1 to the 1991 Act, such order shall be equivalent to a hospital order made under the MHA 1983, section 37, to which there *may* be added a restriction under the MHA 1983, section 41, with or without limit of time. A restriction order without limit of time is, however, mandatory in cases where the charge brought against the offender was murder.
(b) To make a guardianship order (see paragraph 13.15, this Chapter).
(c) To make a supervision and treatment order. This order is very similar to a community order with a mental health treatment requirement (see paragraph 13.03, this Chapter), although there are minor differences. A supervision and treatment order may be made only on the evidence of two doctors (not required in the case of a mental health treatment requirement), that the defendant's mental condition is such that it requires and may be susceptible to treatment but does not warrant the making of a hospital or guardianship order. The order requires the defendant to be under supervision for a period specified in the order of not more than two years (the maximum duration of a community order is three years) and, during that period or a specific part of it, to submit to medical treatment, whether as a resident patient, a non-resident patient, or otherwise with a view to the improvement of his mental condition. Such an order may also include residence requirements.
(d) To make an order for the defendant's absolute discharge.

Section 37(3) of the MHA 1983 deals with the anomalous power of a magistrates' court **13.29** to make a hospital order (or guardianship order) where the court is satisfied that the person did the act or made the omission charged, but without proceeding to conviction. This provision gives magistrates' courts a power which is similar to the Crown Court's powers to return a special verdict of not guilty by reason of insanity or to make a finding that the accused is unfit to plead, neither of which are available in the magistrates' courts. It was confirmed in *Horseferry Road Magistrates' Court, ex parte K* [1997] QB 23 that a defence on insanity is available in the magistrates' courts, but there it leads to a full acquittal, rather than to the special verdict. It has been held that the power in section 37(3) should be very sparingly used (see *Lincoln (Kesteven) Justices, ex parte O'Connor* [1983] 1 WLR 335). However, in *R (Surat Singh) v Stratford Magistrates' Court* [2008] 1 Cr App R 2 the Divisional Court held that a defendant in the magistrates' court is not entitled to a trial on the issue of insanity, and in all cases where an order under section 37(3) is a possibility the court should conduct the fact-finding exercise required. If it not satisfied that the act was done or omission made then the defendant is entitled to a full acquittal. If it is not so satisfied and the conditions for making an order under section 37(3) are met, the court may make such an order. Alternatively it may try the issue of insanity, and if the accused is acquitted the defence prevails. If a magistrates' court makes an order under section 37(3) the person so dealt with has the same right of appeal to the Crown Court as if he was appealing against conviction and sentence (MHA 1983, section 45(1)).

14

SENTENCING FOR A RANGE OF OFFENCES

'What sentence will I get for this if I am convicted?' asks the defendant before the trial. 'Is **14.01** it worth appealing against this?' asks the offender after he has been sentenced. These commonly asked and very natural questions prompt a third question: to what extent can the general principles of sentencing, the range of sentencing measures available to the courts, and the pervasive effect of sentencing guidelines in channelling the discretion of judges and magistrates be pulled together to predict the sentence which will be imposed on the offender or his chances of appealing successfully against whatever sentence has been passed upon him? The purpose of this Chapter is to indicate the approach which has been set out in sentencing guidelines and approved by the Court of Appeal to sentencing a variety of commonly encountered criminal offences. Wherever sentencing guidelines are in place, prominence is given to what the guidelines say. If there are no sentencing guidelines, reference is made to the leading decision or decisions of the Court of Appeal which offer appellate guidance.

14.02   The Chapter is necessarily limited in scope. A full analysis of the sentencing guidelines and relevant appellate case law could easily amount to a book by itself. Indeed, the great majority of David Thomas's *Current Sentencing Practice* encyclopaedia, which runs to four volumes and to thousands of pages, covers precisely that material in exhaustive detail. Only an outline can be offered here—but, in keeping with the title of the book, this is a pared-down practical guide to the key considerations when sentencing for a range of the most commonly encountered offences. When reading what follows it is important to remember the general principles applicable to the community sentence and custodial sentence thresholds and the way in which sentencing guidelines should be used. This material was covered in Chapter 2. That Chapter also contains the lists of general aggravating and mitigating factors supplied by the SGC in its guideline on *Seriousness*. These factors should always be borne in mind whatever offence guideline is being considered, as well as aggravating and mitigating factors specifically listed in the particular offence guideline. Some of the matters which may be relevant to personal mitigation are also dealt with in Chapter 2, and again these are additional to those specifically mentioned in the individual offence guidelines.

A   SENTENCING FOR HOMICIDE AND RELATED OFFENCES

Murder

14.03   Murder carries a mandatory penalty of life imprisonment (Murder (Abolition of Death Penalty) Act 1965, section 1(1)). If a murder is committed by a person aged under eighteen at the time of the offence (whatever their age at the date of conviction) the mandatory sentence is detention during Her Majesty's Pleasure (PCC(S)A 2000, section 90). Since this is a mandatory sentence there is no appeal against it. The offence of attempted murder carries a discretionary life sentence.

14.04   In every case of murder the judge is required to fix a minimum term, which must be served in full by the offender before he can first be considered for early release. Since there is no discretion over the sentence for murder, the real decision which the judge has to make is over the appropriate minimum term. By the CJA 2003, section 271 an offender may appeal against an order specifying his minimum term, and by the CJA 2003, section 272 the Attorney General may refer a minimum term imposed in a murder case to the Court of Appeal on the ground that it was unduly lenient. The CJA 2003, section 269 and schedule 21 sets out a very detailed scheme of 'general principles' to guide the judge in setting the minimum term in murder cases, applicable to all murders committed after December 2003. Although described as 'general principles' the scheme is similar to the form of sentencing guidelines which were produced by the Sentencing Guidelines Council, and in effect schedule 21 is a guideline scheme. It should be noted that it is the only such scheme which is incorporated directly by statute rather than being created after consultation by the normal guidelines process. In schedule 21 'child' means a person under eighteen, 'minimum term' means the part of the sentence to be specified by the sentencer under section 269(2), and a 'whole life order' means an order under section 269(4). The meaning of 'racially or religiously aggravated' is the same here as in section 28 of the Crime and Disorder Act 1998 and the meaning of 'sexual orientation', 'disability', and 'transgender identity' is the same here as in the CJA 200s, section 146. Section 269 says that unless the judge makes an order under section 269(4) that the offence of murder is so serious that the early release provisions should not apply to the offender and he must spend the rest of his life in prison (a 'whole life' order), the judge must order that the early release provisions will apply to the offender once he has completed the minimum term. An order under section 269(4) cannot be made unless the offender is aged twenty-one or over. An offender may appeal against such an order (CJA 2003, section 271).

The early release provisions are set out in section 28 of the Crime (Sentences) Act 1997. **14.05**
Release is certainly not automatic at the expiry of the minimum term—release is a matter for the Parole Board, and they will direct the offender's release only when satisfied that 'it is no longer necessary for the protection of the public that the prisoner should be confined' (section 28(6)). The Board will consider the case for release at the expiry of the minimum term and if release is not ordered at that point the Board will reconsider the case for release every two years thereafter. If that risk endures, then an offender may continue to be refused his release, so that the effect is that he will die in prison. The duration of the minimum term depends on the seriousness of the offence and is that part of the sentence which reflects the appropriate punishment and deterrence. The indeterminate part of the life sentence which continues once the minimum term in served is designed to ensure that the person is released only when it is safe to do so. Assessment of the continuing nature of risk posed by the offender is a matter for the Parole Board and not the sentencing judge (*Leigers* [2005] 2 Cr App R (S) 654).

Schedule 21 is set out as follows: **14.06**

> Criminal Justice Act 2003, schedule 21, paragraphs 4 to 11
>
> Starting points
> 4. —
>   (1) If—
>   (a) the court considers that the seriousness of the offence (or the combination of the offence and one or more offences associated with it) is exceptionally high, and
>   (b) the offender was aged 21 or over when he committed the offence, the appropriate starting point is a whole life order.
>   (2) Cases that would normally fall within sub-paragraph (1)(a) include—
>   (a) the murder of two or more persons, where each murder involves any of the following—
>   (i)   a substantial degree of premeditation or planning,
>   (ii) the abduction of the victim, or
>   (iii) sexual or sadistic conduct,
>   (b) the murder of a child if involving the abduction of the child or sexual or sadistic motivation,
>   (c) a murder done for the purpose of advancing a political, religious, racial or ideological cause, or
>   (d) a murder by an offender previously convicted of murder.
> 5. —
>   (1) If—
>   (a) the case does not fall within paragraph 4(1) but the court considers that the seriousness of the offence (or the combination of the offence and one or more offences associated with it) is particularly high, and
>   (b) the offender was aged 18 or over when he committed the offence, the appropriate starting point, in determining the minimum term, is 30 years.
>   (2) Cases that (if not falling within paragraph 4(1)) would normally fall within sub-paragraph (1)(a) include—
>   (a) the murder of a police officer or prison officer in the course of his duty,
>   (b) a murder involving the use of a firearm or explosive,
>   (c) a murder done for gain (such as a murder done in the course or furtherance of robbery or burglary, done for payment or done in the expectation of gain as a result of the death),
>   (d) a murder intended to obstruct or interfere with the course of justice,
>   (e) a murder involving sexual or sadistic conduct,
>   (f) the murder of two or more persons,

    (g) a murder that is racially or religiously aggravated or aggravated by sexual orientation, disability or transgender identity, or

    (h) a murder falling within paragraph 4(2) committed by an offender who was aged under 21 when he committed the offence.

5A. —

  (1) If—

    (a) the case does not fall within paragraph 4(1) or 5(1),

    (b) the offence falls within sub-paragraph (2), and

    (c) the offender was aged 18 or over when the offender committed the offence, the offence is normally to be regarded as sufficiently serious for the appropriate starting point, in determining the minimum term, to be 25 years.

  (2) The offence falls within this sub-paragraph if the offender took a knife or other weapon to the scene intending to—

    (a) commit any offence, or

    (b) have it available to use as a weapon,

and used that knife or other weapon in committing the murder.

6. If the offender was aged 18 or over when he committed the offence and the case does not fall within paragraph 4(1), 5(1) or 5A(1), the appropriate starting point, in determining the minimum term, is 15 years.

7. If the offender was aged under 18 when he committed the offence, the appropriate starting point, in determining the minimum term, is 12 years.

Aggravating and mitigating factors

8. Having chosen a starting point, the court should take into account any aggravating or mitigating factors, to the extent that it has not allowed for them in its choice of starting point.

9. Detailed consideration of aggravating or mitigating factors may result in a minimum term of any length (whatever the starting point), or in the making of a whole life order.

10. Aggravating factors (additional to those mentioned in paragraph 4(2), 5(2) and 5A(2)) that may be relevant to the offence of murder include—

    (a) a significant degree of planning or premeditation,

    (b) the fact that the victim was particularly vulnerable because of age or disability,

    (c) mental or physical suffering inflicted on the victim before death,

    (d) the abuse of a position of trust,

    (e) the use of duress or threats against another person to facilitate the commission of the offence,

    (f) the fact that the victim was providing a public service or performing a public duty; and

    (g) concealment, destruction or dismemberment of the body.

11. Mitigating factors that may be relevant to the offence of murder include—

    (a) an intention to cause serious bodily harm rather than to kill,

    (b) lack of premeditation,

    (c) the fact that the offender suffered from any mental disorder or mental disability which (although not falling within section 2(1) of the Homicide Act 1957) lowered his degree of culpability,

    (d) the fact that the offender was provoked (for example by prolonged stress),

    (e) the fact that the offender acted to any extent in self-defence or in fear of violence,

    (f) a belief by the offender that the murder was an act of mercy, and

    (g) the age of the offender.

The starting points in schedule 21 are set out as amended by later legislation. It should be noted that for an offender who was under eighteen when he committed the murder, the starting point is always twelve years. An offender aged eighteen, nineteen, or twenty cannot attract a whole life starting point but may, in a case where the seriousness of the offence is 'particularly high' attract a starting point of thirty years. Otherwise the starting point is fifteen years.

The Court of Appeal has made it clear on several occasions that judges must not apply the **14.07** scheme in schedule 21 in a mechanistic way. In *Jones* [2006] 2 Cr App R (S) 19 the Court said that every case will depend upon its own facts and while the judge must have regard to schedule 21 in some cases it may be appropriate to depart from them, the judge giving reasons for doing so. The Court pointed out the huge gaps which exist between the various starting points and said that it was difficult to separate out the choice of starting point from the aggravating and mitigating factors in the case. In effect all relevant matters had to be looked at together, and there was considerable flexibility within the scheme, but care should be taken not to 'double-count' a factor as aggravating sentence where it had already been factored in to the higher starting point in schedule 21. The Court has emphasized paragraph 9 of the schedule, which makes it clear that detailed consideration of the aggravating and mitigating factors applicable in the case may result in a final minimum term of any length. The crossing of a particular age range (eighteen or twenty-one years) should not be regarded as part of a mathematical scale within schedule 21. Birthdays were not necessarily indicative of an offender's level of understanding and maturity (*Peters* [2005] 2 Cr App R (S) 101). According to *Martin* [2010] 1 Cr App R (S) 38 it is not the case that the offender moves automatically to a higher starting point when he turns eighteen. On the other hand it was held in *Davies* [2009] 1 Cr App R (S) 79 that if the presence of a particular feature of the case (such as whether it involved sexual or sadistic conduct, attracting a thirty-year rather than a fifteen-year starting point) was in issue, that feature had to be proved by the prosecution to the criminal standard.

The list of aggravating and mitigating factors in schedule 21 is not exhaustive. In *Blue* [2009] **14.08** 1 Cr App R (S) 6 the Court said that the judge had been entitled to find that a murder had been aggravated by a racial element but not of such importance that it justified a move from the fifteen-year to the thirty-year starting point. The fact that a killing took place in view of the public was an aggravating factor (*Pile* [2006] 1 Cr App R (S) 131), as was the fact that the offender was one of a group who hunted down and killed the victim (*Allardyce* [2006] 1 Cr App R (S) 98). The vulnerability of the victim is always an aggravating factor (paragraph 10(b)), but each case turns on its own facts (see *Morley* [2010] 1 Cr App R (S) 44). The judge is very capable of making his own assessment of this issue, and of the degree of vulnerability (*Latham* [2006] 2 Cr App R (S) 64). In line with all guideline schemes, the relative weight to be given to matters of aggravation and mitigation is a matter for the sentencing judge. 'Lack of intent to kill' is specified as a mitigating factor, but the Court has noted that the potency of this factor varies very much from case to case. It may provide mitigation, but need not do so. In a case where a high level of violence has been inflicted the absence of a specific intent to kill may be of little moment (*Connor* [2008] 1 Cr App R (S) 89). Some specific phrases in schedule 21 have been considered by the Court, such as whether the offender 'took the knife or other weapon to the scene' in paragraph 5A. In *Kelly* [2012] 4 All ER 687 the Court noted that a wide range of circumstances might exist, ranging from where the offender carried the knife from his home a considerable distance to the victim's home, to a case where the offender simply carried the weapon from the kitchen to the lounge. Where a secondary party was unaware that the principal offender had a knife it was not appropriate to use the paragraph 5A starting point for the secondary party. Similarly, whether a murder involved 'sexual conduct' depended on all the facts. If the sexual conduct was closely related to the killing (such as where the victim was raped before being murdered) then the case fell within paragraph 5(2)(e) (*A G's References Nos 25 & 26 of 2008* [2009] 1 Cr App R (S) 116). In *Bouhaddou* [2007] 2 Cr App R (S) 23 it was held that a burglar who confronted with the householder, attacked and killed him in order to make good his escape, fell within paragraph 5(2)(c) as much as if the murder had been planned for gain. In *Inglis* [2011] 1 WLR 1110 the Court considered a case of 'mercy killing', where the relevant aggravating features included paragraph 10(a), (b), and (d) factors (planning, vulnerability of victim, and position of trust) but where specific mitigating features included paragraph 11(f) (belief that the killing was a matter of mercy). Lord Judge CJ said that the 'prescriptive statutory regime' in schedule 21 had caused difficulty and dilemma, and that on the particular facts of the case the identified aggravating factors should not be taken to aggravate the murder. If it were otherwise the express and very important mitigating factor would be deprived of any practical effect. The minimum term was reduced from nine years to five years.

14.09 In a number of cases the Court has reflected on the sentencing for murder of joint offenders, one of whom is under eighteen and attracts a twelve-year starting point but the other is over that age and in the circumstances of the crime attracts a thirty-year starting point. In *Taylor* [2007] 1 Cr App R (S) 59 it was said that this outcome was the result of the statutory scheme and could not as such form the basis for an appeal, but in *Taylor (Joel)* [2008] 1 Cr App R (S) 4 the Court said that such a divergent outcome was unjust and it would be wrong for the sentencer to fix minimum terms for the two offenders entirely in isolation from each other. The final outcome should be that any difference was no more than a fair reflection of the age (and any other relevant) difference between them. In *Swellings* [2009] 2 Cr App R (S) 220 the two offenders were aged eighteen- and sixteen-years old at the time of the offence and they were involved with others in an attack on a householder who remonstrated with a group of young men who were causing damage to cars parked in the street. The victim was kicked repeatedly to the head and died. The first offender was sentenced to custody for life with a minimum term of seventeen years and the second received custody for life with a minimum term of fifteen years. The former sentence was upheld, but the latter was changed to detention during Her Majesty's pleasure.

14.10 Appropriate credit must be given for a guilty plea. Obviously the reduction cannot bite on an indeterminate (life) sentence as such, so it must be taken to adjust the length of the minimum term. A 'whole life' minimum term cannot attract a reduction for plea, but the Court has said that if there has been a plea of guilty then that is one factor which may militate against the imposition of a whole life order (see *Mullen* [2008] 2 Cr App R (S) 88). The issue of giving credit for a plea of guilty in murder cases is considered in detail in the SGC guideline on *Reduction of Sentence for a Guilty Plea*, paragraphs 6.1 to 6.6. The reduction should not exceed one-sixth of the minimum term and will never exceed five years. The reason for specifying 'one-sixth' in relation to murder, when the normal maximum reduction for a guilty plea in relation to a determinate sentence is 'one-third' is because the offender will serve the minimum term *in full* whereas he will serve *half* of a determinate custodial sentence in custody and be subject to licence thereafter. The effect of the reduction is, therefore, the same.

Attempted murder

14.11 The maximum penalty for attempted murder, an offence under the Criminal Attempts Act 1981, section 1, is life imprisonment. This is a serious offence for the purposes of the CJA 2003, section 224 (dangerous offenders).

14.12 The SGC guideline, *Attempted Murder* applies as from 27 July 2009 and supersedes earlier guidance in *Ford* [2005] EWCA Crim 1358. Level 1 offences include those which (if the charge had been murder) would have come within paragraphs 4, 4A, or 5 of schedule 21. This offence always involves very high culpability since an intention to kill must be proved, but the harm occasioned may at the top of the scale be extremely grave and irreversible injury or at the bottom of the scale no physical injury at all, such as where the attempt miscarries in some way or is thwarted by the police. Where serious and long-term physical or psychological harm has occurred the starting point is thirty years (range twenty-seven to thirty-five years); where some physical or psychological harm has occurred the starting point is twenty years (range seventeen to twenty-five years) and where little or no physical or psychological harm has occurred the starting point is fifteen years (range twelve to twenty years). At level 2 (other planned attempts to kill) where the equivalent degree of injury has been done to the victim, the starting points and ranges are twenty years (seventeen to twenty-five years); fifteen years (twelve to twenty years) and ten years (seven to fifteen years). At level 3 (other spontaneous attempts to kill) where an equivalent degree of injury has been done to the victim, the starting point and ranges are fifteen years (twelve to twenty years); twelve years (nine to seventeen years) and nine years (six to fourteen years). Specific (but non-exhaustive) aggravating and mitigating factors are set out in the guideline.

Manslaughter (diminished responsibility)

14.13 The maximum penalty for manslaughter is life imprisonment (Offences Against the Person Act (OAPA) 1861, section 5). This is a serious offence for the purposes of the CJA 2003, section 224 (dangerous offenders). There are no sentencing guidelines for this form of manslaughter.

14.14 Long-standing guidance was issued by the Court of Appeal in *Chambers* (1983) 5 Cr App R (S) 190. Leonard J explained that in diminished responsibility cases there are various courses open to a judge. If the inevitable psychiatric reports recommend and justify it and there are no contrary indications, a hospital order may well be the right sentence. Where a hospital order is not recommended or is not appropriate, and the defendant constitutes a danger to the public for an uncertain period of time the sentence will be an indeterminate term of imprisonment, such as a life sentence. In cases where the evidence shows that the defendant's responsibility for his acts was so grossly impaired that his degree of responsibility for them was minimal, then a lenient course such as a non-custodial sentence, will be open. There will however be cases where there is no proper basis for a hospital order but the defendant's degree of responsibility is not minimal. Then the judge should pass a determinate sentence of imprisonment, the length of which will depend on the degree of the offender's responsibility and the period of time for which the offender will continue to represent a risk to the public.

14.15 The general approach in *Chambers* was reconsidered and broadly endorsed more recently in *Wood* [2010] 1 Cr App R (S) 6. In that case the Court said that there were some diminished responsibility cases where the offender's reduced culpability was small and others where it was very significant and, subject to that particular matter, there was plainly a link to the principles set out in schedule 21 to the 2003 Act, relating to sentencing for murder. The Court was also concerned to emphasize that in cases where the offender would remain dangerous for an uncertain period of time, a life sentence should only be used where other forms of the indeterminate sentence, such as imprisonment for public protection, were available. However, since imprisonment for public protection has since been abolished in 2012, this part of the decision in *Wood* is of less importance. Further guidance is awaited.

Manslaughter (loss of control)

14.16 The maximum penalty for manslaughter is life imprisonment (Offences Against the Person Act 1861, section 5). This is a serious offence for the purposes of the CJA 2003, section 224 (dangerous offenders). The SGC guideline, *Manslaughter by Reason of Provocation* applied to cases of manslaughter by provocation. The substantive law was changed by the Coroners and Justice Act 2009, section 54 and section 55, which replaced the partial defence of provocation by the partial defence of loss of control. No sentencing guidelines exist for the new partial defence.

14.17   The SGC guideline on *Provocation* applies to a 'first time offender' aged eighteen or over convicted after a trial. A 'first time offender' is someone who does not have a relevant past conviction by virtue of the CJA 2003, section 143(2). Appropriate reduction for a guilty plea must always be made. The *Provocation* guideline has three categories. The highest category is 'low degree of provocation occurring over a short period', which has a starting point of twelve years within a range of ten years to life; the middle category is 'substantial degree of provocation occurring over a short period', which has a starting point of eight years within a range of four years to nine years; and the lowest category is 'high degree of provocation occurring over a short period' which has a starting point of three years within a range of 'if custody is necessary' up to four years. Additional aggravating and mitigating factors are set out. In *Thornley* [2011] 2 Cr App R (S) 361, the Court of Appeal said that the guideline must be read in light of the statutory change to the partial defence as well as the indirect impact of schedule 21 to the 2003 Act on the sentencing of murder, especially the starting point relevant to cases where an offender has taken a knife to the scene and killed the victim. Lord Judge CJ said that the *Provocation* guideline provided an ample sentencing bracket for the case of *Thornley* itself, such that any sentence within the appropriate range would be consistent with the proper application of the guideline. Specific (but non-exhaustive) aggravating and mitigating factors are set out in the guideline. Several of the mitigating factors set out in the guideline, such as 'spontaneity and lack of premeditation', previous experience of abuse and/or domestic violence', 'evidence that the victim presented an on-going danger to the offender or another', and 'actual (or reasonably anticipated) violence from the victim' do fit well with the rationale for revision of the substantive law and the introduction of the loss of control partial defence. Revision of the *Provocation* guideline to take account of the changes to the defence is awaited.

Manslaughter (unlawful act)

14.18   The maximum penalty for manslaughter is life imprisonment (Offences Against the Person Act 1861, section 5). This is a serious offence for the purposes of the CJA 2003, section 224 (dangerous offenders). There are no sentencing guidelines for this form of manslaughter.

14.19   These offences vary very widely in terms of culpability and circumstances, since they cover the whole range of homicide between murder and accidental death. The main difficulty in sentencing is to attain a proper balance between a sentence which reflects culpability (which may in some cases be low) but which also marks the fact that a life has been taken. In the leading decision of *A G's Ref (No 60 of 2009)(Appleby)* [2010] 2 Cr App R (S) 311 the Court of Appeal reviewed a large number of cases of unlawful (or constructive) manslaughter where the victim had been killed as a result of violence where no weapon had been used and in which, but for the death of the victim, the appropriate charge would have been as assault under the Offences Against the Person Act 1961, section 47 or section 20. Lord Judge CJ said that general references to sentencing for 'one-punch manslaughter' were apt to mislead, and sentences around twelve months' imprisonment should be confined to cases of the lowest culpability where death was almost accidental. Regard must now be given to the problem of gratuitous violence in streets and city centres which was a significant aggravating factor in many cases of unlawful act manslaughter. What was now required, without diminishing the importance of the offender's culpability, is for more attention to be given to the consequences of those actions. One of the offenders dealt with in *Appleby* is Cowles, where sentences of seven years were upheld in a case where the victim had tried to intervene in an attack by the two offenders on another man. The victim had been seized, held in a headlock, and repeatedly punched to the face. He never regained consciousness. Lord Judge CJ said that such a case had nothing whatsoever to do with one-punch manslaughter. Sentencing for manslaughter of a child involving the use of violence including the shaking of a baby was reviewed in *Burridge* [2011] 2 Cr App R (S) 148. In that case culpability was high, with intent falling just short of that necessary for murder. The injury had been inflicted in a temper, and the offender had previously been warned and advised. He lied to the hospital and to the police. A sentence of ten years was imposed. The Court stressed in *A G's Ref (No 125 of 2010)* [2011] 2 Cr App R (S) 534 that the higher sentencing levels for manslaughter which had been signalled in *Appleby* also applied in the present context. A sentence of three-and-a-half years was increased to five years where the offender had lost his temper and had either shaken or thrown his infant son causing brain damage and death.

Where the unlawful manslaughter has involved use of a weapon, such as where a knife **14.20** has been taken to the scene and used to kill the victim, a sentence in the range of ten to twelve years before allowance for plea is generally appropriate, even where some element of provocation is present (*Carter* [2003] 2 Cr App R (S) 524). Twelve years following a trial was upheld in *Bishop* [2012] 1 Cr App R (S) 60 where the offender had sought out a man who had been harassing his girlfriend and stabbed him seven times. Higher sentences are also appropriate where manslaughter is committed in the course of another offence, such as robbery or burglary. In *Jumah* [2011] 2 Cr App R (S) 200, an offender who planned and organized a robbery and was present at the scene when another offender stabbed and killed the store manager had his sentence increased from fourteen years to eighteen years.

Manslaughter (gross negligence)

The maximum penalty for manslaughter is life imprisonment (Offences Against the Person **14.21** Act 1861, section 5). This is a serious offence for the purposes of the CJA 2003, section 224 (dangerous offenders). There are no sentencing guidelines for this form of manslaughter.

Sentences vary widely to cover the great range of circumstances in which this offence can **14.22** be committed. In common with other areas of manslaughter the Court of Appeal in *Barrass* [2012] 1 Cr App R (S) 450 confirmed that the more severe sentences appropriate in manslaughter cases following *Appleby* (paragraph 14.19, this Chapter) also apply in relation to gross negligence manslaughter. *Barrass* was a case where a socially inadequate offender failed to summon medical attention for his sister who became immobilized at their home after a fall. A sentence of two years and eight months was upheld. A forty-four-year-old medical consultant urologist was convicted after a trial in *Garg* [2011] 2 Cr App R (S) 59. He failed to ensure the safety and proper treatment of a patient admitted to the ward over the weekend, and he made changes to hospital records in the hope of avoiding liability. A sentence of two years was upheld.

Child destruction, infanticide, and abortion

The maximum penalty for child destruction is life imprisonment (Infant Life (Preservation) **14.23** Act 1929, section 1), for infanticide it is also life imprisonment (Infanticide Act 1938, section 1), and also for procuring an illegal abortion (OAPA 1861, section 58). These are all serious offences for the purposes of the CJA 2003, section 224 (dangerous offenders). There are no sentencing guidelines for any of these offences and no recent appellate guidance.

The proper approach to sentencing for infanticide was considered in *Sainsbury* (1989) 11 **14.24** Cr App R (S) 533. The offender gave birth without medical assistance on the floor at her boyfriend's flat. The baby was then drowned in a river. A sentence of twelve months' imprisonment was varied by the Court of Appeal to a community order, the Court noting that although the offence was serious the mitigating factors were overwhelming.

Causing or allowing the death of a child or vulnerable adult

14.25 The maximum penalty for this offence is fourteen years (Domestic Violence, Crime and Victims Act 2004, section 5). This is a serious offence for the purposes of the CJA 2003, section 224 (dangerous offenders). There is a lesser form of this offence where serious injury, rather than death, results. There are no sentencing guidelines for either form of this offence.

14.26 In *Ikram* [2008] 2 Cr App R (S) 648 a sentence of nine years was upheld for each of two adults convicted after a trial. The death of their child was caused by deliberately inflicted violence but the prosecution was unable to prove which of the offenders had actually caused the fatal injuries. The Court of Appeal said that the general approach to sentencing for manslaughter of a child (see 14.19) was useful when considering sentence for this offence.

Causing death by dangerous driving

14.27 The maximum penalty for this offence is fourteen years. This is a serious offence for the purposes of the CJA 2003, section 224 (dangerous offenders). The offence carries a mandatory driving disqualification for at least two years, with a compulsory extended re-test. The SGC guideline on *Causing Death by Driving* applies. As with all SGC guidelines, it applies to a 'first time offender' aged eighteen years or over convicted after a trial. A 'first-time offender' is someone who does not have a relevant past conviction by virtue of the CJA 2003, section 143(2). Appropriate reduction for a guilty plea must always be made.

14.28 The guideline indicates three levels based predominantly on the standard of driving displayed. Level 1 (the highest) covers 'the most serious offences encompassing driving that involved a deliberate decision to ignore (or a flagrant disregard for) the rules of the road and an apparent disregard for the great danger being posed to others'. A level 1 offence has a starting point of eight years (range seven to fourteen years). Level 2 covers 'driving that created a *substantial* risk of danger' (emphasis in the original), which has a starting point of five years (range four years to seven years). Level 3 covers 'driving that created a *significant* risk of danger' (emphasis in the original), which has a starting point of three years (two years to five years). The guideline also adds: '[w]here the driving is markedly less culpable than for this level, reference should be made to the starting point and range for the most serious level of causing death by careless driving'. It can be seen that the ranges for levels 2 and 3 overlap. This is deliberate. 'to allow the breadth of discretion necessary to accommodate circumstances where there are significant aggravating factors'.

14.29 Additional aggravating factors are:

(a) previous convictions for motoring offences, particularly offences that involve bad driving or the consumption of excessive alcohol or drugs before driving,

(b) more than one person killed as a result of the offence,

(c) serious injury to one or more victims in addition to the death(s),

(d) disregard of warnings,

(e) other offences committed at the same time, such as driving other than in accordance with the terms of a valid licence or driving while disqualified or driving without insurance or taking a vehicle without consent or driving a stolen vehicle,

(f) the offender's irresponsible behaviour in failing to stop, falsely claiming that one of the victims was responsible for the collision, or trying to throw the victim off the car by swerving in order to escape, or

(g) driving off in an attempt to avoid detection or apprehension.

Additional mitigating factors are:

(a) alcohol or drugs consumed unwittingly,

(b) offender was seriously injured in the collision,

(c) the victim was a close friend or relative,

(d) actions of the victim or a third party contributed significantly to the likelihood of a collision occurring and/or death resulting,

(e) the offender's lack of driving experience contributed to the commission of the offence, or

(f) the driving was in response to a proven and genuine emergency falling short of a defence.

The guideline also states that sentencers should take into account relevant matters of **14.30** personal mitigation, in particular good driving record, giving assistance at the scene, and remorse. The Court of Appeal in *Oughton* [2011] 1 Cr App R (S) 390 made it clear that where an offender has had an impeccable driving record prior to the incident a larger than normal discount to reflect that might be justified.

Causing death by careless driving while under the influence of drink or drugs

The maximum penalty for this offence is fourteen years. This is a serious offence for the **14.31** purposes of the CJA 2003, section 224 (dangerous offenders). The offence carries a mandatory driving disqualification for at least two years, with a compulsory extended re-test. The SGC guideline on *Causing Death by Driving* applies. As with all SGC guidelines, it applies to a 'first-time offender' aged eighteen years or over convicted after a trial. A 'first-time offender' is someone who does not have a relevant past conviction by virtue of the CJA 2003, section 143(2). Appropriate reduction for a guilty plea must always be made.

The guideline takes the form of a matrix where the applicable starting point and sentence **14.32** range depends on the interaction of two variables—the standard of driving displayed and the extent to which the offender was over the legal alcohol limit or the quantity of drugs ingested. The legal limit of alcohol is 35 micrograms in breath, 80 milligrams in blood, and 107 milligrams in urine. At the highest (most serious) level, where the offender had 71 micrograms or above of alcohol or the equivalent, or had ingested a high quantity of drugs, or where there had been deliberate non-provision of a specimen where there was evidence of serious impairment, the following apply:

(a) in a case of careless driving arising from momentary in attention with no aggravating factors, the starting point is six years (range five years to ten years),

(b) in other cases of careless driving the starting point is seven years (six years to twelve years), and

(c) in a case of careless driving falling not far short of dangerous the starting point is eight years (seven years to fourteen years).

Where the level of alcohol or drugs was lower, in the equivalent scenarios (a) to (c) the applicable starting points and ranges are correspondingly lower.

Additional aggravating factors are (a), (b), (c), (e), and (f) set out at paragraph 14.29, this Chapter, and additional mitigating factors are (a), (b), (c), (d), and (f) set out in that paragraph.

The guideline also states that sentencers should take into account relevant matters of personal **14.33** mitigation, in particular good driving record, giving assistance at the scene, and remorse.

Causing death by careless driving

14.34   The maximum penalty for this offence is five years. The offence carries a mandatory driving disqualification for at least one year, with a discretionary re-test. The SGC guideline on
Causing Death by Driving applies. As with all SGC guidelines, it applies to a 'first time offender' aged eighteen years or over convicted after a trial. A 'first-time offender' is someone
who does not have a relevant past conviction by virtue of the CJA 2003, section 143(2).
Appropriate reduction for a guilty plea must always be made.

14.35   The guideline indicates three levels based predominantly on the standard of driving displayed. Level 1 (the highest) covers 'careless driving falling not far short of dangerous driving'. A level 1 offence has a starting point of fifteen months (range thirty-six weeks to three
years). Level 2 covers 'other cases of careless driving', and has a starting point of thirty-six
weeks (community order (high) to two years). Level 3 covers 'careless driving arising from
momentary inattention with no aggravating factors', which has a starting point of community order (medium), range (community order (low)—community order (high)). Additional
aggravating factors are (a), (b), (c), (e), and (f) set out at paragraph 14.29, this Chapter, and
additional mitigating factors are (b), (c), (d), (e), and (f) set out in that paragraph. In *Smith*
[2011] EWCA Crim 2844 the Court said that the consumption of alcohol and the careless
nature of the driving were constituent elements of the offence and not in themselves aggravating features of the case.

14.36   The guideline also states that sentencers should take into account relevant matters of
personal mitigation, in particular good driving record, giving assistance at the scene, and
remorse. In *Thorogood* [2010] EWCA Crim 2123 the Court said that it was appropriate to
take the age of the offender into account where appropriate as personal mitigation and that
this might require a further reduction from the sentence starting point before applying the
normal recommended reduction for a guilty plea.

Causing death by driving: unlicensed, disqualified, or uninsured driver

14.37   The maximum penalty for this offence is two years. The offence carries a mandatory driving disqualification for at least one year, with a discretionary re-test. The SGC guideline on
Causing Death by Driving applies. As with all SGC guidelines, it applies to a 'first time offender' aged eighteen years or over convicted after a trial. A 'first-time offender' is someone
who does not have a relevant past conviction by virtue of the CJA 2003, section 143(2).
Appropriate reduction for a guilty plea must always be made.

14.38   The guideline indicates three levels. Level 1 (the highest) covers 'the offender was disqualified from driving OR the offender was unlicensed or uninsured plus two or more
aggravating factors from the list apply'. A level 1 offence has a starting point of twelve
months (range thirty-six weeks to two years). Level 2 covers 'the offender was unlicensed
or uninsured plus at least one aggravating factor from the list applies' and has a starting
point of twenty-six weeks (community order (high) to thirty-six weeks). Level 3 covers
'the offender was unlicensed or uninsured, and no aggravating factor' which has a starting point of community order (medium), range (community order (low)—community
order (high)).

14.39   The aggravating factors (which in this offence feed directly into the sentencing levels as
explained earlier) are (a), (b), and (c) set out at paragraph 14.29 in this Chapter, plus 'irresponsible behaviour such as failing to stop or falsely claiming that someone else was driving' and additional mitigating factors are (b), (c), and (f) set out in that paragraph plus 'the
offender genuinely believed that he or she was insured or licensed to drive'.

B SENTENCING FOR NON-FATAL OFFENCES AGAINST THE PERSON

Threats to kill

The maximum penalty for this offence is ten years (CLA 1977, schedule 12). This is a ser- **14.40** ious offence for the purposes of the CJA 2003, section 224 (dangerous offenders). There are no sentencing guidelines for this offence.

Sentences seem to range downwards from a high mark of about five years. Higher sen- **14.41** tences are reserved for cases where the threat is not uttered on the spur of the moment but is calculated to strike terror in the person threatened, especially where accompanied by an immediate physical threat to the victim. In *Martin* (1993) 14 Cr App R (S) 645 a sentence of four years was upheld in a case where the offender sent the victim two anonymous notes stained with blood. In *Patel* [2013] 1 Cr App R (S) 617 the offender threatened his former partner that he would kill their young son, and then sent her a text saying that he had done so. Four years was reduced to twenty months in that case.

Wounding or causing grievous bodily harm with intent

The maximum penalty for this offence is life imprisonment (OAPA 1861, section 18). This **14.42** is a serious offence for the purposes of the CJA 2003, section 224 (dangerous offenders). The Sentencing Council guideline *Assault* applies. It applies to offenders aged eighteen years or over who have been convicted after a trial. The offence range for this offence is three to sixteen years. A sentence passed outside this range is a departure from the guideline and the court must give reasons why it would be contrary to the interests of justice to sentence within the offence range (CJA 2003, section 174(6)). If the offence is committed in a domestic setting the SGC guideline on *Domestic Violence* also applies.

As with all SC guidelines the court must at step 1determine the offence category by assess- **14.43** ing the degree of harm (greater or lesser) and the level of culpability (higher or lower). A closed list of factors is provided in the guideline. Category 1 is greater harm (serious injury must normally be present) and higher culpability. Category 2 is greater harm (serious injury must normally be present) and lower culpability, or lesser harm and higher culpability. Category 3 is lesser harm and lower culpability. Category 1 for this offence has a starting point of twelve years (range nine to sixteen years), category 2 has a starting point of six years (range five to nine years), and category 3 has a starting point of four years (range three to five years). At step 2 the court must then consider the non-exhaustive list of factors set out in the guideline as increasing seriousness or as reducing seriousness or reflecting personal mitigation. The presence of aggravating or mitigating factors entitle the judge in a particular case to move up or down within the category range or to move into a different category from that selected at step 1. At step 2 the court must make any appropriate upward adjustment to reflect the presence of relevant previous convictions, or downward movement to reflect their absence. At step 4 an appropriate reduction should be made for a guilty plea.

The Court of Appeal has considered the sentencing guidelines for this offence in several **14.44** subsequent cases. Of interest is *Collis* [2012] EWCA Crim 1335 where the forty-year-old defendant used a kitchen knife to stab the victim in the neck after the victim, who lived in a neighbouring flat, forced his way into the defendant's flat and attacked the defendant's wife. The defendant, who had many previous convictions, pleaded guilty on the basis that he had not armed himself in advance. The Court said this was a case of greater harm having regard to the life-threatening nature of the injury, but was at the borderline of higher and lower culpability. The case was therefore at the borderline of categories 1 and 2, requiring a starting point of nine years. After taking account of mitigation and the early plea of guilty, the final sentence was six years. In *Fadeiro* [2012] EWCA Crim 1292 the nineteen-year-old defendant stabbed a seventeen-year-old youth in the face with a knife, causing a deep penetrating injury close to his eye. By great good fortune no permanent or serious damage was done. The judge selected a starting point at the lower end of category 1 (greater harm and higher culpability), imposing a sentence of eleven years' detention in a young offender institution. The Court of Appeal agreed with the sentence, but preferred to say that it was a category 2 case given that greater harm (in the context of the offence) had not been caused. Culpability was high and there were a number of important aggravating features, not least the fact that the defendant had a previous conviction for robbery in which a knife had been produced. In *Karakas* [2013] 1 Cr App R (S) 46 (p 261) the defendant, a man of previous good character, stabbed the victim four times following a series of disputes. The femoral artery was severed, there were injuries to bladder and bowel, and the victim lost five pints of blood and was in hospital for two months. Following a guilty plea, the judge passed a sentence of ten years based on a starting point of fifteen years. The Court of Appeal agreed that this was a category 1 case, but that in light of personal mitigation the sentence was reduced to eight years.

Inflicting grievous bodily harm/unlawful wounding

14.45   The maximum penalty for this offence is five years (OAPA 1861, section 20). This is a specified offence for the purposes of the CJA 2003, section 224 (dangerous offenders). The Sentencing Council guideline *Assault* applies. It applies to offenders aged eighteen years or over who have been convicted after a trial. The offence range for this offence is community order up to four years. A sentence passed outside this range is a departure from the guideline and the court must give reasons why it would be contrary to the interests of justice to sentence within the offence range (CJA 2003, section 174(6)). If the offence is committed in a domestic setting the SGC guideline on *Domestic Violence* also applies.

14.46   As with all SC guidelines the court must at step 1 determine the offence category by assessing the degree of harm (greater or lesser) and the level of culpability (higher or lower). A closed list of factors is provided in the guideline. Category 1 is greater harm (serious injury must normally be present) and higher culpability. Category 2 is greater harm (serious injury must normally be present) and lower culpability, or lesser harm and higher culpability. Category 3 is lesser harm and lower culpability. Category 1 for this offence has a starting point of three years (range two-and-a-half to four years), category 2 has a starting point of one-and-a-half years (range one to three years), and category 3 has a starting point of high-level community order (low-level community order to fifty-one weeks). At step 2 the court must then consider the non-exhaustive list of factors set out in the guideline as increasing seriousness or as reducing seriousness or reflecting personal mitigation. The presence of aggravating or mitigating factors entitle the judge in a particular case to move up or down within the category range or to move into a different category from that selected at step 1. At step 2 the court must make any appropriate upward adjustment to reflect the presence of relevant previous convictions, or downward movement to reflect their absence. At step 4 an appropriate reduction should be made for a guilty plea.

14.47   The case of *Morrison* [2012] 2 Cr App R (S) 594 was decided after the Sentencing Council's guideline came into effect. The defendant struck the victim on the head with a bottle. The bottle broke, and the victim received several fractures to the skull and eye socket which required an operation to repair. The defendant pleaded guilty on the day of the trial. The judge found this to be a category 1 case, and took a starting point of four-and-a-half years. The Court of Appeal said that there was clearly greater harm, but in terms of culpability the use of the weapon had to be set against lack of premeditation. Whether one took the case as falling within category 1 or on the cusp between categories 1 and 2, the combination of aggravating and mitigating factors took the case to a starting point of three-and-a-half years. The final sentence, allowing for the late plea, was three years. In *Marsh and Stokes* [2012] 2 Cr App R (S) 178 the female defendants became involved in a fight with a sixteen-year-old girl. One defendant held the girl's arms behind her back while the second cut the girl's face with a key, causing a 4 centimetre laceration which would leave a permanent scar. The Court of Appeal agreed with the judge that this was a category 1 case, given that this was a cold-blooded attack which caused physical and psychological damage. Coulson J said that it was important that all the various factors in the guideline were looked at in the round. Sentences of two years' imprisonment and twenty months' detention in a young offender institution were upheld.

There is an aggravated form of this offence, which is Racially or Religiously Aggravated **14.48** Grievous Bodily Harm/Unlawful Wounding. The maximum penalty for this offence is seven years (Crime and Disorder Act 1998, section 29). This is a specified offence for the purposes of the CJA 2003, section 224 (dangerous offenders). The Sentencing Council guideline *Assault* applies. If the offence is committed in a domestic setting the SGC guideline on *Domestic Violence* also applies. When applying the SC guideline the court should determine the sentence for the 'basic' offence without taking account of the element of aggravation and then make an addition to the sentence considering the level of aggravation involved. In doing so it may be appropriate to move outside the identified category range taking into account the increased statutory maximum.

Assault occasioning actual bodily harm

The maximum penalty for this offence is five years (OAPA 1861, section 47). This is a spe- **14.49** cified offence for the purposes of the CJA 2003, section 224 (dangerous offenders). The Sentencing Council guideline *Assault* applies. It applies to offenders aged eighteen years or over who have been convicted after a trial. The offence range for this offence is fine to three years. A sentence passed outside this range is a departure from the guideline and the court must give reasons why it would be contrary to the interests of justice to sentence within the offence range (CJA 2003, section 174(6)). If the offence is committed in a domestic setting the SGC guideline on *Domestic Violence* also applies.

As with all SC guidelines the court must at step 1 determine the offence category by assess- **14.50** ing the degree of harm (greater or lesser) and the level of culpability (higher or lower). A closed list of factors is provided in the guideline. Category 1 is greater harm (serious injury must normally be present) and higher culpability. Category 2 is greater harm (serious injury must normally be present) and lower culpability, or lesser harm and higher culpability. Category 3 is lesser harm and lower culpability. Category 1 for this offence has a starting point of one-and-a-half years (range one to three years), category 2 has a starting point of twenty-six weeks (range low-level community order to fifty-one weeks), and category 3 has a starting point of medium-level community order (range band A fine—high-level community order). At step 2 the court must then consider the non-exhaustive list of factors set out in the guideline as increasing seriousness or as reducing seriousness or reflecting personal mitigation. The presence of aggravating or mitigating factors entitle the judge in a particular case to move up or down within the category range or to move into a different category from that selected at step 1. At step 2 the court must make any appropriate upward adjustment to reflect the presence of relevant previous convictions, or downward movement to reflect their absence. At step 4 an appropriate reduction should be made for a guilty plea.

14.51 There is an aggravated form of this offence, which is Racially or Religiously Aggravated Actual Bodily Harm. The maximum penalty for this offence is seven years (Crime and Disorder Act 1998, section 29). The offence range is fine to three years. This is a specified offence for the purposes of the CJA 2003, section 224 (dangerous offenders). The Sentencing Council guideline *Assault* applies. If the offence is committed in a domestic setting the SGC guideline on *Domestic Violence* also applies. When applying the SC guideline the court should determine the sentence for the 'basic' offence without taking account of the element of aggravation and then make an addition to the sentence considering the level of aggravation involved. In doing so it may be appropriate to move outside the identified category range taking into account the increased statutory maximum.

Common assault

14.52 The maximum penalty for this offence is six months (summary only) (CJA 1988, section 39). The Sentencing Council guideline *Assault* applies. It applies to offenders aged eighteen years or over who have been convicted after a trial. The offence range for this offence is discharge to six months. A sentence passed outside this range is a departure from the guideline but note that in this case the top of the offence range coincides with the maximum penalty. If the offence is committed in a domestic setting the SGC guideline on *Domestic Violence* also applies.

14.53 As with all SC guidelines the court must at step 1 determine the offence category by assessing the degree of harm (greater or lesser) and the level of culpability (higher or lower). A closed list of factors is provided in the guideline. Category 1 is greater harm (injury or fear of injury must normally be present) and higher culpability. Category 2 is greater harm (injury or fear of injury must normally be present) and lower culpability, or lesser harm and higher culpability. Category 3 is lesser harm and lower culpability. Category 1 for this offence has a starting point of high-level community order (range low-level community order to 6 months), category 2 has a starting point of medium-level community order (range band A fine to high-level community order), and category 3 has a starting point of band A fine (range discharge to band C fine). At step 2 the court must then consider the non-exhaustive list of factors set out in the guideline as increasing seriousness or as reducing seriousness or reflecting personal mitigation. The presence of aggravating or mitigating factors entitle the judge in a particular case to move up or down within the category range or to move into a different category from that selected at step 1. At step 2 the court must make any appropriate upward adjustment to reflect the presence of relevant previous convictions, or downward movement to reflect their absence. At step 4 an appropriate reduction should be made for a guilty plea.

14.54 There is an aggravated form of this offence, which is Racially or Religiously Aggravated Common Assault. The maximum penalty for this offence is two years (Crime and Disorder Act 1998, section 29). The offence range is discharge to six months. This is a specified offence for the purposes of the CJA 2003, section 224 (dangerous offenders). The Sentencing Council guideline *Assault* applies. If the offence is committed in a domestic setting the SGC guideline on *Domestic Violence* also applies. When applying the SC guideline the court should determine the sentence for the 'basic' offence without taking account of the element of aggravation and then make an addition to the sentence considering the level of aggravation involved. In doing so it may be appropriate to move outside the identified category range taking into account the increased statutory maximum.

C SENTENCING FOR CERTAIN PROPERTY OFFENCES

Robbery

The maximum penalty for this offence is life (Theft Act 1968, section 8). This is a serious **14.55** specified offence for the purposes of the CJA 2003, section 224 (dangerous offenders). The SGC guideline *Robbery* applies. There are separate guidelines for adult offenders and for offenders aged under eighteen years old. The guidelines apply to first-time offenders who have been convicted after a trial. The offence range for this offence when committed by an adult is up to three years to twelve years, and when committed by a young offender it is community order to ten years. A sentence passed outside this range is a departure from the guideline and the court must give reasons why it would be contrary to the interests of justice to sentence within the offence range (CJA 2003, section 174(6)).

The robbery guidelines apply to the following three categories of robbery only: **14.56**

(a) street robbery or 'mugging'
(b) robberies of small businesses
(c) less sophisticated commercial robberies

Violent personal robberies in the home are not covered. In that context relevant appellate guidance can be found in *O'Driscoll* (1986) 8 Cr App R (S) 121, *AG's References (Nos 38, 39, & 40 of 2007)(Crummack)* [2008] 1 Cr App R (S) 319, and *Poynter* [2013] 1 Cr App R (S) 33. These cases suggest sentences of between ten and fifteen years after a trial, and overlap with cases of aggravated burglary (see paragraph 14.60). Professionally planned commercial robberies are not covered in the SGC guideline either. Court of Appeal authorities include *Jenkins* [2009] 1 Cr App R (S) 109 (sentences of up to a maximum of twenty-five years for multiple armed robberies), and *Lawrence* [2011] EWCA Crim 2609 (daytime violent smash-and-grab raids in jewellery shops; sentences of eleven or twelve years after a trial). Another example is *AG's Reference (No 13 of 2012)(Bouhaddon)* [2012] EWCA Crim 1066, where the court said that the judge should not have been invited to sentence a case involving violent cash in transit robberies within the SGC guidelines. It is also clear that the SGC guideline is not apposite to deal with cases of ram-raiding, whether these are charged as theft, robbery, or burglary (*Lawlor* [2013] 1 Cr App R (S) 532).

For *adult offenders* the guidelines identify three categories: **14.57**

Where the victim is caused serious physical injury by the use of significant force and/or the use of a weapon, the starting point is eight years (range seven to twelve years). Where a weapon is produced and used to threaten, and/or force is used which results in injury to the victim, the starting point is four years (range two to seven years). Where the offence incudes the threat or use of minimal force and removal of property the starting point is twelve months (range up to three years). Offence-specific aggravating factors include more than one offender, offence pre-planned, wearing a disguise, offence committed at night, vulnerable victim targeted, targeting of large sums of money or valuable goods, and possession of weapon.

In *Peloe* [2011] 1 Cr App R (S) 96 the defendant accosted a woman in the street, and **14.58** grabbed her bag with sufficient force to cause her to fall over. He struck her three times in the face and took her bag. He was arrested two hours later. He had twenty previous convictions for fifty offences, including robbery. The judge treated this as a level 2 offence in the guidelines and passed a sentence of six years following a trial. The Court of Appeal agreed. Significant force was used and there was an element of persistence in the violence although the offence was opportunistic. The criminal record was a significant aggravating feature.

The sentence was high but not wrong in principle. By comparison in *Hume* [2011] 2 Cr App R (S) 268 the defendant approached a seventy-six-year-old lady who had just collected her pension. When she got into her car the defendant pulled the door open, reached across her, and grabbed her bag from her grasp. The victim suffered minor injury to her fingers. A sentence of four years following a plea of guilty was reduced to thirty-two months. The judge had been entitled to conclude that the victim had been targeted, and the defendant had a poor record.

14.59   For *young offenders* the guidelines identify three categories.

Where the victim is caused serious physical injury by the use of significant force and/or the use of a weapon, the starting point is seven years (range six to ten years). Where a weapon is produced and used to threaten, and/or force is used which results in injury to the victim, the starting point is three years (range one to six years). Where the offence includes the threat or use of minimal force and removal of property the starting point is community order (range community order to two months). Offence-specific aggravating factors are the same as for adult offenders. Specific mitigating factors include age and immaturity of offender, and peer-group pressure.

Aggravated burglary

14.60   The maximum penalty for this offence is life (Theft Act 1968, section 10). This is a serious specified offence for the purposes of the CJA 2003, section 224 (dangerous offenders). The Sentencing Council guideline *Burglary Offences* applies. It applies to offenders aged eighteen years old or over who have been convicted after a trial. The offence range for this offence is one to thirteen years. A sentence passed outside this range is a departure from the guideline and the court must give reasons why it would be contrary to the interests of justice to sentence within the offence range (CJA 2003, section 174(6)).

14.61   As with all SC guidelines the court must at step 1 determine the offence category by assessing the degree of harm (greater or lesser) and the level of culpability (higher or lower). A closed list of factors is provided in the guideline. Category 1 is greater harm and higher culpability. Category 2 is greater harm and lower culpability, or lesser harm and higher culpability. Category 3 is lesser harm and lower culpability. Category 1 for this offence has a starting point of ten years (range nine to thirteen years), category 2 has a starting point of six years (range four to nine years), and category 3 has a starting point of two years (range one to four years). At step 2 the court must then consider the non-exhaustive list of factors set out in the guideline as increasing seriousness or as reducing seriousness or reflecting personal mitigation. The presence of aggravating or mitigating factors entitles the judge in a particular case to move up or down within the category range or to move into a different category from that selected at step 1. At step 2 the court must make any appropriate upward adjustment to reflect the presence of relevant previous convictions, or downward movement to reflect their absence. At step 4 an appropriate reduction should be made for a guilty plea. Offence-specific aggravating factors include child at home when offence committed, offence committed at night, abuse of power/abuse of trust, and gratuitous degradation of victim.

Domestic burglary

14.62   The maximum penalty for this offence is fourteen years (Theft Act, section 9). If committed with intent to inflict grievous bodily harm on a person or to do unlawful damage to a building or anything in it, this is a serious specified offence for the purposes of the CJA 2003, section 224 (dangerous offenders). The Sentencing Council guideline *Burglary Offences* applies. It applies to offenders aged eighteen years or over who have been convicted after a trial. The offence range for this offence is community order to six years. A sentence passed outside this range is a departure from the guideline and the court must give reasons why it would be contrary to the interests of justice to sentence within the offence range (CJA 2003, section 174(6)). When sentencing the offender for a third qualifying domestic burglary the court must apply section 111 of the PCC(S)A 2000 and impose a custodial sentence of at least three years unless satisfied that there are particular circumstances which relate to any of the offences or to the offender which would make it unjust to do so. The Court of Appeal has said in *Andrews* [2013] 2 Cr App R (S) 5 and again in *Silvera* [2013] EWCA Crim 1764 that when sentencing a 'three strikes' burglary case the proper approach was to work through the SGC guideline and then to check that the final sentence is not less than the minimum sentence required by section 111. A judge should not take the three-year term in section 111 as the starting point.

As with all SC guidelines the court must at step 1 determine the offence category by assessing the degree of harm (greater or lesser) and the level of culpability (higher or lower). A closed list of factors is provided in the guideline. Category 1 is greater harm and higher culpability. Category 2 is greater harm and lower culpability, or lesser harm and higher culpability. Category 3 is lesser harm and lower culpability. Category 1 for this offence has a starting point of three years (range two to six years), category 2 has a starting point of one year (range high-level community order to two years), and category 3 has a starting point of high level community order (low-level community order to six months). At step 2 the court must then consider the non-exhaustive list of factors set out in the guideline as increasing seriousness or as reducing seriousness or reflecting personal mitigation. The presence of aggravating or mitigating factors entitle the judge in a particular case to move up or down within the category range or to move into a different category from that selected at step 1. At step 2 the court must make any appropriate upward adjustment to reflect the presence of relevant previous convictions, or downward movement to reflect their absence. At step 4 an appropriate reduction should be made for a guilty plea. Offence-specific aggravating factors include child at home when offence committed, offence committed at night, gratuitous degradation of victim, and victim compelled to leave their home. So-called 'distraction burglary' of the elderly or otherwise vulnerable has always attracted higher sentences, especially where the offender has a record of similar offending. In *Brooker* [2012] 1 Cr App R (S) 298, for example, the Court of Appeal upheld sentences totalling six years for a series of distraction burglaries committed at the homes of elderly people, by a man with a long record of drug-related property offences. **14.63**

The guideline says that when sentencing category 2 or 3 offences the court should also consider the custody threshold as follows: (i) has the custody threshold been passed? (ii) if so, is it unavoidable that a custodial sentence be imposed? (iii) if so, can that sentence be suspended? **14.64**

Non-domestic burglary

The maximum penalty for this offence is ten years (Theft Act, section 9). If committed with intent to inflict grievous bodily harm on a person or to do unlawful damage to a building or anything in it this is a serious specified offence for the purposes of the CJA 2003, section 224 (dangerous offenders). The Sentencing Council guideline *Assault* applies. It applies to offenders aged eighteen years old or over who have been convicted after a trial. The offence range for this offence is fine to five years. A sentence passed outside this range is a departure from the guideline and the court must give reasons why it would be contrary to the interests **14.65** of justice to sentence within the offence range (CJA 2003, section 174(6)). In *Bailey* [2013] EWCA Crim 1779 two defendants each received sentences of forty-two months after guilty pleas for a non-domestic burglary. The Court said that without reduction for plea the sentences would have been over five years and therefore outside the guidelines, and that could not be justified on the facts, even though there were aggravating features of the offence and both defendants had very poor records. Another example is *Byrne* [2012] EWCA Crim 418.

14.66   As with all SC guidelines the court must at step 1 determine the offence category by assessing the degree of harm (greater or lesser) and the level of culpability (higher or lower). A closed list of factors is provided in the guideline. Category 1 is greater harm and higher culpability. Category 2 is greater harm and lower culpability, or lesser harm and higher culpability. Category 3 is lesser harm and lower culpability. Category 1 for this offence has a starting point of two years (range one to five years), category 2 has a starting point of eighteen months (range low-level community order to fifty-one weeks), and category 3 has a starting point of medium-level community order (Band B fine to eighteen weeks). At step 2 the court must then consider the non-exhaustive list of factors set out in the guideline as increasing seriousness or as reducing seriousness or reflecting personal mitigation. The presence of aggravating or mitigating factors entitle the judge in a particular case to move up or down within the category range or to move into a different category from that selected at step 1. At step 2 the court must make any appropriate upward adjustment to reflect the presence of relevant previous convictions, or downward movement to reflect their absence. At step 4 an appropriate reduction should be made for a guilty plea. Offence-specific aggravating factors include offence committed at night, particularly where staff present or likely to be present, abuse of a position of trust, and gratuitous degradation of victim.

14.67   The guideline says that when sentencing category 2 or 3 offences the court should also consider the custody threshold as follows: (i) has the custody threshold been passed? (ii) if so, is it unavoidable that a custodial sentence be imposed? (iii) if so, can that sentence be suspended? When considering category 3 offences the court should also consider whether the community order threshold has been passed.

Handling stolen goods

14.68   The maximum penalty for this offence is fourteen years (Theft Act, section 22). Sentencing guidelines for this case can be found in the Court of Appeal case of *Webbe* [2002] 1 Cr App R (S) 82. The Court said that the value of the goods is often a helpful indication of the seriousness of the offence, but not the determining factor. Aggravating features are the closeness of the handler to the primary offence, high value of the goods, sophistication, high level of profit made, and handler providing a regular outlet for stolen goods. Less serious offences would typically involve low-value goods, a one-off offence, little or no benefit to the offender.

Theft

14.69   The maximum penalty for this offence is seven years (Theft Act 1968, section 1). The SGC guideline *Theft* applies. There are separate guidelines for theft in breach of trust, theft in a dwelling, theft from the person, and theft from a shop. The guidelines apply to first-time offenders aged eighteen years or over who have been convicted after a trial.

14.70   For theft in breach of trust the offence range is fine to six years. There are four categories: where there is theft of £125,000 or more, or theft of £20,000 or more in breach of a high degree of trust the starting point is three years (range two to six years). Where there is theft of £20,000 or more but less than £125,000 of theft of less than £20,000 in breach of a high degree of trust the starting point is two years (range one year to three years). Where there is theft of £2000 or more but less than £20,000 or theft of less than £2000 in breach of a high degree of trust the starting point is eighteen weeks (range community order (high) to one year). Finally, for theft of less than £2000 the starting point is community order (medium) and the range is fine to twenty-six weeks. Specific aggravating factors are long course of offending, suspicion deliberately thrown on others, and offender motivated by intention to cause harm or out of revenge.

For theft in a dwelling the offence range is fine to three years. There are three categories: **14.71** where there is theft from a vulnerable victim involving intimidation or the use or threat of force (falling short of robbery) or the use of deception, the starting point is eighteen months (range one year to three years). Where there has been theft from a vulnerable victim the starting point is eighteen weeks (range community order (high) to one year). Where there has been theft in a dwelling not involving a vulnerable victim the starting point is community order (medium) (range fine to eighteen weeks). Specific aggravating factors are intimidation or face-to-face confrontation with victim, use of force etc, use of deception etc, and offender motivated by intention to cause harm or out of revenge.

For theft from the person the offence range is fine to three years. There are three cat- **14.72** egories: where there is theft from a vulnerable victim involving intimidation or the use or threat of force (falling short of robbery) the starting point is eighteen months (range one year to three years). Where there has been theft from a vulnerable victim the starting point is eighteen weeks (range community order (high) to one year). Where there has been theft from the person not involving a vulnerable victim the starting point is community order (medium) (range fine to eighteen weeks). Specific aggravating factors are intimidation or face-to-face confrontation with victim, use of force etc, high level of inconvenience caused to victim, and offender motivated by intention to cause harm or out of revenge.

For theft from a shop the offence range is fine to four years. There are four categories: where **14.73** there is theft by an organized gang/group and intimidation or the use or threat of force the starting point is one year (range thirty-six weeks to four years). Where there is theft involving significant intimidation, or threats or use of force resulting in slight injury, or very high level of planning, or significant related damage, the starting point is six weeks (range community order (high) to thirty-six weeks). Where the theft involves low-level intimidation or threats, or some planning eg a session of stealing on the same day, or going equipped, or some related damage the starting point is community order (low) and the range is fine to community order (high). Finally, where there is little or no planning or sophistication and the goods taken are of low value the starting point is a fine (range conditional discharge to community order (low)). Specific aggravating factors are child accompanying offender involved in or aware of theft, professional offending, victim particularly vulnerable (eg small independent shop), and offender targeted high-value goods.

Fraud

The SGC guideline *Fraud—Statutory Offences* applies. There are separate guidelines for **14.74** confidence fraud, possession etc articles for use in fraud, banking and insurance fraud, and benefit fraud. Only the guidelines for confidence fraud and benefit fraud are considered here. The guidelines apply to first-time offenders aged eighteen years or over who have been convicted after a trial.

Confidence fraud is a generic description rather than a specific offence. The guideline **14.75** assumes that it will be prosecuted under the Fraud Act 2006, section 1, where the maximum penalty is ten years, or false accounting under the Theft Act 1968, section 17, where the maximum penalty is seven years. The offence range for sentencing confidence fraud is fine to eight years. The guideline is a matrix based on two main factors: the nature of the offence and the sum of money involved.

14.76 Where there is a large-scale advance-fee fraud or other confidence fraud involving the deliberate targeting of a large number of vulnerable victims, the starting point based on a sum of £750,000 is six years (range five to eight years), the starting point based on a sum of £300,000 is five years (range four to seven years), the starting point based on a sum of £60,000 is four years (three to six years), the starting point based on a sum of £10,000 is three years (two to five years).

14.77 For lower-scale advance-fee fraud or other confidence fraud characterized by a degree of planning and/or multiple transactions the starting point based on a sum of £750,000 is five years (range four to seven years), the starting point based on a sum of £300,000 is four years (range three to six years), the starting point based on a sum of £60,000 is three years (two to five years), the starting point based on a sum of £10,000 is eighteen months (range twenty-six weeks to three years).

14.78 For a case involving single fraudulent transaction confidence fraud involving targeting of a vulnerable victim the starting point based on a sum of £60,000 is twenty-six weeks (community order (high) to eighteen months), the starting point based on a sum of £10,000 is six weeks (range community order (medium) to twenty-six weeks).

14.79 For a single fraudulent transaction confidence fraud not targeting a vulnerable victim and involving no or limited planning the starting point based on a sum of £60,000 is twelve weeks (community order (medium) to thirty-six 36 weeks), the starting point based on a sum of £10,000 is community order (medium) (range fine to six weeks).

14.80 *Benefit fraud* is a generic description rather than a specific offence. The guideline assumes that it will be prosecuted under the Fraud Act 2006, section 1, where the maximum penalty is ten years, or false accounting under the Theft Act 1968, section 17, or false representation to obtain benefit under the Security Administration Act 1992, section 111A(1), or failing to disclose a change in circumstances under the 1992 Act section 111A(1A), (1B), (1D), or (1E) where the maximum penalty is seven years. The offence range for benefit fraud is fine to seven years. The guideline is a matrix based on two main factors: the nature of the offence, and the sum of money obtained or intended to be obtained.

14.81 Where the fraud is fraudulent from the outset, professionally planned, and either fraud carried out over a significant period of time or multiple frauds, the starting point based on a sum of £750,000 is five years (range four to seven years), the starting point based on a sum of £300,000 is four years (range three to five years), the starting point based on a sum of £60,000 is two years (eighteen months to three years.

14.82 Where the fraud is fraudulent from the outset and either fraud carried out over a significant period of time or multiple frauds the starting point based on a sum of £750,000 is four years (range three to seven years), the starting point based on a sum of £300,000 is three years (range two to four years), the starting point based on a sum of £60,000 is fifteen months (eighteen weeks to thirty months), the starting point based on a sum of £12,500 is twelve weeks (range community order (high) to one year), the starting point based on a sum of £2500 is community order (high) (range community order (low) to six weeks).

14.83 For a case not fraudulent from the outset and either fraud carried out over a significant period or multiple frauds, the starting point based on a sum of £750,000 is three years (range two to six years), the starting point based on a sum of £300,000 is two years (range one to three years), the starting point based on a sum of £60,000 is thirty-six weeks (twelve weeks to eighteen months), the starting point based on a sum of £12,500 is six weeks (range community order (medium) to twenty-six weeks), the starting point based on a sum of £2500 is community order (medium) (range fine to community order (high)).

For a single fraudulent transaction, fraudulent from the outset, the starting point based **14.84** on a sum of £60,000 is twenty-six weeks (six weeks to twelve months), the starting point based on a sum of £12,500 is community order (high) (range fine to eighteen weeks), the starting point based on a sum of £2500 is community order (low) (range fine—community order (medium)).

For a single fraudulent transaction, not fraudulent from the outset, the starting point based **14.85** on a sum of £60,000 is twelve weeks (community order (medium) to thirty-six weeks), the starting point based on a sum of £12,500 is community order (medium) (range fine to six weeks), the starting point based on a sum of £2500 is a fine (range fine to community order (low)).

D SENTENCING FOR CERTAIN DRUGS OFFENCES

The Sentencing Council guideline *Drug Offences* applies. It applies to offenders aged **14.86** eighteen or over who have been convicted after a trial. This guideline covers importation (fraudulent evasion of a prohibition by bringing into or taking out of the UK a controlled drug under the Misuse of Drugs Act 1971, section 3 and the Customs and Excise Management Act 1979, section 170(2)), where the maximum penalty (for Class A drugs) is life imprisonment; supplying or offering to supply a controlled drug under the MDA 1971, section 4(3) or possession of a controlled drug with intent to supply under the MDA 1971, section 5(3), where the maximum penalty (for Class A drugs) is life imprisonment; production of a controlled drug under the MDA 1971, section 4(2)(a) or (b), where the maximum penalty (for Class A drugs) is life imprisonment; cultivation of a cannabis plant under the MDA 1971, section 6(2), where the maximum penalty is fourteen years; permitting premises to be used, under the MDA 1971, section 8 where the maximum penalty (for Class A drugs) is fourteen years; and possession of a controlled drug under the MDA 1971, section 5(2), where the maximum penalty (for Class A drugs) is seven years. Only the guidelines for possession with intent to supply and possession are considered here, and only in relation to Class A and Class B drugs.

The Court of Appeal in *Healey* [2013] 1 Cr App R (S) 176 provided a detailed explanation **14.87** of the proper approach of the courts to the *Drug Offences* guideline. Hughes LJ said that the task of the sentencer was to read the guidelines for what they were, and it was not open to a judge to prefer and apply appellate guidance which pre-dated the guidelines. His Lordship also said,

> [t]he format which is adopted by the Sentencing Council in producing its guidelines is to present the broad categories of offence frequently encountered pictorially in boxes. It may be that the pictorial boxes which are part of the presentation may lead a superficial reader to think that adjacent boxes are mutually exclusive, one of the other. They are not. There is an inevitable overlap between the scenarios which are described in adjacent boxes. In real life, offending is found on a sliding scale of gravity with few hard lines. The guidelines set out to describe such sliding scales and graduations. In these guidelines, as in almost all such, there is a recognition that the two principal factors which affect sentencing for crime can broadly be collected together as, first, the harm the offence does, and secondly, the culpability of the offender…Quantity, which is a broad appreciation of harm, may well colour participation, which is a broad appreciation of culpability, and vice versa. What we have just said about

sliding scales applies equally to both elements, both to culpability and to harm. In neither case do the boxes have hard edges.

14.88 These remarks were endorsed Lady Justice Hallett in *A-G's Refs (Nos 15, 16 & 17 of 2012)* [2012] EWCA Crim 1414, where it was said that the Council's choice of words in categorizing the role of an offender within a drugs hierarchy (leading, significant, lesser) was not intended to be a change in substance from earlier sentencing practice.

Possession of controlled drug with intent to supply

14.89 The maximum penalty (Class A) is life imprisonment, and the offence range is community order to sixteen years. For Class B drugs the maximum penalty is fourteen years and the offence range is fine to ten years. For Class C drugs the maximum penalty is fourteen years and the offence range is fine to eight years. A sentence passed outside this range is a departure from the guideline and the court must give reasons why it would be contrary to the interests of justice to sentence within the offence range (CJA 2003, section 174(6)). As with all SC guidelines the court must at step 1 determine the offence category by assessing the degree of harm (greater or lesser) which in this case is based on an indicative quantity of the drug involved and the level of culpability (higher or lower) which in this case is demonstrated by the offender's role in the offence. In this guideline there are four categories of harm and three categories of culpability: leading role, significant role, and lesser role for each class of drug, leading to a matrix with twelve cells for each class of drug. A closed list of factors is provided in the guideline. At step 2 the court must then consider the non-exhaustive list of factors set out in the guideline as increasing seriousness or as reducing seriousness or reflecting personal mitigation. The presence of aggravating or mitigating factors entitle the judge in a particular case to move up or down within the category range or to move into a different category from that selected at step 1. At step 2 the court must make any appropriate upward adjustment to reflect the presence of relevant previous convictions, or downward movement to reflect their absence. At step 4 an appropriate reduction should be made for a guilty plea.

14.90 For Class A cases, section 110 of the PCC(S)A 2000 provides that a court should impose a minimum sentence of at least seven years' imprisonment for a third Class A drug trafficking offence except where the court is of the opinion that there are particular circumstances which relate to any of the offences or to the offender and would make it unjust to do so in all the circumstances.

14.91 For Class A drugs for category 1 the starting points are fourteen years for a leading role (range twelve to sixteen years), ten years for a significant role (range nine to twelve years), and seven years for a lesser role (range six-to-nine years). For category 2 the starting points are eleven years for a leading role (range nine to thirteen years), eight years for a significant role (range six-and-a-half years to ten years), and five years for a lesser role (range three-and-a-half to seven years). For category 3 the starting points are eight-and-a-half years for a leading role (range six-and-a-half years to ten years), four-and-a-half years for a significant role (range three-and-a-half years to seven years), and three years for a lesser role (range two to four-and-a-half years). For category 4 the starting points are five-and-a-half years for a leading role (range four-and-a-half years to seven-and-a-half years), three-and-a-half years for a significant role (range two years to five years) and eighteen months for a lesser role (range high level community order three years).

14.92 For Class B drugs for category 1 the starting points are eight years for a leading role (range seven to ten years), five-and-a-half years for a significant role (range five to seven years) and 3 years for a lesser role (range two-and-a-half years to five years). For category 2 the starting points are six years for a leading role (range four-and-a-half years to eight years), four years for a significant role (range two-and-a-half years to five years), and one year for a lesser role (range twenty-six weeks to three years). For category 3 the starting points are four years for a leading role (range two-and-a-half years to five years), one year for a significant role (range twenty-six weeks to three years), and high-level community order for a lesser role (range low-level community order to twenty-six weeks). For category 4 the starting points are eighteen months for a leading role (range twenty-six weeks to three years), high-level community order for a significant role (range medium-level community order to twenty-six weeks) and low-level community order for a lesser role (range band B fine to medium-level community order).

The Court of Appeal has made it clear in *Dyer* [2013] EWCA Crim 2114 that appellate **14.93** cases which pre-dated the sentencing guidelines should not be relied upon, especially the cases of *Dhajit* [1999] 2 Cr App R (S) 142 and *Afonso* [2005] 1 Cr App R (S) 99, which had been prominent in the pre-guideline decisions. The Court said that the drug guidelines were designed to achieve more consistent sentencing in cases involving drugs. Provided judges followed and applied the guidelines properly different sentencing outcomes between co-defendants or amongst defendants arrested as part of a particular police operation, or in different cases across the country, could form no basis for an appeal based upon disparity of sentence. Decisions of the Court of Appeal subsequent to the guidelines might help to interpret the guideline, and provide practical illustrations of its application including circumstances where the interests of justice might require a departure from it. Leveson LJ in *Dyer* also stressed the particular provision in the guideline on possession with intent to supply, which was that in cases of 'street dealing' (including sale of drugs to undercover police officers) the harm caused was not quantified by the amount of the drug involved. Such cases went immediately into category 3. A street dealer who was funding his own habit was motivated by financial advantage and therefore played a significant role for the purposes of assessing his culpability under the guideline. That leads (assuming Class A drugs) to a starting point of four-and-a-half years and a category range of three-and-a-half years to seven years. Drug purity becomes relevant at step 2 in the guideline, together with all relevant aggravating and mitigating factors (including but not limited to those listed). Supply of a controlled drug to a serving prisoner is a significant aggravating factor. See *AG's Reference (No 34 of 2011)* [2012] 1 Cr App R (S) 288 and *Sanchez-Canadas* [2013] 1 Cr App R (S) 588 for examples. Then, of course, there should be appropriate reduction for a guilty plea.

Possession of controlled drug

The maximum penalty (Class A) is seven years, and the offence range is fine to fifty-one **14.94** weeks. For Class B drugs the maximum penalty is five years and the offence range is discharge to twenty-six weeks. For Class C drugs the maximum penalty is two years and the offence range is discharge to community order. A sentence passed outside this range is a departure from the guideline and the court must give reasons why it would be contrary to the interests of justice to sentence within the offence range (CJA 2003, section 174(6)). As with all SC guidelines the court must at step 1 determine the offence category, in this case based on the class of drug involved. At step 2 the court must then consider the non-exhaustive list of factors set out in the guideline as increasing seriousness or as reducing seriousness or reflecting personal mitigation. The presence of aggravating or mitigating factors entitles the judge in a particular case to move up or down within the category range or to move into a different category from that selected at step 1. At step 2 the court must make any appropriate upward adjustment to reflect the presence of relevant previous convictions, or downward movement to reflect their absence. At step 4 an appropriate reduction should be made for a guilty plea.

14.95 For category 1 (possession of Class A drug) the starting point is a band C fine (range band A fine to fifty-one weeks). For category 2 (possession of Class B drug) the starting point is a band B fine (range discharge to twenty-six weeks). For category 3 (possession of Class C drug) the starting point is band A fine (range discharge to medium-level community order). The guideline says that where appropriate the court should consider the custody threshold as follows: (i) has the custody threshold been passed? (ii) if so, is it unavoidable that a custodial sentence be imposed? (iii) if so, can that sentence be suspended? Where appropriate the court should also consider whether the community threshold has been passed.

E SENTENCING FOR CERTAIN SEXUAL OFFENCES

14.96 The Sentencing Council guideline *Sexual Offences* applies. It applies to offenders aged eighteen or over who have been convicted after a trial and who are sentenced on after 1 April 2014, when the guideline took effect. This guideline covers more than fifty sexual offences. A press release issued by the Sentencing Council on 12 December 2013 said that the intention of the new guidelines was to reflect more fully the psychological and longer-term effects on the victim. Some offences have higher starting points and ranges than the previous SGC guidelines provided. For example, in relation to rape (see paragraph 14.97, this Chapter) the new guideline allows top category sentences with a starting point of fifteen years. The previous guideline only allowed sentences with this starting point for multiple rapes. In addition the worst cases of assault by penetration can now receive the same sentence as rape. The guideline on indecent images of children has been simplified to place more emphasis on what the offender does with the images—possessing, distributing, or creating—rather than concentrating on the number of images.

Rape

14.97 The maximum penalty for this offence is life (SOA 2003, section 1) This is a serious specified offence for the purposes of the CJA 2003, section 224 (dangerous offenders). The offence range for this offence is four to nineteen years. A sentence passed outside this range is a departure from the guideline and the court must give reasons why it would be contrary to the interests of justice to sentence within the offence range (CJA 2003, section 174(6)). The rape guideline states that offences may be of such seriousness (for example, involving a campaign of rape), that sentences of twenty years and above may be appropriate. As with all SC guidelines the court must at step 1 determine the offence category by assessing the degree of harm (which in this case may fall into one of three categories) and the level of culpability (described as A or B, rather than higher or lower, as in other SC guidelines). Within the harm categories, category 2 provides a closed list of relevant factors—severe psychological or physical harm, pregnancy or STI as a consequence of offence, additional degradation/humiliation, abduction, prolonged detention/sustained incident, violence or threats of violence (beyond that which is inherent in the offence), forced/uninvited entry into victim's home, or victim is particularly vulnerable due to personal circumstances. The harm falls within category 1 where the extreme nature of one or more category 2 factors or the extreme impact caused by a combination of category 2 factors may elevate it to category 1. Category 3 applies where the factor(s) in categories 1 and 2 are not present.

A case falls within culpability level A where there is a significant degree of planning, the offender acts together with others to commit the offence, use of alcohol/drugs on victim to facilitate the offence, abuse of trust, previous violence against victim, offence committed in course of burglary, recording of the offence, commercial exploitation and/or motivation, offence racially or religiously aggravated, offence motivated by, or demonstrating hostility to the victim based on his or her sexual orientation (or presumed sexual orientation) or transgender identity (or presumed transgender identity), or offence motivated by, or demonstrating, hostility to the victim based on his or her disability (or presumed disability). A case will fall into culpability level B if the factor(s) in category A are not present.

These combinations of harm and culpability generate a matrix. For the offence of rape category 1 harm has a starting point of fifteen years (range thirteen to nineteen years) where the culpability falls within A and a starting point of twelve years (range ten to fifteen years) where the culpability falls within B. Category 2 harm has a starting point of ten years (range nine to thirteen years) where the culpability falls within A, and a starting point of eight years (range seven to nine years) where the culpability falls within B. Category 3 harm has a starting point of seven years (range six to nine years) where the culpability falls within A, and a starting point of five years (range four to seven years) where the culpability falls within B. **14.98**

At step 2 the court must then consider the non-exhaustive list of factors set out in the guideline as increasing seriousness or as reducing seriousness or reflecting personal mitigation. The presence of aggravating or mitigating factors entitle the judge in a particular case to move up or down within the category range or to move into a different category from that selected at step 1. At step 2 the guideline stresses that the court must make any appropriate upward adjustment to reflect the presence of relevant previous convictions. At step 4 an appropriate reduction should be made for a guilty plea. **14.99**

Assault by penetration

The maximum penalty for this offence is life (SOA 2003, section 2) This is a serious specified offence for the purposes of the CJA 2003, section 224 (dangerous offenders). The offence range for this offence is community order to nineteen years. A sentence passed outside this range is a departure from the guideline and the court must give reasons why it would be contrary to the interests of justice to sentence within the offence range (CJA 2003, section 174(6)). As with all SC guidelines the court must at step 1 determine the offence category by assessing the degree of harm (which in this case may fall into one of three categories) and the level of culpability (described as A or B, rather than higher or lower, as in other SC guidelines). Within the harm categories, category 2 provides a closed list of relevant factors: severe psychological or physical harm, penetration using large or dangerous objects, additional degradation/humiliation, abduction, prolonged detention/sustained incident, violence or threats of violence (beyond that which is inherent in the offence), forced/uninvited entry into victim's home, or victim is particularly vulnerable due to personal circumstances. The harm falls within category 1 where the extreme nature of one or more category 2 factors or the extreme impact caused by a combination of category 2 factors may elevate it to category 1. Category 3 applies where the factor(s) in categories 1 and 2 are not present. **14.100**

A case falls within culpability level A where there is a significant degree of planning, offender acts together with others to commit the offence, use of alcohol/drugs on victim to facilitate the offence, abuse of trust, previous violence against victim, offence committed in course of burglary, recording of the offence, commercial exploitation and/or motivation, offence racially or religiously aggravated, offence motivated by, or demonstrating hostility to the victim based on his or her sexual orientation (or presumed sexual orientation) or transgender identity (or presumed transgender identity) or offence motivated by, or demonstrating, hostility to the victim based on his or her disability (or presumed disability). A case will fall into culpability level B if the factor(s) in category A are not present.

14.101   These combinations of harm and culpability generate a matrix. For the offence of assault by penetration category 1 harm has a starting point of fifteen years (range thirteen to nineteen years) where the culpability falls within A and a starting point of twelve years (range ten to fifteen years) where the culpability falls within B. Category 2 harm has a starting point of eight years (range five to thirteen years) where the culpability falls within A, and a starting point of six years (range four to nine years) where the culpability falls within B. Category 3 harm has a starting point of four years (range two to six years) where the culpability falls within A, and a starting point of two years (range high-level community order to four years) where the culpability falls within B.

14.102   At step 2 the court must then consider the non-exhaustive list of factors set out in the guideline as increasing seriousness or as reducing seriousness or reflecting personal mitigation. The presence of aggravating or mitigating factors entitle the judge in a particular case to move up or down within the category range or to move into a different category from that selected at step 1. At step 2 the guideline stresses that the court must make any appropriate upward adjustment to reflect the presence of relevant previous convictions. At step 4 an appropriate reduction should be made for a guilty plea.

Sexual assault

14.103   The maximum penalty for this offence is ten years (SOA 2003, section 3). The offence range for this offence is community order to seven years. A sentence passed outside this range is a departure from the guideline and the court must give reasons why it would be contrary to the interests of justice to sentence within the offence range (CJA 2003, section 174(6)). As with all SC guidelines the court must at step 1 determine the offence category by assessing the degree of harm (which in this case may fall into one of three categories) and the level of culpability (described as A or B, rather than higher or lower, as in other SC guidelines). Within the harm categories, category 1 provides a closed list of relevant factors: severe psychological or physical harm, abduction, violence or threats of violence, forced/uninvited entry into victim's home. Category 2 provides a closed list of relevant factors: touching of naked genitalia or naked breasts, prolonged detention/sustained incident, additional degradation/humiliation, or victim is particularly vulnerable due to personal circumstances. Category 3 applies where the factor(s) in categories 1 and 2 are not present. A case falls within culpability level A where there is a significant degree of planning, offender acts together with others to commit the offence, use of alcohol/drugs on victim to facilitate the offence, abuse of trust, previous violence against victim, offence committed in course of burglary, recording of the offence, commercial exploitation and/or motivation, offence racially or religiously aggravated, offence motivated by, or demonstrating hostility to the victim based on his or her sexual orientation (or presumed sexual orientation) or transgender identity (or presumed transgender identity), or offence motivated by, or demonstrating, hostility to the victim based on his or her disability (or presumed disability). A case will fall into culpability level B if the factor(s) in category A are not present.

14.104   These combinations of harm and culpability generate a matrix. For the offence of sexual assault category 1 harm has a starting point of fifteen years (range thirteen to nineteen years) where the culpability falls within A and a starting point of twelve years (range ten to fifteen years) where the culpability falls within B. Category 2 harm has a starting point of eight years (range five to thirteen years) where the culpability falls within A and a starting point of six years (range four to nine years) where the culpability falls within B. Category 3 harm has a starting point of four years (range two to six years) where the culpability falls within A, and a starting point of two years (range-high level community order to four years) where the culpability falls within B.

At step 2 the court must then consider the non-exhaustive list of factors set out in the guide- **14.105** line as increasing seriousness or as reducing seriousness or reflecting personal mitigation. The presence of aggravating or mitigating factors entitle the judge in a particular case to move up or down within the category range or to move into a different category from that selected at step 1. At step 2 the guideline stresses that the court must make any appropriate upward adjustment to reflect the presence of relevant previous convictions. At step 4 an appropriate reduction should be made for a guilty plea.

Indecent photographs of children

There are two possible offences here: possession of an indecent photograph of a child **14.106** (CJA 1988, section 160), and indecent photographs of a child (Protection of Children Act 1978, section 1). The maximum penalty for the former offence is five years. The offence range is community order to three years. The maximum penalty for the latter offence is ten years. The offence range is community order to nine years. A sentence passed outside the offence range is a departure from the guideline and the court must give reasons why it would be contrary to the interests of justice to sentence within the offence range (CJA 2003, section 174(6)). As with all SC guidelines the court must at step 1 determine the offence category by assessing the degree of harm (which in this case may fall into one of three categories A, B, or C, based upon the nature of the images) and the level of culpability (based upon the offender's involvement in the offence as being possession, distribution, or production of the images). Distribution includes possession with a view to distributing or sharing the images. Production includes the taking or making or any image at source, but making an image by simple downloading should be treated as possession for sentencing purposes.

These combinations of harm and culpability generate a matrix. For these offences category **14.107** A is concerned with images involving penetrative sexual activity or images involving sexual activity with an animal, or sadism. For possession, the starting point is one year (range twenty-six weeks to three years), for distribution the starting point is three years (range two to five years) and for production the starting point is six years (range four to nine years). Category B is concerned with images involving non-penetrative sexual activity. For possession, the starting point is twenty-six weeks (range high-level community order to eighteen months), for distribution the starting point is one year (range twenty-six weeks to two years) and for production the starting point is two years (range one to four years). Category C is concerned with other images not falling within A or B. For possession, the starting point is high level community order (range medium level community order to twenty-six weeks), for distribution the starting point is thirteen weeks (range high-level community order to twenty-six weeks) and for production the starting point is eighteen months (range one to three years). The guideline says that when sentencing appropriate category 2 or 3 offences the court should consider the custody threshold as follows: (i) has the custody threshold been passed? (ii) if so, is it unavoidable that a custodial sentence be imposed? (iii) if so, can that sentence be suspended?

At step 2 the court must then consider the non-exhaustive list of factors set out in the guide- **14.108** line as increasing seriousness or as reducing seriousness or reflecting personal mitigation. The presence of aggravating or mitigating factors entitle the judge in a particular case to move up or down within the category range or to move into a different category from that selected at step 1. Specified aggravating factors include age and/or vulnerability of child depicted, discernible pain or distress suffered by child depicted, period over which images were possessed, distributed or produced, high volume of images possessed, distributed or produced, placing images where there is the potential for a high volume of viewers, collection includes moving images, active involvement in a network, commercial exploitation and/or motivation, large number of different victims. At step 2 the guideline stresses that the court must make any appropriate upward adjustment to reflect the presence of relevant previous convictions. At step 4 an appropriate reduction should be made for a guilty plea.

F SENTENCING FOR CERTAIN OTHER OFFENCES

14.109 On offences relating to public order, there are no sentencing guidelines but the leading decisions of the Court of Appeal are *Caird* (1970) 54 Cr App R 499 on the offence of riot, and on public disorder more generally see *Blackshaw* [2012] 1 WLR 1126.

14.110 On offences relating to firearms there are no sentencing guidelines, but the leading decision of the Court of Appeal is *Avis* [1998] 1 Cr App R (S) 420, as qualified in relation to the most serious offences by *Wilkinson* [2010] 1 Cr App R (S) 628. On possession of offensive weapons the leading authority is *Celaire* [2003] 1 Cr App R (S) 610, as refined and developed in *Povey* [2009] 1 Cr App R (S) 228 especially in relation to the carrying of knives.

14.111 On offences against the administration of justice, there are no sentencing guidelines but the leading decisions of the Court of Appeal are *Archer* [2003] 1 Cr App R (S) 446 on perjury in the face of the court, *Mitchell* [2003] 1 Cr App R (S) 508 on perverting the course of justice, *AG's Reference No 16 of 2009(Yates)* [2010] 2 Cr App R (S) 64 on assisting an offender, *Purchase* [2008] 1 Cr App R (S) 338 on escape from lawful custody, and *AG v Dallas* [2012] 1 WLR 991 on contempt by a juror.

14.112 On offences involving corruption there are no sentencing guidelines but the leading decision of the Court of Appeal is *Dougall* [2011] 1 Cr App R (S) 227.

14.113 On offences involving misuse of computers there are no sentencing guidelines but the leading decisions of the Court of Appeal are *Martin* [2013] EWCA Crim 1420, and *Lewis* [2010] 2 Cr App R (S) 666 (the latter charged as misconduct in public office).

14.114 On immigration offences there are no sentencing guidelines but the leading decision of the Court of Appeal is *Le and Stark* [1999] 1 Cr App R (S) 422 on assisting illegal entry, applied in *Oliveira* [2012] EWCA Crim 2279 in the context of sham marriages. Guidance on sentencing for the offence of trafficking people for exploitation was provided in *AG's References (Nos 37, 38, & 65 of 2010)* [2010] EWCA Crim 2880.

KEY DOCUMENTS[1]

David Thomas, *Current Sentencing Practice*, 4 volumes, (London: Sweet & Maxwell, 2013).

Criminal Justice Act 2003, schedule 21.

Sentencing Guidelines Council, Definitive Guideline, *Overarching Principles: Seriousness* (effective December 2004).

Sentencing Guidelines Council, Definitive Guideline, *Manslaughter by Reason of Provocation* (effective 29 November 2005).

Sentencing Guidelines Council, Definitive Guideline, *Robbery* (effective 1 August 2006).

---

[1] All sentencing guidelines can be found on the Sentencing Council website: <http://sentencing council.judiciary.gov.uk/>.

Sentencing Guidelines Council, Definitive Guideline, *Domestic Violence* (effective 18 December 2006).

Sentencing Guidelines Council, Definitive Guideline, *Causing Death by Driving* (effective 4 August 2008).

Sentencing Guidelines Council, Definitive Guideline, *Theft* (effective 5 January 2009).

Sentencing Guidelines Council, Definitive Guideline, *Attempted Murder* (effective 27 July 2009).

Sentencing Guidelines Council, Definitive Guideline, *Fraud—Statutory Offences* (effective 26 October 2009).

Sentencing Council, Definitive Guideline, *Assault (Crown Court)* (effective 13 June 2011).

Sentencing Council, Definitive Guideline, *Burglary Offences* (effective 16 January 2012).

Sentencing Council, Definitive Guideline, *Drugs Offences* (effective 27 February 2012).

Sentencing Council, Definitive Guideline, *Sexual Offences* (effective 1 April 2014).

15

SENTENCING APPEALS AND THE STATUTORY CONSEQUENCES OF CONVICTION

15.01 This Chapter considers the arrangements for appeal against sentences passed by the magistrates' courts and by the Crown Court. The Court of Appeal is for most purposes the final court in determining appeals in sentencing matters. Very few cases reach the Supreme Court. The main reason for that is that appeal to the Supreme Court is only possible where the case raises a point of law of general public importance. This is rare in sentencing cases, since normally the issue is whether the judge has very substantially over-sentenced or under-sentenced the offender. That is a matter of the proper application of sentencing guidelines and the proper exercise of judicial discretion, rather than a matter of law. Many Court of Appeal decisions are narrowly confined to that issue in relation to the case before the court. Sometimes, however, as we saw in Chapter 14, the Court will take the opportunity to issue more general comment and guidance on a particular sentencing issue which involves travelling well beyond the instant facts of the case or cases before it. These decisions are of particular importance, and many such cases have been referred to in earlier chapters of this book. It is time now to consider in more detail the operation of appeals in sentencing cases.

15.02 This Chapter also covers a number of statutory provisions which apply automatically once a person has been convicted of an offence. Some of these apply in every case, while others apply only where conviction for a particular offence, or the imposition of a particular form of sentence, has occurred. We deal with sex offender notification, disqualification from working in future with children or vulnerable adults, and other automatic consequences such as removal of the right to vote from convicted prisoners. The provisions of the Rehabilitation of Offenders Act 1974 are also considered.

A APPEAL AGAINST SENTENCE PASSED BY A MAGISTRATES' COURT

Most appeals against sentence passed by a magistrates' court are heard by the Crown **15.03**
Court. A small minority are heard by the Administrative Court. These methods of appeal
are the same whether the sentence was passed for a summary offence or for an offence
triable either way, and irrespective of whether the sentence was passed in the youth court
or the adult magistrates' court. It should be noted that appeals against sentence imposed
by the magistrates' court lie on behalf of the convicted and sentenced defendant only. The
prosecution has no right of appeal as such against a sentencing decision of the lower court.
Save for a narrow exception involving the prosecution taking the matter to the High Court,
there is no possibility of a prosecution appeal against an unduly lenient sentence passed by
the magistrates. It is thus a one-sided system of appeal. This may be thought somewhat odd,
in that if a sentence was incorrect it should be amenable to remedy irrespective of whether it
was too high or too low. A possible answer is that within a system where for time and other
practical reasons only a limited number of appeals can be catered for, it is more important
to remedy mistakes which are to the detriment of the individual offender rather than those
which disappoint society more broadly.

Appeals to the Crown Court

Only the offender may appeal, and he may be appealing solely against sentence or he may **15.04**
be appealing against conviction and sentence. As we have seen there is no right of prosecution appeal. The offender's right of appeal is automatic, and lies without any requirement
of obtaining leave to appeal (Magistrates' Courts Act (MCA) 1980, section 108). Appeal
lies against a sentence on the ground that it was too high, or that in some respect it was
unlawful or invalid. Notice has to be given to the clerk of the magistrates' court which
passed the sentence, within twenty-one days of being sentenced, that the offender intends
to appeal. Further detail is provided by the Criminal Procedure Rules (CPR), rule 63.3 and
63.4. The appeal notice must be in writing and must specify the sentence or order about
which the offender wishes to appeal, summarize the issues, and say whether the magistrates' court has been asked to reconsider the case. The clerk of the magistrates' court must
serve on the Crown Court officer the appeal notice, details of the parties, and a copy of
the relevant entry from the register of the magistrates' court which made the order. Section
108 provides that the offender can appeal against any sentence or order made by the magistrates, apart from:

(a) an order to pay prosecution costs (*Tottenham JJ, ex parte Joshi* (1982) 75 Cr App R 72),
     or
(b) an order made in pursuance of any enactment under which the court has no discretion
     as to the making of the order or its terms (an example might be a referral order by a
     youth court where the compulsory referral conditions are made out).

For the avoidance of doubt, appeal does lie against a magistrates' court's decision to:

(a) impose an absolute or conditional discharge (MCA 1980, section 108(1A)), notwith-
     standing the PCC(S)A 2000, section 14 (under which a conviction for which an ab-
     solute or conditional discharge is passed is deemed not to be a conviction except for
     certain purposes);
(b) make a declaration of relevance within the meaning of section 23 of the Football
     Spectators Act 1989 (MCA 1980, section 108(3));
(c) impose a surcharge under section 161A of the CJA 2003 (MCA 1989, section 180(4)).

15.05 Amongst the *many* other specific sentencing provisions granting a right of appeal to the Crown Court are those relating to disqualification from driving (Road Traffic Offenders Act 1988, section 34 or section 35); making a recommendation for deportation (Immigration Act 1971, section 6(5)); making a hospital order without proceeding to conviction (MHA 1983, section 45(1)); imposing a financial order on a parent or guardian of a young offender (PCC(S)A 2000, section 137(7)); imposing a parenting order (Crime and Disorder Act (CDA) 1998, section 10(1)); binding over the offender to keep the peace (Magistrates' Courts (Appeals from Binding Over Orders) 1956, section 1); imposing a restraining order consequent upon conviction or acquittal (Prevention of Harassment Act 1997, section 5 and section 5A); or ordering the destruction of an animal (Animal Welfare Act 2006, section 37(4)).

15.06 The appeal will always be heard by a Crown Court judge, who will usually be a circuit judge or a recorder (who must of course be approved or 'ticketed' to hear appeals) sitting with no fewer than two and not more than four lay justices. Almost always two justices take part. The involvement of the lay justices in the appeal process is important to ensure that the judge is fully aware of the relevant magistrates' court sentencing guidelines and sentencing practice more generally. Of course neither of the justices must have been involved in the original decision. The position is slightly different if the appeal is from a youth court, in which case each justice of the peace present must be qualified to sit as a member of the youth court and the Crown Court bench must include at least one man and one woman (unless the judge decides that the appeal can proceed with only one justice present or without the bench including a man and a woman because the appeal will otherwise be delayed unreasonably). Further detailed rules are set out in the CPR, rule 63.10. Any objection to the constitution of the Court must be made before proceedings begin (Senior Courts Act 1981, section 8(2)). Whenever a Crown Court judge sits with lay justices the latter should take a full part, and be seen to take a full part, in the proceedings. In the event of disagreement, the majority view prevails. Thus in theory the magistrates can out-vote the judge. The magistrates must, however, accept any directions from the judge on any point of law which arises in the appeal (*Orpin* [1975] QB 283).

15.07 An appellant may abandon the appeal by serving an appropriate notice before the hearing of the appeal begins. After the hearing has begun the appeal may be abandoned only with the permission of the Crown Court (RSC, rule 63.8). A failure on the part of the appellant to turn up at the Crown Court (which happens not infrequently) is not an abandonment of the appeal (*R (Hayes) v Chelmsford Crown Court* (2003) 167 JP 65). In those circumstances, even where the appellant's legal representative is present, the almost inevitable outcome is that the Court dismisses the appeal and requires the appellant to pay the prosecution costs incurred. However, if no notice of abandonment has been given and the appellant's lawyer is in court, the Crown Court may decide to hear the appeal in the appellant's absence (*Croydon Crown Court, ex parte Clair* (1986) 83 Cr App R 202).

15.08 The appeal takes the form of a re-hearing of the sentencing stage of the trial, so that it is not, as such, a review of the original decision. There may be additional evidence before the court that was not available to the magistrates, or a new or updated report. Arguments which were not canvassed by the lawyers in the lower court may be relied upon in the appeal. This leads to the logical conclusion (as set out in the *Criminal Practice Directions*, 63A.3) that 'reasons for the sentence imposed should be omitted' from the documents before the appellate court. Sometimes the appellant appears unrepresented. It is the usual etiquette for the lawyer acting for the respondent to make clear to the court (if the appellant is unable to do so) what point the appellant relies upon. The court may also assist an unrepresented appellant in making their point, but it is not for the judge to argue either side of a case if a lawyer has not been instructed, or fails to appear (*Wood Green Crown Court, ex parte Taylor* [1995] Crim LR 879). Section 83 of the PCC(S)A 2000, which places restrictions on a court imposing a custodial sentence on an unrepresented offender, also applies in this context (*R (Ebert) v Wood Green Crown Court* [2013] EWHC 917 (Admin)).

The Crown Court may confirm the sentence which was originally passed and dismiss the **15.09** appeal, or it may reduce the sentence, or it may *increase* it up to the maximum sentence which the magistrates could have imposed at first instance (Senior Courts Act 1981, section 48). Unlike the Court of Appeal, the Crown Court enjoys the power to increase sentence on appeal. Any part of the original sentence can be increased, even though the appellant has not appealed against that part. The power to increase sentence may not be exercised very often but, given that no leave to appeal is required, the possibility of increasing sentence on appeal probably acts as a deterrent to frivolous appeals. Further, whenever an appeal fails the unsuccessful appellant can be ordered to pay the prosecution costs. The Crown Court should not increase sentence without first giving a warning of its intention to do so (*R (Tottman) v DPP* [2004] EWHC 258 Admin). If the Crown Court takes the view early on in the appeal that the appeal is without merit and that the appellant was, if anything, leniently dealt with, the court may remind the appellant's advocate of the court's power to increase sentence. That may focus the mind, and prompt an abandonment of the appeal. Once abandoned, however, the Court cannot alter the sentence. All of these points apply equally where the appellant does not turn up, but their legal representative does, and the Crown Court decides to press ahead and decide the appeal.

In announcing its decision on an appeal from the magistrates' court the Crown Court will **15.10** normally give brief oral reasons which are not reported. Occasionally in a more complex case the court may issue a more detailed judgment, sometimes in written form, but again such judgments are not reported. It can be seen that appeal to the Crown Court provides a quick and convenient way of correcting sentencing errors made by the lower court. A note of the Crown Court's decision and a short summary of the reasons for that decision will be sent from the Crown Court to the clerk of the magistrates' court concerned. The clerk may wish to show this to the magistrates who made the original decision. Beyond that, since these appellate decisions are unreported, they provide no general sentencing guidance for the lower courts. An unsuccessful appellant may well be required to pay the prosecution's costs (Prosecution of Offences Act 1985, section 18(1)(b)). A successful applicant may be awarded his costs (section 16(3)).

A decision of the Crown Court on an appeal from the magistrates may itself be appealed by **15.11** way of case stated in the same circumstances as a decision by magistrates may be appealed. Judicial review may also be available.

Appeal to the High Court: case stated

Either the offender or the prosecution may appeal to the Divisional Court of the Queen's **15.12** Bench Division of the High Court against a sentencing decision made by a magistrates' court. The appeal must be on either of the grounds that the sentence was wrong in law or that it was in excess of jurisdiction (MCA 1980, section 111). Appeals to the High Court are relatively rare because whilst many offenders might claim that they were sentenced by the magistrates more severely than they should have been, only a handful could claim that the magistrates demonstrably approached their sentencing task on the wrong legal basis or passed a sentence which was beyond their lawful powers. If the offender's complaint is simply that he was sentenced too severely, his proper recourse is to appeal to the Crown Court. Indeed, if an appellant loses his right of appeal to the High Court he closes his right of appeal to the Crown Court (MCA 1980, section 111(4)). The threshold is high.

An appellant will succeed in such an application only where the sentence imposed by the magistrates was 'harsh and oppressive' or 'truly astonishing' (*Tucker v DPP* [1992] 4 All ER 901). The imposition of such a sentence shows that the magistrates must have made an error of law.

15.13   This method of appeal is known as appeal by 'case stated'. The magistrates, on application by the appellant made within twenty-one days, are required to draw up a document listing the facts which they found proved, the question of law or jurisdiction upon which the view of the High Court is sought, and their own ruling on the matter. In practice this task will be undertaken by the clerk to the justices, assisted by the bench which made the decision, although if the court which made the original decision contained a district judge no additional legal advice may be necessary. The twenty-one-day period is strict, and cannot be varied, even by the High Court itself (MCA 1980, section 111(2)). The application must specify the decision in issue, specify the proposed question on which the opinion of the High Court is sought and indicate the proposed grounds of appeal. The procedure for the serving of an application is dealt with in some detail in the Criminal Procedure Rules, rule 64. It is open to the magistrates to refuse to state a case on the basis that the application is frivolous, but such refusal is rare.

15.14   The hearing in the High Court generally takes the form of legal argument based on the facts set out in the case which the magistrates have stated (rather than being a re-hearing). The High Court must consist of at least two High Court judges (Supreme Court Act 1981, section 6(3)). Often three judges sit, and may include the Lord Chief Justice and, at his request, Lords Justices of Appeal. There is then a considerable overlap of personnel between the Administrative Court and the Court of Appeal. Full, reasoned judgments are given, which are reported. If a two judge court is evenly divided, the appeal fails (*Flannagan v Shaw* [1920] 3 KB 96). Section 111 of the MCA 1980 also states that, in addition to the offender and the prosecution, '[a]ny person who...is aggrieved by the conviction, order, determination, or other proceeding of the court' may state a case for the Administrative Court. It is thus possible that the victim of an offence who feels aggrieved by the sentence passed by the magistrates, or by their failure to make a compensation order in the victim's favour, might take a complaint to the High Court in this way.

15.15   In disposing of an appeal the High Court may 'reverse, affirm or amend' the magistrates' decision, remit the matter to them with their opinion thereon, or make any other order it thinks fit (SCA 1981, section 28A). Thus, to take an example frequently encountered in practice, if the prosecution appeals against the magistrates' refusal to disqualify for an offence carrying obligatory disqualification, the High Court could send the case back to the magistrates with its opinion that the facts relied upon by the motorist concerned were not capable in law of amounting to special reasons for not disqualifying. The magistrates would then have to disqualify for at least the minimum period. In other cases, where it is plain what the proper sentence should have been, the High Court may simply substitute the correct sentence for the original sentence.

15.16   A decision of the Crown Court on appeal from a magistrates' court may be appealed by way of case stated in the same circumstances as a decision by the magistrates may be appealed (Senior Courts Act 1981, section 28). An application for judicial review might also be made (SCA 1981, section 29).

Application to the High Court: Judicial Review

15.17   One of the tasks of the High Court is to supervise the work of lower tribunals. In doing so the High Court exercises its powers of judicial review to control the way on which a wide variety of courts, tribunals, and other persons who are under a duty to act judicially, exercise their powers. The relevant orders are a mandatory order, compelling the lower court to exercise its proper jurisdiction, a prohibiting order, to restrain it from proceeding improperly, and a quashing order, to quash any order which has been made improperly. Judicial review is available in respect of all decisions taken by magistrates, including sentencing decisions. It is also available with respect to decisions of the Crown Court, but only when that court is not exercising its jurisdiction in relation to a trial on indictment. That means that judicial review is not available in respect of a sentencing decision made by the Crown Court at first instance (*R (CPS) v Guildford Crown Court* [2007] 1 WLR 2886). As an alternative to appealing by way of case stated, a person having 'sufficient interest' in the matter (which certainly includes the offender and the prosecution) who considers that a sentence passed by a magistrates' court or by the Crown Court on appeal from the magistrates, was outside the scope of the court's powers, may apply for judicial review of the decision which was made. While the offender and the prosecution clearly have sufficient interest to make an application, it seems that other persons, such as the victim of the offence, might have such an interest. The application is to the Divisional Court of the Queen's Bench Division of the High Court, which may quash the sentence and replace it with whatever sentence it considers appropriate (SCA 1981, section 31(5) and section 43). As with appeal by case stated, the normal appeal process should have been exhausted before such an application is made.

The permission of the High Court must be obtained before a claim for judicial review **15.18** is made. A claim must be made promptly, and in any case within three months after the grounds to make the claim first arose.

Although applications for judicial review are not usually an appropriate means of appeal- **15.19** ing against sentence (*Allen v West Yorkshire Probation Service* [2001] EWHC 2), there are some cases where sentencing decisions have been quashed in this way. A sentence can be quashed if an error of law has clearly been perpetrated (*Liverpool Crown Court, ex parte Baird* (1985) 7 Cr App R (S) 437) or the decision is irrational (*Chelmsford Crown Court, ex parte Birchall* (1989) 11 Cr App R (S) 510). It was held in *St Albans Crown Court, ex parte Cinnamond* [1981] QB 480 that if magistrates pass a sentence which is far above the normal level of sentence for the offence in question, such that it may fairly be described as 'harsh and oppressive', they thereby err in law or act in excess of jurisdiction, and consequently the Divisional Court has power to reduce the sentence, even though it was within the magistrates' statutory powers.

On the face of it, the case stated and judicial review procedures are available in very similar **15.20** circumstances, and are likely to produce the same result. It seems that where both case stated and judicial review might be available to an applicant, the former is the preferable course to choose because it enables the facts found by the magistrates, or by the Crown Court, to be placed more conveniently and squarely before the High Court. The upshot of *R(P) v Liverpool City Magistrates* (2006) 170 JP 453 is that, for many cases involving alleged error of law, case stated is the normal route. It would be wrong to pursue judicial review simply to take advantage of the less stringent time limits. The same point was made in *R (White) v Blackfriars Crown Court* [2008] 2 Cr App R (S) 542, where Richards LJ said that the Court should be slow to entertain an application for judicial review as an alternative to an appeal by case stated just because the time limit for an appeal has been missed even if (as in that case) the fault lay with the applicant's solicitors and not with the applicant personally. Judicial review should be available in such a case only where 'serious injustice' would otherwise occur.

B APPEAL BY OFFENDER AGAINST SENTENCE PASSED BY THE CROWN COURT

15.21   Appeals against sentences passed by the Crown Court are heard by the Court of Appeal (Criminal Division). This is so whether the sentence was passed following the offender's conviction on indictment or following his summary conviction and committal to the Crown Court for sentence.

15.22   All the Lords Justices of Appeal are members of the Court of Appeal (Criminal Division) (SCA 1981, section 2(2)). In addition, the Division has certain ex officio members, notably the Lord Chief Justice, who is its president (SCA 1981, section 3(2)). Although all the Lords Justices are entitled to sit in the Criminal Division, in practice only a minority do so, chiefly those who have had experience of the criminal courts either at the Bar or as a judge of first instance. The Lords Justices are assisted by High Court judges who may be requested (in effect, required) to act as judges of the Criminal Division (section 9(1)). Much of the Division's work is, in fact, carried out by High Court judges. Of course a judge is not allowed to be involved in any way in the disposal of an appeal against sentence which he imposed when sitting as a Crown Court judge (section 56(2)). Any number of courts of the Criminal Division may sit at any one time (section 3(5)). For the purposes of determining an appeal against sentence, a court is validly constituted if it contains at least two judges qualified to sit in that Division (section 55(4)). Decisions may be taken by a majority, but if a two-judge court is divided the case must be reassigned and re-argued before three judges (section 55(5)). Only one judgment is given, that being pronounced either by the senior judge or such other member of the court as he directs to pronounce it (section 59). It is also common also for senior circuit judges, experienced in criminal matters, to be invited to sit in the Criminal Division. It should be noted that many ancillary decisions connected with an appeal (eg granting leave to appeal) do not have to go before a court but may be taken by a single judge, either a Lord Justice or a High Court judge, as requested by the Lord Chief Justice to act as a judge of the Criminal Division (see Criminal Appeal Act 1968, section 31). The administration of the Division's work is in the hands of an official, the Registrar of Criminal Appeals, and his staff. The duties of the Registrar in relation to the handling of criminal appeals including appeals against sentence, are set out in the Criminal Procedure Rules.

15.23   As a result of the broad definition of 'sentence' contained in the CAA 1968, section 50(1), almost any order made by a Crown Court judge in respect of a convicted offender is capable of being the subject of an appeal to the Court of Appeal. This is so whether the order is a punishment or is an ancillary order. For the avoidance of doubt, all of the following sentences or orders are capable of being the subject of an appeal by virtue of the definition in section 50(1):

(a)   a hospital order, with or without a restriction order, an interim hospital order, and a hospital direction and a limitation direction, all under the MHA 1983;

(b)   a recommendation for deportation;

(c)   a financial reporting order (*Adam* [2008] EWCA Crim 914);

(d)   a deferment of sentence (*A-G's Reference (Nos 36 and 38 of 1998)* [1999] 2 Cr App R (S) 7);

(e)   a surcharge (*Stone* [2013] EWCA Crim 723).

15.24   It seems that the only sentence against which there is no possibility of an appeal is the mandatory sentence of life imprisonment, custody for life, or detention at Her Majesty's pleasure which, depending on the age of the offender, must be passed on an offender convicted of murder. Although the sentence as such cannot be appealed, the minimum term set by the trial judge can be the subject of an appeal, whether by the offender on the basis that it was too high or by the Attorney General on the basis that it was too low. See *Sullivan* [2004] EWCA Crim 1762. The passing of a mandatory sentence for murder may also be subject to appeal where an issue of compliance with the ECHR is said to arise. Thus the Grand Chamber of the European Court of Human Rights has held that the imposition of a 'whole life minimum term' in a murder case contravenes Article 3 of the ECHR (*Vinter v UK* [2013] ECHR 645), but the Court of Appeal in *A-G's Reference (No 69 of 2013)* [2014] EWCA Crim 188 has disagreed. The Court found that the Secretary of State's power to release a life sentence prisoner in exceptional circumstances on compassionate grounds was sufficient to ensure that English law was compliant with the Convention.

Subject to obtaining the Court of Appeal's leave to appeal, an offender convicted on indictment may appeal to the Court of Appeal against any sentence passed on him for the offence (CAA 1968, section 9). Appeal lies against the imposition of a restraining order, consequent upon conviction or acquittal (Prevention of Harassment Act 1997, section 5 and section 5A). Again subject to obtaining leave an offender who was convicted or pleaded guilty in the magistrates' court and was then committed by magistrates to the Crown Court to be sentenced may appeal to the Court of Appeal against the Crown Court's sentence, but only if: **15.25**

(a) the sentence was one of custody for six months or more;
(b) a suspended sentence was brought into effect;
(c) the offender was disqualified from driving;
(d) a recommendation for deportation was made, or
(e) the sentence is one which the convicting court had no power to pass (CAA 1968, section 10).

Where the Crown Court has passed two or more sentences on the offender an application for leave to appeal against any one of the sentences is treated as an application in respect of all of them (section 11(2)). Appeals to the Court of Appeal normally require the leave of that Court (CAA 1968, section 11). It seems that leave is needed, even in a case where the trial court did not have power to pass the sentence that it did. The only exception to the requirement for leave is the unusual situation where the Crown Court judge who has just passed the sentence then grants a certificate that the case is fit for an appeal against sentence without the leave of the Court of Appeal (section 11(1) and (1A)). This occurs very infrequently (an exceptional case is *Grant* (1990) 12 Cr App R (S) 441). Another possible example is where the judge has interpreted legislation in a way which may be incompatible with a convention right under the ECHR, and grants a certificate in order for the Court of Appeal to consider whether a declaration of incompatibility might be made (which the Crown Court does not have power to make). So, for all practical purposes, leave of the Court of Appeal is always required. The granting of leave is customarily considered by a single judge. The procedure is set out in the Criminal Procedure Rules, rule 68. The appellant (or his solicitor) must serve an appeal notice on the relevant officer at the Crown Court where the sentence was passed not more than twenty-eight days after it was passed (section 28). The Court of Appeal does have power to extend the time limit, and will do in a case where there is good reason for the delay, such as an error in sentencing not being identified until after the passage of time. The appeal notice must specify the sentence or order, identify each ground of appeal on which the appellant relies, identify the relevant sentencing powers of the Crown Court, and list any relevant authorities. The *Criminal Practice Directions*, Appeal, paragraph 68C2 states that '[a]dvocates should not settle grounds or support them with written advice unless they consider that they are properly arguable. Grounds should be carefully drafted . . . set out and particularised'. A copy of the advocate's positive advice about the merits should be attached as part of the grounds. The Registrar   **15.26** of Criminal Appeals then obtains all the relevant documents, such as a transcript of the sentencing remarks together with copies of reports which were before the Crown Court judge at the time of sentence. These documents, and the notice and grounds of appeal are handed to the single judge, who considers whether there is a reasonable possibility that an appeal might succeed and, if so, leave to appeal is granted. Otherwise, it is refused. In the latter case the applicant may renew the application for leave to a full court of the Criminal Division, provided the Registrar is served with a further notice within fourteen days from the date of refusal. One variation to this procedure is that sometimes, to save time, an application for leave to appeal is referred at once to the full court without going first to a single judge and the court may then treat the application for leave as the hearing of the appeal and deal with the sentencing appeal issue forthwith.

15.27   At the hearing of the appeal the Court of Appeal will have before it the documents considered by the single judge, plus possible additional documents, such as an up-to-date pre-sentence report or medical report or, if the offender was given a custodial sentence, a report as to his progress within the custodial setting. Some judges may feel aggrieved that their sentences are altered on appeal on the basis of material which was not available to them at the time, but obviously the Court must look at all relevant matters at the time of the appeal. Counsel for the appellant will present the arguments for sentence to be reduced. In a run-of-the-mill appeal against sentence the prosecution is unlikely to be represented, but in a more complex case the Court will hear argument from both sides. The *Criminal Practice Directions* Appeal, paragraph 68A.3 states that the Registrar will notify the relevant prosecution authority in the event that leave to appeal against sentence is granted, giving the prosecution an opportunity to be represented at the hearing if they wish. The prosecution are always invited to appear and to respond as a matter of course in any case involving an appeal against a confiscation order, or where the court is considering issuing sentencing guidelines.

15.28   In disposing of an appeal their Lordships may quash the sentence or order appealed against and replace it with whatever they consider appropriate, provided that:

(a)   the replacement sentence or order is one which the Crown Court had power to make when dealing with the appellant; and

(b)   the appellant, taking the case as a whole, is not dealt with more severely on appeal than he was at the Crown Court (CAA 1968, section 11(3)).

In other words the Court of Appeal may reduce but not increase sentence on an appeal by the offender against sentence. This may be contrasted with the power of the Crown Court to increase sentence when dealing with an appeal against sentence imposed by the magistrates (see paragraph 15.09). However, provided that the total effect of what the Court does is not to increase the aggregate sentence, their Lordships may make the sentence for one of several offences for which the offender was dealt with at Crown Court more severe. Or, where two orders were imposed on sentence for a single offence they can both be adjusted (*McLaren* (1983) 5 Cr App R (S) 332, where the offender's fine was increased but his driving disqualification reduced). In *Stone* [2013] EWCA Crim 723 Pitchford LJ pointed out that if the requirement to impose the statutory surcharge had been overlooked in the Crown Court that omission could not normally be remedied by the Court of Appeal on appeal against sentence because of section 11(3). However, if the Court allowed the appeal against sentence it might be possible then to add the appropriate surcharge, provided that, taking the case as a whole, the appellant was not more severely dealt with. An example is *Taylor* [2013] EWCA Crim 1704 where the Crown Court judge had made no allowance for time spent by the offender under a qualifying curfew and had also omitted to impose the relevant surcharge. The Court was able to remedy both mistakes because the resulting sentence was less severe than before. There are several cases which have considered what does or does not amount to being more severely dealt with on appeal against sentence. It was held in *Whittaker* [1967] Crim LR that a sentence of imprisonment for a fixed term of years could not be varied to a life sentence on appeal. This would still apply today. In *Bennett* (1968) 52 Cr App R 514 the offender pleaded guilty to indecent assault and received a sentence of three years' imprisonment. The Court of Appeal allowed the appeal and substituted a hospital order with a restriction order. The Court said that a hospital order designed to treat and cure the offender could not be regarded as more severe than imprisonment, although the duration of the hospital order might turn out to be longer than the custodial term. It has also been held that an immediate term of imprisonment is more severe than a suspended sentence, even if the immediate term is much shorter than the suspended term (*Thompson* (1977) 66 Cr App R130). This is an old case, dealing with a different form of suspended sentence than exists today (which might include onerous community requirements), and it is possible that a different view might now be taken. Much more recently, in *Eaton* [2006] EWCA Crim 794, the Court had to deal with a case where a community order plus a sexual offences prevention order had been passed on an offender who had pleaded guilty to making indecent images of a child. The sexual offences prevention order had been imposed for three years, which is unlawful because the minimum period is five years. The Court of Appeal, considering the limitation on its powers imposed by section 11(3), found itself unable to increase the length of the order to five years so as to make it a lawful order. The result was that the order had to be quashed altogether. This is an unfortunate outcome, to say the least. It could perhaps have been avoided if the community order had been adjusted at the same time so as to make the overall sentence no more severe.

It may appear that the lack of general power in the Court of Appeal to increase sentence **15.29** on appeal means that there is no bar to unmeritorious appeals. There is one way, however, in which the Court of Appeal may penalize an appellant for commencing such an appeal. That is to direct that some or all of the time the offender has spent in custody between the submission of the grounds of appeal and the dismissal of his application of leave to appeal shall not count towards service of any custodial sentence imposed on him by the Crown Court (CAA 1968, section 29). This is known as a direction for loss of time. Section 29 is unaffected by the change made in 2012 whereby time served by the offender on remand in custody is deducted automatically from the custodial sentence imposed by the court (section 240ZA of the CJA 2003). Although in the past such a direction would not be made in a case where counsel (rather than the appellant himself) has settled the grounds of appeal and the appellant has pursued his appeal to the single judge on counsel's advice that there were reasonable grounds to do so, the Court indicated a change of practice in *Hart* [2006] EWCA Crim 2329. In that case applicants and counsel were reminded of the Court's power to make a direction for loss of time, together with a clear indication that such a direction will be made in respect of an application totally without merit, irrespective of counsel's advice. Further details on the exercise of the direction for loss of time can be found in the *Criminal Practice Directions* Appeal, paragraph 68E1.

Where an appellant is appealing against a custodial sentence, the single judge has power **15.30** to grant bail pending determination of the appeal (CAA, sections 19(1)). If bail is refused application may be made to a court of the Criminal Division. The procedure for making an application for bail, pending appeal, is set out in the CPR 2013, rules 68.8 and 68.9. Unless the sentence appealed against is very short there is reluctance to grant bail. This approach derives from the old case of *Watton* (1979) 68 Cr App R 293 where it was said that there had to be exceptional circumstances to justify the granting of bail pending appeal, but that these *might* include the fact that a custodial sentence would have been completed before the appeal was heard. Consequently the majority of appellants have spent several weeks, if not months, in custody before their appeals are heard. It quite often happens that the Court of Appeal will allow the appeal and reduce the custodial term to one which will permit the appellant's immediate release from custody. Such cases are unreliable guides as to the appropriate level of sentence for the type of offence in question. It may be that their Lordships really think that a custodial sentence need not have been imposed in the first place, but prefer not to say so. Sometimes they may think that the period already served represents the proper penalty. Sometimes they may think that the original sentence was appropriate but in light of a favourable report as to the offender's progress in custody, that the offender has now learned his lesson and should, as an act of clemency, now be released.

15.31   When the Court of Appeal has dealt with the appeal a note is sent to the judge who passed the original sentence giving brief reasons for upholding or varying the sentence. If leave to appeal is refused by the single judge and the matter is pursued no further again a brief note is sent to the sentencing judge giving reasons.

C REFERENCE BY THE ATTORNEY GENERAL

15.32   By virtue of sections 36 and 36 of the CJA 1988 the Attorney General has power to refer a sentence passed in the Crown Court to the Court of Appeal for a review of that sentence where the Attorney considers that the sentence was 'unduly lenient'. This is subject to:

(a) the Court of Appeal giving leave; and
(b) the offence for which the sentence was passed was either one which is triable only on indictment or one which is triable either way and is specified in an order made by the Home Secretary by statutory instrument (CJA 1988, section 35(3)); and
(c) the sentencing judge has been unduly lenient or has erred in his powers of sentencing or has failed to impose a sentence required to be passed under any one of the prescribed sentences under the PCC(S)A 2000, section 110 or 111, or the PCA 1953, section 1A(5), or the CJA 1988, section 139AA(7), or the FA section 51A(2), or the CJA 2003, section 224A, 225, or 226.

This amounts, to all practical purposes, to a prosecution appeal against sentence imposed in the Crown Court, subject to the important limitations cited earlier. The possibility of a prosecution appeal from the Crown Court stands in contrast to the lack of a power for the prosecution to appeal a sentence imposed in the magistrates' court which they believed to be unduly lenient (see paragraph 15.01, this Chapter). For the purposes of a sentencing reference the word 'sentence' has the same wide meaning as it has under the CAA 1968, section 50(1), except that it does not extend to an interim hospital order (CJA 1988, section 35(6)).

15.33   For the avoidance of doubt, it has been held that the following orders made by the Crown Court may be appealed by the prosecution:

(a) a conditional discharge (*A-G's Reference (No 57 of 1995)* [1996] 2 Cr App R (S) 159) and, by implication an absolute discharge,
(b) a deferment of sentence (*A-G's Reference (No 22 of 1992)* [1994] 1 All ER 105), and
(c) the setting of a minimum term in a life sentence.

15.34   Any person is entitled to draw the attention of the Attorney General to a sentencing decision in the Crown Court which that person believes to have been unduly lenient. This is not infrequently done in cases attracting a high level of public interest. A recent example is the sentence imposed in 2013 on the broadcaster Stuart Hall for a number of historical sexual offences committed against young women and girls. The original sentence of fifteen months' imprisonment was increased to thirty months by the Court of Appeal, by ordering that two of the fifteen-month sentences should run consecutively rather than concurrently. The decision whether to refer the matter to the Court of Appeal is, however, for the Attorney General to make. It was said by the Court of Appeal in *A-G's Reference (No 14 of 2003)*, *The Times*, 18 April 2003, that the Attorney General must always personally consider the matter and decide for himself whether to seek leave to appeal. The Court has also said that the reference procedure is not the same as a general right of prosecution appeal against sentence, and the distinction between a lenient sentence and an unduly lenient one must always be borne in mind. Judges should not step back from imposing a lenient sentence where that is the right course to take (*A-G's Reference (No 8 of 2007)* [2008] 1 Cr App R (S) 1). A difficult issue can arise where, under the *Goodyear* principle, the sentencing judge gave an indication of sentence which then prompted a plea of guilty and the prosecution now seeks to appeal on the basis that the sentence indicated was unduly lenient. Even if prosecution counsel at the trial has taken no exception to the course being taken or the sentence indicated the Court of Appeal is not precluded from considering a reference by the Attorney General (*A-G's Reference (No 48 of 2006)* [2007] 1 Cr App R (S) 90). It was pointed out by Latham LJ in this case that defence counsel should always warn his client, and prosecution counsel should where appropriate remind the judge, that the procedure in *Goodyear* leaves open the possibility of the Attorney General referring the matter to the Court of Appeal.

If the Court of Appeal does give leave for reference, in disposing of the appeal it will, **15.35** in contrast to appeals against sentence brought by offenders, hear argument from both sides. Upon an Attorney General's sentencing reference the Court of Appeal may quash the sentence passed by the Crown Court and replace it with the sentence which it thinks is appropriate. It is specifically provided in section 36(2) that the Attorney General may refer a sentence to the Court of Appeal if he considers that the judge has erred in law, but the powers of the Court of Appeal to review the sentence go much wider than that. In the majority of cases the judge has understood his powers correctly, but has chosen in his discretion to pass a sentence that appears to the Attorney General to be too lenient in all the circumstances of the case. The replacement sentence must be one which the Crown Court would have had power to pass on the offender (section 36(1)). Of course the judge whose sentence is under consideration cannot sit in the appeal (section 36(4)). The relevant procedure for referring a case is set out in the CJA 1988, schedule 3 and the CPR 2013, rule 70. The Attorney General must, not later than twenty-eight days after sentence was passed, serve on the Registrar of Criminal Appeals a notice giving all relevant details and including an application for leave.

The Court of Appeal has set out its approach to the disposition of references under section **15.36** 36 in a number of cases, and the matter now seems to be quite settled. The leading case is *A-G's Reference (No 4 of 1989)* (1989) 11 Cr App R (S) 517, as modified in later decisions. The following are the key points which arise:

(a) The Court of Appeal will only increase a sentence which is clearly 'unduly lenient'. Leniency is not necessarily a bad thing. It is not enough that the members of the Court of Appeal would themselves have imposed a more severe sentence. To be unduly lenient a sentence must fall outside the range of sentences which the judge, applying his mind to all the relevant issues, could reasonably consider appropriate. Thus a sentence can be 'lenient', but not 'unduly lenient'. In making their assessment the Court of Appeal will, of course, have regard to the applicable sentencing guidelines. If there are no applicable sentencing guidelines the Court will consider any relevant previous decisions of the Court. These matters should have been before the sentencing judge. As with an appeal by the offender, the appellate court will also have before it the documents considered by the single judge, plus possible additional documents, such as a progress report on the offender under the community order which, it is argued, was an unduly lenient disposal. The Court has stressed on many occasions that the sentencing judge is very well placed to weigh the competing considerations before passing sentence, especially where the judge has presided over a contested trial.

(b) When considering an appeal against sentence by an offender, we have seen that the Court will sometimes consider material which was not available to the sentencing judge at the time. In the context of a prosecution appeal, however, the Court has usually taken the view that the task of the Court is to consider whether the sentence was unduly lenient on the basis of all the facts known to the judge (*A-G's Reference (No 84 of 2009)* [2011] 1 Cr App R (S) 85). If the Court decides that the sentence was unduly lenient it may then look at any additional material to help it to decide what the proper sentence now ought to be (*A-G's Reference (No 74 of 2010), The Times,* April 1 2011).

(c) The Court has established over the years that when it does increase sentence it will bear in mind the fact that the offender has undergone the additional stress of having to be sentenced twice over. This may especially be the case where the Court of Appeal, in the event, varies a non-custodial sentence to a custodial one. Some discount from the properly justified sentence is generally regarded as being appropriate—a principle sometimes referred to in this context as 'double jeopardy'. In *A-G's Reference (Nos 14 & 15 of 2006)* [2007] 1 Cr App R (S) 40, the Court of Appeal said that discounts for double jeopardy should be near the upper end of the range, said to be about 30 per cent, where a custodial sentence was now being substituted for a non-custodial one, or where the offender had completed the custodial sentence imposed by the judge or was about to be released. In other cases the double jeopardy principle was of less relevance and in some cases could properly be ignored. There is a statutory exception to this principle when the Court of Appeal is dealing with an Attorney General's reference with respect to a minimum term, set in a mandatory life sentence for murder or a discretionary life sentence. Section 36(3A) states that in such a case the Court of Appeal 'shall not, in deciding what sentence is appropriate for the case, make any allowance for the fact that the person to whom it relates is being sentenced for a second time.' This is a complete exclusion, irrespective of the circumstances of the case.

15.37 These points mean that the value of a Court of Appeal decision on a reference by the Attorney General is of limited value in providing guidance for sentencers in the future. A decision by the Court of Appeal not to interfere with sentence does not mean that the original sentence is viewed by the Court as having been correct; merely that it is not so far wrong as to justify correction. Further, the general approach that the Court should have regard to 'double jeopardy' also tends to dilute the guidance value of these cases. Typically, when the court does increase the sentence, it says that it has made such an allowance but it does not make clear what discount has been allowed for double jeopardy. When no figure is given for this the sentence selected by the Court of Appeal is hardly a reliable guide for future cases. It would be helpful in all cases for the Court to indicate clearly what the proper sentence should have been, and then either to dismiss the appeal on the basis that the difference between that sentence and the one actually imposed is not sufficient to justify any variation, or to increase the sentence, making it clear what discount has been allowed to the offender in all the circumstances.

D APPEAL TO SUPREME COURT AGAINST SENTENCE

Appeal lies to the Supreme Court against the decisions of both the Court of Appeal **15.38** (Criminal Division) and the Divisional Court of the High Court under the CAA 1968, section 33 and the Administration of Justice Act 1960, section 1(1)(a) respectively. In the case of the Divisional Court a direct appeal to the Supreme Court is possible only if the decision in question was taken in a criminal cause or matter, but that obviously will be so where the decision relates to sentencing. The right of appeal to the Supreme Court is not restricted to the offender. In particular, if the offender sentenced in the Crown Court successfully appealed to the Court of Appeal, the prosecutor could in theory appeal to the Supreme Court to have the original sentence reinstated. However, in practice in sentencing matters an appeal to the Supreme Court is restricted to cases where (by section 33(2)):

(a) the lower court certifies that there is a point of law of general public importance; and
(b) either the lower court or the Supreme Court gives leave to appeal.

It is the first restriction which makes appeals to the Supreme Court on sentencing matters so rare. Sentencing rarely raises points of law (as opposed to sentencing principle), let alone points of law of general public importance. Moreover the argument that an exceedingly harsh sentence necessarily raises a point of law was rejected in *Ashdown* [1974] 1 WLR 270. It was said in that case that, provided the sentence was within the sentencing court's powers, the propriety of the sentence could never raise a point of general public importance. The rarity of sentencing appeals which reach the Supreme Court is neatly illustrated by the remarks of Lord Diplock in *Courtie* [1984] AC 463, in which he said that the case came before the House of Lords (as it then was) in the guise of an appeal against sentence only, but in fact raised questions of substantive law. He then continued: 'I cannot myself recall any criminal appeal confined to sentence only having come before this House since I started to sit here in 1968'. Any application for leave to appeal to the Supreme Court must be made within twenty-eight days from the date on which the Court of Appeal made its decision or (if later) the date on which the Court gave reasons for its decision (CAA 1968, section 34(1) and (1A)). The Supreme Court may either deal with the matter itself, or remit the case to the Court of Appeal to be dealt with there (CJA 1988, section 35(3)).

Where a sentencing matter has gone to the Court of Appeal on a reference by the Attorney **15.39** General (see paragraph 15.04, this Chapter) and the Court of Appeal has concluded its review and either upheld an allegedly unduly lenient sentence or has varied it, the Attorney General or the person to whose sentence the reference relates may refer a point of law involved in the sentence to the Supreme Court for their opinion (CAA 1968, section 36(1)). The Supreme Court may either deal with the matter itself, or remit the case to the Court of Appeal to be dealt with there (CJA 1988, section 36(5)). Such a reference to the Supreme Court can only be made with the leave of the Supreme Court or the Court of Appeal, and leave requires that there is a point of law of general public importance involved in the case (CAA 1968, section 36(6)). No such cases have yet been reported.

Although not appeals against sentence as such, there are many decisions of the Supreme **15.40** Court (or House of Lords) which are closely related to sentencing and have had important indirect impact on the law and practice of sentencing. These are dealt with in their appropriate places in this book.

E REFERENCE BY THE CRIMINAL CASES REVIEW COMMISSION

The Criminal Cases Review Commission (CCRC) was established under section 8 of the **15.41** Criminal Appeal Act 1995. Sections 17 to 21 set out the extensive investigatory powers of the Commission. The CCRC is centrally concerned with miscarriages of justice, in the sense of wrongful convictions, but they also have power to refer to the Court of Appeal a sentence which was imposed in the Crown Court or refer to the Crown Court a sentence imposed in the magistrates' court.

15.42 Under section 9 of that Act the CCRC may refer a conviction on indictment, or sentence imposed in relation to that conviction, to the Court of Appeal. The CCRC may only refer a case if there appears to be a 'real possibility' that the Court of Appeal will quash the original conviction or sentence. A reference will normally only be made where new information has come to light which was not available to the court at the time or not raised when it should have been (section 13), although in exceptional circumstances the CCRC may refer a case where this does not apply. Applicants should usually have appealed first. According to the Annual Report of the CCRC for 2012–13, 21 cases were referred to the Court of Appeal in that year, of which only five related to sentence only. In 2011–12 some twenty-six CCRC references were considered by the Court of Appeal. There were only two sentence-only matters, and in both cases the Court quashed the original sentence. In one of these, *Pleasants* [2012] EWCA Crim 3022 it was agreed that it had been unlawful for the judge to make an order returning the offender to serve part of an unexpired sentence under the PCC(S)A 2000, section 116. The case had already been before the Court on an earlier occasion, when the most recent custodial sentence had been reduced in length, but nobody had noticed the section 116 problem. The power under section 116 has since been abolished.

15.43 By the Criminal Appeal Act 1995, section 11, where a person has been convicted of an offence in a magistrates' court the Commission may refer that conviction to the Crown Court and (whether or not they refer the conviction) may refer the sentence imposed. Such a reference is treated for all practical purposes as an appeal under the MCA 1980, section 108 (see paragraph 15.04). References by the CCRC to the Crown Court on sentencing matters appear to be rare.

F PARDON AND RELEASE ON COMPASSIONATE GROUNDS

15.44 As an act of grace, the Sovereign may either grant a free (or conditional) pardon or remit the rest of the offender's sentence. This is known as the prerogative of mercy (CAA 1968, section 49). In practice these powers are not exercised personally by the Sovereign, but are now administered on her behalf by the Secretary of State.

15.45 A pardon is normally granted only where it has been established that the original conviction was unjustified, such as where a miscarriage of justice is shown to have occurred. It is clear that a pardon 'does not in any sense eliminate the conviction', although it relieves the subject of the effect of any penalties as a result of that conviction (*Foster* [1985] QB 115). In that case the Court of Appeal held that the appellant, a man who had been pardoned in respect of an offence of rape, following later confession to that offence by another man, might properly still bring an appeal against his conviction. A pardon may have great symbolic importance to those concerned, so that pardons are sometimes sought by an offender's family long after the offender's death. See, for example, the famous case of *Secretary of State for the Home Department, ex parte Bentley* [1994] QB 439. There the Court of Appeal indicated that the prerogative was a 'flexible power', and that the grant of a conditional, rather than a free pardon was appropriate where 'a mistake had been made' and the offender should not have been executed. A person pardoned may receive compensation under the CJA 1988, section 133, but the criteria for doing so are quite strict (see *R (Adams) v Secretary of State for Justice* [2012] 1 AC 48). The Criminal Cases Review Commission (paragraph 15.41, this Chapter) has power to conduct investigations and, where appropriate, request the Court of Appeal to reconsider a case where there appears to the Commission to be a real possibility that the verdict or sentence will not be upheld in the light of new information not available at the trial.

In contrast to the grant of a pardon, remission of an offender's sentence by executive au- **15.46** thority does not imply that the original conviction was unjustified: it means merely that the rest of the sentence need not be served. Remission of the remainder of a custodial sentence is generally used for one of two reasons. The first is where a prisoner has given particular help to the authorities in the detection of other offences or the apprehension of other offenders. The second is in cases where the offender is discovered to be suffering from a terminal illness and has a short time left to live. Sentence is remitted so that the person need not die in custody. Sometimes the Court of Appeal makes reference to the possibility of release on compassionate grounds when upholding a custodial sentence on a seriously ill offender. See further paragraph 2.52 at point (iv). Of particular importance here is the Crime (Sentences) Act 1997, section 30, which provides that the Secretary of State may at any time release a life sentence prisoner on licence if he is satisfied that exceptional circumstances exist which justify the prisoner's release on compassionate grounds. The possibility that an offender sentenced by way of life imprisonment with a 'whole life' minimum term might be released on compassionate grounds is the critical issue when considering whether such a sentence infringes Article 3 of the ECHR. The Grand Chamber of the European Court of Human Rights in *Vinter v UK* [2013] ECHR 645 has taken the view that compliance with Article 3 requires that the sentence must always attract the possibility of review and ultimately the possibility of release. The Court of Appeal in *A-G's Reference (No 69 of 2013)* [2014] EWCA Crim 188, however, has disagreed with this conclusion, and found that the power which exists under section 30 of the 1997 Act offers the possibility of review and release even for an offender with a whole life minimum term, such that English law is compliant with the European Convention.

There is also the possibility of remission of non-custodial sentences. A community order **15.47** may be remitted in circumstances where very good progress has been made by the offender, and a fine may be remitted where the financial circumstances of the offender have deteriorated significantly since the penalty was imposed.

G DISQUALIFICATIONS UPON CONVICTION

While not part of sentence as such, a wide range of disqualifications apply automatically **15.48** on persons convicted of certain offences. They are considered here because they are closely associated with the sentencing decision and because they may have a very significant impact upon the defendant after conviction.

Sex offender notification

A person who is convicted of an offence which is listed in schedule 3 to the Sexual **15.49** Offences Act 2003 is subject to the notification requirements of that Act. Care must be taken when using this schedule, which is complex. Several of the offences listed attract the notification requirements only in certain circumstances, such as the offender having received a custodial sentence of at least twelve months' duration, or a community sentence of at least twelve months, and also dependent upon the age of the offender, and in some cases the age of the victim. See further section 132 of the Act. In *Davison* [2009] 2 Cr App R (S) 76 it was held that a community order for twelve months with an unpaid work requirement was a community sentence of at least twelve months for the purposes of the notification requirements, even though the offender had completed his hours of unpaid work in a much shorter time. Notification requirements also apply to persons found not guilty of the offence by reason of insanity, or persons cautioned for the offence (SOA 2003, section 80). An offender who is subject to the notification requirements (also referred to as 'sex offender registration') is referred to in the Act as a 'relevant offender'. The basic notification requirements are set out in section 83. They are that the offender must, within the period of three days of the conviction, notify to the police his date of birth, national insurance number, name (and any aliases), home address, and any other address at which he regularly stays. Subsequent changes to these details must also be notified to the police (section 84). The person may also be required to inform the police of the details of any planned travel arrangements outside the UK (section 86). The Secretary of State has power to add further notification requirements by statutory instrument. In *R (Prothero) v Secretary of State* [2013] EWHC 2830 the Divisional Court considered the Sexual Offences Act 2003 (Notification Requirements) (England and Wales) Regulations 2012 which, among other things, require an offender to provide details of his bank, debit, or credit card accounts. The Court rejected an argument that this requirement infringed Article 8 of the ECHR, holding that it was not inappropriate or disproportionate. Persons who were formerly subject to registration under the Sex Offenders Act 1997 are now made subject to the notification requirements under the SOA 2003 (section 81).

15.50   The notification periods depend on the sentence which was imposed for the listed offence, and they are set out in section 82 of the Act. In summary, an offender sentenced to imprisonment for a term of thirty months or more is subject to an indefinite notification period; an offender sentenced to imprisonment for more than six months but less than thirty months is subject to a notification period of ten years; an offender sentenced to imprisonment for six months or less is subject to a notification period of seven years. For a person cautioned the period is two years; for a person conditionally discharged the period is the duration of the discharge; and for a person sentenced in any other way the period is five years. If the offender was aged under eighteen on the relevant date these periods of time are halved. Since an indefinite period cannot be halved, it will be seen that for a young offender the difference between a sentence of twenty-nine months and one of thirty months is the difference between five years and life (see *M* [2010] EWCA Crim 592, at paragraph 15.52, this Chapter). A person sentenced to a detention and training order is to be treated as if he had been sentenced to a custodial term of half the duration of the order (*Slocombe* [2006] 1 WLR 328; *M* [2010] EWCA Crim 42).

15.51   The European Court of Human Rights held in *Ibbotson v UK* [1999] Crim LR 153 that sex offender registration was not a 'penalty' within the meaning of Article 7(1), so that registration could properly include offenders who had been convicted and sentenced before the legislation came into force. The notification requirements extend to offenders who have been sentenced by way of conditionally discharge (*Longworth* [2006] 1 WLR 313). The Supreme Court in *R (F (A Child)) v Secretary of State for the Home Department* [2011] 1 AC 331 found that certain notification requirements under the Act which would endure for an indefinite period with no provision for review, were disproportionate and infringed Article 8 of the ECHR. The Act was accordingly amended in 2012 by the insertion of sections 91A to 91E to provide for review and make the provisions compliant with the ECHR.

15.52   It is important to be clear that the notification requirements of the 2003 Act are automatic upon conviction of a listed offence. They are not an additional form of punishment, and so in principle should not be taken into account when determining the sentence to be passed (*A-G's Ref (No 50 of 1997)* [1998] 2 Cr App R (S) 155). Since the provisions are automatic in their effect in principle they do not strictly require the judge to make reference to them, although informing the offender is now required by the *Criminal Procedure Rules*, rule 42.3. The Rules do not state what the consequence of a failure to do so would be, but it is clear that the notification requirements would take effect in any event. The SOA 2003, section 92 provides that, where a sentencer states in open court that an offender has been convicted of a listed offence and certifies those facts, the certificate shall be sufficient evidence of those facts. There is in fact no 'sex offender register' (despite this phrase being in common and popular usage), and so it is a myth that an offender convicted of a relevant offence is required to 'sign' it. Although the notification requirements are not part of sentence, sometimes judges have been concerned about the additional burden of the notification requirements on the particular offender. That is what happened in *A-G's Ref (No 50 of 1997)* [1998] 2 Cr App R (S) 155 where the judge, on discovering that the nine-month prison sentence which he was about to impose would trigger a notification period of ten years, reduced sentence to six months so to require seven years' notification instead. Following a reference by the Attorney General the Court of Appeal said that judges must impose the appropriate sentence for the offence and should not concern themselves with the impact on the period of notification under the SOA. The Court has not always been consistent in its approach, however. In *Banham* [2010] EWCA Crim 448 a community order was varied to a conditional discharge in part because the community order would trigger a notification period of five years and on the facts the offender did not represent a risk of re-offending. Further, in *M* [2010] EWCA Crim 592 the Court reduced a sentence of two years and nine months' detention to one of two years and two months in light of fresh material before the court about the mental state of the offender which meant that notification for life was inappropriate. The sentence as varied attracted a notification period of five years on the young offender instead.

Where a young offender is convicted of an offence listed in schedule 3 and is sentenced in **15.53** a way which results in triggering the notification requirements of the Act, the court may direct that the obligation shall be treated as the obligation of the parent rather than that of the young offender. This is known as a parental direction (under section 89(1) of the Act), and is the only aspect of the notification scheme which involves the court making an order. The parent must ensure that the young offender attends the police station as well when notification is being given. Such a direction has immediate effect and lasts until the young offender attains the age of eighteen or for such shorter period as the court may direct. Application may later be made by the young offender, the parent, or the chief police officer for the area in which the young offender resides, for the parental direction order to be varied, renewed, or discharged.

It is an offence for a person subject to the notification requirements of the SOA 2003 to fail **15.54** without reasonable excuse to comply with those requirements, or to furnish false details. The offence, under section 91 of the Act is punishable with up to five years on indictment or to six months, a fine, or both on summary conviction.

Disqualification from working with children or vulnerable adults

Offenders convicted of any of a long list of offences specified in the Safeguarding of **15.55** Vulnerable Groups Act (SVGA) 2006 are subject to being barred from working in the future with either children, or with vulnerable adults, or both. The Independent Barring Service is responsible for managing these arrangements. The specified offences are to be found in the schedule to the SVGA 2006 (Prescribed Criteria and Miscellaneous Provisions) Regulations 2009 (SI 2009 No 27), as amended. The four paragraphs in the schedule list the offences which will result in automatic inclusion on one or other (or both) lists of person who are so barred, either with or without the right to make representations. This process happens automatically upon conviction for a specified offence.

15.56   The sentencing judge is required to explain to the offender that he will be, or (depending upon the offence conviction) may be barred, and the offender will be handed a notice setting out the effect of the consequences of this conviction. Judges no longer have the power to order that the offender should be disqualified from working with children, a power contained in section 28 of the Criminal Justice and Court Services Act 2000 but repealed with effect from 17 June 2013.

Other forms of disqualification

15.57   A number of other forms of disqualification apply automatically upon conviction, depending upon the nature and duration of the sentence passed and the period of time which has expired since the conviction.

(a) By the Representation of the People Act 1983, section 3(1), while detained in custody following conviction for any offence, any person is legally incapable of voting at any parliamentary or local government election. The ban does not extend to prisoners held on remand. The Grand Chamber of the European Court of Human Rights in *Hirst v UK (No 2)* (2006) 42 EHRR 849, held that this provision amounted to a violation of the rights of the applicant (a serving prisoner) under Article 3 of the First Protocol. Despite much debate since this decision Parliament has not yet changed the law to bring it into line with the Convention.

(b) By the Local Government Act 1972, section 80(1)(d), any person who has been convicted of an offence and had imposed upon him a custodial sentence of three months or more, whether suspended or not, is disqualified from being, or being elected, a member of a local authority for a period of five years from the date of conviction.

(c) By the Firearms Act 1968, section 21, a person convicted of an offence for which he has received a custodial sentence of three years or more is prohibited from possessing or acquiring any firearm or ammunition for life.

(d) By the Juries Act 1974, schedule 1, part II, an offender who has served at any time a custodial sentence of five years or more, or within the last ten years has served a custodial sentence of any length, or within the last ten years has had imposed on them a suspended prison sentence or a community order, is disqualified from jury service.

H REHABILITATION OF OFFENDERS

15.58   The basic principle of the Rehabilitation of Offenders Act 1974 is that, after the passage of time convictions may become 'spent', and a convicted person may consider himself 'rehabilitated'. When a conviction is spent, the offender is treated for a range of purposes as if he had never been convicted of the offence concerned. While the ROA 1974, section 7(2) strictly excludes from its scope the operation of criminal proceedings, the *Criminal Practice Directions*, paragraph 35A.1, nonetheless requires that spent convictions which appear on the offender's criminal record should be marked as such, and that nobody should refer in open court to such spent convictions without the authority of the judge. This matter was considered in Chapter 1, at paragraph 1.71. The underlying rationale of the Act is that, for most offenders, when their sentence comes to an end and a period of time has then followed during which the person has remained conviction-free, should be able to return to their lives and make a positive contribution to society. As was observed by the Court of Appeal in *Meyers* [1996] 1 Cr App R (S) 249, 'it is in the public interest that persons should renounce a life of crime and that they should take up honest work and live a proper life'.

This important public interest has been increasingly compromised in recent years, however, because of concerns over the continuing future risk which may be posed by certain offenders, especially sex offenders. This has resulted in legislation which significantly cuts across the basic principle. The requirements of sex offender notification and the setting up of agencies to bar offenders from entering any kind of work which would pose a risk to children and vulnerable adults, were referred to in paragraphs 15.49 and 15.55 above.

The protection of the 1974 Act extends to all convictions except one which has resulted in **15.59** a sentence which is excluded from rehabilitation (see paragraph 15.60). Section 4(1) of the Act states that 'a person who has become a rehabilitated person for the purposes of this Act in respect of a conviction shall be treated for all purposes in law as a person who has not committed or been charged with or prosecuted for or convicted of or sentenced for the offence or offences which were the subject of that conviction'. The term 'conviction' is given a broad meaning in the Act, but does not extend to cover the imposition of a bind over to keep the peace imposed at any time except as part of the sentence. An offence for which an order for absolute or conditional discharge is made does not count as a conviction for a variety of purposes (the PCC(S)A 2000, section 14) but section 1(4) of the Act provides that discharges are sentences which may be the subject of rehabilitation. In some situations the protection afforded by section 14 of the 2000 Act may be greater than that of the 1974 Act. In *Kitt* [1977] Crim LR 220, for example, the offender applied to renew a shotgun licence and stated on the form that he had not been convicted of an offence since the last renewal. In fact he had in the meantime been convicted of handling stolen goods, and was conditionally discharged. The form stated that spent convictions must be revealed and he was convicted of making a false statement on the form, contrary to the Firearms Act 1968. The conviction was overturned, on the basis that section 14 (or, at least, an earlier identically-worded provision) permitted him to say that he had not been convicted at all.

Rehabilitation periods

The impressively broad phrasing of section 4(1) is not quite what it seems. The Act must be **15.60** read in context of the numerous exceptions which apply to it in the employment context. Also, certain sentences fall outside the scope of the Act and an offender who has been so sentenced can never become rehabilitated with respect to that conviction. Currently those sentences are any form of custodial sentence for life or an extended sentence, or any determinate custodial term exceeding forty-eight months.

The rehabilitation periods are set out in section 5(1) of the Act. The following summary **15.61** includes only those forms of sentence which are currently available to the courts, but the Act lists rehabilitation periods for many other forms of sentence which are now abolished but still appear on the criminal records of offenders.

Where more than one sentence is imposed for an offence then the longer or longest rehabilitation period applies (section 6(2)). A person who has been convicted can only become rehabilitated under the Act if he is not reconvicted within the relevant period of an indictable offence (section 6(5) and (6)). If he is reconvicted within the relevant period the effect is that he will not be rehabilitated under the Act until the longer of the two rehabilitation periods (for the original offence and the new offence) has expired. The practical effect of this rule is that persistent offenders tend to have few spent convictions because the fresh offences keep the old ones alive.

The rehabilitation periods have recently changed in March 2014 when section 139 of the **15.62** LASPOA 2012 was brought into force. These periods replace the periods as set out in the original legislation, but they have retrospective effect, so that all previous convictions, whenever they were acquired by the offender, will be subject to the revised rehabilitation periods. It will be seen that, in contrast to the periods as set out in the original Act, which all ran for a specified period from the date on which the sentence was imposed, the new periods for the most part finish on the expiry of a specified period after the sentence is *completed*. This is of particular importance in relation to custodial sentences. In each case the completion of the custodial sentence means the conclusion of the whole sentence, including the licence period, and not the conclusion of the custodial part of the sentence before early release. Overall, the effect of the LASPOA 2012 changes is to reduce the applicable rehabilitation periods. The applicable periods now are:

(a) for a custodial sentence of more than thirty months up to and including forty-eight months, seven years from the date on which the sentence is completed for an adult, and forty-two months for a young offender;

(b) for a custodial sentence of more than six months up to and including thirty months (including a suspended sentence), forty-eight months from the date on which the sentence is completed for an adult, and twenty-four months for a young offender;

(c) for a custodial sentence of more than six months or less (including a suspended sentence), twenty-four months from the date on which the sentence is completed for an adult, and eighteen months for a young offender;

(d) for a fine, twelve months from the date of conviction for an adult, and six months for a young offender;

(e) for a community order or a youth rehabilitation order, twelve months from the last day on which the order is in force for an adult, and six months for a young offender;

(f) for a 'relevant order', which includes a conditional discharge, a bind over to keep the peace, a hospital order with or without a restriction order, a referral order, or any order which imposes a disqualification, disability, prohibition or other penalty (but not a reparation order) the day when the order ceases to have effect.

It should be noted that under these provisions there is no rehabilitation period for an absolute discharge.

Exceptions to the Act

15.63 The practical effect of the Act is much affected by the far-reaching exceptions which apply to it. The relevant law can be found in the Rehabilitation of Offenders Act 1974 (Exceptions) Order 1975, which has been added to by many subsequent statutory instruments. The exceptions have the effect that none of the provisions of section 4 of the Act apply, and so details of spent convictions must be revealed in relation to any questions asked by persons in the course of their office or employment in order to assess the suitability of an applicant for a wide range of professions, offices or employments, regulated occupations, and the granting of licences. The details of the Order fall outside the scope of this book.

KEY DOCUMENTS

Criminal Practice Directions [2013] EWCA Crim 1631 (effective 7 October 2013), amended by [2013] EWCA Crim 2328 (effective 10 December 2013).

Criminal Procedure Rules (SI 2013, No 1554) (effective 7 October 2013).

European Convention on Human Rights, Articles 3 and 7.

Criminal Cases Review Commission <http://www.justice.gov.uk/about/criminal-cases-review-commission>.

Disclosure and Barring Service <http://www.gov.uk/government/organisations/disclosure-and-baring-service>.

INDEX

9 780199 695812